Completely Revised and Updated 2nd Edition

THE

TEACHER'S

Complete & Easy

GUIDE TO THE

INTERNET

Ann Heide   Linda Stilborne

Web Site Resource Materials developed by Val Johnston

Teachers College
Columbia University
New York and London
http://www.tc.columbia.edu/~tcpress

D1502069

Published in the United States of America by Teachers College Press
1234 Amsterdam Avenue, New York, NY 10027
http://www.tc.columbia.edu/~tcpress

Published in Canada by Trifolium Books Inc.

Copyright © Trifolium Books Inc. 1996, 1999

Published in agreement with Trifolium Books Inc.

Library of Congress Cataloging-in-Publication Data

Heide, Ann, 1948-
    The teacher's complete & easy guide to the Internet / Ann Heide, Linda Stilborne. – 2nd ed.
        p. cm.
    Includes bibliographical references and index.
    ISBN 0-8077-3779-8
    1. Internet (Computer network) in education. 2. Education—Computer network resources.
3. Teaching—Computer network resources. I. Stilborne, Linda. II. Title
    LB1044.87.H45 1998   98-21513
    370'.285.678—dc21   CIP

ISBN 0-8077-3779-8

Manufactured in Canada

02 01 00 99   2 3 4 5

Editing: Wendy Thomas
Production Coordination: Gaynor Fitzpatrick
Text design & layout: Jack Steiner
Cover design: Blair Kerrigan
Cartoons: Scot Ritchie (pages 81, 213, 280). The cartoons on pages 120, 143, 166 were
produced with the permission of Unisys Corporation.

Acknowledgments

The authors and publisher would like to thank the Unisys Corporation for granting permission to include its excellent Glossary entitled *Information Superhighway Driver's Manual:
Key terms and concepts that will put you in the passing lane* in our book. Special thanks to
James B. Senior and Michael Heck of Unisys Corporation for providing us with all the material we needed on such a timely basis, and to Jim Chiponis for his delightful cartoons.

    We thank the many educators and friends who took the time to provide valuable reviews.
We also thank the Lafayette County School District for sharing their Acceptable Use Policy
with all of us on the Internet. Lastly, the many teachers who shared their ideas with us on the
Internet are warmly thanked for their important contributions.

    Trifolium Books Inc. acknowledges with gratitude the generous support of the
Government of Canada's Book Publishing Industry Development Program (BPIDP).

About This Book

It is challenging and sometimes frustrating to keep up with the constantly changing environment of the Internet. For teachers, an even greater challenge is integrating this technology into their classrooms in a meaningful way. Teachers who have used the first edition of the *Teacher's Complete & Easy Guide to the Internet* found it to be an invaluable resource for learning about this technology and locating relevant curriculum resources. In this new edition, we provide even more information to help teachers further explore classroom resources and online learning environments.

The second edition offers an updated and expanded view of the Internet. We explain the range of ways that the Internet can be used to enhance learning, with many lesson ideas, practical tips, and step-by-step instructions for both new and experienced users. Here are some of the questions you will find answers to in the second edition:

- **What impact is the Internet having on learning?**
  See Chapter 1, which explains why the Internet is an increasingly important tool for educators and how telecommunications technologies have the potential to transform the ways in which teachers teach and students learn.

- **How can the Internet be integrated into the curriculum in a meaningful way?**
  Find out how to organize student Internet projects, from keypals to global classrooms — and how to ensure that the use of the Internet results in a meaningful learning experience for students. Learn about WebQuests as a practical model for curriculum-based projects that promote active learning.

- **How are teachers in the early, middle, and higher grades using the Internet for student projects?**
  You'll find ideas throughout this book, but see especially the Project Ideas features. Project Ideas are provided for most grade levels. Some are cross-curricular, and many projects can be extended or adapted for use with younger or older students.

- **How are teachers dealing with controversial and unacceptable material on the Internet?**
  Student security issues (such as acceptable use) are a major issue with teachers and with parents. Chapter 3 discusses acceptable use policies (AUPs) and offers practical guidelines for safe and productive online learning. (See also Appendix A, which contains a sample AUP.)

- **What are some strategies for using the Internet with special needs students?**
  Chapter 3 identifies some of the ways in which the Internet can provide support for special needs students and identifies a range of useful resources for helping students with disabilities.

- **What are the newest tools and resources available on the Internet?**
  Chapters 4 through 6 will provide you with the latest information about the World Wide Web. Find out about alternative browsers, such as the award-winning Opera browser and how to customize your browser. In Chapter 8 you will be able to learn about some older and some newer Internet applications, including telnet, audio, and video on the Internet and off-line browsers.

- **How can I use the Web more efficiently?**
  If you sometimes feel overwhelmed by too much information on the Internet, Chapter 4 will introduce you to strategies for finding what you are looking for quickly and easily. In Chapter 5 you will find guidelines for evaluating and citing Web resources.

- **How can I create effective Web pages for class activities and school communications?**
  Chapter 7 provides simple explanations for developing your own Web pages. In this chapter you will also find tips for developing school Web pages, great sources for graphics, and software options for editing Web pages.

- **How can I connect with other teachers on the Net?**
  See Chapter 7 for a discussion of e-mail, as well as suggestions for listervers (discussion forums) and newsgroups of particular interest to teachers. You can also find out where to obtain free e-mail accounts.

- **Where can I find curriculum-related information on the Internet?**
  Many of the best Web sources for curriculum and student projects are cited in Chapters 2, 3, 4, and 5 as well as in the hints and Teaching Tips that appear throughout the book. You will also find a list of selected sources in Appendix B and a more extensive list on the CD-ROM that comes with the book.

- **Where can I get information on technological planning?**
  See Chapter 9 for resources that can help administrators and teachers meet the continuing challenge of implementing technological change.

- **How can I get my classroom involved if funding is limited?**
  Funding is another challenge for integrating the Internet into the classroom. Chapter 9 also offers practical suggestions for enlisting corporate, government, and community support to make the Internet a reality in your school.

- **What additional opportunities exist for teachers outside of the classroom?**
  Find out about initiatives that support homeschoolers and provide distance education. In Chapter 10, you can learn about ways that teachers are using distance education for professional development and as a new teaching venue.

About This Book's Features

We have designed *The Teacher's Complete & Easy Guide to the Internet* in a way that we think will make good sense to teachers. We explain all the basics on how to use the Internet and provide practical tips and project ideas that will help teachers turn the Internet into a useful tool for the classroom.

Here are some of the exciting features of this book:

Getting Started... with. We're aware that you need to gain a level of comfort with new technology before launching into class projects, so we include structured learning exercises specifically designed to help teachers master basic concepts and skills.

Project Ideas. We think this is one of the most exciting features of this book! These take you step by step through a range of Internet projects that you can use in the classroom. Projects are included for all grade levels and for varying levels of connectivity. You'll be able to implement some of these with just a basic Internet connection.

A Sampling of... Great Internet Sites. Our "site samplers" identify many of the very best educational sites currently on the Internet. We've also provided space for you to add your own personal favorites, as your list of exciting educational resources on the Internet continues to grow.

HINT Scattered throughout the text, these highlight extra suggestions for learning about the Net and using it effectively.

Teaching Tips. These time-saving tips will help you and your students make the most of your time online as you integrate the Internet into your classroom.

Tech Talk. These are technical points that are not essential, yet are useful to know about. If a particular point seems obscure at first, you can highlight it and return to it once you've gained more experience. It's not necessary to understand everything all at once. In fact, we hope this guide will continue to be useful to you over the long term.

Teacher Quotes. Our teacher quotes (most of them culled from the Internet!) offer practical hints and insights into the value of this technology for learning. We hope you'll find these as exciting, motivating, and helpful as we did.

Glossary. Check the back of the book for an excellent glossary of Internet terms from Unisys Corporation.

Acceptable Use Policy. Appendix A shows you how one school has addressed the issues of student safety and acceptable use of Internet access.

Curriculum Links: Online Resources. Appendix B lists links that will lead you to resources in your specific teaching area. We include everything from Art to the Environment to Special Needs. The list is designed to help teachers link the Internet to practical learning outcomes. Even teachers who are already familiar with the Internet will find this list of selected curriculum resources invaluable.

Education sites on CD-ROM. This comprehensive resource includes and extends the sites listed in Appendix B, by providing capsule summaries of hundreds of important education links for teachers and covering primary through secondary grade levels and more than fifteen curriculum areas. The CD-ROM will help you quickly link to special needs resources, technology planning resources, professional references for teachers, and activities for students.

Opera browser. The CD-ROM also includes shareware version 3.21 of the Opera browser for Windows 3.1x, Windows 95, Windows 98, and Windows NT. Because Opera is particularly fast and works well on machines that are not so up-to-date, we feel that many teachers may be interested in sampling this browser. You can visit the Opera Web site at **http://www.operasoftware.com** for additional information about Opera, to access alternative versions of the browser (including versions in languages other than English), or to subscribe to the Opera mailing list.

Note that the Opera browser is an evaluation copy. If you intend to use it on an ongoing basis, you will need to pay a modest registration fee. Information about Opera costs and alternative versions of the browser are available at **http://traviata.nta.no/opera.htm**.

How to begin?
We suggest you read Chapter 1 first because it gives an overview of the ways that the Internet can be used in the classroom. Even if you are an experienced Internet user, Chapter 1 will help you learn more about the role of technology in schools and generate new ideas about how the Internet can be used to support learning.

Chapters 2 through 9 offer down-to-earth instructions on "how to" that you can explore in whichever order works best for you. Use the Table of Contents and the Chapter Goals to help determine which chapters will be most immediately useful to you. Some teachers may want to focus initially on using electronic mail, while others will prefer to start by sampling some of the curriculum resources on the World Wide Web. Be aware that Chapters 6 and 9 are somewhat more technical than the other chapters. You may want to explore these two chapters after you have mastered basic Web navigation. If you are an experienced user, these may be among the first chapters you'll want to delve into.

The CD-ROM can serve as a helpful tool throughout your learning, and as a starting point whenever you are planning your own classroom Internet activities.

Our most important goal in designing *The Teacher's Complete & Easy Guide to the Internet* has been to try to make it work for individual teachers. Thus, we have relied on the suggestions, ideas, and experiences of teachers like yourself. Their input has helped us to identify many issues that need to be addressed for the Internet to be successfully implemented in schools. We welcome your comments and suggestions about sections of this book that you have found particularly useful.

If you have ideas you would like to share with others, please send them to

Trifolium Books Inc.
250 Merton Street, Suite 203
Toronto, ON M4S 1B1

Or, e-mail your suggestions to Trifolium's president at **trifoliu@ican.net**.

"I am proud to be able to use the Internet as a way of speaking to people all over the globe to help provide quality education to my future students! We've only just begun!"

Cheryl Janik, Elementary School Teacher, currently a graduate student in the Elementary Education Program at the University of New York at Buffalo.

About the People Behind This Book

Ann Heide, author. Ann received a Prime Minister's Award for Excellence in Teaching Math, Science and Technology and participated in Northern Telecom's National Institute in 1994. After several years as a classroom teacher and technology consultant, she recently enjoyed a year travelling (without a computer!). In 1998-1999 Ann will be teaching Educational Technology courses at the Faculty of Education at the University of Ottawa's teacher education program, as well as continuing in her role as consultant with the Ottawa-Carleton Catholic School Board, Ottawa, Ontario.

Linda Stilborne, author. Linda is a learning technology consultant and distance learning specialist. She has taught at Deer Park High

Linda Stilborne (left), Ann Heide (right)

School in Cincinnati, Ohio, and St. Joseph's High School in St. Thomas, Ontario. Her classroom subject specialties are English and computers. As a member of the technical support team for Canada's SchoolNet, she conducted research into the educational applications for the Internet, with a particular focus on classroom integration issues. Linda has also served as an Eastern Region representative to the Ontario Colleges' Computer Based Learning Project and as a research project co-ordinator for the Education Network of Ontario.

Val Johnston. A classroom teacher and librarian with the Oxford County Board of Education for more than 20 years, Val has been devoted to promoting students' use of computers at school and at home. Spreading the word about computers, she's worked with adults in night courses, run a children's summer computer camp, and worked with E.S.L. teachers to develop methods to teach their students about computer use. She currently maintains Web site and Internet curriculum materials for the Ontario Ministry of Education and the Educational Computing Organization of Ontario.

Contents

Acknowledgments ii
About This Book iii
About This Book's Features v
About the People Behind This Book viii

Introduction   1
Ten Tips for Internet Success 4

Chapter **1 The Role of the Internet in Today's Classroom**   6

The Internet today 7
Technology and learning theory 8
Technology and schools 9
Keys to using the Net 14
Learning through connectivity 18
Learning through online resources 19
Learning by becoming involved 23
Learning to learn 23
Summing up 26

Chapter **2 Tapping into Existing Projects**   27

Types of projects 28
Learning through connectivity 28
Learning through online resources 33
Learning by becoming involved 39
Learning to learn 43
Joining an existing project 46
Direct instruction 49
Student experts 49
Practice activities 50
Learning together 51
Summing up 52

Chapter **3 Planning Your Own Projects**   53

Planning your project 53
Students with special needs 62
Student Internet accounts 66
Security and viruses 66
Child safety 67
Software that limits access to inappropriate sites 68

Acceptable use policies 72
Sample acceptable use policies 73
Responding to inappropriate material 75
Resources re child safety 76
Summing up 77

Chapter 4 **Exploring the World Wide Web**   **78**

The Web as a tool for learning 78
World Wide Web: overview 79
Web browsers: Netscape vs. Explorer 81
Basic navigation 84
URLs 84
Making friends with your browser 86
Searching the Web 91
Search engines 95
Metasearch tools 99
Hints for searching the Internet 99
A sampling of educational Web sites 104
Summing up 111

Chapter 5 **Bringing the World Wide Web
into the Classroom**   **112**

Evaluating online resources 127
Copyright 133
Citing Internet sources 134
Using online newspapers and magazines 135
A sampling of good Internet news sources 136
Online traveling 140
A sampling of Internet travel guides 140
WebQuests 154
Ideas for WebQuest Learning Tasks 160
Summing up 161

Chapter 6 **Developing Web Pages for Learning 162**

Introduction to HTML 163
Developing a Web page 165
Basic HTML tags 165
Adding colors and images 168
Web graphics 170
HTML editors 171
Where to learn more about HTML 172

School Web pages   173
Posting Web pages   178
Student Web projects   179
Summing up   181

Chapter 7 **Communicating Over the Net**   182

Electronic mail: overview   184
Using Netscape Mail   189
Listservers: discussion groups via e-mail   192
Finding out more about Usenet news   201
FAQs   201
Online forums   202
Summing up   215

Chapter 8 **Additional Internet Tools**   216

FTP   217
Compressed files   220
Sites for downloading software and educational
    resources   223
Telnet   227
Gophers   228
Real-time discussion on the Web   28
Other chat environments   231
CU-SeeMe   232
Streaming audio   234
Other helper applications   235
Installing viewers   237
Offline browsers   238
Summing up   238

Chapter 9 **Bringing the Internet into Schools**   239

What is a connection?   240
Establishing a SLIP/PPP connection   242
Models for schools   247
School implementation planning   252
Training   253
Staying current   261
Funding   262
Business-education partnerships   266
Private grants, awards and contests   270
Time   271
Summing up   273

Chapter **10** **Beyong the Classroom Walls** **274**

Homework helpers 274
Plagiarism 278
Homeschooling 279
Distance education 282
New directions 288

Glossary 291

Appendix A 301
Sample Acceptable Use Policy

Appendix B 306
Curriculum Links: Online Resources

Bibliography 335

Notes 336

Index 337

Introduction

> **"**I want my students to know how to live satisfying, productive lives. Technology is an increasingly important part of living and working and playing in the world today. The essential role for teachers, as I see it, is to introduce students to some of the possibilities of this new culture, to give students the opportunity to participate and to belong.**"**
> — JOHN GRAVES, PARENT HOME SCHOOLER, SAN DIEGO, CA, USA

In education today, we find ourselves in exciting and challenging times characterized by constant change. While the Internet brings us closer to being able to deliver on the promise of technology to re-shape our education systems, we know that educational media alone do not influence the achievement of students.

In this book, we examine the use of the Internet within the overall context of educational reform, in which the integration of technology is neither simply to speed up the process of learning nor to teach new technology skills. Rather the intent is to combine technology use with other reform efforts (e.g., new instructional strategies, new uses of time and staffing), in helping schools become environments that empower students to successfully attain new learning goals. This book is for any teacher who wants to learn more about how to use the Internet to enhance student learning. It is especially for teachers who approach the Internet with reluctance and perhaps with a touch of skepticism about its value in the classroom.

Your guide
The Teacher's Complete & Easy Guide to the Internet is intended to help you, the teacher, experience the excitement that the Internet can bring to your classroom. It explains key concepts and helps you learn to use basic Internet tools. Learning the mechanics of using new tools is just one element of technology in education reform; another is developing lesson plans and projects that incorporate the resources available over the Internet into curriculum. You do not have to do all this yourself; this book tells you where to find some of the best educational resources on the Net. Most importantly, it will help you to discover how the Internet can help your students learn.

The global village

We read and hear a great deal these days about how the world is shrinking. Traditional political, economic, and social boundaries are being redefined almost daily. As we search for common values and a common understanding, we develop an appreciation for the complexities of managing a world of profoundly different cultures and social structures.

Education will be the key to resolving economic and cross-cultural problems, and it is the younger generations that will need to find solutions. We are all aware that we have a responsibility to provide today's students with the skills they will need to succeed in a workplace that is increasingly information based. These skills certainly include knowing how to use computers; even more important are the personal and social skills that must be developed.

Veterans of the education technology movement say teachers learn best from each other. Fortunately, teachers who have ready access to the Internet are discovering, inventing, and sharing the kinds of practices and programs in their own classrooms that illustrate true education reform. And because the Internet is an incredibly effective communications tools, these teachers are finding one another, sharing with one another, and organizing collegially in new ways. In the past few years there have been substantial efforts aimed at making the Internet a more teacher- and student-friendly place. Resource lists and lesson plans have sprung from a variety of sources both public and private; we highlight some of the best in this book.

A central skill
We feel strongly that the Internet is a powerful force for helping students develop a sense of personal responsibility for their own learning. Students expand their horizons by learning how to communicate, how to collaborate, and indeed, how to learn. Teachers who understand that the world is changing also understand that classroom learning needs to change in response. Schools must play an integral role in bringing about the necessary social adjustments as we move from an industrial to an information-based economy. The Internet will be a vital tool for bringing about such change. It is increasingly clear that we as teachers must think about the impact telecommunications can have on education and respond in positive ways to it.

Educators who have begun using the Internet as a learning tool know the critical role it can play in linking students to the world of telecommunications and information technology. Others are excited by the vastness of the information resources on the Internet. More than anything, teachers who have begun to explore the Internet with their classes are thrilled by its potential as a communications tool.

The opportunity
A major challenge is that much of this technology is new to almost everyone. Even seasoned "Internauts" are still struggling to improve the technology and sort out the technical, political, and pedagogical

issues. Major improvements need to be made to our telecommunications infrastructure to accommodate increasingly complex applications, such as multimedia and video-conferencing. Then there are the serious social questions, such as "Should there be complete freedom of information on the Internet?" Educators must play a part in helping to resolve some of these issues. We have a unique opportunity to ensure that knowledge and understanding, rather than power and greed, are the forces that will steer the growth of the information highway.

A team approach

As you and your class become familiar with the Internet's many resources, learning can become a team effort in which everyone is encouraged to share knowledge, skills, and new discoveries. A team approach to learning is one of the things that makes the Internet fun for students. One innovative geography teacher has even involved her class in designing learning units for other classes—including establishing learning outcomes and evaluating learning. A team approach also allows students to become active in their own education and reinforces the value of personal responsibility.

The three keys to keeping this dynamic environment manageable are

- committing enough time to become reasonably familiar with Internet tools
- seeking out others who can help when you get stuck
- moving slowly enough to make sure that you understand each stage before moving on to the next.

You are about to embark on an adventure that will change the way you teach and the way your students learn. It will also change the ways in which you—and they—see and respond to the world. It is our hope that *The Teacher's Complete & Easy Guide to the Internet* will help to make this adventure a mutually exciting and satisfying one.

Ann Heide
Linda Stilborne

Learning about the Internet will:

- be exciting
- take time
- sometimes be frustrating
- change the way you solve problems
- change the way you teach
- give you new confidence
- broaden your horizons

Most importantly,

- Using the Internet will ensure that you and your students have a place in a global world.

Ten tips for Internet success :-)

Here are some approaches you and your students can use to get started quickly and avoid common pitfalls. Many of these suggestions are based on the idea of sharing expertise, which is the best way to master the Internet. Because integration of technology into the curriculum is a requirement of the educational reform that is occurring everywhere, you are not alone. Take advantage of what other teachers, students, administrators, and the broader community are offering to help you bring this technology into your classroom.

1. **Consult others before proceeding on your own;** if you know someone who is using the Internet, ask him or her to help you get started. Check with your local school district resource people, teacher organizations and national as well as provincial/state online networks to find out what existing projects are already available for your students to join. If other teachers in your school have experience using the Internet, offer to help them manage an Internet project.

2. **Find a learning partner,** possibly another teacher in your school who also wants to use the Internet. You can compare notes on resources and encourage each other. (If you find yourselves complaining to each other, find a different partner!)

3. **Sign up for any local courses** that promise to help you learn more about the Internet and its tools. Your school district may offer such courses or may be willing to fund a course, particularly if you agree to share some of what you learn with your colleagues. (Hint: Taking a course with a partner is also a good way to ensure you don't miss key points.)

4. **If your school does not have Internet access,** get your own account. Shop around for a service provider until you find one who is willing to provide help with the installation. If possible, seek out Windows- or Macintosh-based access, since these bring you the best of the Internet's marvelous graphics.

5. **If you know of any student technowizards at your school,** ask them to help with such tasks as installing a modem. As you may have discovered, many students (particularly those in the upper grades) are already knowledgeable about the Internet, and are eager to share what they know.

6. **Visit your school or local university** library to see what books and magazines are available about using the Internet in education. Many educational journals such as *Electronic Learning, Leading and Learning with Technology, American Journal of*

Distance Education, and *Electronic School and Journal of Computer Assisted Learning* focus on the role of technology in education reform and provide lesson plans, projects, and useful advice from teachers.

7. **Once you're online,** seek out online tutorials and education resources. This book suggests many helpful sources.

8. **Don't try to master everything at once;** take time to explore. In particular, give yourself ample time to learn before beginning a classroom project. If you spend even thirty minutes a day learning something new, you'll be amazed at what you've mastered in a month.

9. **Once you're comfortable with electronic mail,** join one of the educational listservs such as INCLASS or Kidsphere. (See Chapter 4 for more information about these.)

10. **Although Net browsers let you keep track of resources online,** keep a small notebook or card file of some of the interesting resources you find. A personalized, computer-based card file or database is great for quick searching.

Hope you find our hints helpful! We will provide more useful tips throughout this book.

If you live in a country where the grade levels K–12 are not used, please note the following approximate ages of students at each grade level. This chart will permit you to see readily which projects in the book are at the appropriate level for your own students.

kindergarten (K)	grade 1	grade 2	grade 3	grade 4	grade 5	grade 6
ages 5–6	ages 6–7	ages 7–8	ages 8–9	ages 9–10	ages 10–11	ages 11–12

grade 7	grade 8	grade 9	grade 10	grade 11	grade 12
ages 12–13	ages 13–14	ages 14–15	ages 15–16	ages 16–17	17–18

The Role of the Internet in Today's Classroom

"I asked my daughter, 'What would be the number one thing you would want us to teach you if you were heading off for college today?' Her answer was immediate: 'Teach me to use the Net!'**"**

— JOHN DALTON, TEACHER, JENNIFER MERCHANT TAIPEI AMERICAN SCHOOL, TAIPEI, TAIWAN

Marshall McLuhan, the communications visionary of the sixties, said that new technologies are always used to do the old job—that is, until some driving force causes them to be used in new ways. It can be argued that, so far, this has been our experience with computers in education. Today there are computers in schools, but as yet they have not significantly changed the nature of teaching or of learning. Computers can deliver learning in novel ways, but they still fall far short of delivering the kinds of school experiences we want for our children. With the advent of the Internet, this situation is changing and very quickly. Again, it was McLuhan who captured the concept that is now the driving force behind the Internet—as well as behind an impending revolution in education. The concept is that of the *global village*. Since Marshall McLuhan coined the term in the 1960s, few of us have truly understood what the term "global village" means. Most of us have been impressed with CNN's instantaneous global video broadcasting, but the passive medium of television gives few of us the feeling of much involvement beyond our favorite reclining chair. Yet today, thousands of children in dozens of countries around the world are living the reality of the global village in personal, hands-on interactive ways. Through the medium of networking and telecommunication technologies, these students are for the first time learning to think of themselves as global citizens, seeing the world, and their place in the world, in ways much different than their parents.

This chapter looks at the Internet and its potential to bring about revolutionary social change in education and society. The availability of so much information and so many opportunities to share and communicate with people at a distance may not at first appear to be sufficient justification for schools to spend the amounts of money needed to link classrooms to the Internet. This chapter discusses some of the reasons why the Internet is an increasingly important tool for educators and shows how telecommunications technologies have the potential to transform the ways in which teachers teach and students learn.

Chapter goals

- ■ **To provide an overview of the Internet**
- ■ **To consider the role of the Internet in education**
- ■ **To introduce some specific Internet tools that teachers can use**
- ■ **To examine some practical ways in which the Internet can help students learn**

The Internet today

The Internet is an extensive network of interlinked yet independent computer networks. In less than two decades, the Internet has gone from being a highly specialized communications network used mostly for military and academic applications to a massive electronic bazaar. Today, the network includes

- educational and government computers
- computers from research institutions
- computerized library catalogues
- businesses
- homes
- community-based computers (called *freenets*)
- a diverse range of local computer bulletin boards.

Anyone who has an account on one of these computers can send electronic mail throughout the network and access resources from hundreds of other computers on the network.

The phenomenal growth of the Internet is one indicator of the impact that this technology will ultimately have. For the past six years, the Internet has doubled in size each year. That means that each year, there are as many new people connecting to the Internet as there are existing users.

> "StatsCan reported earlier this year that 45% of homes with children under 18 (1.7 million) had home computers and estimated that 20% of them are surfing the Net....That figure will grow to 40% by the end of the century. The Internet is penetrating homes as fast as television did in the 50s," says Don Tapscott, author of *Growing Up Digital: The Rise of the Net Generation* (1997).

Because of the free-wheeling culture of the Internet and its overall lack of structure and external controls, it is tempting to dismiss it as a novelty. Those who take time to learn about it soon discover, however, that the Internet is actually a microcosm of our society. Most of what happens in the real world is in some way reflected on the Net. On the Internet you can find libraries, radio programs, and shopping malls. You can meet friends, take courses, subscribe to magazines, and obtain medical or gardening information. The Internet can be a source of news, a forum for dialogue with other people about current events, a place to find out about government activities and about jobs. For students, the Internet offers pen-friends (known as *keypals*), learning resources, a place to share their thoughts and ideas, a place to collaborate with peers, and opportunities to publish their own stories and pictures.

Technology and learning theory

How do we educate today's child, born into a world of instant information with a host of resources available at the press of a button? For students to assemble and modify ideas, to access and study information, the traditional classroom tools of pencils, notebooks, and texts are still required, but they are inadequate. Computers, video, and other technologies engage students with the immediacy they are used to in their everyday lives, but the key is not what technology is available in the classroom, rather how it is used. Like anything else, the value of technology in education is derived entirely from its application.

Early uses of computers to aid instruction through drill and practice were based on the work of behaviorists such as B.F. Skinner. In this paradigm, technology was relegated to a secondary, supplemental role that failed to capitalize on its true strengths. It is no surprise that research has failed to show consistent improvements in student learning through this use of technology. In contrast, constructivist theories predominate in the literature today. In a constructivist view of learning, learners actively construct knowledge as they make sense out of their experiences. Constructivist learning is active and student-centered and tends to be project-oriented. Current theories put technology into the hands of learners to assist in their developing higher order cognitive skills and speak of technology's power to access, store, manipulate, and analyze information, thus enabling learners to spend more time reflecting and understanding. "In general, goals of instruction in a constructivist environment center around problem-solving, reasoning, critical thinking and the active use of knowledge. Additionally, constructivists see collaboration, metacognition and student centered instruction as essential elements of the learning environment." (Grau and Bartasis, 1995) Learners' accessibility to information using the Internet allows them to develop their own styles of information retrieval and organization. Using the Internet as a tool, students can explore environments, generate questions and issues, collaborate with others, and produce knowledge rather than passively receiving it.

Technology and schools

In fact, the Internet offers only a bare suggestion of the role that telecommunications will ultimately play in the lives of today's students. Significant global changes are occurring rapidly and political boundaries are becoming less distinct. Issues such as the environment, terrorism, and inflation affect all the citizens of the world. Job market skills and employment requirements are changing. Communication skills are becoming essential to earning a living, yet students are not coming to the workforce adequately prepared. The skills they will require to navigate this environment must be learned today. It is generally agreed that in the twenty-first century, technology will be pervasive. Futurists predict that by the end of this century, approximately two-thirds of all work will involve some form of computerized information. It is therefore important that all students today learn to access, analyze, and communicate electronic information effectively.

It has been suggested that if someone who died one hundred years ago were to visit North America in the last decade of the twentieth century, the only thing recognizable would be the schools. Although technology has radically changed factories, offices, banks, and hospitals, most of our classrooms might appear unchanged.

There has been change, of course. Teachers know that the whole philosophy of learning has changed radically in recent years. As a result, both the way students are taught and the kinds of skills they acquire in today's classroom are very different from the methodology and curriculum of even a decade ago. In fact, schools must change continually to accommodate the society in which they operate. For example, junior kindergartens, school lunch programs, resource teachers, and sex education—all unheard of fifty years ago—are commonplace today. Because information technology is currently *the* driving force in our culture and in our economy, it is time to incorporate it into the curriculum in a meaningful way. When teachers and students are connected to the world, teaching and learning strategies change. When teachers change how they teach, moving from "instructional deliverers" to "side-by-side learners," we see technologies employed in drastically different ways—more like the ways they are used in other segments of our society. The world is available as a curriculum resource: NASA scientists, aviation professionals and hobbyists, biologists mapping the human genome, Middle Eastern scholars studying the Dead Sea Scrolls, musicians, dissident Chinese refugees—and teachers and their students can all be found on line, along with the information generated by their research and activities. The implications for schools are profound.

When students communicate with people in distant and foreign places, they begin to understand, appreciate, and respect cultural, political, environmental, geographic, and linguistic similarities and differences. Their view of the world and their place in the world changes and curriculum content becomes current, relevant, and integrated from a multi-disciplinary, global perspective.

There are a number of reasons why some schools and teachers have been less than enthusiastic about bringing the Internet into the classroom. These reasons include

- a systemic lack of awareness of the appropriate uses of technology in schools
- the apparent complexity of the Internet
- the absence of new forms of assessment with which to measure new forms of learning
- the lack of telephone or data lines in schools
- reduced funding for public education
- concerns about child safety on the Internet
- the lack of both time and training opportunities for teachers.

As well, sometimes there is a lack of administrative support, and occasionally, colleagues may resist a teacher's attempt to explore new methods. There is also the problem that—at least at first glance—the Internet may seem to be dominated by technowizards who appear to be more concerned about what the technology can do than about how it can improve the teaching and learning processes. Some teachers may be daunted by the fact that their students know so much more than they themselves do about the Internet. "This has never happened before in human history— that children are an authority about a central issue in society." (Tapscott, 1997) These are all real problems, but they are problems that must somehow be overcome. The Internet—or, more precisely, the broader world of computers and telecommunications, of which the Internet is only a part—is restructuring society. It is a phenomenon that challenges some of our assumptions about how the world works. Consider the following examples, which signal the reality of the new global village. Via the Internet:

- A North American company can hire programmers in countries as distant as India or Russia.
- Within minutes of the 1994 earthquake in Los Angeles, people around the world were able to obtain first-hand accounts of the event. Because telephone calls to Los Angeles were not possible, the Net became a critical means of relaying information to and from the disaster area. In one poignant case, a family asked anyone within the disaster zone to check on their grandmother, whom they could not reach. Within a couple of hours, a response was posted on the Internet: "I couldn't get through to

your grandmother, so I went to the apartment building and found her. The building didn't hold up very well, but your grandmother did. She's fine."

- An owner of a small bookstore in Nova Scotia, Canada, turned his business around virtually overnight by tapping into the global marketplace. Currently, there are twenty to thirty million potential consumers on the Internet who can purchase everything there from pet food to automobiles. Each month, more than 1500 new companies connect to the Net.
- Large companies are increasingly involved in collaborative research with other companies to develop new products in a rapidly evolving marketplace. Global competition and multinational corporate ventures are fueling the need for Internet connectivity and an increasingly sophisticated telecommunications infrastructure.

Education is also taking its place in the global village.

- Hundreds of distance education courses are now available over the Internet. A high school in Oregon offers anyone with Internet connectivity the opportunity to acquire a diploma through distance learning. Some school districts, particularly those serving rural populations, are investigating delivery of elementary-level classes.
- Students join scientists on board NASA's Kuiper Airborne Observatory as it flies at 41,000 feet to study planets, stars, and galaxies with its infrared telescope.

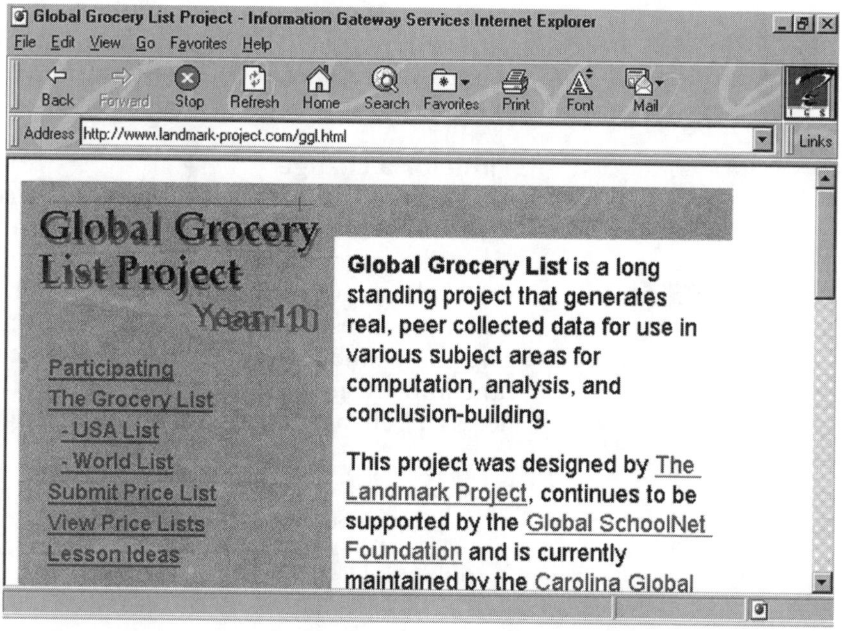

Figure 1-1
The Global Grocery List stimulates a discussion with Japanese students who are surprised that their diet staple, rice, is so much more expensive than in other parts of the world. Students in Japan and America discover principles of protectionist trade policies.

- A student in Cold Harbor Springs, New York, interviews Russian Jewish immigrants in Brooklyn. He recruits online acquaintances in Moscow and Jerusalem to interview Russian Jews in those places and send him the results, so he can compare the stories from all three places in his high school sociology project.
- During the 1994–95 school year, students across the United States carried on a continuous dialog with scientists journeying to Antarctica.

> "I've never seen a project that was so alive with the breath of what it means to do the work of science...."
>
> — *Parent of a middle schooler from New Jersey, U.S.A., talking about* Live from Antarctica

- Students in New York collect relief supplies to send to their on-line friends devastated in the Florida hurricane.
- Students all over the world share their excitement at the Mars landing and use the Internet to view the first pictures as they arrive from the surface. This event is just one example of the real-time experiences made possible by the Internet.

Through the computer, students can converse with other students in remote classrooms. With video-capture technology, students can participate in a dynamic fashion in events as they happen around the globe. Students who have the opportunities described here have already begun to make their own paradigm shifts regarding their place in the world and how to relate to it. As adults, these students will have advantages in their skills, experiences, and outlook over those who were confined within their own classrooms and communities. Through telecommunications, the walls of the classroom recede and learning about the world becomes more immediate, personal, and real.

Time for a change

The technological revolution has produced a generation of students who have grown up with multidimensional, interactive media sources, a generation whose understandings and expectations of the world differ from those preceding them. Only by revising educational practices in the light of how our culture has changed can we give these students an appropriate education. Technology consultant and award-winning teacher Alan November describes the necessary changes to our schools as changing "job descriptions":

> "The job descriptions of everyone in school will fundamentally change because of the [information] highway. Students will move from working in the test-preparation business to building information products that can really be used by 'clients' around the world. For teachers, perhaps the most difficult job change will be that we'll no longer be at the center of learning for our students. We'll become brokers—connecting our students to others across the nets who

will help them create and add to their knowledge in a way that one teacher alone could only dream of."

— Quoted by Thérèse Mageau (1994, May/June), "Will the superhighway really change schools?" Electronic Learning, 13(8):24.

Some teachers might raise an eyebrow at November's unconventional views, but others would insist that the reality he envisions is not far off. Classroom use of the Internet is already a reality. One set of figures indicates that between 1991 and 1993, educational use of the Internet grew by an astonishing 23,000 percent, and that much of this growth was in elementary and secondary schools. By December 1994, there were nearly 200 elementary and secondary school Internet servers. By July 1995, this figure had increased to 450, and by December 1995, there were more than 1900 schools with their own home page posted on the World Wide Web.

It is often the case that, at least initially, people approach new technologies with the thought that they are somehow replacing something more familiar. Sometimes this perception proves to be true. Television has in large part replaced radio, just as the car has replaced the horse and buggy. We may worry that the Internet has the potential to replace the textbook, the school library, and, ultimately, the classroom teacher. Undoubtedly the role of the classroom teacher will change, but teachers will not become redundant. In fact, the best guarantee that teachers, and not technology, will be at the heart of the classroom of the future is to ensure that we as the teachers of today master new tools for learning, such as the Internet. "For teachers, technology should be a means to new ends, to more dynamic learning, but technology should not be the issue. The real issues are about new forms of perception and awareness required by change, new definitions of what it means to produce knowledge, and a willingness to abandon old forms of authority for the more democratic assets found in a true learning community." (Rowe, 1994) With access to the Internet, the classroom becomes an even greater cooperative learning environment in which the teacher provides focus, guidance, and inspiration.

In 1996, President Clinton articulated a clear vision for improving 21st century education through the use of technology in American schools. Defining "Four Pillars" as part of his Technology Literacy Challenge, the President called for broadening educational technology objectives to include not only hardware and connectivity, but also digital content and professional development. More American schools have internal networks and access to the outside world than ever before. From 1994 to 1996, the number of schools reporting Internet access nearly doubled. In schools serving students from low income homes, Internet access jumped 71% from 1995 to 1996.

—CEO Forum on Education and Technology, http://www.ceoforum.org/report97/pillars.html, 02/12/97

	Old model	New model	Implications for learners
Figure 1-2 **New models for learning**	Teacher centered	Learner centered	Students are empowered as learners
	Passive absorption	Learner participation	Student motivation is enhanced
	Individual work	Team learning	Team building skills are developed; learning is enhanced through sharing
	Teacher as expert	Teacher as guide	Framework for learning is more adaptable to a fast-changing world
	Static	Dynamic	Resources for learning (textbooks, existing knowledge base) are replaced by an online link to the real world. Resources can be adapted to immediate learning needs
	Prescribed learning	Learning to learn	Development of skills for the information age

"Today, more than ever, we need teachers who are able and willing to become side-by-side learners with their students. Teachers who are not afraid to acknowledge, 'I don't know,' and then can turn around and say, 'Let's find out together.' These teachers need to know how to use various technologies to shape and process and manage information, to look for relationships, trends, anomalies, and details, which can not only answer questions, but create questions as well. We need teachers who understand that learning in today's world is not just a matter of mastering a static body of knowledge, but also being able to discover the rapidly changing ideas about that knowledge itself."

—*Al Rogers. TheFailure and the Promise of Technology in Education, Global SchoolNet Foundation,* **http://www.gsn.org,***03/10/97.*

Figure 1-2 outlines some of the shifts between the old and the new models of learning, together with their implications for students.

Keys to using the Net

As with any learning venture, success depends on mastering the basics and then gradually expanding knowledge through practice. Although the Internet is a huge and ever-expanding universe of information, the good news is that you don't have to know it all. For teachers, the key to using the Internet successfully is to learn to use a few basic tools—and then to focus on using a few key educational resources.

This chapter briefly describes some basic Internet tools. Subsequent chapters will discuss each of these in detail. The paragraphs that follow are intended to give a preview of some of the ways that you can access educational resources over the Internet. With the exception of the World Wide Web (described below), most of these applications are possible even on an outdated computer with a relatively slow connection.

World Wide Web

The World Wide Web, along with special software called Web browsers (such as Netscape, Opera, or Microsoft's Internet Explorer), provides point-and-click access to text, graphics, sound, and sometimes video files, often integrated around a specific topic. The World Wide Web provides easy access to a vast array of information. A Web page can be a "clickable" children's book, an online museum exhibit, an art gallery display, a government information resource, a lesson from a distance learning course, a weather map, or even an interactive frog dissection. The World Wide Web also provides a great opportunity for students to publish their own information.

You can use a Web browser as a communications tool to send e-mail or to participate in on-line discussions. Technologies such as *Web conferencing*, in which messages are posted to the Web for ongoing discussions, and *push technology*, which allows customized data delivery, have greatly enhanced the relatively static presentation of text and graphics. Increasingly, Internet applications that have traditionally been separate and distinct are now all accessible through the World Wide Web. Newsgroups, FTP (File Transfer Protocol) sites, and even online "chat groups" are all available through the Web. For many teachers, the Web is the real focus of the Internet, to the point where some people have come to think (erroneously) that the Web and the Internet are synonymous.

E-mail

Electronic mail, or e-mail, rivals the Web as the most common Internet application, as well as one of the most powerful. Electronic mail allows you to send and receive messages over the Internet. Using electronic mail, you can communicate with anyone else who has an Internet address. You can also send messages through "gateway" services to other systems, such as bulletin boards or CompuServe. Many classroom projects may use electronic mail, which provides an opportunity for interactions with students and teachers around the globe.

In addition, through electronic mail you can join worldwide discussion groups. There are literally hundreds of discussion groups for educators on the Internet. Favorites among elementary and secondary school teachers include Kidsphere, an international discussion group for teachers; Edtech, which focuses on the use of technology in the classroom; and Kidlit-L, a discussion group that explores children's literature. There is a wide range of discussion groups with a specific curriculum focus. Such groups include **K12.lang.art**, for language arts education; **k12.ed.soc-studies**, for social science teachers; and **k12.ed.life-skills**, for school counselors.

You will be amazed at the number of projects you and your students can undertake using e-mail. Chapters 2, 3, and 6 provide a wealth of examples and ideas.

Audio and interactive video

With the proper computer setup (including speakers, a sound card, and Web phone software, which you can buy at your local computer store), you can use the Internet in place of the telephone. While this technology is not yet common, it is estimated that more than one million people currently use it.

You can also have instant access to radio and other audio broadcasts with technologies such as RealAudio. Desktop videoconferencing and video over the Internet are still limited on slower-speed networks (such as those that depend on ordinary telephone lines), but new techniques for compressing and transmitting data may make these high-end applications widely available in just a few years.

The proliferation of cable television services, set-top boxes (for Internet access via your television), and satellite communication technologies may help develop an all-purpose tool that will one day bring interactive audio, video, and broadcast services to average technology users.

Other Internet applications: FTP, telnet and Gopher

FTP stands for *File Transfer Protocol*. This process is used to transfer files across the Internet. FTP can be used to transfer all kinds of files from a remote computer to the local computer where your own account resides. Resources available through FTP include educational software, text files of sample lesson plans, electronic books, research reports, and graphics files. Using FTP you can quickly bring many useful resources into the classroom. Canada's SchoolNet is one example of an FTP site that offers resources specifically for teachers.

Telnet is a way of connecting to a computer at a remote location and using that computer as if you were actually at that remote site. Although telnet is not used as commonly as it once was, you might use telnet to get to another site such as an online library catalog located at a university. When you telnet to a remote location, you basically use the telnet command and provide the Internet address of the location you wish to access. Once you reach that location, you complete the logon information. The Big Sky Telegraph bulletin

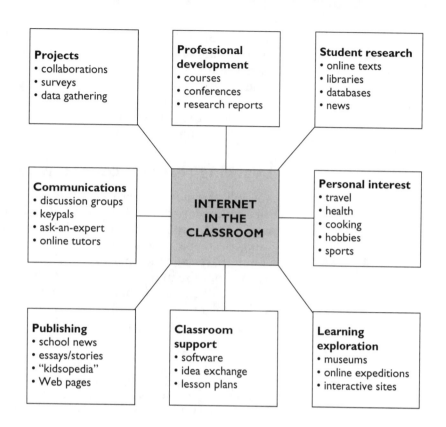

Figure 1-3
The Internet in the class-room

Projects
• collaborations
• surveys
• data gathering

Professional development
• courses
• conferences
• research reports

Student research
• online texts
• libraries
• databases
• news

Communications
• discussion groups
• keypals
• ask-an-expert
• online tutors

INTERNET IN THE CLASSROOM

Personal interest
• travel
• health
• cooking
• hobbies
• sports

Publishing
• school news
• essays/stories
• "kidsopedia"
• Web pages

Classroom support
• software
• idea exchange
• lesson plans

Learning exploration
• museums
• online expeditions
• interactive sites

board, which serves as a clearinghouse for some school telecommunications projects, is accessible through telnet.

Gopher is an Internet tool that allows you to go to hundreds of sites on the Internet through a straightforward menu structure. You maneuver your way through the Internet by selecting items listed on a menu. Gopher can still be useful for accessing information if you do not have a graphical (i.e., Windows or Macintosh) connection to the Internet.

Your success in using the Internet will depend on your understanding of exactly how it relates to the classroom. Figure 1-3 suggests some of the ways in which the Internet can be tied to teaching and learning.

Internet

Each Internet tool has a specific function, and most teachers exploring the Net will want to become familiar with all of them. For teachers, these tools can be used to provide students with exciting opportunities to access and interpret the world around them. Teachers in a traditional classroom often have to create an artificial world, from whatever resources are available, to create learning opportunities that capture some dimension of the real world. But such resources have always been limited, and the classroom environment has never been quite "real." By becoming familiar with a few basic Internet navigation tools, teachers can bring the real world into the classroom. Following are some examples of typical Internet learning activities.

Learning through connectivity

Possibly the most powerful feature of the Internet is its potential as a communications tool. Students delight in being able to connect with people around the world. A fairly simple educational activity using electronic mail involves linking individual students with their counterparts in other places. This is an excellent way for them to learn about life in other countries, to develop and improve their language skills, and to share their thoughts on contemporary issues and problems.

> "When the earthquake happened in San Francisco, we read about tidal waves in kids' swimming pools, earth movement in soccer fields, and kids being thrown down stairways—kids' perceptions of what it was like to be in an earthquake. When the Berlin Wall came down, we had classes in Berlin that were giving us day-by-day reports on what it was like to be there. When the Gulf War was going on, kids in Saudi Arabia's schools talked about the crocheted gas mask backpacks that their mothers made."
>
> — *Margaret Riel, Consultant, AT&T Learning Network*

Being able to see world events at the same level of detail at which ordinary people actually experience them is one way that students can discover the basic humanity they share with people around the globe.

Students can also use e-mail to involve other classes in a project. One seventh-grade class used e-mail to conduct a survey. They wanted to know how much time other students their age spent watching television, so they designed an electronic questionnaire and distributed it to other students over the Internet. This project provided students with an opportunity to learn about gathering and analyzing data. The project was also an interesting way to explore an important social issue.

A somewhat younger group of students used e-mail to find out about food resources around the world. Through a single e-mail account, they requested that students in other countries send them messages about what foods were native to their area. The responses they received provided the basis for developing a classroom map on which foods from various regions were displayed. Being able to interact with other students around the globe in this way brings a new and exciting dimension to learning.

Finally, electronic mail connectivity is a powerful tool for accessing experts and tutors. Purdue University in Indiana operates an online writing lab (OWL) that provides some excellent writing resources as well as human writing coaches. Along a similar line, the Canadian-based Writers In Electronic Residence has professional writers reviewing student writing samples. Other programs link students with scientists and researchers to help with class projects and units of study. Students themselves can even become mentors for their peers, using a rubric to evaluate writing samples or comparing solutions to a common math problem submitted by e-mail.

Connectivity is also a powerful tool for teachers. Global classrooms, in which several classes from around the world work on a common theme, allow teachers to collaborate on lesson planning, student activities, and assessment techniques. Many hours of preparation time can be saved by taking advantage of shared resources and strategies. Professional growth is a natural outcome as teachers learn together and benefit from one another's expertise. The Marsville project challenged students in many locations to research, design, and build a Martian colony. Organized into teams, students designed one of the eight support systems needed to establish a colony on Mars: air supply, communications, food production and delivery, recreation and leisure, temperature control, transportation, waste management, and water supply. A Marsville Web site allowed the students to post messages, read updates, and view designs from other participating schools. Communication via phone, fax, video e-mail, and video-conferencing enhanced the excitement and collaboration of the participating schools. (**http://www.enoreo.on.ca/mars97/index.htm**)

Learning through online resources

As classrooms are able to connect to Internet resources, learning can become an endless adventure. Not only are there substantial text-based resources on topics ranging from planets to politics, but a wide range of resources is available for electronic field trips involving pictures, text, sound, and sometimes interactivity. Here is a sampling of some recent online exhibits sponsored by museums and other educational institutions.

- Honolulu Community College offers a fascinating dinosaur exhibit that features pictures, textual information, and an opportunity to take a narrated tour of the exhibit.

- The Institute of Physics in Naples offers an exhibit of some early instruments used to study physics. Specialized exhibits of this type abound on the Internet, and many of them are exhibits that few people would have a chance to visit otherwise.

- The Smithsonian Institution makes available its exhibit, Oceans of the Earth. Students electronically visiting the exhibit electronically can learn about fascinating sea creatures and about how the oceans affect climate. Teachers can download video clips from the Undersea Flyby or access educational resources such as the *Killer Whale Teacher's Guide*.

- At another exhibit sponsored by the French Ministry of Culture, students can learn all about the discovery of a Paleolithic painted cave. The University of California at Berkeley sponsors the online Museum of Paleontology with exhibits on geology, fossils, and pre-history. A computer server in Oxford, England, provides a gateway to these and many other museum sites.

- Classes can visit the Louvre and other art galleries as well as photography exhibits. Students can download graphics and incorporate them into their own printed or electronic reports. They must first ensure that their teacher allows the use of such graphics and that no copyright laws are being broken by reproducing them. Of course, students must correctly reference all materials taken from the Internet.

- At Questacon, Australia's hands-on science center, students can explore current exhibits, read about intriguing science discoveries and applications, practice problem-solving skills with something called Puzzlequest, and actually try experiments online. Like many resources on the Internet, these are available at no cost, apart from the cost of basic connectivity.

You'll find the addresses to these and other great sites in upcoming chapters, as well as on the CD that accompanies this book. In addition to Web sites, which offer multimedia and interactivity, a great many less exciting but equally useful text-based resources are available on the Internet. These include online books, magazines, and references sources (such as an online dictionary and table of chemical elements). Selected news features, back issues of popular magazines, and full-text encyclopedias are increasingly available on the Net. Extensive archives of historical topics and online documentation of current events provide a depth and breadth of learning resources unmatched by anything previously available in even the best-equipped schools. The Internet is a very good resource for students researching current events, science, or social science topics. In addition, many discussion groups publish basic information about their area of interest. From these resources students can obtain information on topics ranging from pet care to astronomy to ballet. While the Internet falls somewhat short of having information about "everything," it is a substantial information resource. In most

Figure 1-4
Hands-on learning from Questacon, Australia

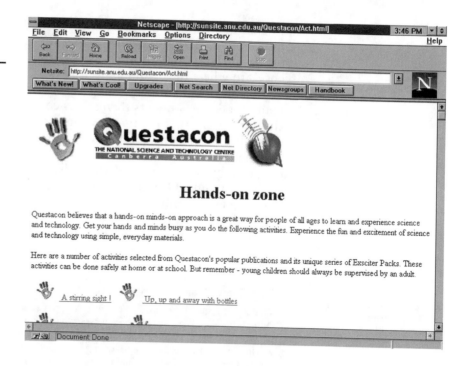

communities, it is a welcome supplement to the generally limited resources available in a local library.

Students can also construct knowledge by collecting and sharing information with one another. In one cooperative project, students analyzed the quality of rivers in their area and compared the data they collected with data gathered by other students in their state. In another project, students reported on when various wildflowers started to bloom in their area, with data being collated centrally.

Perhaps one of the most rewarding ways to use the Internet in a classroom is actually to participate in a real-world adventure. An interesting example of how this can happen is the MayaQuest project. This was an online experience through which students could interact with archeologists investigating the ancient world of the Maya. The project took place in 1995–96. It enabled students to follow a team of researchers on a trek through southern Mexico and northern Central America. Students and teachers could participate in this project in many different ways.

A major component of the project involved the researchers regularly posting on the Internet narratives of their experiences; they described not only details of the ruins they encountered, but geographical conditions and local customs in the areas they visited. In addition, photographs of the journey could be viewed online or downloaded and printed. Newsgroup discussions allowed students to pose questions to the researchers as well as offer their opinions on just about everything, from whether the researchers should consider eating in restaurants (not exactly an authentic Mayan travel experience!) to where the team might head next.

In addition to the teaching resources on the Maya that were made available, students themselves could test their learning by participating in an online scavenger hunt. The scavenger hunt presented them with questions designed to help them review what they had learned about the ancient Mayan civilization and to think deductively about some of their discoveries (see Figure 1-5). The project culminated with satellite broadcasts of video footage from the expedition, and classrooms with appropriate equipment could access this video over the Internet. The material gathered from the project is now a resource base for information about the Maya—

Figure 1-5
Sample questions from the MayaQuest Scavenger Hunt

MayaQuest Scavenger Hunt

This scavenger hunt will inspire children to learn about the region and its rich Mayan culture. It will also give them the necessary background to form their own theory as to why the ancient Mayan civilization collapsed, and to draw parallels to today's world. To find answers to the following questions, students can conduct their own research and can follow the expedition. We encourage participants to share and discuss their ideas in the MayaQuest discussion forum. At the conclusion of the expedition, the MayaQuest team members will post their answers.

1. Find three sites where ancient environmental abuse is apparent. What shape did it take? (clear-cut forest, slash-and-burn agriculture, pollution) In what century did it start occurring? Why did it happen?
2. Find three sites where there is clear evidence of warfare. What does it look like? (fortresses, violent scenes on glyphs) Where are they located? Are they pre-classic, classic, or post-classic?
3. Find evidence of modern-day warfare. What does it look like? How has it affected the surrounding environment and the lives of the people?
4. Find three sites where there is evidence of ancient overpopulation. What is the evidence? Are there any other related signs? (cut rain forests, smaller skeletons)
5. Find three examples of modern-day overpopulation. How are overpopulated cities affecting rural areas? social tensions? the environment?
6. Find three clues that ancient natural disasters occurred. (collapsed temples, stelae scenes depicting disasters...)
7. Research the remains of a modern-day natural disaster. What sort of damage did the last hurricane that hit the coast leave? Have there been earthquakes? What happened to the homes? Did people flee or rebuild? Did sickness or social unrest follow? What did the event do to the environment?
8. Find three Mayan stories or myths. These must be collected from village elders. They will be transmitted in Spanish and English. What clues do they hold about ancestors of modern Maya?
9. Read the interviews with the presidents of Honduras, Belize, Mexico, or Guatemala. Give your reaction to their comments.

and a wonderful example of the new learning experiences in which students using the Internet can actually participate in scientific research.

Learning by becoming involved

Electronic publishing can provide an authentic audience for student writing. Online magazines and newspapers, catering to all ages of students, abound on the Web. Some focus on current events, others on current issues relevant to students of particular ages, still others on book reviews or artistic creations. Some evidence has been gathered showing that students who write for a distant audience of their peers, as compared to those who write for their teachers

- are more fluent
- are better organized
- state and support their ideas more clearly
- include content that is more substantive and better supports their thesis
- consider the limits and needs of their audience
- enjoy writing more
- are more willing to write, proofread, revise, and edit their work
- are more careful about their spelling, punctuation, grammar, and vocabulary. (Cohen and Riel, 1989)

School home pages are also used as a forum for publishing student work. Parents and families appreciate this easy access to examples of exemplary student products.

Many classes use the Internet to facilitate and organize collections of traditional music, games, folk tales, or customs from around the world. Because physical barriers such as race, gender, and disability do not exist in a virtual online world, these information exchanges promote multicultural acceptance and appreciation of diversity. The isolation experienced by some rural schools can also be addressed by having the students become involved in virtual events. A few years ago, 12,000 children from nine countries competed with one another in track-and-field events without having to leave their own schoolyards. This one-day event, which was billed as a "virtual" Olympics, was facilitated by the Internet.

Learning to learn

An important development in current thinking about education is that we now acknowledge the need for students to develop skills for lifelong learning. The Internet is an ideal mechanism for encouraging students to assume responsibility for their own learning. In accessing the diverse range of learning resources on the Internet, students become active participants in their quest for knowledge.

"By going online, students can delve into special libraries, develop relationships that dissolve the barriers of age and distance, and share the enthusiasm of experts who love their careers. Over the Internet, pupils from different schools and backgrounds work together on projects and publish their results for thousands to view. Together, they are opening a window onto a vital world that might otherwise exist only as a flickering two-dimensional image on a television screen. As a result, many educators are rethinking the three traditional 'Rs' and adding resources and relationships to reading, writing, and 'rithmetic."

— *"The Internet Style of Learning." http://io.advanced.org/ThinkQuest/i-style html*
(January 8, 1996)

Incorporating the Internet into classroom learning gives students significantly more opportunities to structure their own learning than are available in traditional classrooms. Years ago, in the days of the one-room schoolhouse, it was assumed that there was more knowledge inside the schoolroom than outside. Today, there is much more knowledge outside the classroom. Moreover, given the diversity of learning styles, it is difficult if not impossible to "repackage" the world of knowledge to suit individual learner needs. More and more, the role of the teacher is to facilitate learning, not to prescribe it. Learning becomes an evolving process rather than a prescribed set of tasks, and the teacher's relationship to the students shifts from that of an all-knowing authority to that of a facilitator, a counselor, and a guide.

Students learn to define their learning needs, to find information, to assess its value, to build their own knowledge base, and to communicate their discoveries. Having them create their own lessons is one way of facilitating this process. All the higher-order skills come into play—defining the question, gathering resources, sifting and sorting them, and figuring out how to present them in a way that is meaningful to somebody else. And the result is something of genuine value: high-quality student work helps fill the need for well-vetted content in the online world. In the ThinkQuest Project, teams of students and coaches are encouraged to build educational tools through their own Web pages to help them and other students prepare for the future. Submissions are collected in ThinkQuest's online library of entries. A recent peek into this library revealed the following lessons:

- An in-depth analysis of *Macbeth*
- Anatomy of a murder: A Trip Through Our Justice System
- CHEMystery: An Interactive Guide to Understanding Chemistry
- Chernobyl: A Nuclear Disaster
- Collab-O'-Write
- Creative Nexus—the center for artistic expression
- Economics and Investment: A Stock Market Simulation
- Interactive Tour of the Cell

- Science and Beauty of Fractals
- Science Quest: An Exploration of Experiments
- Shadowball: The Story of the Negro Leagues
- Southern Native American Pow Wows
- The Spanish Missions of California
- Stamp on Black History
- Tangerine! Poetry Site Extraordinary
- WarEyes

Opportunities for problem solving of all kinds—mathematics, games, quizzes, design and technology—are easy to find on the Internet. Students can get involved individually or in collaborative groups. Online tutorials provide "just-in-time" training for virtually any technology-related skill you and/or your students need to learn. Teachers equipped with a computer, modem, and a phone line can tap into hundreds of project ideas on the Internet. Online discussions expand a teacher's network of colleagues to include teachers from around the world. This is especially important for teachers in small schools or in rural communities who may not otherwise have the opportunity to interact with teachers in their area of specialty. The Internet is a source for electronic books and journals, for educational research, and for professional development opportunities in the form of conferences and courses.

Figure 1-6
The Think Quest Project gives students an opportunity to create knowledge and share it with others.

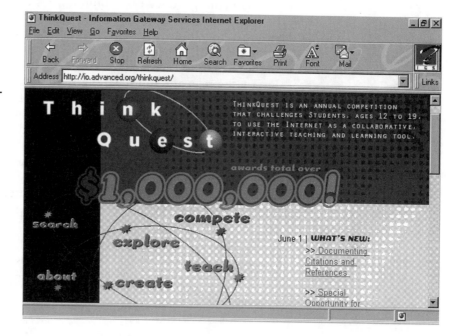

These are comments from classes that participated in the Weber-Malakov expedition, a project that had students use electronic mail to interact with a research team exploring the Arctic. The team was led by a Canadian and a Russian, and the project generated student interest in the respective cultures. Here are some of the learning experiences that stemmed from this event.

"We have discovered among our students technical experts who have all kinds of Internet knowledge, way more than their teachers! These students are now busy training their classmates on how to send e-mail and 'surf the Net'."

"We have established a team of students who correspond with children in Russia. They are learning to communicate at an appropriate level as they share common interests. Do you know that seven-year-old Sergei in Russia knows who Van Halen is and enjoys this 'heavy metal' music as much as fifteen-year-old Kevin in Canada?"

"We have learned how students at a school in the Northwest Territories track a herd of caribou by monitoring the whereabouts of three cows that have transmitters attached to their ears. These students too are using satellite data. The topic of caribou and the use of technology in remote areas tied in nicely with our study of Farley Mowat's novel, *Never Cry Wolf*."

"We have learned to question, to reflect on and wonder about matters beyond a superficial level. We wondered what time the sun got up when Richard and Misha first left for the pole, or did it get up at all? When did or when will twenty-four hours of daylight begin? How will sunlight affect the trip and the explorers themselves?"

Summing up

The Internet as a learning tool is an ongoing work in progress, one that is being produced by communities of learners, many of whom have come together through new ways of communicating made possible by the Internet itself. The educational value of the Internet ultimately will depend on what we put into it and what we do with the information we take out of it. The best way to ensure that the Internet is relevant and meaningful in your own classroom is to join with other learners in becoming familiar with the range of its resources. Technology literacy facilitates growth, change, empowerment, independence, knowledge building, collaboration, and communication. Once you know what is available and how it can benefit your students, you will be confident in developing original projects and ideas. This chapter has examined some interesting ways in which teachers are using the Internet. The chapters that follow will present many more exciting examples of classroom Internet use.

"To have students who are explorers, we need teachers who encourage exploration. To deal with the Information Age in and out of the classroom, we need teachers who can teach students how to manage information through available technologies and who can aid students in turning information into knowledge."

— *Nancy Hechinger and Melissa Koch (1993), "Beyond the lightbulb."*
Technos: Quarterly for Education and Technology, 2(1): 23.

Tapping into Existing Projects

> "In a world often over enamored of change for change's sake ... advocates of technology in our schools should have a compelling answer to the question, 'Technology for what?' The answer, we suggest, is twofold: to promote equal educational opportunity for all our children; and to raise the academic achievement of all children. Technology can advance both equity and excellence in education."
>
> — DIANE RAVITCH (1993, JANUARY), "THE PROMISE OF TECHNOLOGY: EIGHT WAYS TO TAKE FULL ADVANTAGE OF TECHNOLOGY." *ELECTRIC LEARNING*, 50.

Educational technology will continue to advance at an ever-increasing pace. As educators, it is our job to plan for and implement the use of technology in ways that are best for all our students. Technology must be understood in a context; in education, the context is learning. This means integrating Internet use into the curriculum in a meaningful way and incorporating it into current successful classroom practices such as outcomes-based education, cooperative learning, active learning, and student portfolios. Internet projects can provide an authentic context in which students develop knowledge, skills, and values. Knowing how to use the Internet is not an end in itself; rather, it is a gateway to lifelong learning.

> "I am involved in a totally online school .... The students dial up from their homes via modem, download their specified lessons for the day, then upload them to a computer or to the teacher of the class. There are also group discussions in the specified disciplines. I am currently examining their learning with standardized tests, and our faculty is amazed at their progress. We even have parents now enrolled. I think it's the way of the future, and it's happening now."
>
> — *Kevin Gerrior, Teacher, California, U.S.A.*

Perhaps the easiest way to begin is to participate in an Internet project started by others that meets your educational goals. These goals should include developing social and cooperative learning skills in addition to knowledge and task-related skills. This chapter describes some different types of projects and provides concrete examples of how teachers are using the Internet to enhance student learning. Helping students learn to use some basic Internet tools will be critical to your success. The strategies included in this chapter come from teachers who have had learned from experience.

■ **To describe some ongoing Internet projects that invite participation**

■ **To provide strategies for helping students learn how to use Internet tools**

Types of projects

As you investigate other teachers' projects in your reading and online explorations, you will discover a wealth of Internet activities to satisfy many styles of learning and student interests.

Learning through connectivity

Keypals

This is the electronic equivalent to penpals and is probably the most common of all school telecomputing activities, though not always the best as a beginning project. Individual students can be paired; the students communicate about themselves and share their interests and activities or a specific school project. Other keypal projects involve sending more general mail to a class rather than using one-to-one communication. Group-to-group exchanges are easier to manage than person-to-person messages with regard to quantities of e-mail. A suggested timeline for an introductory keypal activity could be:

- Week 1—write introductory letters stating name, age, grade, and one special interest

- Week 2—respond with a second letter giving information about family, school, hobbies, other interests

- Week 3—discuss a special topic, e.g., pets, jokes, creative writing, a curriculum theme

- Week 4—decide if communication will be ongoing or regularly scheduled, or if you wish to get involved together in a collaborative project

The following are some Web sources for matching classes of students.

K12Pals

For elementary and secondary students seeking keypals.
　　listserv@suvm.syr.edu

eMail Classroom Xchange

A Web site where you can search for classroom partners for e-mail exchanges or post your own request.
　　http://www.iglou.com/xchange/ece

HINT Listservers, commonly known as listservs, are special-interest groups available through the Internet. Members post messages to the list owner, and listserv software distributes these to all members of a given discussion group. To join a listserv, you need only know how to send an e-mail message and specific information about how to subscribe to any given list. Chapter 7 discusses listservs and how to subscribe.

Global Kids Commons
Global Commons Inc. offers the "Electronic Sister School Program" through which schools are matched with other schools around the world. Schools then communicate with each other to set up either project or keypal exchanges.

http://www.kids-commons.net/index.html

Keypals: Classroom to Classroom Connection
Messages from teachers looking for keypals for their classes are organized by grade level at this site.

http://www.teachnet.com/pals.html

Pitsco's Launch to Keypals/Penpals
This meta-list has links to over fifty WWW sites that focus on key-pals. They include listserv archives that circulate keypal requests, WWW sites where requests for keypals may be posted and others specific to a particular keypal project.

http://www.pitsco.inter.net/p/keypals.html

"Our French classes are corresponding with students in the French Alps who are studying English. They compare lifestyles, pleasures, and problems they experience. The students use a teacher's e-mail address; they incorporate several students' letters into a single document as attachments. They have also sent pictures to France as attached files."

— *Rick Pyles, Teacher, Tyler Consolidated High School, Sisterville, West Virginia, U.S.A.*

Figure 2-1
Kidlink's Global Youth Dialogue

Kidlink has several different forums for youth aged ten to fifteen. This truly international site can be accessed in approximately seventy languages.

http://www.kidlink.org/english/kidcafe.html

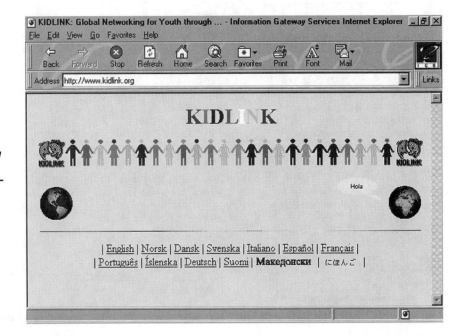

Tips for Keypal Exchanges

- Be clear about the curriculum focus and desired outcomes.
- When looking for keypals, be sure to leave enough time for people to reply to your request. Some flexibility may be required but be clear with your expectations. Send out your request several times and repeat the message one or two weeks before the desired start date.
- Consider using a listserv to advertise for possible keypal partners. You will want ten to fifteen classes to respond to your project to ensure that students get replies to their letters.
- Sample survey questions help younger students get started—e.g., sports, weather, seasonal activities, countries of origin, wishes, favorite books.
  (Educational Network of Ontario, **http://www.enoreo.on.ca/students/keypal.htm**, 03/09/97)

Electronic postcards and greeting cards have added a twist to traditional keypal activities by allowing you to send an image along with your message. Electronic postcards add variety and creativity to student exchanges, but there is a catch. Because the various graphics formats don't always travel well over the Net, the card doesn't just magically pop up on the recipient's computer screen. Instead, he or she must visit an electronic post office to view it.

To send an electronic postcard, you must first locate a World Wide Web site that offers the service. Here are just a few of the many free sites available:

The Electric Postcard

This is one of the best card collections, offered by the Massachusetts Institute of Technology. You can choose images from categories such as famous paintings, photographs, and science.
   http://postcards.www.media. mit.edu/postcards/

Marlo

This excellent site features award certificates in addition to postcards and greeting cards. There is a good selection of cards for special occasions such as Halloween, Christmas, Hanukkah and Martin Luther King Day. You can add a bit of music to your card also.
   http://www.marlo.com

Warner Brothers

Warner Brothers provides several cards featuring their cartoon characters.
   http://www.warnerbros.com/ postoffice/

Family Planet House of Cards

Disney's favorite characters are found here.
   http://www.family.com/ WebObjects/DCard

Multimedia Greeting Cards

Multimedia Greeting Cards allow you to add links and sound to your greeting.
   http://kmmc.harvard.net/ link902.htm

To find other sites, type "postcards" into a search engine and browse through the results.

Simply follow the instructions at the site for selecting, addressing, and sending a card. It's free. Soon after you send the card, the recipient will be notified by e-mail that a card is waiting. Using the address and password provided, he or she can then log onto the appropriate site and view the postcard. The cards are stored for about two weeks from the date they are sent.

Global classrooms

There can be much more to student use of e-mail than keypal exchanges. You can link up with numerous Internet-based activities in which classes from different parts of the globe work together on the same project. Sometimes classes conduct certain activities in their own school (e.g., exploring a common theme, writing and exchanging book reports) and then share the results with others in the group by e-mail. Teachers share activities by e-mail or by posting them at a Web site they've created, thus saving valuable planning time. The Canadian National Marsville Project described in Chapter 1, in which students from across North America collaboratively researched and planned their own colonies on Mars, is an excellent example of the role of telecommunications in helping students to become active learners, problem solvers, researchers, and designers. Flat Stanley, based on the book by Jeff Brown, is a smaller scale example of such a project. It began with Dale Hubert's Grade 3 students exchanging paper "Flat Stanleys" with travel journals and has expanded to a Web site at which teachers can find activity ideas for their classroom unit based on the theme.

FLAT STANLEY THEME

I have a grade 3 class. I plan on having kids make their own Stanleys during the first week or two of the new school year. They will take these home and keep personal journals that will be shared aloud with the rest of the class each day. I will be able to point out good examples of journal writing and encourage students to recognize quality writing. After some time of doing this, they will do an in-class exchange. They will take a classmate's Stanley home, keep a daily journal, then share it with the class each day. This will serve as practice before actually sending Stanleys to other sites.

After the students develop skills at daily journal writing I plan on having them divide into groups and each group member will make a contribution, either in art or text, etc. This collaborative Stanley will be sent out, and another will be started.

In order to get good responses it is helpful to provide good information. Therefore, students will be encouraged to do some research on their city, their school and local information in order to send out a quality Stanley. When a flat visitor arrives a group will be chosen to host it. Hopefully, with the large number of participants, each group will get lots of opportunities to look after a Stanley from afar.

If your school system is similar to mine you are expected to cover and assess reading, writing, math, technology, music, art, social studies, etc. If you like themes, Flat Stanley can touch on all of these areas.

SEND FLAT STANLEY AND HIS JOURNAL TO FAMOUS PEOPLE: The Blue Jays, the Simpsons, the Premier, the Prime Minister, Oprah, etc.

FLAT FOOD—HEALTH: Make a list with your students of all the foods we eat that are flat. Invite a parent to come in and prepare pancakes, cheese on crackers or whatever. Talk about healthy snacks and you've done some Health.

FLAT RACERS—DESIGN AND TECHNOLOGY: The challenge is to help Stanley get from one end of a plank to the other end, two meters away. At the end of the plank is a cereal box into which Stanley must fit. If the plank is inclined students could make go carts from toilet paper rolls, put on some wheels, put in FS and let him roll. Or make a small paper box with the bottom open. Put it over a marble. The marble will roll and move the box. Tape Flat Stanley to the box. Time the races. Try heavier and lighter. Change the incline and record the results. On a level board students would have to come up with sources of power. Electric motors or elastic bands or balloons that deflate like a rocket could be used. Record the results, come up with ways of

---

improvement. Why did one way work and another one not? Use graphs to plot the success and use ratios. For example, you might have a 1-in-3 success rate. It's the Scientific Method and Mathematics in action!

GROW A FLAT GARDEN—SCIENCE: Get those plastic sleeves that banks put your bank statement book in. Make a stand to hold it vertically. Fill 2/3 with potting soil. Plant seeds and watch the roots grow. Instead of the plastic sleeve, use overhead projector acetates or plastic lunch bags held in a popsicle-stick frame. Turn the bag after the plant begins to grow. Do the roots change direction? Experiment with varying light and water. Try different seeds. Record the results. Compare the results to the predictions the students recorded earlier.

MAKE KITES AND PAPER AIRPLANES— SCIENCE AND TECHNOLOGY: What is the smallest kite that can be made that will fly? How far can a paper airplane fly? How long can it stay in the air? Predict, then record. Compare results to the predictions and account for any discrepancies. Try again.

MAKE A FLAT CITY—SOCIAL STUDIES: On a piece of stiff cardboard lay out a town and build facades of buildings. Plan for a park. Consider traffic flow. Do you want the school near the park or near downtown? Why? Are there bike trails? Is there mass transportation? Make flat figures and attach paper clips to their feet. By holding a magnet under the board the students could move their figures through the town. Is the scale right? Are the doors the right size? Is the library wheelchair accessible? Does the school have play equipment?

FLAT WRITING—LANGUAGE ARTS: With the exchange of journals writing is probably the most obvious application in the FS Project. Consider adding poetry, songs, imaginary trips and Stanley's description of what it is like traveling in an envelope.

FLAT STANLEY MATH: As Stanleys arrive from other schools measure and record and sort and categorize their dimensions. Estimate how many cubes would cover his head, how many Stanleys placed end to end would reach down the hall, etc.

FLAT STANLEY MEASUREMENT: Identify several Flat Stanley mailing sites and determine their distance from you. Which one is farthest? By how much? How far would he travel to make return trips to each one? How could he visit all of the sites in a round trip that would cover the least or most distance?

ACTUALLY USING THE FLAT STANLEY PROJECT IN THE CLASSROOM

I favor the Contract Approach. This is the Flat Stanley Contract I made to give the students choices while still meeting the curriculum outcomes. Students are to select at least two topics from the Research and Writing and at least two topics from the Creative Writing sections. They select at least one topic from each of the remaining sections. There will therefore be a minimum of eight components to the Flat Stanley Project.

FLAT STANLEY CONTRACT

Name: _____

Research & Writing	Inventions	Modelling	Arts & Crafts	Drama	Creative Writing
daily journal	flat racer	box sculpture	Flat Stanley	puppet play	puppet play
information about city	flat flyer	Plasticene & clay	painting	speech	write a speech
pen pal notes	shadow shapes	paper clothes	play	write a play	game/game board
e-mail notes	animated roll up	envelope	songs	write a song	
flat recipes		shoe box theater		describe being flat	add a chapter to the book

Mentors

Specialists in a variety of fields make themselves available to students via the Internet. Some examples are Ask Dr. Math, Ask Dr. Science, Ask a Geologist, and Electronic Innovators in the Schools.

A good place for your students to look for an expert is at Pitsco's Ask an Expert site at **http://www.askanexpert.com/askanexpert/**. This directory of links includes over 300 Web sites and e-mail addresses where they can find experts who have volunteered their time to answer questions. Students can select from twelve categories (such as religion, science/technology, career/industry, international/culture, and arts) or they can conduct a search for their specific topics.

Sometimes experts respond to listserv postings from students; however, it is unwise to count on this.

> "One team spent hours in libraries looking for documents on sundials. They found nothing. After posting a request for information on the Internet, they received recommendations from distinguished professors from several renowned universities. Even when expert-student collaboration is brief, it really boosts student morale."
>
> — *Mathieu Dubreuil, Teacher, École Secondaire Dorval, Quebec, Canada*

Learning through online resources

Information collection. Data can be collected from multiple sites and analyzed in the classroom. The simplest type of activity might involve students electronically issuing a survey, collecting responses, analyzing the results, and then reporting their findings to all participants. Students can gather information by conducting their own online surveys and polls or by collecting statistics, comparative prices, or athletic records. Some examples include:

- measuring water acidity at various sites and comparing with others

HINT www.statcan.ca is your direct route to statistical information profiling Canada's business, economy, and society. It should be your first stop for the latest numbers.

ASK AN EXPERT SITES

Ask a Composer
Students can e-mail questions to **dfroom@osprey.smcm.edu**

Ask a Curator at
http://www.rain.org
Sponsored by the Santa Barbara Museum of Natural History, this is the site to visit if you're looking for answers to questions about natural history or Native American culture.

Ask a Dinosaur Expert at
http://denr1.igis.uiuc.edu
Administrator Russ Jacobson at Dino Russ's Lair, part of the Educational Extension program of the Illinois State Geological Survey, can tell you anything you want to know about dinosaurs and paleontology. You can also explore many links to other dinosaur sites.

Ask a Doc! at
http://www.rain.org
At Ask a Doc! you can look through the FAQ (frequently asked questions) archives or write to one of the Medical Mall specialists with a question of your own.

Ask a Geologist at
http://walrus.wr.usgs.gov
These scientists at the United States Geological Survey answer questions about topics such as earthquakes and volcanoes. Send your questions to **Ask-A-Geologist@usgs.gov** , and they will be answered in a few days.

Ask a Librarian at
http://ipl.sils.umich.edu
This service is offered by the Internet Public Library Reference Center. You can ask your questions by e-mail, interactive form, or "live" assistance at their MOO (Multi-User Object Oriented Environment). The Internet Public Library also provides a list of the most frequently asked reference questions.

Ask a Meteorologist at
http://www.weather.com
At The Weather Channel's Web site, you can have your weather-related questions answered by a Weather Channel meteorologist. Each week a featured meteorologist chooses the most interesting questions submitted and posts them along with the answers. There is also an archive of questions and answers from the past.

Ask a Musician at
http://www.sln.fi.edu
The "What Makes Music" Web page is sponsored by the Franklin Institute Science Museum. Curator Paul M. Helfrich invites you to send your questions about the science of sound and music.

Ask a Volcanologist at
http://volcano.und.nodak.edu
Expert scientists from the University of North Dakota will answer your questions about anything having to do with volcanoes.

Ask Dr. Internet at
http://promo.net
You can add your own questions to this Project Gutenberg site or browse the archived issues for answers to questions about the Internet.

Ask Dr. Math at
http://forum.swarthmore.edu
Dr. Math is part of the Geometry Forum at Swarthmore College. Students can ask Dr. Math questions about any math topic. Teachers can ask for help with math concepts and classroom strategies. This site also contains a collection of previously asked questions and answers on a variety of topics from elementary, middle, and secondary levels.

Ask Dr. Tooth at
http://www.dentistinfo.com
Dr. Tooth will answer dental-related questions. Responses to your questions will arrive via e-mail.

Ask Kids! at **http://plaza. interport.net**
Educator Sachiko Oba's Kids' Space hosts the Ask Kids bulletin board, where you can post questions and find out the opinions and thoughts of other kids.

Dr. Jim's Virtual Veterinary Clinic at **http://rampages. onramp.net**
Dr. Jim provides a list of frequently asked questions about dogs and cats, and other useful pet-related links. The information on this Web page is based on answers to questions Dr. Jim has received on a national radio talk show.

The Mad Scientist Network at
http:// pharmdec.wustl.edu
The Mad Scientist Network at Washington University describes itself as "a collective cranium of scientists from around the world," who are happy to answer your science questions submitted at their Web site or by e-mail at **YSP@pharmdec.wustl.edu**

Ask a Woman Artist
Students can e-mail to **athene@ webhippie.com**

- global grocery lists to compare prices of common items around the world
- wildlife studies that track migration paths of butterflies, whales, and birds
- election projects in which students vote electronically and compare their choices with national returns
- Olympics projects in which schools conduct Olympic-like events and submit their statistics for a competive comparison

What starts as an information collection project will often lead naturally to additional online experiences, as shown in Dalia Naujokaitis's project, "Buy Nothing Day: Be a Consumer Hero."

BUY NOTHING DAY: BE A CONSUMER HERO!

Grade: 4-9
Project Leader: Dalia Naujokaitis
St. Elizabeth School
Ottawa, ON, Canada
Web Site: **http://www3.sympatico.ca/st.elizabeth1/**
E-mail: **st.elizabeth2@sympatico.ca**

Timeline: Starts: December 1996
Ends: January 1997 — ongoing

Curriculum
Main Subject: Consumer Education
Integrated Subjects: Computer and Information Technology, English Language Arts, Communications and Media Studies, Global Studies, Environmental Studies

Participation Summary
Number of participating students: 100
Number of participating teachers: 5
Number of participating schools: 20+

The site was developed as a resource for other students to learn about the International Buy Nothing Day and to participate in the "choose your own adventure stories." The main participants as a result were from the Gifted program at St. Elizabeth School, which comprises twenty-two schools from the Ottawa Roman Catholic Separate School Board (so in a sense twenty-two schools participated through our e-mail account **st.elizabeth2@sympatico.ca**). We have had hundreds of visitors but we don't have their e-mail. The survey was and continues to be taken by kids in North America mainly and we do not keep the e-mail addresses for that since we are only interested in the data.

Description
Buy Nothing Day is an interdisciplinary project on consumer consciousness for students from Grades 4 to 9. Built around the celebration of the International Buy Nothing Day, the theme of the project as expressed in the slogan "Be a Consumer Hero! Stand up against the pressure to BUY! BUY! BUY!" provides the student and teacher with a framework for investigating the impact of advertising on consumer spending and overconsumption as a primary environmental problem in the world today. The students will

- research the origins, purpose and impact of the International Buy Nothing Day
- analyze the impact of overconsumption on the state of the environment
- conduct and participate in the Buy Nothing Survey
- create interactive stories on environmental/consumer consciousness themes "Fuz Gets Frazzled" and "Didi's Dilemma"
- discuss and create action plans for implementing the six R's of environmental and global citizenship (Reduce consumption of resources, reuse goods, recycle, reconsider our values, restructure our economic system, redistribute our wealth)

- create the Buy Nothing Day Web site to serve both as a resource and a forum to which the global community can contribute.

Student Centered

The project is run by students for students. The students will :

- conduct and participate in the Buy Nothing Survey (created by the Grade 6 students at St. Elizabeth School)
- construct, read, and interpret tables, charts and graphs
- use a variety of technologies to develop skills in information retrieval and analysis, creative writing and publishing (interactive stories)
- work cooperatively and effectively with others in the creation of a WWW resource
- manage e-mail and all telecommunications

Main Steps:

- Post a call for others to participate in educational listservs.
- Students at St. Elizabeth School create the framework of Buy Nothing Day on the WWW, providing links, information, survey and main outlines for "Choose Your own Adventure " type stories.
- Classes register to participate in the survey.
- Classes participate in the survey by e-mail or on the Buy Nothing Day Web site.
- Survey results are posted on the Web site.
- Classes participate in creating the endings for "Didi's Dilemma" or "Fuz Gets Frazzled." Endings or variations for stories are published on the Web.
- Students from the global community are encouraged to participate in building and expanding the Web site through their contributions of essays, research, and "Choose Your Own Adventure" stories.

Internet Usage

The Internet will be used in the project both for communication and publishing of information. E-mail will be the main vehicle for sharing information among the participants. The Web site, Buy Nothing Day, will contain the resources, interactive stories to which students can contribute, the Buy Nothing Survey, and the results when the survey is completed. The Media Awareness Network will create links to our pages and the results of the survey. The SchoolNet listserv will be used as the main means of informing the global community of the project and its progress.

Buy Nothing Survey

1. How old are you?
2. Are you a boy or girl?
3. Do you get an allowance?
4. If you do, how much allowance do you get per week?
5. What do you spend your allowance on?
6. Do you think we buy more things than we really need?
7. Do you feel you just have to have things you see advertised on TV?
8. Do you think commercials make us want things we would otherwise not ?

How it involves and attracts others

Teachers will be attracted to this project because of its multidimensional approach and the seamless integration of media literacy into the curriculum. The site can be used as a tool for further discussion and analysis of consumer habits and values of students at different ages. Students by nature are curious and concerned with the state of the planet. This project will provide ample opportunities for them to reflect on their own lifestyles and the impact of advertising in particular on the choices they make as consumers.

Information Technologies

- e-mail with attachments for file exchange
- the World Wide Web as a publishing and analysis tool
- spreadsheets for data input and creation of pie charts and graphs
- word-processing software for story creation
- the WWW as a search and research tool

Summary Report

What did you do to draw participation from other teachers and classes?

- Posted the "Call to Participate" in the project on the SchoolNet and Hilites lists.
- The Media Awareness Network also provided a link to our "Buy Nothing" Web site so that more students would be able to participate in the survey.

What Internet resources were used, listed in order of usefulness?

- Adbusters Website (**http://www.adbusters.org/ Pop/buynothingday.html**)
- Media Awareness Network Website
- SchoolNet listserv

What impact did your project have on students' learning?

The students at St. Elizabeth School (Grades 4/5/6) were enthusiastic researchers using the WWW. The students looked at the issue of overconsumption and then wrote factual profiles on the impact of this on the environment. Their idea of writing a "choose your own adventure" story involved much planning both of the content and the HTML needed to make this work. The project encouraged lots of problem solving, collaboration and decision making. Some students became writers, others illustrators, while those more comfortable with technology created the Web site. Perhaps the greatest impact was in the awareness that the students gained both in understanding consumerism and their resolve to be in control of it rather than be controlled by the need to "have" more and more. They became "activists" through the Web site, rather than be taken in by commercialism.

What aspects of the project would you do differently and why?
Perhaps the one main drawback was the very short lead

time for informing others about the Web site. The fact that our service provider was also updating their server at the same time made access to the Web site problematic.

What recommendations would you give other teachers wanting to run your project(s)?
Give at least six weeks of lead time for others to get involved in the project and don't be disappointed if the response is slower than you expected. This is a new way of doing business for many teachers and everyone is just beginning to get their "sea legs" for using telecommunications as part of the learning/teaching process. When it does happen, it's tons of fun!
— D. Naujokaitis. Buy Nothing Day: Be a Consumer Hero
http://www.schoolnet.ca/grassroots/ , August 22, 1997

Figure 2–2
GlobaLearn mounts live expeditions all over the world. Participating students interact with remote expedition teams via their World Wide Web site.

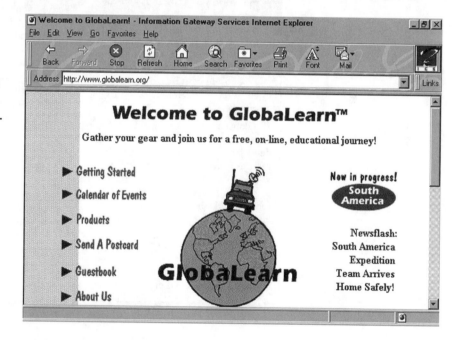

Online field trips. These can be as simple as sharing information about the community or as complex as monitoring an expedition to reach the North Pole by dogsled. Students can share observations and experiences made during local field trips with teachers and students from other cities and countries by posting trips for others to see and asking relevant questions. Yahoo's virtual field trips site at **http://www.yahoo.com/Recreation/Travel/Virtual_Field_Trips/**

Tour Canada without Leaving Your Desk is at **http://www.cs.cmu.edu/ Unofficial/Canadiana/ Travelogue.html**. This site has pointers to national and provincial locations such as parks, cities, and tourist information centers.

One place to find online expeditions is GlobaLearn at **http://www. globalearn.org/**. GlobaLearn, Inc. is a nonprofit company that was incorporated in August 1993 to prepare children for global citizenship and to develop in them the skills, awareness, and determination necessary to become responsible stewards of the earth. GlobaLearn is founded on the belief that learning should draw on all fields of discipline; should be thematic; should result in a tangible product or performance; and, most importantly, should be relevant to the daily lives and personal experiences of students. The GlobaLearn program seeks to:

- engage children in learning;
- promote a greater understanding of the world's diverse lands and cultures;
- instill in students and educators basic technology and communication skills;
- bring students and educators from around the world together in a resource- and content-rich learning environment.

GlobaLearn mounts live expeditions all over the world. Participating students interact with GlobaLearn's remote expedition teams via their World Wide Web site. At each stopping point, the team is hosted by a local school child who offers a personal introduction to the local community. The host child serves as the starting point for ensuing investigations into the history, traditions, industries, and physical resources of the community. Using laptop computers and digital cameras and recorders, the explorers capture their discoveries daily and send them, via satellite uplink, to GlobaLearn's server in Connecticut. In minutes, GlobaLearn's home staff formats the materials for the Web site. Once the materials are posted, they can be viewed by anyone with access to the World Wide Web.

GlobaLearn works closely with educators to develop and make available curriculum activities that facilitate integrating the program into the classroom. These activities exist to ensure that students actively participate in the expedition process, becoming explorers and using the remote field teams as their extensions to investigate the historical, cultural, and physical features of the world's communities. Students are also encouraged to use the expeditions as a model for the kind of explorations they can conduct in their own communities. Using the interactive areas of the Web site, students can supplement the data generated by the field teams and make dynamic comparisons between their lives and the lives of others in different countries.

The program has been designed to serve a broad range of disciplines, teaching styles, and classroom setups. GlobaLearn makes content materials and resources available; suggests ways in which these materials and resources can be used; develops opportunities for their use (interactive areas); and the rest becomes the decision and work of the user.

(GlobaLearn, **http://www.globalearn. org/**, 03/09/97)

provides links to online tours such as Amazon Adventure, Odyssey in Egypt, and Live from Antarctica.

An online trip could be to a museum or gallery anywhere in the world. Each group or pair of students could visit a different institution and summarize their findings. This compilation of visits and ratings makes a good reference source for future individual student research. Museums, galleries, and other educational institutions offer text, pictures, sound and sometimes even interactivity.

"My favorite project focused on virtual museums visits. These allow learners to experience the multimedia strength of the World Wide Web. The esthetic and other curriculum goals that can be enhanced by multimedia museum visits have great learning potential. My favorite museum listing can be found at http://www.comlab.ox.ac.uk/archive/other/museums.html."

— *Robert Christina, Associate Professor, Oakland University, Rochester, Michigan, U.S.A.*

Learning by becoming involved

Electronic publishing

You will find wonderful writing by high school students published on many of their school Web sites. Students can also publish their original works in an online newspaper, anthology, or magazine. One of the most popular is Midlink, an electronic magazine for middle school students at **http://longwood.cs.ucf.edu/~MidLink**. A recent issue featured a survey of what makes a great school, recipes from around the world, and student dreams.

Electronic process writing is facilitated by programs such as the Writers In Electronic Residence program sponsored by York University in Canada. Writers In Electronic Residence (WIER) connects students across Canada with writers, teachers, and one another in an animated exchange of original writing and commentary. The writers, who are all well-known Canadian authors, join classrooms electronically to read and consider the students' work, offer reactions and ideas, and guide discussions between the students. (**http://www.wier.yorku.ca/wierhome/**) Another variation is having students from several schools work on collaborative writing of the same piece. More publishing sites for students include:

Inkspot Web   Inkspot includes links to workshops and writing associations, publications seeking young writers, online contests, and publications about writing for student authors. You will also find lots of links to school publications and school-based electronic magazines here.
http://www.inkspot.com

Stone Soup   This site features writing and artwork from students up to age thirteen. Since Stone Soup accepts only about one percent of all work submitted, this would be of most interest to especially talented student writers.
http://www.stonesoup.com/

Book Reports   Students can publish their favorite book reports and read those of others.
http://i-site.on.ca/Isite/Education/Bk_report/

The Little Planet Times   The Little Planet Times is an interactive newspaper for kids, by kids. Each issue has a central theme for children to read about, write about, and discuss.
   http://www.littleplanet.com/

E-LINK Magazine   This electronic elementary magazine, published four times each year, welcomes submissions of stories, art work, riddles, and more from students aged five to eleven.
   http://www.inform.umd.edu/MDK_12/homepers/emag/

Children's Express   The Children's Express motto is "By Children for Everybody." Here students can write an editorial or story to be published in the Online Newsroom (choosing from relevant topics such as Juvenile Justice, Animals and Us, or Kids and the Media), respond to monthly poll questions, give feedback on articles, or subscribe to a listserv.
   http://www.ce.org

"We shared students' writing among various schools in our province. Students had the opportunity to analyze and critique each other's writing. This was a great experience for them, since we are a small school and students don't often get the opportunity to see much writing by students their own age."

— *Jill Colbourne-Warren, Teacher, H.L. Strong Academy,*
Springdale, Newfoundland, Canada

Information exchanges

Many classes organize or contribute to compilations of games, folk tales, music, holidays, or recycling practices from around the world. This sharing of information is intrinsically interesting for children and provides an excellent way to foster international acceptance and an appreciation of cultural diversity. This type of activity can also involve many classes without becoming too overwhelming. Karen Walkowiak's project, "Connected to the World/The Teddy Bear Exchange," exemplifies a creative approach to student information exchange, especially for the beginner internaut.

Virtual events

Students who participate at their local school in athletic events, read-a-thons, or collections can submit their results to a larger arena. This is a good way to overcome the isolation of some rural schools.

"A host school runs the virtual track meet. The students create and send out entry forms to the schools interested in being involved. A certain number of participants are allowed per event, with age and gender categories. A deadline is set as to when results are sent back to the host school (e.g., results for the high jump or 100-m sprint). The students of the host school then figure out the placings and send back their results sheet."

— *Margot Alwich, Teacher, Lindsay Place High School, Pointe Claire, Quebec, Canada*

CONNECTED TO THE WORLD/THE TEDDY BEAR EXCHANGE

Grades: K-6

Project Leader: Karen Walkowiak
Holy Redeemer Catholic School
Kanata, Ontario, Canada

Participation Summary
Number of participating students: Holy Redeemer (approx. 325)/Partner Classes (approx. 300)

Number of participating teachers: Holy Redeemer — 17 / Partner Teachers — 14
Number of participating schools: 14, from Canada, U.S.A., Australia, Israel,

Timeline:
September–June of each school year, beginning with 1996

Description

This project involves the creation of a "Teddy Bear Exchange" hosted on the Holy Redeemer School Web site, which will:

- Allow all interested classes at Holy Redeemer Catholic School to participate in a plush animal exchange with a class in another part of the world;

- Facilitate the creation of partnerships between other schools interested in beginning a plush animal exchange project;

- Provide online resources and suggested classroom activities for teachers interested in running a Teddy Bear Exchange in their own classroom. Participating teachers are encouraged to add their own ideas and comments!

The "cornerstone" of this project was the exchange of plush animals between the Grade 1/2 class at Holy Redeemer Catholic School in Ottawa, Canada, and the Grade 1/2 class at Bose School in Kenosha, Wisconsin, U.S.A. Other interested classes at Holy Redeemer Catholic School had the opportunity to be partnered with classes across the world. The cost of shipping the animals by airmail was absorbed by a local travel agency that agreed to be our partners for this project. In return for this expense, the Teddy Bear Exchange Web page provided a link to the travel agency home page.

The project began with the creation of a home page. This Web site described the project in detail and encouraged interested schools to initiate contact with Holy Redeemer classes. Interested schools completed an online form on the Web page, giving all necessary school information (school name, location, grade level, class size, e-mail address, etc.) and a brief description of why they wished to take part in this project. This information was then organized according to grade level, and teachers were encouraged to make contact with prospective partner classes. Once a partnership was formed between schools, the students decided what animal they would send to their partner school, named the animal, and filled its "knapsack" with a travel journal and Canadian sou-

venirs such as flags, bookmarks, money, photographs, letters from the children, maps, gifts for hosts, an audiotape of the national anthem, storybooks, local newspapers, etc. The students justified each item, and provided relevant reasons for their selections. When the plush animal arrived in the host classroom, e-mail was sent to confirm the animal's safe arrival, and described any travel experiences. A "travel journal" was kept in the animal's knapsack, and each evening, the animal was sent home with a different student. The parents participated by writing in the animal's journal, to be dictated by the student (at the primary level). The partner schools followed similar format with the Holy Redeemer animals. There was a regular e-mail exchange between the partner schools.

The Teddy Bear Exchange runs for a period of time predetermined by the teachers involved (about two months). At the end of the exchange, the teddy bears were returned and the students exchanged "summary" letters describing the overall exchange.

Main Steps

- Design and post a Teddy Bear Exchange Web page. This page allowed teachers to learn about the project, form partnerships, and exchange ideas. There was no student involvement at this point.
- Submit a posting to teacher listservs (e.g., Teachers.net, Highlights, Classroom Connect).
- Confirm dates and details of partnership between Holy Redeemer Catholic School and partner schools.

September

- Introduce students to the project. The students decide upon a teddy bear, name it, and brainstorm a list of items to go in the knapsack.
- Begin e-mail exchange between classes to prepare for exchange date.
- Partner other classes at Holy Redeemer School with various schools.
- Assess the initial success of the "partnership database" and make any necessary modifications.
- Add links to other schools taking part in the animal exchange to the page.

- Teachers communicate through e-mail to ensure project is proceeding correctly and troubleshoot problems as they arise.

October–November, 1996
- Exchange plush animals through airmail.
- Establish classroom routines of rotating animal among students and keeping journal (both written and online).
- Continue to exchange e-mail postcards between the students in partner classrooms. (Postcards concern both plush animal updates, and other classroom activities.)
- Teachers communicate through e-mail to ensure project is proceeding correctly and troubleshoot problems as they arise.
- Other classes at Holy Redeemer School are partnered with various schools and follow the steps outlined above.
- Teachers post all learning activities associated with plush animal exchange to teacher forum section of plush animal page.

December, 1996
- Return plush animals to schools through airmail.
- Students write "follow-up / conclusion" for individual plush animal links.
- Continue to exchange e-mail between students in partner classrooms.
- Participating teachers assess success of project. Comments and suggestions for improvement are added to plush animal information and teacher forum links.

Summary Report

What did you do to draw participation from other teachers and classes?
- The staff of Holy Redeemer were invited to join in the "Teddy Bear Exchange," which consists of each class choosing one teddy bear to represent their class, school and country as an ambassador of our Canadian culture.
- Our Web site address was posted at sites that are available to other teachers, such as Web66, School World, Classroom Connect, and Canada's SchoolNet.
- Postings promoting our project were also sent to Kidsphere listserve and individual teachers sent requests to schools posted at Web66.

Principal student activities in this project:
- Students chose and named their class teddy bears and collected souvenirs (e.g., Canada flags, pins, maps, postcards, hockey items) that they wanted to share with their partner classes.

- The Junior level classes studied "Canada" as a curriculum theme for the first term of the school year.
- Students made dossiers of themselves, introducing themselves to their partner classes. These took the form of pendants and letters of introduction.
- Students participated in teddy bear craft-making at all grade levels.
- Picture taking for class photo albums was a highlight for each class.
- Students gained a knowledge of other places in the world and put their map and globe skills as well as research skills to use.
- Students were shown how to navigate through the school Web pages in our computer lab.

What Internet resources were used in order of usefulness?
- Kidsphere Listserv
- Web66
- Classroom Connect
- Canada's SchoolNet
- SchoolWorld
- The Education Place

What impact did your project have on students' learning?
Since this was an entire school initiative, there was an incredible enthusiasm that students and staff shared! The children were eager to initiate and maintain contact with their partner classes and were thrilled to host visiting teddy bears. They were especially excited about taking the visiting teddy bears home to share with their families as well as document the teddy bears' adventures in the travel journals. The children enjoyed sharing their journal entries with their peers. This was also an excellent medium for enhancing computer literacy skills. A group of eighteen students who had been trained as "computer troubleshooters" edited the school Web pages prior to submission and took an active role in suggesting changes. At the time, although our lab does not yet have Internet access, all children had the opportunity to experience what being on the Internet would "feel" like, by navigating the Web pages using general "point and click" skills. This project was also versatile in that our French teachers were also able to integrate it into their curriculum so that children were able to share both English and French cultures with their partner classes.

What aspects of the project would you do differently and why?
The one thing that I would have changed was the date that the project was to begin. We received our e-mail and Internet access later than anticipated, thus, the project was not actually totally underway until November

1996. I would also submit our requests for partner classes to listservs immediately. This was an excellent vehicle for establishing a connection with other classes.

What recommendations would you give other teachers wanting to run your project?

- Collaborative planning, leadership, organization, time management and team building are essential to the success of this project.
- Observe "netiquette."
- Respond to all requests promptly.
- Train teachers on the basics of sending and receiving e-mail as well as using the Internet, and provide ongoing support.
- Raise funds for shipping the teddy bears (grants, donations, fundraising) before the project is initiated.

- Get administrative support. Our administration was actively involved and supportive from the initiation of the project, and kept well-informed throughout the duration.
- Publicize the project. This is a wonderful way to link to the parent community, to promote enthusiasm among the children and to elevate awareness of the possibilities of integrating computer technology into the curriculum.

— K. Walkowiak, Connected to the World/The Teddy Bear Exchange
http://www.schoolnet.ca/grassroots/, August 22, 1997

Learning to learn

Games and quizzes

Students enjoy learning through interactive games that revolve around a curriculum topic. Such projects are extremely motivating to most students of all ages. Students can learn a game and share it with others from a site such as Clever Games for Clever People at **http://www.cs.uidaho.edu/~casey931/conway/games.html**, which features games from John Conway's book, *On Numbers and Games* (New York: Academic Press Inc.).

> "The activity, Insect Wacky Facts, is quite simple. Participants are told about unusual or 'wacky' insect behavior. They must identify the strange creature, suggest an explanation for its behavior, and cite any sources consulted. Sometimes there is more than one 'right' answer. Bob [the online science teacher] then writes back, giving supplementary information in a straightforward, or sometimes tongue-in-cheek, way."
>
> — *Christian Dufour, Teacher, Small Schools Network, Quebec, Canada*

Problem-solving activities

Similar problems can be presented to students in various locations, or two or more classes can take turns presenting problems for peers in other locations. Teams of students use telecommunications technology to plan strategies, discuss progress, share results, and solve problems collaboratively. They might even produce a joint final report. Most focus on mathematics and logic problems, but Odyssey of the Mind at **http://www.odyssey.org/** involves students at all levels in solving problems in a variety of areas, from building mechanical devices such as spring-driven vehicles to giving their own interpretation of literary classics.

Here are some math-oriented problem-solving sites for students.

MathSoft Puzzler
Puzzles and their solutions for high school students.
http://www.mathsoft.com/puzzle.html

MegaMath
Graphs, stories, and games with lots of helpful teacher resources.
http://www.c3.lanl.gov/mega-math/workbk/graph.html

Word Problems for Kids
Elementary school students can tackle these problems in pairs and check their answer when they've completed them.
http://juliet.stfx.ca/people/fac/pwang/mathpage/math1.html

Problem of the Week
The goal of this site is to challenge elementary students with non-routine problems and to encourage them to verbalize their solutions. Student submissions are answered by "Visiting Math Mentors" and students also have an opportunity to act as mentors themselves. All those who correctly answer the challenge appear on the Web site, and the most creative solutions are highlighted.
http://forum.swarthmore.edu/sum95/ruth/elem.pow.html

"A group presents a complex task as a challenge or contest. Participants attempting to complete the task e-mail requests for specific help as needed. For example, a math problem may be posed and the solution is required to be described in words; or a physics experiment may be explained and the distant students are asked to repeat the experiment within a defined error tolerance."

— *Shelley Martin, Student, Department of Graduate Studies, Carleton University, Ottawa, Ontario, Canada*

Social action projects
When students focus on a real-life problem, the Internet truly becomes a tool for learning. Students electronically research solutions to local or global issues and often get involved in awareness projects or fund raising as a result. For example, students might participate in a social justice issue such as the Canadian children's letter-writing campaign to the prime minister regarding child poverty (http://www.ualberta.ca/~ckunzle/results/). The following activity, Environmentally Friendly Community, is another example of how students can get involved in authentic issues.

"Several of my students have been using Internet Relay Chat to speak with people around the world. Social studies students listen to the nightly news for foreign events, such as the recent earthquake in Russia, and then try to contact individuals from the countries mentioned in the hope of hearing from people who are involved."

— *Rick Pyles, Teacher, Tyler Consolidated High School, Sisterville, West Virginia, U.S.A.*

ENVIRONMENTALLY FRIENDLY COMMUNITY

Description
Students will discover what it takes to make their community more environmentally friendly. They will research what is presently being done with respect to reducing and recycling waste and then determine what further action is needed.

Grade level: 6-12

Learning outcomes
Students will
- research the roles required to run a community
- find out how their municipal government deals with environmental issues
- access Web resources related to environmental issues
- take photos using a digital camera
- use e-mail to communicate with community members
- create an environmental checklist for their community
- examine forms of energy available in their community
- investigate energy or water use in the home or school and record results in a spreadsheet
- produce a graph from a spreadsheet
- explore methods of reducing energy or water consumption
- assess the effectiveness of local energy or water conservation programs
- prepare a report on the environmental health of the community

Class management ideas
- Students work in small groups, with each group responsible for researching and reporting on one aspect of the community.
- Each team prepares a report to share with the whole class.
- Consider using a *jigsaw model* in which students become experts in their chosen field and share their knowledge with other teams.
- Students could take on roles such as environmental engineer, environmental officer, environmental health specialist, environmental scientist, environmental lawyer, biologist, naturalist.

Scenario
Friends of your family are planning to move to an area near your community. They are members of an environmental awareness organization and are most concerned that the community is environmentally friendly. They have asked you and your family to help them make the decision as to where they should purchase a house. They have given you some very specific topics to investigate.

Problem
Create a plan for determining how your community addresses environmental issues. You will need to find out how the municipal government deals with these issues:
- waste management
- water protection
- transportation
- sewage treatment
- green space
- recreation
- alternative forms of energy

Prepare a report suitable for your friends. Outline how your community stacks up.

Internet resources
Locate Web resources concerning your local community as well as surrounding communities of a similar size and composition. Visit ecology and environment sites to prepare tips for your local government.

Ask a Naturalist at **http://www.web.net/fon/ask.htm** Federation of Ontario Naturalists will answer questions on a variety of issues.

Ask the Eco Expert at **http://www.gbr.org/econet/askeco.htm** Ask questions about ecological and environmental issues.

Canadian Department of the Environment at **http://www.doe.ca/envohome.html** Canadian information on the environment.

Charlotte's Energy Page at **http://www. swiftly.com/apase/charlotte/energy.html** Activities, information, career material on energy.

Cool Environmental Sites at **http://www.ccinet.ab.ca/dc/cool.htm** Links to many sites worldwide.

Energy Probe at **http://www.nextcity.com/EnergyProbe/** Information about the wise use of energy, alternative sources of energy, energy in the home.

Envirolink at **http://envirolink.org/** Wide variety of issues and links to other sites.

Environmental Organization Web Directory at **http://www.webdirectory.com/** Large list of Web sites on environmental issues.

Environmental Careers at http://www. schoolnet.ca/math_sci/env_geol/careers/ contents.htm
Examples and explanations of many environmental careers.

Evergreen Foundation at http://www. evergreen.ca/home.html
Links, activities for green environments, school projects.

Environmental Solutions at **HYPERLINK** http://strategis http://strategis. ic.gc.ca/sc_indps/canenvir/engdoc/loc_eng.html
Industry Canada's Web site on environmental solutions.

Greenpeace at http://www.greenpeace.org/
Information about the organization and links.

Municipalities on the Web at http://www.arch.buffalo.edu/cgi-bin/pairc/ loc_can
Site for finding Web sites for some local municipalities.

Urban Agricultural Notes at http://www. cityfarmer.org/
Links to many sites related to environmental city living.

Urban Forest Centre at http://www.utoronto.ca/forest/ufc_intr.html
Information on planting trees in urban settings, landscaping benefits.

Suggested student activities:
- Brainstorm in your group the elements needed for a community and the issues related to making it environmentally friendly. Record your ideas in an electronic journal.
- Research the roles required to run a community. Use a class database to record your findings.
- Carry out Internet research into one of the major topics. Prepare a report for your team members. Add it to the electronic journal for sharing and use it in the final report.
- Create an environmental checklist for the community. Go on a walking tour and record your findings. Take pictures using a digital camera (or scan photos) for your database and presentation.
- Examine the forms of energy available in the community and determine the advantages and disadvantages of each. Using e-mail, contact representatives to ask for information about current practices and future plans.
- Investigate how energy consumption (or water usage) is measured in your home or school and calculate how much energy (or water) is used in a week, month and year. Record your results in a spreadsheet and turn it into a graph.
- Explore methods for reducing the amount of energy or water consumed. Consider asking an expert for information; use e-mail.
- Look at energy conservation programs in your community and determine how effective they have been. Create a chart or graph to demonstrate your findings.
- Examine water management programs in your community and others. Explain the reasons for the different methods and e-mail your findings to the local politicians and water facilities.
- Determine the importance of green space in maintaining environmental quality, and identify public interest groups that work to preserve urban green space. E-mail them to find out their opinions about the health of your community.

Final activity
Create a final report on the environmental health of your community for your friends, considering creative methods of demonstrating your findings. Prepare a report to be submitted to various environmental agencies and your local municipality.
— Sheila Rhodes (1998), *Connecting the Web: Successful Student Internet Activities,* Trifolium Books Inc.

Joining an existing project

Once you start looking around, you'll be delighted by the number and variety of projects that students can join. Some are specific to a particular age or grade level, while others are more general. All you need to get involved in an interactive Internet project is access to Internet e-mail. As we will discuss in Chapter 8, you can get this easily through a commercial service such as CompuServe, America Online, or Prodigy, through a local Internet service provider, or through your community freenet. Once you are online, look for

1. Before going online

- Locate a collaborative project you want to join.
- Introduce the topic to the class by presenting background information, holding a class discussion, visiting the local library, and/or inviting local guest speakers.
- Send home a note describing the collaborative research project students will be conducting and inviting parents to participate or contribute in any way they can.
- Divide the class into groups of four or five students.
- List and describe each of the tasks needed to conduct the project.
- Assign each student within the group a job title and task to accomplish.
- Review proper online behavior and Net etiquette.
- Have students sign an AUP (Acceptable Use Policy) stating they have read the rules and will follow them.
- Have parents also sign an AUP form indicating that they have reviewed the online rules with their children and will assist the teacher in enforcing those rules.

2. During the collaborative project

- Begin your activity with a "hello" greeting message. Rather than have each student write a separate hello message, it is more effective if groups of two or three students create different sections of the message. For example, one group might write about their school; another can describe their city; another can tell nearby places to visit, and so on. The result is a single collaborative document that reflects the input of all the individual students.
- Have all students keep a written or typed log of their activities describing their research, their explorations, and their findings (this helps ensure that students are staying on task).
- Schedule students to meet periodically and report the highlights of their activities to their group and the entire class.
- Exchange lesson plans with other teachers and discuss ways to refine and improve the project.

3. After the collaborative activity

- Write thank-you notes to project partners.
- Prepare a list of questions about the collaborative project and practice answering them by interviewing one another (students could videotape each other).
- Make presentations about the project to other classes and to the community.
- Organize the findings in a shareable format (including images, audio, and video clips) and post the information on the Internet.

— Yvonne Marie Andres, *Electronic Learning*, March 1995

forums, conferences, or special interest groups related to education. You can also subscribe to one of many listserv groups, which are discussion groups interested in a specific topic. When you subscribe to one of these mailing lists, you receive all messages posted to the list by other subscribers around the world.

When reviewing the many available projects, look for one that is consistent with the learning outcomes you have in mind for your students. You might begin by selecting a curriculum-specific project that focuses on process writing, geography skills, or science. Consider simple projects before trying more complex ones: you might begin by participating in a survey, exchanging writing samples, or responding to keypal requests.

"Getting students online can be frustrating at first because everything is new— the hardware, the software, and all the tools of the Net. But don't get discouraged. Make sure you know some good resources that will help the kids get started."

— *Sholom Eisenstat, Teacher, Earl Haig Secondary School, Toronto, Ontario, Canada*

As your students become more comfortable with the technology and see what is possible, they will be eager to get involved in more sophisticated projects, such as tracking an expedition or working cooperatively with others to address an environmental problem. Once you are involved in a project, learning outcomes that you had not anticipated are likely to emerge. Be sure to document and assess the skills and values your students develop as they proceed.

You'll find many examples of projects you can join throughout this book.

Teaching students how to use Internet tools

Many students today know what the Internet is all about, but younger students may know the language without truly understanding how the Internet works. Consider inviting a guest speaker from your community to provide an overview, or do a quick introduction yourself.

> "I tell my kids that the Internet is an international network of computers, connected to each other by modems and telephone/fiber optic cables. I explain the different machines that are connected over the Internet, such as the servers, which 'serve' people the information they need in many different ways: mail servers, file servers, Gopher servers, FTP sites, and HTML file servers, or Web sites. This is easiest to do with a diagram. I then explain the various tools available across the Internet, and how students should use these tools depending on what they are looking for and where they wish to go. My lab has TurboGopher, Fetch, InterNews, Eudora, and Netscape on each computer. Although each program works differently, all navigate the international network of computers to help people trade information. I explain that the WWW is just a small subset of the Internet, specifically the patch of Internet traffic conducted and controlled by HTML. My third to sixth graders seem to 'get it' just fine."
>
> — *Sally Grant, Teacher, Sewickley Academy,*
> *Sewickley, Pennsylvania, U.S.A.*

Your students need both direct instruction and skill-building activities to learn how to use the Internet and its tools effectively. Explain, demonstrate, and illustrate each skill you expect them to use in their project. Then provide exercises and allow time for them to practice before expecting them to use the skill independently.

> "The first time you introduce students to The Weather Underground, you might lead them step-by-step to the site, show them how to locate the current temperature of a given city, then how to successfully leave the site. Next, you might have them attempt to return to the site on their own and locate weather conditions in a city of their choice. You might allow teams of students to compete in scavenger hunts to locate information. All of these activities help students practice the needed retrieval skills. Once they know how to retrieve the information, they will be ready to put the available information to real instructional use."
>
> — *Patricia Ross (1995, February), "Relevant telecomputing activities."*
> The Computing Teacher, 28–30.

Direct instruction

Several expensive tools are available that facilitate whole-class direct instruction. You may be fortunate enough to have access to one of these in your school. Special projectors allow you to project your computer screen onto a large screen for whole-class lessons. An LCD (liquid crystal display) tablet, used on an overhead projector, also allows projection from the computer. Alternatively, a TV/video cable can be used to display your computer screen onto a larger TV screen. On the other hand, direct instruction may require that students gather around a single computer, if that's all you have. Rather than try to show thirty students at once, you could divide the class into groups of four or five and have a student expert, helping teacher, or parent volunteer assist with the instruction.

> "The grandfather of one of my students was wonderful! For six weeks during our whales unit, he came every morning. He worked with pairs of students, helping them to find information about whales and to contact scientists. By the time the unit was complete, everyone had used the Internet and we had many great resources to share!"
>
> — *Joanne Dillon, Teacher, Elmridge School, Gloucester, Ontario, Canada*

The technical skills necessary to navigate the Internet cannot be taught in a vacuum. Introduce and practice each skill only as it is needed to accomplish a curriculum task. For example, an isolated lesson on how to do a Web search is soon forgotten if students are not involved in a related activity. However, teaching that same lesson while students are engaged in researching earthquakes provides them with a valuable tool to use immediately for a specific purpose.

Along with directly teaching students how to use Internet tools through lessons and discussion come the other important issues that students must learn: netiquette, copyright rules, and citing of Internet resources. These are addressed in Chapter 5.

Student experts

You don't have to teach the whole group yourself. Identify student experts in each class, train them, and let them teach others. Everyone benefits from this experience. Explain and discuss the learning outcomes you expect in these roles. Look for students who have leadership skills and will attend the school for a few years to come. Get a long-term commitment from them. Some schools award bonus marks or course credits for such services. Having one student teach another is also an authentic evaluation tool, since the ability to teach a particular skill is a demonstration of how completely it has been mastered. Use cooperative learning strategies to take advantage of the strengths of the technowizards in your class

Internet Driver's License is a program available for US$99 from Classroom Connect. It outlines the steps and provides classroom resources to teach students the "rules of the road" for Internet usage.

If you teach young children, you can find a great lesson plan from Loogootee Elementary School in Indiana. It's called "Surfing for ABC's" for kindergarten and first grade and is at **http://www.siec.k12.in.us/~west/abcless.htm**. One called "Surfing Safely on the Internet" for second and third grade students is at **http://www.siec.k12.in.us/~west/surfless.htm**.

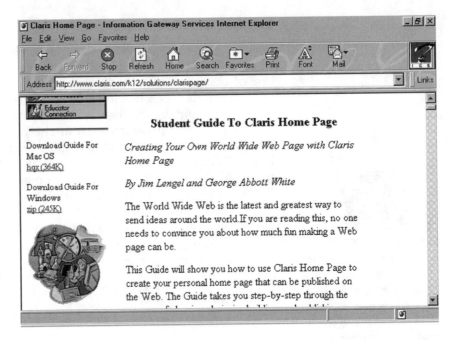

by distributing them among the groups to act as leaders during the technology-related parts of the project.

Some of the many Internet courses and tutorials available on the Internet itself are appropriate for student use. Take a look at one or more of these if students are learning to create Web pages:

- **Introduction to HTML** at **http://www.cwru.edu/help/introHTML/toc.html**
- **NCSA's HTML Primer** at **http://www.ncsa.uiuc.edu/General/Internet/WWW/HTMLPrimer.html**
- **The 8-minute HTML Primer** and **Putting Pictures on your Page** at **http://web66.coled.umn.edu/Cookbook/**

Practice activities

Games, simulations, and scavenger hunts allow students to have fun while practicing skills. You can design your own practice activities or take advantage of those you find on the Internet itself. Centennial Regional High School in Greenfield Park, Quebec, Canada, received the Roy C. Hill Award (given to teachers for developing new ideas to use in the classroom) for their Cyberspace Treasure Hunt. You can find out more about it at **http://www.infobahnos.com/~crhs/crhs.treasure.hunt.html**. Scavenger hunts based on curriculum themes developed by creative elementary school teachers can be found at **http://www.crcssb.edu.on.**

ca:1080/~red/htm/scaven.htm. Some treasure hunts even offer prizes, such as the CANARIE/SchoolNet 1997 Internet Treasure Hunt in which twenty-five puzzle pieces were hidden throughout the World Wide Web. Students had to find the pieces and put them together to figure out a secret message. (**http://www.canarie. ca/frames/starth3_e.html**)

> "Don't overwhelm your students by creating projects that are too big or that have too many parts. Take a couple of preparatory weeks practicing how to use a browsing tool such as Netscape or any multimedia software *before* launching the project. Then, make sure you've identified the main ideas and reviewed how to take notes."
>
> — *Terrie Gray, Teacher, Chico Junior High School, Chico, California, U.S.A.*

Learning together

Some school systems have initiated training sessions or courses that include teachers, students, and parents. The groups could be mixed or handled separately, but all learners gain expertise at approximately the same rate. Working as a community reinforces the goal of lifelong learning and breaks down some of the traditional barriers between home and school.

> "I created a system that targets entire school families for Internet training to 'jump-start' as many educators, students, and parents as possible. I bundle teacher training, student training, and parent training into a five-part, ten-hour series I call the Internaut Academy. I cover Net basics, classroom management, and other practical issues, and rotate the teacher, student, and parent sessions in order to maintain equity among the groups. Ten hours is enough to launch people in individual directions."
>
> — *Mike Abbiatti, Teacher, Woodlawn High School/Louisiana State University, Shreveport, Louisiana, U.S.A.*

The change process

Integrating the Internet into regular classroom use will be a continuing challenge, and every experience won't be a success. Change is a journey, a non-linear trip loaded with uncertainty and excitement. Educational experts in implementation and the change process state that

- change takes place over time,
- change involves anxiety,
- change involves learning new skills through practice,
- successful change involves pressure,
- the people who must implement the change need to see why the new way works better,
- problems are our friends,
- connection with the wider environment is critical for success,
- both top-down and bottom-up strategies are necessary,
- every person is an agent for change.

Summing up

Once you have participated in a project or two, you'll be eager to continue incorporating the Internet as an exciting component of many subjects and units of study. As you and your students become more familiar with Internet tools, you can design your own project and invite participants from around your community or around the world. In the next chapter, you'll find some strategies for planning successful projects.

Planning your own projects

*"*It's not about buying the best equipment. It's not about what will make the school look good. It's about enhancing students' learning, and inspiring and supporting teachers in doing what they already do well.*"*

— What's working in education (an online companion to *the learning connection*) **http://www.benton.org/practice/edu/,** 17/02/98

After participating in at least one project organized by others, you may be eager and ready to try initiating your own project. This is an exciting venture for both students and teachers, and there's plenty of help available from others who are eager to share their ideas and tips. Careful planning will be essential to the success of your project. In this chapter, we've synthesized information from experienced teachers to put together a series of logical steps that will help you to be assured of providing a valuable, meaningful learning experience for your students. If you have not already done so, you will also want to make decisions about student accounts and establish some classroom routines for acceptable Internet use before you begin. These issues are addressed in the pages ahead.

Chapter goals
- **To outline strategies for developing original projects**
- **To establish student procedures for accounts and use of Internet tools**
- **To examine issues of acceptable use**

Planning your project

Step 1: Select a topic.
A teacher's choice of topics is usually controlled by curriculum set in place by the school or school district. Working within these guidelines, involve your students as much as possible in selecting a topic, giving them scope to pursue their own related interests. If you are planning to invite participation from others, give your project a snappy title that reflects its process or its content goals: "Fast Food Flash," "Great Gourmet Gastronomy," "Taming the Tube." Your students will enjoy creating novel project names.

Step 2: Establish learning outcomes.
Effective use of the Internet in education requires standards and outcomes for student learning. Without specific learning expectations

for Internet-based activities, students will lack direction and focus and will be overwhelmed by the sheer quantity of information available to them. Learning outcomes define the criteria by which to measure both student progress and teacher effectiveness in using the Internet as a tool. Learning outcomes related to Internet use in the classroom fall into two broad categories:

- those associated with the knowledge, skills, and values of the curriculum unit (e.g., "Students will describe regional, national, and global environmental problems related to the use of technology and investigate ways of sustaining life in the future")
- those related to effective use of the technology itself (e.g., "Students will send e-mail letters to peers in other parts of the country").

Whether learning outcomes are teacher-selected or designated by the core curriculum, keep them foremost in mind as you plan your Internet project. Ask yourself the following questions:

- What learning outcomes do I want the students to achieve?
- Are these outcomes clear, specific, and measurable?
- Am I trying to fit the outcomes to the technology, or am I using the technology as a tool to meet the outcomes?
- To what extent will Internet use assist students in achieving the desired learning outcomes?
- Could these learning outcomes be achieved just as effectively or more effectively using other methods?

Step 3: Investigate other projects.

Examine other teachers' successful projects and identify the common elements that contributed to their success. Consider the timelines and number of classes involved. Look for situations that parallel your own with regard to anticipated learning outcomes, student ability, access to computers, time available, and teacher experience. Find a good project that has already been tried, and then improve it by customizing it to suit your own needs. You can find many good sites to look for projects throughout this book.

Step 4: Decide the type of activity and plan a timetable.

Choose the type of activity—keypal, information exchange, etc.— and decide how much time you plan to devote to it, keeping in mind the amount of Internet access time available to your students. Peak use on an educational network is geared to traditional cycles of the school calendar. October through December, February through May, and July (with summer school) are very busy times on the network. However, most of the successful networking activities were planned, and announcements posted, six to eight weeks before the actual project was to begin. Carefully consider the types of

Have students working on the same project use the same diskette. Several letters, poems, or reviews can be combined into a single document as pages 2, 3, 4, and so on. This ensures that teachers don't spend unnecessary time getting students' material onto one diskette (or retyping).

teaching/learning strategies that are appropriate for your students and the type and amount of Internet access available in your school and classroom.

- **Whole-class activities.** If you're a beginner, start with a teacher-directed whole-class activity, especially if you have a limited number of computers with Internet access. Corresponding with another class either locally, nationally, or internationally is a good way to introduce students to the Internet. E-mail can be integrated into just about every subject and grade: reading, writing, social studies, science, business, second language learning. You can use e-mail as a vehicle for teaching both curriculum-related skills (such as letter-writing, devising questions, or improving punctuation) and Internet-related skills (such as addressing, formatting, and sending e-mail, and online etiquette). Once students have mastered electronic messaging in the group setting, they will be able to use it individually as a tool for other assignments.

You don't have to limit yourself to e-mail. Information gathering related to a particular theme or project can be done by a pair of students who then report back to the whole class.

Not only is whole-class instruction an effective means to learn the basic skills of Internet use: it is also an appropriate forum for exploring such topics as

- sources of information found on the Internet
- accuracy of information found on the Internet
- evaluation of Web sites
- copyright issues
- citing Internet sources
- security issues
- acceptable use.

The issues of evaluation, copyright, and citing are discussed in detail in Chapter 5.

If you're counting on all students accessing the Web simultaneously in a lab setting, be sure to have an alternative offline activity in mind should something go wrong. Also, don't expect all students to be able to access the same Web site without very long delays.

- **Cooperative learning activities.** In a well-structured, active learning environment, the Internet can become one of a number of tools that a group of students (or one or two members of each group) can use for a specific purpose, as in the Environmentally Friendly Community project described on page 45 in Chapter 2. In such a setting, student experts emerge and peer tutoring happens naturally. Most Internet projects involve a great deal of learning offline. This might involve manipulating graphics or information files that have been gleaned from the Internet, or developing e-mail messages in a word-processing package for uploading later. It can also include posting new findings on a bulletin board, or tracking responses to a questionnaire on a graph or map. Each student in the group can play an important role, yet all need not have access to the Internet.

Computer networks allow us to look at cooperative learning in a new way. Students can learn to work in teams whose members are separated by distance. This reflects the reality of our changing world of work. Before getting involved in a cooperative Internet activity, you can simulate this situation using your school's local area network. For example, while one team member gathers observational data about reptiles in the science lab, another might research the topic in the library, and another might scan drawings and diagrams in the multimedia room. Team members communicate strictly via computer.[1] Following this experience, students will be eager to try collaborating with others in more distant places.

"When student teams work in collaboration with other schools (virtual grouping), they know that the other group is counting on them and that they have to trust them."

— *Mathieu Dubreuil, Teacher, École Secondaire Dorval, Dorval, Quebec, Canada*

- **Individual activities.** You'll need a lot of student access if you expect all students to engage individually in an Internet activity as a mandatory course requirement. However, many schools are fortunate enough to have all their computers online. To be fair, ensure that all students have mastered the basic skills of Internet use, have attained a certain level of expertise through practice, and can get help when they need it. One of the great strengths of individualization, of course, is that no two students learn in exactly the same way. While one may approach an information search in a step-by-step manner, another may prefer to "surf" through a variety of sites. There is no right or wrong way, as long as the final goal is achieved within the specified timeframe.

Students need large blocks of time for Internet use. If you have explored the Internet at all yourself, you know how fast time goes while you're using it. It is very frustrating to get to the site you've been searching for only to find that there is not enough time left to download the information you want. It is also difficult to predict how long it will take to get to a particular site, or even if you can get there when you want to. Thus, it is inadvisable to create rigid timeframes. Involve your students as much as possible in establishing realistic time limits for the completion of projects, and try to keep your timetable flexible. By observing carefully, you can identify students who are off task and those who are using their time wisely. Have students keep a list of any sites they have used, with a brief description of their contents. If all are working on the same topic, share findings at the end of each computer session. This fosters collaboration and saves time for everyone. By the end of the

If you have a computer with Internet access in your classroom, use it as a learning center that students access as one component of a unit. For example, in a study of whales, allow each student an opportunity to find the answers to specific questions about whales using the World Wide Web whale watching site (**http://www.physics.hel sinki.fi/whale/**). Visit the site yourself first to compose your questions.

term, you will have developed an excellent resource package. Don't forget to build in time for sharing the finished products, whatever form they take.

"Be patient. Don't be discouraged. Things may not go as planned: they may go a lot slower, or they may not go at all. It's all part of the learning experience."

— *Sharon Lewis, Teacher, Red Deer, Alberta, Canada*

If you teach in a setting where subjects are strictly segregated, team with another teacher. Your two subject areas can complement each other (e.g., language and history; math and science), and students can devote time from both classes to the project.

Step 5: Define roles of participants.
It's important to decide which staff will take a leadership role in initiating, managing, and monitoring a project. The most common method is for the adventurous and innovative teachers to be pioneers and then to encourage others. If you are eager to get involved in a project, brainstorm with interested colleagues and assign tasks according to the individual strengths of the team members. For example, classroom teachers might look after overall organization and student groupings; the computer resource teacher might schedule computer use and manage technical problems; selected students might act as Internet researchers and resource people; parent volunteers might supervise and assist individual students as they work; and the librarian might print a variety of the best projects and display them in the library. Discover your classroom and school student experts and tap into their knowledge by facilitating peer mentorship either in a formal or an informal way. If possible, try your project out with a close colleague first, on a small scale. This run-through can help you overcome technical problems as well as problems with the basic project design. You will find that having a sympathetic colleague available to discuss and solve problems will be a big help.

Are you ready to consider trying electronic student portfolios? Take a look at Tammy's Tech Tips at **http://www.essdack.org/tips**. You will also find useful ideas for classroom computer management, computer projects, and integration of the Internet in the classroom.

Step 6: Incorporate evaluation.

How will you evaluate the student learning outcomes you established for your project? How will you evaluate the usefulness of the Internet as a tool, perhaps even the primary medium, for your project? Teacher, peer, and self evaluation are all appropriate tools in an active, student-centered, technology-enhanced classroom. Develop checklists (see Figure 3-1) and rubrics (see Figure 3-2) of observable performance indicators to use as assessment criteria. Involve students in this process as much as possible. Use observational data, teacher-student conferencing, and a portfolio of work samples for formative evaluation. End your project with a tangible product such as an oral presentation, written report, video, or student/class portfolio that can be used for summative evaluation purposes.

Step 7: Outline the details of the project.

The following information will be required by other educators who wish to participate in your project:

Figure 3-1
Sample telecommunications skills record sheet

OUTCOMES	JANICE	ABDUL	GUY	SARAH
1. Student understands network concepts				
• describes how physical connections are made				
• identifies hardware components: server, terminal, modem				
• uses terminology: user ID, password, account, logon, logoff, online, upload, download, e-mail, attachment, netiquette				
2. Student accesses and uses local bulletin board				
• logs on and off				
• reads e-mail				
• sends e-mail				
• reads conference mail				
• uploads a file				
• downloads a file				
• uses appropriate netiquette				
3. Student accesses and uses Internet services				
• logs on and off				
• navigates the main menu				
• sends and receives e-mail				
• retrieves information using a Web browser				
• creates and uses bookmarks				
• uses a search tool (e.g., Web Crawler) to locate information				

The Teacher's Complete & Easy Guide to the Internet

Figure 3-2
Sample rubric

OUTCOME	LEVEL 1	LEVEL 2	LEVEL 3
Students will select appropriate technologies and use them effectively for a variety of purposes.	Uses a range of technology as suggested by the teacher for purposes within the school.	Uses a broad range of technology as suggested by teacher and peers for purposes both within and outside the school.	Selects appropriate technology independently and uses it competently for both academic and personal purposes.
Students will use an extensive range of media as sources of information.	Uses a range of media texts; discusses content and expresses personal opinions about the material.	Uses a broad range of media texts to acquire information; uses material to clarify and extend point of view.	Uses sophisticated media to locate and analyze specific information related to social, political, economic, and cultural issues.

- contact person's information (name, school, e-mail address, school address, and phone number)
- project title
- grade levels involved
- curriculum links (list as many as are relevant)
- anticipated student learning outcomes
- number of schools/classes to be involved
- summary of project including specific timelines
- registration details
- sharing of information at conclusion of project.

If you are applying for funding for your project, these details will be the basis of your proposal.

"For a successful cooperative project, be clear about your objectives, be sure the students understand the purpose, plan how you are going to manage the project, and be sure to follow through on your commitments to others."

— *Connie Mark, Teacher, Pearl City, Hawaii, U.S.A.*

Step 8: Invite others to participate.

Create your "Call for Participation" and post it to the curriculum conferences, Web sites, and/or listservs you have selected. Set definite starting and ending dates, and announce these when you call for participation. You may find that you need to advertise for participants several times, so the earlier you start, the better. Also, one teacher may see your project idea and think that it's great, but may need to pass it on to another. This takes time. It also takes time to gather and compile student input and prepare students to begin. If you expect submissions such as data or student writing, set realistic deadlines and stick to them, but set timelines that are broad enough to allow flexibility. You might provide examples of the

Ten Useful Tips from Doug Walker

1. Start Small if Necessary

A school does not need many Internet connections. Most student work on an Internet project is done offline using existing school resources. Material developed on word processors can quickly be uploaded or downloaded. In our school, only one of our computers connects to the Internet. While two or three more would have made things easier, we've been able to manage the complexities of our Internet projects without difficulty. If you have only one or two computers that connect to the Internet, think about where to put these machines. Our school finally decided on the library. That way, the Internet computer could be available to everyone in the school.

2. Keep Your Teacher's Eyes Open

Explore the Internet with your teacher's eyes wide open. I'm always on the lookout for ideas to use in the classroom. In my Internet travels, I enjoy exploring its nooks and crannies. I like to build a project with the Internet resources I discover. I've come across thousands of Usenet newsgroups on every imaginable subject, with their remarkable FAQs ("Frequently Asked Questions"). Besides the monthly dozen or so huge NASA FAQs on recent developments in space science, you'll discover FAQs on lots of things students are already interested in: pets, "Star Trek," sports, hobbies, genealogy. Because FAQs appear at frequent intervals, not only do they contain very up-to to-date information, bibliographies, and answers to readers' questions, but they also list where to get resources on the Internet—articles, software, pictures, and sound files.

While wandering the Internet, you'll also discover fascinating and helpful e-mail discussion lists (listservs). Some listservs are general; others are very specific. While your classes participate in Internet projects, alert yourself to useful spinoff ideas for creating your own projects to share with other Internet schools.

3. Set Clear Goals

Once you have the equipment and the Internet connection, and are familiar with some Internet resources, you are ready to begin planning your project. We structured the project around Grade 6 meteorology. Above all, we wanted our sixth-grade students to engage in scientific inquiry. We also wanted our students to use the Internet as a tool to develop their information literacy skills, and to empower them to learn about the world by communicating with students in other countries and cultures. That the whole school should feel part of our project, that everyone would perceive themselves as part of a community of knowledge discovery was another important project goal.

We banned the word "about" from our project. Since this was to be a science project, we were careful to make sure it wasn't "about" science—no theatrical magic-trick style "science experiments," no laboriously reproduced canned "experiments," where everything is known beforehand, making originality and thinking for oneself irrelevant. Students will learn if they can see that they are involved in doing something real. To learn science, let them really be scientists. They had specific tasks to perform and data to analyze.

We also banned "about" from learning the Internet. We were not too keen on hauling classes into the library to tell them "about" the Internet, have them take copious notes, and test them on a bunch of definitions. Having students passively learn about something as alive and changing as the Internet would be counterproductive. Why should students have to be content with passive learning, when they could learn by doing?

4. Brainstorm Your Project

Transform the goals of your project into concrete plans by brainstorming with staff. For example, at a staff meeting for a recent project, I asked for volunteers. Seven educators immediately expressed interest, but there was understandable uneasiness at the outset. Some of the team were uncomfortable with computers, and only our librarian had experience using the Internet. The problem disappeared, though, when we encouraged everyone on the team to choose an area in which he or she was most comfortable.

We decided to train students to be our school's Internet researchers and resource people, continuously passing on to others what they learned. We developed investigative teams of student journalists. Finally, wanting the whole school to "own" the project, we dreamed up a vast "Weather Wall" for the library, where beautiful art work, displays, maps, and constantly updated bulletins would keep everyone informed about our project and the world of weather.

5. Be Realistic!

In planning an effective Internet project, it's important to keep your feet on the ground. Many projects don't succeed because practical matters are ignored. That's why we chose Grade 6 meteorology as the basis for our project. It offered the potential to do real hands-on scientific observation in the field. Yet, it didn't require expensive instruments. A barometer, thermometer, and rain and wind gauges were not difficult for students to read and use. If need be, students could always make their own weather instruments.

6. Be Organized
In most projects, many things have to come together. Make a flow chart so students can see how the parts relate to the whole and so they can understand how their contributions fit in.

7. Show, Don't Tell, Your Students
In library visits and moments from planning periods, we showed small groups of students the basics of using Ottawa's Free-net, Usenet newsgroups, and WWW resources. A morning group would watch like hawks as the demonstration unfolded. By the afternoon, the new group already knew what to do, mysteriously having learned—during recess—from students in the earlier group.

8. Look at Problems Positively
Don't get discouraged. In the course of any project there are bound to be obstacles. Think positively. And go back to the list of tips.

9. Involve Other Schools
How other schools participate in your project is not within your direct control. They can simultaneously duplicate it, if they wish, or they can share doing your school's research. If you do wish to involve other schools in your project, advertising is essential. You must send out a "Call to Participate" outlining your project, with goals, materials, and a detailed time line. The call ought to be issued several weeks before the project starts, so other schools will have time to get ready for the project.

Encourage students and teachers to post messages about current happenings as your project progresses. Frequently post your most interesting letters, one per class. Too many messages of dubious clarity obscure the goals of the project. Send out only your best stuff.

10. Evaluate the Project as It Unfolds
Keep your project well tuned. Keep your eyes open. Listen to your feelings. Find creative ways to bring out the best in one another. Be alert to independent thinking and encourage it as it cautiously emerges. Real talent must not be wasted. Be brave. Let your students astonish you with the depth of their insight, with the beauty of their art work, with the intensity of their writing. Don't neglect your Internet partners as you delight in your school's love of learning. Heighten their participation by advertising, by increasing interaction. If you're careful to design your Internet project to make a real difference in how teachers teach and how students learn, it will.

— Doug Walker (1994) The Grassroots Program, Canada's SchoolNet
http://www.schoolnet.ca, 01/10/97

kinds of writing or data collection that students will submit. Phased deadlines establish a sense of accountability to the other participants in the project and make it easier to ensure that they follow through. Even if the teacher is inclined to drop out, students who know the deadlines will often hold their own teachers accountable to complete the project.

> "In cooperative projects, be clear on your expectations from other schools. If they lack the time to meet all project requirements, perhaps they can participate to a lesser degree."
>
> — *Sharon Lewis, Teacher, Red Deer, Alberta, Canada*

As soon as people respond to your call, send them a reply acknowledging their request for participation and a more detailed outline of the project that includes specific timelines and registration procedures. Keep track of the replies and registration details in a special file or folder; if you have enough classes before the registration date closes, be sure to respond to all requests stating that the project is full.

Step 9: Share your plans with parents.

Let parents know what you're planning and indicate that you would welcome their suggestions and assistance. This is a good way to identify contacts in your community who are knowledgeable about this new technology. You'll probably find that they will offer to help in a variety of ways, such as donating equipment, advising you of useful Internet sites, or spending time helping students.

> "When our school's old modem finally bit the dust, I made a point of mentioning to my students that we could really use a modem, especially if their parents had upgraded their modems at work. Within a week we received three working modems. We were back online in no time!"
>
> — *Chris McQuire, Teacher, Pope John XXIII School, Nepean, Ontario, Canada*

Step 10: Evaluate and bring closure to your project.

At the conclusion of the project, share the results with all participants. If you publish any student writing, send a copy to all who participated. Involve your students in writing a summary that describes the project, what they did, what they learned, and what changes they would make. Post the summary on the network for others to see, not just the project participants. Have your students send a thank-you message to all participants. You might also want to send a copy of your summary and a thank you to the principal of each school that participated in order to reinforce the value of using the Internet to achieve educational goals.

Students with special needs

The Internet is highly motivating for most students, and it can be used to implement and complement proven strategies in working with students with special needs. It can free the special student from a history of negative experiences with more traditional education and provide control and autonomy that may previously have been missing.[2] The Internet can open up the world to the student who is confined by socioeconomic or physical limitations. The multimedia technologies of the World Wide Web are powerful tools for meeting the needs of learning-disabled students and those with specific auditory or visual needs.

Teachers can individualize Internet activities to suit special-needs students by giving them a specific task to do online, such as searching an encyclopedia to make a list of the ten biggest cities in the world. Cooperative learning strategies support them as they participate in the regular program. Cooperative learning doesn't have to be limited to students within the class, as telecommunications links students throughout the community and the world. Cooperative problem solving, information exchanges, and pooled data analysis involve and engage all students as peers. One of the advantages of electronic communication is that gender, race, age, and physical

characteristics are invisible. In online communication, we focus on what people say in their writing, not how they appear.

> "I became aware that my students of low socioeconomic status had a harder time dealing with computers than those who had computers and video machines at home. We need to expose kids to technology at an early age in school. When pairing kids for computer use, I try to place them with kids at their own level, rather than with a more capable student who might unknowingly 'take over'."
>
> — *Heddi Thompson, Teacher, Chase County Elementary School, Cottonwood Falls, Kansas, U.S.A.*

Here are some further strategies for students with special needs.

- Provide a learning partner or buddy to assist the student who has difficulty reading, following instructions, or staying on task.
- Encourage parents to use the Internet at home with the student, if possible.
- Provide opportunities for individual electronic mentoring such as online projects in which students submit original writing to professional writers, teachers, and other students and receive personal feedback.
- Use Internet resources such as learning games, puzzles, scavenger hunts, and simulations for skill development.

You might want to check out some Internet resources associated with special needs, such as the following.

National Center for Learning Disabilities
This center's mission is to promote understanding and public awareness of children and adults with learning disabilities. It includes

such things as fact sheets, behavioral signs, legal rights, and lists of resources.

http://ncld.org/

KidSource OnLine
Here you will find articles about a variety of learning disabilities, links to student and parent sites such as homework helpers, and online forums.

http://www.kidsource.com/kidsource/pages/education.disabilities.html

The Learning Disabilities Home Page
This site provides useful links to references concerning Attention Deficit Disorder, autism, auditory and visual deficits, teaching LD students, and technology for special-needs students.

http://www.westvikingc.nf.ca/Westvik.htm

Learning Disabilities Association of Canada
The Canadian national organization is a focal point for articles of general information, research, legal issues, and links to other sites.

http://eduss10.educ.queensu.ca/~lda/ldac/ldachome.html

Learning Disabilities Association of America
LDA is a national organization of parents, professionals, and individuals with learning disabilities created to help parents and individuals of potentially normal intelligence who manifest handicaps of a perceptual, conceptual, or coordinative nature. They provide fact sheets, resources, and publications as well as links to other sites.

http://www.ldanatl.org/

Deaf World Web
Deaf World Web is the central point of information on deafness on the Internet, with deafness-related information on all subjects from resources to references around the world.

http://deafworldweb.org/

International Dyslexic Association
Of special interest here is the technology section, which includes assistive technologies, technology resources, and commercially available products and services.

http://www.interdys.org/

National Centre to Improve Practice in Special Education through Technology, Media and Materials
From this interesting site, you can visit two exemplary early childhood classrooms, explore the use of voice recognition technology to address writing difficulties, look at an online workshop about assis-

tive technology for students, or view a video of students using assistive technologies.

http://www.edc.org/FSC/NCIP

Bobby

This is a free Web-based service that will help you to make Web pages accessible to people with learning disabilities.

http://www.ldresources.com/

The Arc of the United States

The Arc of the United States is the nation's largest voluntary organization committed to the welfare of mentally retarded children and adults and their families. This home page provides links to support groups, reading lists, other disability-related sites such as dyslexia and autism, parenting information, assistive technology and software, and funding sources.

http://fohnix.metronet.com/~thearc/welcome.html

Children and Adults with Attention Deficit Disorders

This is an extremely well-organized site that provides resources and links related to children and adults with Attention Deficit Disorder.

http://www.chadd.org/

listserv@ukcc.uky.edu

E-mail to this address. Type SUBSCRIBE DEAFBLIND <your name> to join this deaf-and-blind discussion list.

listserv@sjuvm.stjohns.edu

E-mail to this address. Type SUBSCRIBE CEC-TAM <your name> to join a discussion list for technology issues relating to exceptional children. Type SUBSCRIBE AUTISM <your name> to join the discussion list for issues relating specifically to autism.

> "The primary value of using the Internet in my Learning Disabilities classroom is the willingness of my students to do their own research because the Net is (a) up to date, (b) does most of the labor for them (compared with looking through books and magazines), (c) is interactive through the e-mail contacts they make, and (d) is still a novelty with them."
>
> — Gayle Fields, Learning Strategist, Queen Elizabeth Junior/Senior High School, Calgary, Alberta, Canada

> "Adults often worry about socioeconomic, gender, and other issues regarding computer use, but the kids I see in my open-access lab don't show any of these problems. The experienced kids help the new ones, the gamesters defer to the workers, the girls and boys work in absolute equality, the age range in the lab is representative of the school, the Black-White ratio is also representative, and those students who have computers at home help the rest who don't have them. These concerns may stem from adult perceptions or preconceptions of young people rather than from observation of real kids at work. But maybe I'm just fortunate to have worked with an unusually great bunch of kids all these years."
>
> — Elizabeth S. Dunbar, Teacher, Baltimore City College, Baltimore, Maryland, U.S.A.

Student Internet accounts

Accounts and passwords are for your protection, to ensure that someone else will not log on as you and misbehave using your identity. All staff members should have their own accounts. If your type of Internet connection permits it, giving each student an individual account is also a good idea. When students use generic logins and passwords, it's difficult to trace misbehavior and track student usage. On the other hand, when individual students are given the responsibility for acceptable use, you can monitor and track usage. Find out how much control your school's system provides over student access. Some schools require that the e-mail account itself belong to the minor's parents, thus they have the right to examine all materials. In other schools, teacher accounts give staff full access to all Internet resources, while student accounts allow access only to certain sites and/or to certain navigation tools. When students require more than what is available, they need only ask a teacher to assist them.

Some teachers have only a personal account, and don't mind students using it after establishing guidelines for acceptable use. If the computer is in your classroom, it's easy to monitor, and if you work with younger students, you can be sure that someone will "tell" if classroom rules are broken. Naturally, those who abuse the privilege lose the privilege.

> "Students using the Internet should be instructed never to give out home addresses or phone numbers. We use our school address. Personally, I prefer to give my e-mail address to people whom I don't know, rather than my home mailing address."
>
> — *Dean Christie (1995, May 23), "Re: Just to point it out," Kidsphere.*

HINT Take a look at Tammy's Tech Tips: Nuts About the Net at **http://206.252.190.23/ nutsaboutnet/index. html** for advice about physical setup, integration, policy and procedures, and training. Tammy is an experienced technology teacher with lots of good tips and ideas.

Security and viruses

If you use the Internet to exchange data (such as text or pictures), virus infection is generally not a problem. The real concern occurs when you download software programs and run them on your own computer. Any program you download over the network and run could have a virus. All computers, especially those connected to the Internet, should have virus-protection software running on them. Your hardware or software supplier, your service provider, your technical support personnel, or your colleagues should be able to provide more specific information applicable to your site. Virus-checking software is available free over the Internet.

Another useful policy is for each student to be restricted to one personal floppy disk. This way, when students are using computers for school work, such as gathering information for a research project, they save their work on their own disk. Keep these disks in school so that you have control over what gets loaded onto any computer.

Whether you connect directly to the Internet or rely on your service provider to safeguard your security interests, be aware that you are exposing your network activities, online files, and electronic communications to some degree of risk from the "outlaws" of the Internet. A "hacker" is someone who is highly proficient at understanding and manipulating computer systems. A "cracker" is someone who maliciously and/or illegally enters or attempts to enter someone else's computer system.

Computer security is unquestionably important, both in maintaining the security of the school's computers and in ensuring the proper behavior of all who use the network. In this area, not only school policy, but also provincial/state and national laws may apply. The good news is that Internet sites geared to school use have been spared the kinds of attacks you read about in the press. While your school site is unlikely to be of great interest to computer intruders, they remain a possible threat, if only as a nuisance. A successful intrusion can result in theft of files, malfunctions in your system, installation of new and bogus user accounts, the generation of e-mail messages in your name, or the storage of alien files on your system. It is unlikely that you personally will wish to become part of your system's defense service; that is best left to your service provider and your school's system administrator. Nevertheless, keep the following principles of defense in mind, and teach them to your students.

- Choose your password carefully. The best passwords contain at least six characters combining letters, numbers, and symbols. They should be random and meaningless, yet simple to remember.

HINT One good strategy for choosing a password is to model it after a memorable phrase. For example, "A bird in the hand is worth two in the bush" lends itself to the password Bhw2iB.

- Don't let anyone see your password. If you must write it down, don't identify it as such, and don't leave it near your computer.
- Be aware of oddities in your system that you notice but cannot explain, such as your e-mail account filling up with hundreds of new messages from the same source.
- If you do have a problem while online, sever your connection. (When in doubt, pull the plug!)

Child safety

Parents and teachers are understandably concerned about the appropriateness of some of the material available online. The media have made us well aware of online pornography, violence, and racism. Schools that are now online have taken precautions to keep inappropriate material out of the school setting. Those with broad

HINT You can read a very interesting article called "Is the Net Safe?" at **http://www.cnet.com/ Content/features/ Techno/Networks/ss09. html**. Choose "How the Net Works," Question #9.

Internet access usually require more procedures than those that have a single modem access in the school library. Some use special hardware and/or software to limit student access, some allow students to visit only approved sites, while others rely on strict acceptable use policies and close adult supervision. It's important to keep in mind that students who are fully engaged in creative learning activities will have neither the time nor the interest to seek out forbidden areas of the Internet, whereas students who are turned loose with inadequate forethought, preparation, and supervision are likely to find other ways to amuse themselves online.

Software that limits access to inappropriate sites

NetNanny, SurfWatch, and Cybersitter are examples of software designed to protect children on the Internet; such programs are often referred to as filtering software or Internet content screening tools. At the discretion of parents and schools, they monitor and block inappropriate sites and subject matter. In addition to preventing access to pornography, hate literature, and bomb- and drug-making formulas, you can prevent addresses, phone numbers, and credit card numbers from being sent out on the Internet. There are two types of screening tools available today. Client-based systems are designed for end-users, thus the software must be installed individually on each machine. Server solutions reside on a single machine to which all client machines are attached. Students cannot circumvent the screening mechanism as the server is under sole control of the system administrator.

These software babysitters screen and block both incoming and outgoing commands and content in two different ways. Keyword blocking involves blocking Internet sites that contain certain words. For example, if you enter the word "bomb" in your filtering software dictionary and someone sends the latest pipe-bomb recipe via e-mail, the terminal will shut down when the file is accessed. While this allows for good coverage, it also assumes that because one word at the site is objectionable, the entire site contains undesirable content. If a student tries to access **http://www.playboy.com**, a colorful "Blocked by ..." dialog box appears. However, while keeping students out of the Playboy site with the keyword "breast," you also deny them access to breast cancer research. Even though filtering software uses *knowbots* and *spiders* (Internet robots, in effect) to dig up and then filter any site that includes the use of various words, spelling can be changed and other words substituted.

A better way to block undesirable content is by reference to a database of undesirable material. Typically, a database is created, updated on a regular basis, and maintained by the software publisher, listing sites that fall into several categories that you can selectively turn on and off. A good system will offer daily automatic updates, a large database, and the ability to customize the database yourself. For more information about filtering software, visit these Web sites:

CyberSitter
CyberSitter filters and blocks adult-oriented material, graphics, and language from Internet news-groups, chat areas, World Wide Web pages, and e-mail. For standalone PCs and networks.
http://www.solidoak.com/

FoolProof
FoolProof for Windows is a computer security program that allows you to provide multiple layers of protection. You can protect files, limit the creation of directories and new files, disable access to applications, limit or deny access to DOS, and prevent people from changing the program manager. You can also create user groups that allow you to create different levels of security for different users.
http://www.teleport.com/~smrtstuf/fpinfo.html

The Internet Filter for Windows
The Internet Filter monitors, filters, analyzes, and logs Internet access.
http://www.xmission.com:80/~seer/Turner/if.html

NetNanny
NetNanny filters words, phrases, or sites.
http://www.netnanny.com/netnanny

NetShepherd
NetShepherd rates and filters World Wide Web sites and selectively supervises access.
http://www.shepherd.net/

SafeSurf
SafeSurf, a watchdog organization, has suggested a rating standard in which child-friendly sites identify themselves with HTML tags hidden inside the contents of their Web pages. Provided the child is using a SafeSurf browser, all tagless sites are invisible.
http://www.safesurf.com/

SurfWatch
SurfWatch blocks what is being received at any individual computer.
http://www.surfwatch.com/

Web Doggie

From the MIT Media Lab, WebDoggie is a personalized WWW filtering system that attempts to alleviate the information overload problem faced by users. WebDoggie provides you with your own personalized WWW agent that periodically recommends new WWW documents to you based on what WWW documents you have expressed a liking for in the past.

http://webhound.www.media.mit.edu/projects/webhound/

Web Sense

In addition to allowing you to block undesirable sites, Web Sense monitors Internet activity. Web Sense uses a growing database of more than 60,000 URLs, newsgroups, and chatroom addresses that fall into twenty-eight categories. Each site is checked by a person before being added to the database and updates are daily.

http://www.netpart.com

The ongoing costs of filtering software are high, usually requiring an initial investment plus a monthly update, money that might be better spent on learning related software. Filtering software may also create a false sense of security, and schools that claim they can keep students completely safe from controversial material may find themselves more at risk legally than others who make no such claims. Diverse family values and community values must also be considered, along with students' civil liberties. Some parents may question the school's right to restrict student access to information.

"Kid Safe" sites

Some schools post a list of sites known to be safe for the appropriate age of the students, and these are the only sites that students are allowed to visit at school. This strategy is used with young students; older students can surf and search within the guidelines of a good acceptable use policy, as described in the next section. Obviously, close supervision is always required. Here is one such list of sites for very young children.

Berit's Best Sites for Children at
    http://db.cochran.com/li_toc:theoPage.db

Booknook at
    http://I-site.on.ca/Isite/Education/Bk_report/

Carlos Coloring Book at
    http://robot0.ge.uiuc.edu/~carlosp/color/

Hands On Children's Museum at
    http://www.wln.com/~deltapac/hocm.html

Figure 3-3

Berit's Best Sites for Children provides a comprehensive list of sites, frequently updated, for young children.

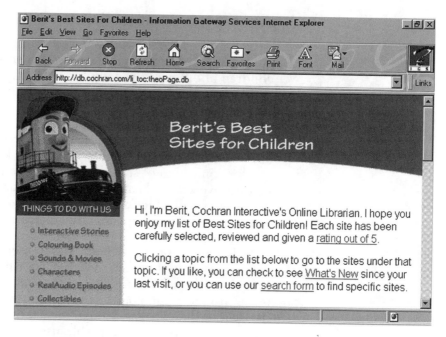

Jellybean Kingdom at
http://www.geocities.com/Enchanted Forest/3737/

KEWL Kids Excellent Web Links at
http://www.cybercomm.net/~teach/

Kids' Wave at
http://www.safesurf.com/wave/sskwave.html

Kids' Web at
http://www.primenet.com/~sburr/index.html

Stage Hand puppets at
http://fox.nstn.ca/~puppets/activity.html

Story Hour at
http://ipl.sils.umich.edu/youth/StoryHour/

The Canadian Kids Homepage at
http://www.onramp.ca/~lowens/107kids.htm

Another approach is to identify curricular and developmentally appropriate sites in advance for each grade level or theme and make these available as "pages" on the World Wide Web server. Students are told they must stay at those sites: no searching, no surfing. Violators suffer loss of Internet privileges or other appropriate consequence. While some teachers may be uncomfortable with this approach, time constraints make it appealing since pointing students toward worthwhile sites saves them time and effort.

Use your browser software to set up your selected **Bookmarks** as the **Home Page** where students begin their explorations. For example, Grade 6 students exploring whales as a class activity open the **Home Page** to see a list of approved sites.

Accceptable use policies

A balanced approach to using the Internet in schools emphasizes guidance rather than censorship. The strategies we use to teach children about risks in daily life work equally well with the risks associated with the Internet. By establishing clear rules and setting boundaries, we teach young children not to run in the school halls, not to talk to strangers, and not to use violence. We make judgments about how much supervision children require at various ages, and when the risk is extremely high, we keep them in sight or we employ some kind of structure such as a fence or a lock. As children mature, we teach them to respect boundaries and values without being physically blocked from entry. We expect our students to begin exercising judgment and restraint as they begin moving toward adult life.

It is important that schools develop clear policies to guide students' use of the Internet and establish rules, and consequences for breaking them. Additionally, schools should consider integrating issues around technology and ethics into the curriculum. To protect the school and to reassure parents, most schools have developed and implemented an acceptable use policy. Such policies are frequently referred to as AUPs. An AUP is an agreement signed by students, their parents, and the teacher. It outlines the terms and conditions of Internet use. Some AUPs are instituted by school boards or districts. Others are school- or even classroom-specific. Find out if your school has an Internet AUP. If not, get together with interested colleagues and parents to develop one before allowing your students to access the Internet. (A typical AUP appears in Appendix A.)

A thorough AUP contains the following:

- a description of what the Internet is,
- an explanation of how students will access the Internet at school,
- examples of how the Internet will be used to enhance student learning,
- a list of student responsibilities while online, which might address such issues as
  — privacy
  — morals and ethics
  — freedom of expression
  — legal constraints
  — safety
  — harassment
  — plagiarism
  — resource utilization
  — expected behaviors/etiquette
  — security issues

The Teacher's Complete & Easy Guide to the Internet

- the consequences of violating the AUP,
- a place for student, parent, and teacher signatures.

Rather than simply sending an AUP home for signatures, consider beginning the school year with a "cyberspace evening" to introduce the community to the Internet. Have students demonstrate some exciting Internet resources and projects. Talk to parents about how you plan to use the Internet in your classroom or school, and explain your AUP in detail. Stress that, with the privilege to use the Internet, students must accept the responsibility for proper use. Some schools adopt a "zero tolerance" attitude while others issue a warning letter after the first violation.

> "Education is the key. We give a unit of Net Etiquette to each student and staff on the responsible use of the Internet account. You can find this agreement on our home page at **http://www.mvhs.fuhsd.org** under resources."
> — *Peg Szady, Teacher, Monta Vista High School, California, U.S.A.*

Sample Acceptable Use Policies

Sample AUPs now abound on the Internet. You might start your search for AUPs at **http://www.pitsco.inter.net/p/accept.html** which is Pitsco's launch to Acceptable Use Policies. There you'll find direct links to many of the sites listed here.

gopher://chico.rice.edu:1170/11/More/Acceptable
Acceptable and unacceptable use of Internet resources.

gopher://ericir.syr.edu:70/11/Guides/Agreements
AskERIC Acceptable Use Policies.

gopher://inspire.ospi.wednet.edu:70/00/Accept_Use_Policies/IN_policies.txt
Developing a School or District "Acceptable Use Policy" for Student and Staff Access to the Internet.

gopher://riceinfo.rice.edu:1170/00/More/Acceptable/bmanning
General information on AUPs by the Internet School Networking Group.

http://kings.k12.ca.us/acceptable.use.policy
Kings County, California.

http://lausd.k12.ca.us/aup.html
Los Angeles Unified School District.

http://mustang.coled.umn.edu/Started/use/Acceptableuse.html
Web 66 Acceptable Use Policies.

http://www.classroom.net/policy.htm
Computer use policies and related discussions along with several examples of policies and an FAQ file.

http://www.eff.org/pub/CAF/policies/
The Electronic Frontier Foundation has a collection of the computer policies of many schools and critiques of some.

http://www.erehwon.com/k12aup/
This site contains materials to assist school districts in developing effective Internet policies and practices.

http://www.firn.edu/firn-use-policy.txt
Florida Education Network Acceptable Use Policy.

http://fromnowon.org/fromay95.html
Creating board or district policies that link acceptable use standards to policies on student rights and responsibilities, thus tying consequences and procedures to those already in effect.

http://www.nmusd.k12.ca.us/Resources/Policies.html
Requirements and conditions that students and parents must agree to before students are permitted access to the Internet in California schools.

http://www.nueva.pvt.k12.ca.us/nnaup.html
The Nueva School, Hillsborough, California.

http://www.rice.edu/armadillo/acceptable.html
For the guidance of students, teachers, administrators, parents, and board members in developing and understanding policy.

http://www.ucalgary.ca/~mueller/hanson.html
http://www.umich.edu/~sstrat/WhatOnWeb.html
http://www.voicenet.com/~crammer/censorship.html
Frequently asked questions about AUPs.

http://www.wentworth.com/classroom/products/stories/aup.htm
Defines what's allowed online, and what's not.

HINT

Books of Internet acceptable use policies for schools

- *An Anthology of Internet Acceptable Use Policies* includes copies of twenty-seven university and K-12 school district policies. It's published by the National Association of Regional Media Centers and is available for US$20 from Don Whitmarsh, NARMC Publications Chair, Area Education Agency 4, 1382 4th Ave. NE, Sioux Center, IA 51250, 712/722-4378.

- *Plans & Policies for Technology in Education: A Compendium* also includes sample plans and policies on other technology-related topics from a total of thirty-eight U.S. school districts. (March, 1995) It's available for US$35 from the National School Boards Association Distribution Center in Maryland, (800) 706-6722.

Responding to inappropriate material

The fact that your school has developed and enforced an AUP doesn't protect you or your students from possible violation from other less considerate Internet users. Though it's a relatively rare event, think about how you would respond if you or a student were to receive an e-mail message, for example, containing language or content that you deem unacceptable. It is then up to the offending student's school to take appropriate action, which might include the submission of a formal apology and suspension of Internet privileges.

"I would treat [abuse of Internet privileges] much as I would treat a child who has been insulted on the playground or while going to or from school: I would counsel the child and try and to deal with the offender.

- I would counsel *all* children about the possibility of this kind of message, so that they are not caught off guard. They should know to report this kind of message immediately to the teacher, who should print the message right away and then forward it to a safe location for future reference.

- I would ensure that all parents understood that this is a risk, but that the school doesn't sanction this behavior and that teachers try to prepare students to deal effectively with this.

- I would write a message to the offending e-mail address, with copies to the system administrator and postmaster complaining about this behavior, with full details of how the student was affected."

— Al Rogers, Executive Director, Global SchoolNet Foundation

Resources re Child Safety

http://www.larrysworld.com/child_safety.html
Child Safety On the Information Highway.

http://www.4j.lane.edu/InternetResources/Safety/Safety.html
Published by the National Center for Missing and Exploited Children, this brochure identifies the benefits, myths, and risks of using the Internet.

http://www.pacificrim.net/~mckenzie/mar96/resource.html
Filtering and Internet Child Safety Information.

http://sunsite.unc.edu/cmc/mag/1995/jun/stratford.html
What's a (Teacher, Parent, Administrator) to Do? How should educators react when confronted in the classroom with unacceptable content or language?

http://www.uoknor.edu/oupd/kidsafe/start.html
A site that uses a question-and-answer format to help children learn to protect themselves in various situations, including on the Internet.

caci-request@cygnus.com
Send an e-mail message to this discussion list called CACI (Children Accessing Controversial Information) if you're interested in joining an ongoing dialog with other educators and parents.

http://netparents.org/
The Center for Democracy and Technology, which opposes government controls on the Internet, has created a Web site called Netparents to make it easier for parents to navigate online "safely" with their children.

http://www.kn.pacbell.com/wired/fil/pages.listkeepingki.html
This site contains online safety guides, filtering software, and search engines for children.

 You will often see this symbol when you visit Web sites. The Recreational Software Advisory Council on the Internet (RSACi) is an independent, non-profit organization based in Washington, D.C, that empowers the public, especially parents, to make informed decisions about electronic media by means of an open, objective, content advisory system. The RSACi system provides consumers with information about the level of sex, nudity, violence, or offensive language (vulgar or hate-motivated) in software games and Web sites. To date, RSACi has been integrated into Microsoft's browser, Internet Explorer, and MicroSystem's Cyber Patrol Software. CompuServe (in the United States and Europe) has also committed itself to rate all its content with the RSACi system... RSACi has been an enthusiastic member of a number of initiatives that would support the protection of free speech on the Web. (http://www.rsac.org)

Summing up

For those who have been teaching for a long time, but equally for beginners, the excitement of getting involved in an online project with other teachers and students around the world is inspirational. The Internet becomes one more tool students use to help them with critical learning; it's an information giver, communication facilitator, and thought provoker. Using the Internet in your classroom projects increases the versatility and value of project-based learning as a curriculum tool by providing a rich environment for individuals and teams to carry out in-depth projects that draw on multimedia and information resources from around the world.

> "So much can go so wrong—a password typed incorrectly, server crashes, pornographic or illegal material. Yet so much can go so right. I can think of a hundred reasons not to get kids involved with the Internet, and I can think of a thousand reasons to get them actively participating. I am willing to put up with the small problems in order to achieve the results that I know will make my students self-motivated, critically thinking, lifelong learners."
>
> — *Robert Steenwinkel, Teacher, Mary Butterworh School, Edmonton, Alberta, Canada*

4

Exploring the World Wide Web

"The modern age has a false sense of security because of the great mass of data at its disposal. But the valid issue is the extent to which [people] know how to form and master the material at [their] disposal."
— JOHANN WOLFGANG VON GOETHE, 1832

The World Wide Web inspires learning. Students and teachers are quickly excited by the vastness of this resource and the discovery of how easy it is to navigate. On the World Wide Web, students can learn about current news events and contemporary science. They can delve into the past and read correspondence from the Civil War or visit a museum that provides a glimpse of an earlier time.

This chapter is an introduction to the World Wide Web. It describes some of the different kinds of applications that you can access over the Web. In addition, this chapter helps you learn how to search for information and introduces you to some good Web resources to help you get started using the Web in your classroom.

Chapter goals

- ■ **To provide an overview of the World Wide Web and its role in the classroom**
- ■ **To provide an overview of Web browsers — options and common features**
- ■ **To introduce the concept of client/server computing**
- ■ **To introduce key concepts related to Web technology**
- ■ **To describe how to search for information on the World Wide Web**
- ■ **To suggest a selection of Web resources for teachers and students**

The Web as a tool for learning

The World Wide Web is an important complement to traditional learning materials, both print and audiovisual. School librarians are constantly challenged to meet broad curriculum needs on limited budgets. Having access to the Web is an excellent way to supplement the school media collection. Ideally, students need to know beforehand how to use both print and Internet resources for their research, and how to assess the value of each for any given project.

In the classroom, the World Wide Web can also be used as a publishing tool, and as such it can be relevant to a broad spectrum of classroom learning activities. An exciting venture for students is to develop their own Web pages. We will talk more about student publishing on the Web in the next chapters.

Understanding the basics of the World Wide Web is the first step to using it effectively in the classroom. Chapter 1 briefly introduced the World Wide Web. In this chapter you will learn more about how it works. You will find that taking time to learn about the mechanics of using the Web will help you to become more confident about using the Web with students.

World Wide Web: overview

The World Wide Web project was developed to provide easy access over the Internet to a variety of media. Web pages can display text, pictures, sound, video, and animated graphics. Web pages display paragraphs about a topic, and also provide links to further information, using a computer technology called *hypertext*.

Hypertext links lead you to more information whenever you choose to follow them. (See Figure 4-1, page 80.) A simple example of a hypertext link would be a situation in which you are reading a document on screen and are given an opportunity to click on a word to find its definition. Or you might be viewing a document about health and nutrition and discover a link to another document that provides in-depth information about vitamins. Hyperlinks can point to other references in the same document or to completely separate files on the Internet. Many educational Web pages or pages developed by individual schools include links to similar sites.

Hypermedia is another term you will encounter on the Web. Hypermedia is similar to hypertext in that both denote the ability to access further information from a document. But hypermedia makes it possible to access other kinds of information, such as pictures or sound files, in addition to text. As you might guess, hypermedia is the basis for many multimedia applications. Web pages are becoming more complex in design, incorporating more sound and video files, so the World Wide Web can be described as a way of delivering multimedia over the Internet.

Client/server technology

A number of Internet applications, including the World Wide Web, are built on *client/server technology*. Client/server is a key concept in the world of the Internet. Simply put, in a client/server environment, two pieces of software work together as a team.

The *client* is responsible for

- the user interface (what the software looks like to you on your desktop),
- initiating the communications process, and
- displaying information sent from the server.

Figure 4-1
Clicking on highlighted hyperlinks will bring up a new page.

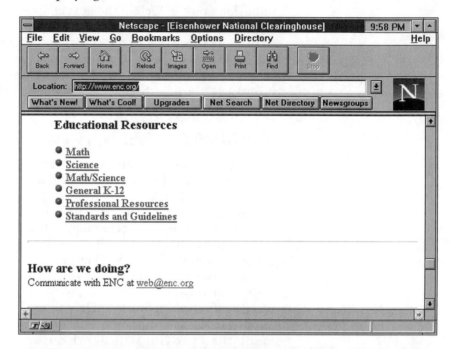

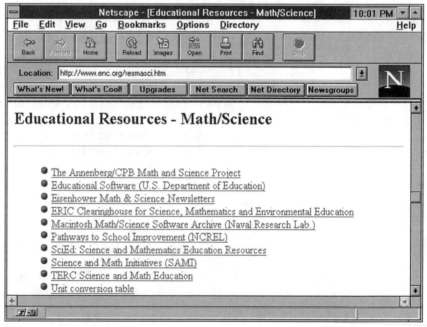

The Teacher's Complete & Easy Guide to the Internet

Figure 4–2
Client/server computing

The *server*
- retains information (menus and file locations),
- analyzes requests coming from the client, and
- responds to requests by sending information back to the client.

In a nutshell, the client is the program that you use locally, and the remote server does what the client says.

A key advantage to client/server computing is that it allows you to use your desktop computing power (the client) while taking full advantage of remote mainframes (the server) to store the massive resources available through the Internet. Another advantage is that it allows information to be passed back and forth over the Internet without the connections between computers having to remain open. The connection on a remote server stays open only long enough to respond to your immediate request for a menu or a file. You, in turn, read the item only after it has been passed to your client computer.

Web browsers: Netscape vs. Explorer

The client software used to access the World Wide Web is called a *browser*. New and improved Web browsers are always on the horizon. The two most popular browsers are **Netscape** (available from **http://www.netscape.com/**) and **Internet Explorer** (available from **http://www.microsoft.com/ie/**), and versions of these browsers are constantly updated. Your access provider may have supplied you with a browser or told you where to obtain the latest versions of these popular Web browsers.

Both Netscape and Explorer offer many of the same features, and versions are available for both Macintosh and Windows operating systems. Both provide a toolbar for easy navigation and accept something called *plug-ins* for accessing many different types of files (such as sound files). With either browser you will be able to

The latest versions of most Web browsers attempt to keep in step with current Internet applications, but not all will support the newest features on the Web. Find out about browser options, and keep up with the newest versions of your favorite browser at David J. Graffa's Browser Watch Page: **http://browserwatch.internet. com/**.

One nice feature of the Opera browser is that it will let you easily view Web pages that you have downloaded from the Web without the need to have Web connectivity software running in the background. Opera offers an Offline Browsing Mode. When this option is selected, the browser will automatically retrieve sites from your disk cache, rather than going online. The cache is a storage space on your hard drive where pages you have recently visited are saved. You can also capture pages for viewing offline by using an offline browser, such as Web Whacker. We discuss offline browsers in detail in Chapter 8.

track sites you've visited in the current session, save and print documents, and save references to sites you want to visit again. If you have configured your browser with information on how to locate news and mail on your Internet service provider's computer, you can also read and post to Internet discussion groups (called newsgroups), and receive and send electronic mail.

The very newest versions of these browsers include features such as the ability to chat and exchange files in real time, and the ability to create Web pages.

Because Netscape and Explorer offer very similar features, the choice between them is mostly a matter of personal preference. When you first start out, it's easiest to stick with the browser that is supplied or recommended by your Internet service provider (ISP), but don't be afraid to download and try another browser.

Other browser options

Although Netscape and Internet Explorer are the browsers of choice for an overwhelming number of users, they may not be ideal for your needs. In a non-graphical environment, you may be using something called **Lynx**, which is a text-only browser, and many Macintosh users prefer to use a browser called **Cyberdog** (**http://cyberdog.apple.com/**). Even if you are using one of the two most popular browsers, you may or may not want to download the latest version. While Netscape Communicator and Internet Explorer 4.0 offer many exciting features, such as the file exchange and real-time conferencing features, some of these may not be suitable for schools if a teacher wants to limit the scope of student opportunities for communications over the Net. In addition, the latest browsers require a lot of disk space and computer memory, which may not be available on a school computer lab.

For many teachers, a browser called **Opera** (**http://www. operasoftware.com**) is a practical alternative to Netscape and Internet Explorer. Opera is not well known, but it is becoming better known because it is a tidy, efficient browser that offers the basics and does so well. Here are several of the features that are available with Opera:

- *Quick loading pages.* (Most people find that Opera will load pages noticeably faster than the mainstream browsers.)
- *Ability to access and view up to four Web pages at once in individual windows.* (This can be a real time saver. You can access several sites at the start of a class period and have other sites you'll be using waiting in the background. This feature will also let you easily compare two or more sites.)
- *Ability to save pages from one session to the next.* (This can be an advantage if your students' computers are located in your own classroom and a project will span several class periods.)

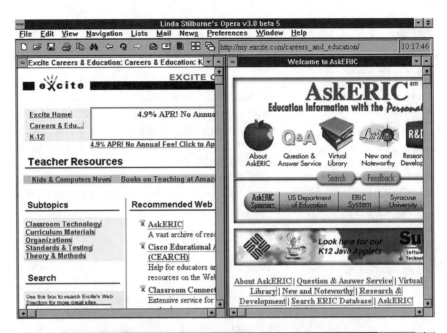

Figure 4-2A
Opera browser displaying two screens simultaneously.

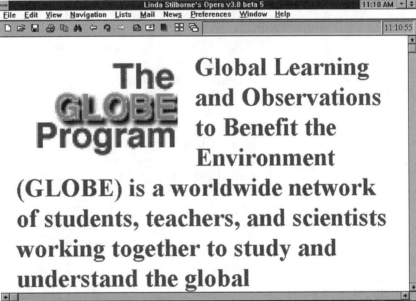

Figure 4-2B
The Opera browser makes it easy to change the size of the display for visually disabled students. Text in this illustration is enlarged on screen to three times its original size.

- *Limited mail access.* (Students can send but not receive mail using Opera. This can be a plus if a teacher wants to limit access to electronic messaging.)
- *Limited requirement for computer disk space.* (This is a very significant feature for schools with older computers.)

- A number of design features (such as a zoom function for graphics and text) have been incorporated into the product, making it well suited for use with students with disabilities.

It's almost impossible to talk about the Opera browser without making some reference to the story of David and Goliath. Opera's entry into the browser marketplace does remind us of the little guy challenging two big giants. It's not likely that Opera will seriously threaten either of the major browsers, both of which are very well established. Opera does, however, offer a number of features that could be particularly valuable for schools. You may want to investigate this browser for yourself or ask your school computer support person to check it out.

Basic navigation

When you first start your Web browser, it will connect to a Web server and display an initial home page (often the home page for the browser company or your Internet provider). From here, you can link to other documents by clicking on the words that are highlighted in some way. They may be a brighter color than other text, and they may be underlined. Once you have followed a particular link and you return to your original page, the links that you have followed will change color. Most new browsers will let you establish your own colors for links, but it's probably most convenient to go with the default settings.

Links are often in the form of clickable images. If you use your mouse to slowly slide the cursor over a Web page, you can detect the hyperlinks by noting when the cursor changes to a grabber hand. Click and wait for a new page to appear. Be cautious about clicking more than once. Pages frequently take a minute or two to download through a modem connection. If a page does not download quickly enough, click on your browser's *Stop* button and try again. If the loading still seems very slow, try again later. When you want to navigate back and forth between pages, you can click on the back and forward arrows displayed at the top of your browser.

URLs

Although at first you'll probably navigate the Web simply by highlighting and clicking on the links that are incorporated into your Web browser or presented on a Web page, you can navigate more efficiently by using URLs (*Uniform Resource Locators*). In effect, URLs are "addresses" that specify the Internet location of computers having different types of information. The first part of the URL (before the colon) indicates the access method or the type of resource you want to retrieve. The part of the URL that follows the double slash (//) specifies a machine name or site. Here are some examples.

http://www.clark.net/pub/robert/home.html This is a Web site (http stands for *h*ypertext *t*ransfer *p*rotocol).

gopher://unix5.nysed.gov This is a Gopher site. Gophers are discussed in Chapter 8.

file://wuarchive.wustl.edu/mirrors/msdos/graphics/gifkit.zip A URL that starts with *file://* is used to access a specific file on the Internet. A slightly different format is used to access a file on your own hard drive. Here is an example of a URL that might be used to retrieve a file from your computer's C drive:

file:///c|filename.htm.

ftp://www.xerox.com/pub/file.txt With the FTP type of URL, you can access and transfer files.

telnet://dra.com The telnet URL will access a login screen for a remote computer.

news:alt.hypertext If your browser has been configured to point to your newserver, an address like this gives you access to newsgroups using your Web browser.

Most of the URLs you will encounter will be for Web pages. (We will explain more about the other types of files and applications in Chapter 7.) You have probably already encountered many references to Web sites. Many agencies, such as businesses, newspapers, and even television programs, now advertise, using an address starting with http:// or www.

The quickest way to access a Web site for which you have a specific address is to clear the window displaying the current URL and put in the URL for the site you want to go to. Most browsers will let you drop the http:// part of the address, but some people prefer to use the complete address. Most browsers locate the URL window at the top of the screen. Opera users can find the address window at the bottom of the screen. You can also use a pull-down menu option or your browser tool bar to open a new location.

HINT Remember that Web sites are constantly changing. In particular, directory names and filenames may quickly go out of date. If a URL does not seem to work, check each character to be sure that you have entered it accurately. Then, try deleting the final filename and/or directories. Once you've accessed a specific location, you can often find the exact information you're searching for just by following the links. If you still are not successful, try finding the item using a search engine such as AltaVista.

HINT ZDNet from the publishers of *PC Magazine* and *MacUser* is a popular source for finding out about new hardware and software options. **http://www5.zdnet.com/**. This site offers advice and how-tos from beginners to advanced. A number of other good sites are linked to print publications. You will find lots of helpful information at Mecklermedia's Internet.com at **http://www.internet.com/** and Wired Magazine's site: **http://www. wired.com**.

Making friends with your browser

Learning about the features available on your own browser is a good investment of time. While it's fairly easy to access links on the Net, many browser features are available to navigate quickly and to help you make the best use of a site once you get there. You can also customize various features on many browsers, such as the size of the print, how many links will be remembered as "followed links," and what program on your computer system you may want to use to display long text files.

To learn about the features on your particular browser, start by exploring the menu options at the top of the screen, and use the Help File for the program. Here are some basic features that are available on most browsers.

- Viewing Web pages, Gopher pages, and accessing FTP sites.
- Viewing many other types of files (such as multimedia files) with the addition of *helper files,* or *plug-ins*.
- Viewing newsgroup discussions and reading electronic mail if you have set up these options. (Some people use separate software for these functions, such as Eudora for reading mail.)

Speeding things up. Here are some things you can do:

- When typing in a URL, you can omit the http://. *Do not do this in electronic mail messages, however, or you will lose the automatic link feature.*
- Turn off image loading.
- Stop the transmission and click on the button to re-load.
- Check to see if another browser window has been opened. This can happen when you go directly to a link from your mail software, or if frames (a technique for splitting a Web display into several parts) are used, a second browser window may have been opened without your realizing it. This is the case when suddenly you find that the Back button doesn't work. You can use the Windows Alt-Tab keys to determine if this has happened. If it has, close the window that is slowing things down.
- It is not always necessary to wait for a page to completely load before clicking on a new link. Be cautious however. Sometime the link you intend to access is farther down on the page that is loading.
- If you are using Opera, you can split the browser screen and access one site while you are viewing another, or keep a search engine ready in a second window.
- If things are really slow — take a break and try again later!

The *right* mouse button offers a number of handy features in a pop-up menu. Try using this feature for moving forward or backward, saving graphics, and setting bookmarks. The options that can be accessed using your right mouse vary from browser to browser, and the menu displayed when you click on your right mouse button will change depending on exactly where your cursor is positioned on a page.

- Setting up bookmarks or favorites that will let you easily return to a site whenever you want to come back to it.
- Using a history file to track sites you've been to before so that you can jump back to a site you had accessed earlier without having to backtrack screen by screen.
- Viewing the source code for a document. This feature will give you a view of all the cryptic-looking codes that go into HTML tagging. You will find that this is a useful feature once you start developing Web pages.
- Setting a number of different options.

- Printing Web pages.
- Cut and copy text from a Web page for pasting into another document.
- Saving Web pages as *HTML* files that include all the formatting codes used by your browser, or as a text file that will then let you import the text content of a site into your word processor. (Note: You can also download HTML pages using an offline browser. Offline browsers are discussed in Chapter 8.)
- Saving images. Saving a graphic from a Web page can be done from most browsers by clicking on the right mouse button when the mouse is positioned on a picture.

Browser options

Many of the options settings for your browser are pre-set and for the most part you will want to stick with them. There are a few, however, that you may wish to change. Here are the most important options to be aware of:

- *Starting page* — Generally, browsers have been preset to load a specific Web page when they are first turned on (commonly that of your access provider). An option is available to change this URL setting to one that you might prefer, such as the URL for your favorite search engine, a good starting point page for a particular unit of study, or a Web page developed by your school or class.
- *Image loading* — Your browser will have a setting for easily turning off the *image loading* and then turning it on again when you want to access the images on a page. If you don't mind viewing pages without all the pretty pictures, this feature can save you time. Find the options menu on your browser and click to toggle the option on or off. With the Opera browser, you can access this feature by clicking on the camera icon at the bottom of the screen.
- *Title bars and button bars* — You can increase the size of the Web page window, by turning off the screen display for these features. Usually this is done by using a toggle selection that allows you to turn a feature on or off with a single click.
- *Visual display* — If you want to increase the size of the print that displays for Web pages, it is possible to do so on most browsers. It is also possible to change the default color setting for the browser background and links.

Tech Talk

A common browser default is to display security messages of various sorts, such as asking you if you want to accept a cookie. A *cookie* is a server device for keeping track of who you are so the computer can send back the appropriate information to you. If, for example, you were taking an online quiz, the server might use a cookie to pass the test results back to your computer. Unless you plan to send your credit card number over the Internet (which we don't really recommend), or your system administrator advises against it, feel free to turn off these warning messages.

Explore the options for setting preferences on your browser. With most browsers you can change font size and colors. There will also be a range of security preferences, such as the option to display or not to display various warning messages and whether to accept "cookies." Don't be afraid to change things. You can always change them back. If you are unsure about some of the options, ask your school technician or a knowledgeable friend to explain.

HINT Use your browser's features for quick navigation. A toolbar at the top of your browser will enable you to move back and forth between pages that you have viewed in the current session. You can also search for text in a currently displayed document and stop the access/transfer process if it's taking too long for a page to load.

Figure 4-3
The Netscape toolbar

Figure 4-4
The Internet Explorer toolbar

Figure 4-5
The Opera navigation bar

HINT In Netscape, if either of the toolbar bars is not visible, pull down the **Options** menu and ensure that the **Toolbar** selection is checked.

The button bar provides one-click access to some additional features. The **Directory** (under Options) selection must be checked to view these.

These display features can be toggled on and off by clicking on the name of the item in the **Options** menu list.

Browser navigation bar

In this example, we describe the range of features available for navigation in Netscape Navigator. In our view, more recent versions of both Netscape and Internet Explorer are not suitable for schools that have less than state-of-the-art equipment (in other words, most schools!), but earlier versions of the browsers are currently standard in many schools. The following functions will be available on all browsers, though the location of the features will not be identical to those on Netscape Navigator, described below.

Back

Brings you back to the pages that you've previously viewed. As it accesses locations, your browser retains information on where you've been (via a history list) and will quickly redisplay pages according to the most recently viewed page when you click on the Back button. Another way to move back is to click on the tiny arrow near the location window. This will display a brief list of sites you have visited in the current session.

Forward

Re-displays a page you have visited prior to using the Back button to retrace your steps.

Home

Brings up the home page. This is the page that automatically loads when you call up Netscape.

Reload

Re-accesses the document you have just viewed and redisplays it on your screen. Use this option when a page appears to have loaded incorrectly.

Images

Reloads images into the current document. If you have turned image loading off, clicking on this button will cause images to be displayed for the current document. On the Opera browser, an on/off button for images is just to the left of the location window that displays the URL.

Find

Searches the text of the current document for a specified character or word. Use this feature to quickly find a specific term on a lengthy page of text.

Stop

Interrupts the data as they come in from the network. On the Opera browser, this option is adjacent to the location window that displays the URL.

Open

Produces a dialogue box that allows you to specify the URL location you wish to access.

The Teacher's Complete & Easy Guide to the Internet

Using a hotlist

Once you start navigating, you will quickly identify sites that you'll want to return to again and again. Luckily, it is not necessary to type in the complete URL each time you want to return to a location. Once you access a site that interests you, you can add it to your list of bookmarks or favorites.

In Netscape, select **Bookmark/Add** on the menu. (Click on your right mouse button for a pop-up menu.) In a subsequent session, when you want to return to that location, you can select **Bookmark/View** and double-click on the entry. When you return to the main Netscape screen, the requested Web page should appear.

The Netscape **Bookmarks** screen also gives you the opportunity to search for, copy, edit, and provide a brief description for your bookmarks. Experiment with the menu options to familiarize yourself with the possibilities for managing your bookmarks.

In Internet Explorer, references are saved as **Favorites**. Click on the right mouse button to add a reference to the list of favorites, and click on the **Favorites** icon in the toolbar to access the list of favorite sites.

Your browser will also let you save or export your bookmark file. In Netscape, a save feature is available from the **Bookmarks** screen under **File | Save**. If you have included a description for your bookmarks, this information will display when the bookmark file is brought into your browser as a Web page. In Internet Explorer, the **Organize Favorites** screen includes an export option. Both browsers will save your bookmarks as an HTML file that can be loaded directly into your browser. If you have saved the file to a diskette, you can share your bookmarks with your colleagues or access the bookmarks from another computer. Use your browser's **File | Open** menu option to access the file from the diskette.

If you're just getting started with Netscape, you can ask another teacher to provide you with a copy of his or her bookmarks, and you can use these as an initial set of pointers. Just load them into the main browser screen with the **File | Open** command, or you can set them up as actual bookmarks by choosing **File | Open** directly from the Bookmarks window (select **Bookmarks | Go to Bookmarks**). Choosing **File | Import** from this screen will let you incorporate a file of additional bookmarks into an exisiting set of bookmarks. Opera also lets you save and import hotlists using menu options from within the **Navigation | Hot List** window.

Bookmarks can be a great help for organizing classroom projects. Because you can easily change them, you can develop one set of bookmarks to distribute to your students and have another working set for yourself. You can develop different bookmark files for different subject areas, such as history or geography. Once you've done this, you can create a *master* set of bookmarks with links to each of the individual bookmark files you have previously created. Just open each individual bookmark file in your browser and add it as a bookmark.

HINT Under Styles, the **Start With** option lets you specify the initial page that will display when you start Netscape. It is possible to specify a bookmark file by typing in the URL for the file (e.g., **file:///c|bookmark. htm)**. You can also point to a Web page that you have previously stored on your hard drive.

Figure 4 - 6
**Netscape Bookmark
Properties**

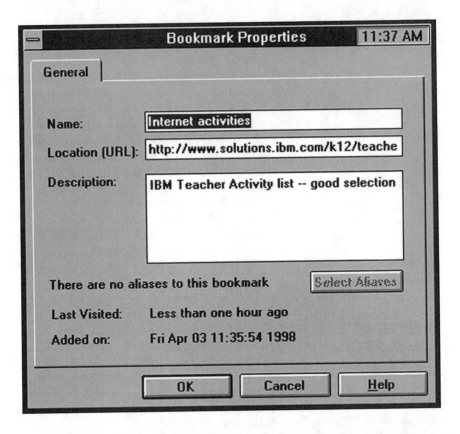

Figure 4 - 6a
**Internet Explorer
Organize Favorites**

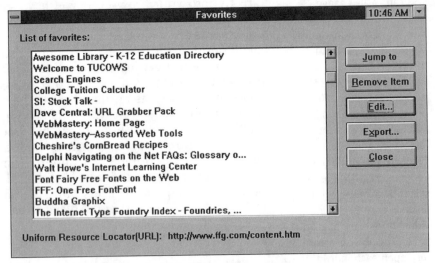

Figure 4-6b
Opera Hot List

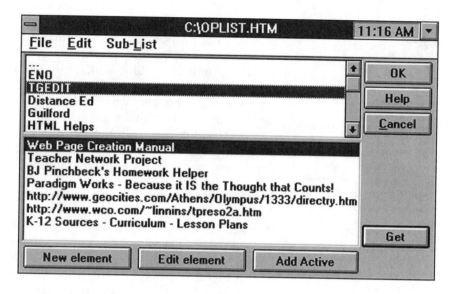

Tech Talk

Lynx is a text-based Web browser. Because it does not capture the multimedia dimension of the Web, it is less ideal, but for schools with limited access to the Internet, it may be the only option. On the plus side, because Lynx does not display images, it can sometimes be a faster way of navigating the Web. Lynx has an excellent **Help** function. Typing **h** for help will give you the opportunity to access several general information guides, an explanation of the various keystroke commands, and the Lynx Users Guide. You can also access the Lynx Users Guide at **http://www.cc.ukans.edu/ lynx_help/Lynx_users_guide. html**.

HINT A number of bookmark utilities can help you manage your bookmarks. QuickLink Explorer for Windows 95 and NT will let you organize your bookmarks into folders and subfolders much like Windows 95 Explorer. There is a freeware version available at **http://www. quiklinks. com**. WebTabs (**http://www.rbal- lance.com/products/**) is a similar shareware program that will let you annotate your bookmarks and add cross-references. You will find other examples of bookmark utilities at TUCOWS (**http://www.tucows. com**).

How to find out more

As you require more detail about specific browser functions and the World Wide Web, use your browser's **Help** menu. The Netscape Handbook option within Netscape's **Help** menu provides a complete overview of Netscape and how to use it. An online tutorial will walk you through the basics, and an alphabetical index lets you look up details on any point you'd like to learn more about. You can also access the Netscape FAQ (Frequently Asked Questions) using the **Help** menu. The Internet Explorer **Help** feature offers a Web tutorial.

Searching the Web

If you have spent any time surfing the Net, you have undoubtedly already discovered that the Internet is chock-a-block full of information and useful resources for teaching. You will also have discovered that finding exactly what you are looking for can sometimes be a daunting task. One long-standing Internet joke compares the Internet to a library with seventeen different card catalogs and "books" that get shuffled around every night. The Internet may be

Tech Talk

As you explore subject trees in areas that interest you, you will undoubtedly find sites you want to return to. You can bookmark these sites, but be warned that bookmark lists can quickly become so long that you can no longer find things easily. A good strategy is to set up bookmark categories that make sense for you — e.g., Lesson Plans, Distance Education, Personal Interest. Include a "temporary" category as well. You can use the temporary category to collect new bookmarks for any given session. Then, at the close of the session, edit your bookmarks by moving new items into an appropriate category, establishing new headings for categories as you need them. Also take advantage of the opportunity to include a brief description of a site if your browser allows space for this on the bookmark edit screen. This will pay off later.

Tech Talk

Your browser keeps track of the sites you have recently visited. Locate the "history" feature in your browser. Clicking on one of the items listed will let you quickly return to that location. While browsing, don't forget that you can bookmark your favorite locations so that you can easily revisit them at a later date.

a great addition to the school library for students' research, but its lack of organization is often a source of frustration. Nevertheless, knowing how to use the Internet effectively as a tool for research is an increasingly important skill, and many teachers are now teaching their students how to find and evaluate information from this resource. Teachers also want to be able to locate useful lessons and learning materials without having to spend hours searching.

Effective Internet searching means knowing about the range of different tools available for searching and mastering techniques for developing and refining your searches.

Subject trees — getting an overview

An important part of finding what you are looking for on the Internet involves taking time to explore some of the resources that are available. There may be forty different repositories for lesson plans on the Internet, but once you become familiar with one or two of them, you may find that that's all you need. Similarly, knowing about a handful of good resources on a subject is a significant advantage when it comes to quickly gathering material for a lesson. A good way to discover useful sites on the Internet is to browse, using a subject tree as a starting point.

Subject trees (sometimes called Web directories) allow you to explore the Internet using an organized list of categories and subcategories. Exploring a subject tree is a good way to become acquainted with what's available on the Web, and many of these sites are combined with a search engine that you can use when you want to find something specific.

Many people feel that one of the best subject trees you can use for exploring the World Wide Web is Yahoo. Yahoo breaks subject information down by broad categories such as Art and Humanities, Science, or Social Sciences, with more specific subject headings under each of these links. To access Yahoo, type the URL **http://www.yahoo.com** in the location display window for your browser and press enter.

To begin browsing, just click on the topics of interest to you that are listed in the directory. Use the Back arrow keys near the top of your browser to return to a previous screen.

Yahoo does not provide links to everything the Web has to offer, but it is an extensive index of some of the best sites and to many indices on specific subjects. If you click on the term *Indices* in any of the Yahoo subject categories, you will find comprehensive lists of sites for specific topics. These are starting-point pages for a particular subject area. For example, in K-12 indices you will find BellSouth.net's Education Gateway. At this site, you can browse for topics that are of high interest to teachers, students, and parents. There are more than thirty K-12 indices available at Yahoo.

Figure 4-7
Click to the right of the location window at the bottom of the screen to access the Opera history list.

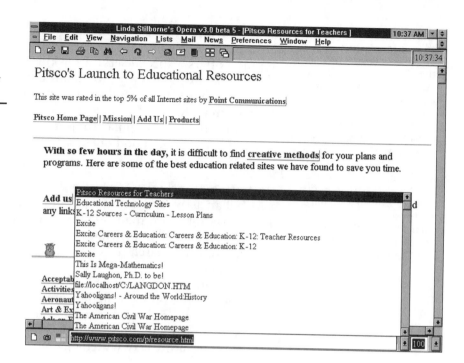

Figure 4-7
Click to the right of the location window at the bottom of the screen to access the Opera history list.

Always "surf" with a purpose. If you are a newcomer to the Internet, it can be valuable for you to spend some time just exploring to get an idea about the kinds of things available on the Net. Always be on the lookout for resources that could be of value in your teaching. When you find something interesting, print a page from the resource as a visual reminder of what's there. File the sheet in a binder, and make an annotation on the page about how you might use the resource in your teaching. When you print from your browser, the URL for the page should automatically appear in the upper right corner of the page, so you won't lose track of where you found the resource.

At some point you might also want to create a printed binder of Web pages as a "where to look" file for students doing research on the Net.

You can also search for items using the Yahoo database by entering a term in the search window and clicking on the *Search* button. Note that the search results will list both Yahoo categories containing your search term and specific sites. Yahoo will also let you confine a keyword search to a specific category once you have accessed a category, such as Education or News and Media. This feature can help you zero in on the type of information you are looking for. Be aware that a Yahoo search is limited to Internet sites that have been preselected by Yahoo, but if you are not satisfied with what you have found on the Yahoo site, you can quickly pass a search through to another search engine. A link to AltaVista is included at the top of the search results page, and you can access a

HINT If you are interested in resources for a particular country, try one of the World Yahoos, such as **http://www.yahoo. ca**, which is a Yahoo page listing Canadian resources. There are Yahoo sites for Canada, Australia, France, Germany, Korea, Japan, and the United Kingdom and Ireland. Some of these can be a great source for foreign-language reading material. You will find links to each of these by scrolling to the bottom of the Yahoo starting page.

number of other search engines by scrolling to the bottom of the results page.

Yahoo offers a special service for kids, called Yahooligans which is located at **http://www.yahooligans.com/**. Yahooligans only lists sources that have been preselected as suitable for students and many have a learning focus.

Yahoo is the most popular subject tree on the Internet, but there are a number of other good ones.

Magellan
http://www.mckinley.com/

Magellan is worth knowing about because it provides ratings and reviews for more than 60,000 Web sites. When you do a keyword search, Magellan provides a brief description for the sites that come up. You can search the entire database, or limit your search to reviewed sites.

If you choose the "Green Light Sites" search option, you can target your search on high-quality sites. This can be a valuable time saver if you are looking for good subject resources for student projects. A similar site offering ratings and reviews is the Britannica Internet Guide at **http://www.ebig.com/**.

Lycos Top 5% Sites
http://point.lycos.com/categories/index.html

For another listing that will help you to quickly find the best of the best, you might also want to visit Lycos Top 5% Sites. This resource rates and classifies a selection of the very best sources from the massive Lycos database (**http://www.lycos.com**). If you perform a search using the key word "education," you will be presented with an eclectic list of sites worth exploring. Some of these, such as Urban Education Web (**http://eric-web.tc.columbia.edu/**), which provides information on inner-city school issues, are jewels that may not be easily found among the plethora of resources offered on many education sites. You can also browse in the K-12 resources area to find Lycos's picks for the top twenty-five in this category. Sites are evaluated for content, design, and overall effectiveness.

LookSmart
http://www.looksmart.com/

One source calls LookSmart a "web directory for non-web-heads." This is a well-designed site sponsored by Reader's Digest. LookSmart eschews technical wizardry in favor of reliable, content-rich sites. LookSmart is easy to navigate, and it also provides a powerful search engine for finding things on the Net.

Argus Clearinghouse
http://www.clearinghouse.net

The Teacher's Complete & Easy Guide to the Internet

HINT Sandi Goldman's Classroom Corners is an excellent guide to classroom and education sources on the Web. You can find it at the Argus Clearinghouse.

A helpful resource for wading through the Net is the Scout Toolkit Surf Smarter page at **http://wwwscout.cs.wisc.edu/scout/toolkit/index.html**. The Toolkit provides links to the best subject catalogs and directories on the Net. Check out SideKicks — quick reference cards for Internet search engines and subject guides and directories. These are quick summaries of searching rules and site features in .pdf format. You can print these and make them available at student workstations.

This is another good place to start browsing. What's different about this source is that it is really a collection of subject guides to the Internet. When you want to get a good overview of what's available in a given subject area, the Clearinghouse is the place to start. Individual guides are put together by subject experts who identify, evaluate, and describe Internet information on a given topic. You will not find a guide on every topic but there are hundreds of guides available and the guides themselves include extensive links to information.

Search engines

Subject trees and guides are good for browsing and for finding general reference information, but the best way to find something specific is to use a search engine. Search engines are tools that let you search for information using keywords that describe your topic. If you were looking for information on a specific topic, such as El Niño, it would probably take you a long time to find something on this by browsing through various weather sites, but you could quickly locate information using a search engine such as AltaVista or Excite. A number of search engines also let you search Usenet News (newsgroup discussions) in addition to the Web, and some will even let you search for newspaper articles.

A number of different search engines are available for searching the Web — and just to make our lives complicated, they all behave a little bit differently. The best way to find out about search engines is to sample a few.

HINT For links to a number of search engine tutorials, go to Search Engine Watch at **http://searchenginewatch.com/tutorials.htm**. Another good source for learning to search the Net is Classroom Connect's Online Guide to Searching which you will find at **http://www.classroom.net/classroom/search.html**.

Microsoft and Netscape both offer quick access to a search page using a browser button. If you are using another browser, you can access these sites using the URL:

http://home.microsoft.com/access/allinone.asp
http://home.netscape.com/home/internet-search.html.

You will also find a good search engine page from the Berkeley Public Library at:

http://infopeople.berkeley.edu:8000/src/srctools.html.

Access one of these sources and sample several of the following search engines. Which is your favorite?

AltaVista

http://www.altavista.digital.com

AltaVista is great for finding the needle in the haystack. In fact, you will probably be amazed at how many needles were waiting to be found. This is a very large, fast, and reliable index and a good source to try when you have not had luck using one of the less comprehensive search engines. If, however, you are using a single search term, results from AltaVista can be overwhelming. You can avoid this problem if you search for phrases using quotation marks (such as "nuclear waste disposal"). To force a word to appear, use a plus sign: "South Dakota" +tornado. A number of special features, such as being able to rank words, find words located near each other, and find documents in a particular language are available through AltaVista's Advanced Search. AltaVista Canada is at **http://www. altavista.ca**.

HotBot

http://www.hotbot.com

HotBot is another fast search engine with a very large database of more than fifty million documents. HotBot has a user-friendly searching screen designed to guide novice users through complex searches.

HotBot lets you limit your search by date, by domain type — for example, you can eliminate commercial sites by including *-.com (minus .com)* in your search and you can restrict your search to a particular media type — such as an image file.

You can also customize settings and save searches to run again at a later point. If you are using a slower modem or an older machine, use **HotBot Lite** at **http://www.hotbot.com/lite/index.html**.

Excite

http://www.excite.com

When you are not sure of the exact term to use for a search, Excite is a good search engine to select. Excite uses something called concept searching. It will search for documents matching the keywords you have put in. It will also try to find related documents based on the *ideas* captured by your terms. When you search the Internet using Excite, the best strategy is to put in a string of three or four terms that describe what you are looking for. For example, if you performed a search using the term *poverty*, Excite will suggest related terms that you might want to include in your search, such as *low-income*. Including additional terms, such as combining the terms *+poverty +nutrition*, would further refine your search. Each document is given a rating according to how well it is thought to match what you are searching for, and the most relevant documents are presented first on the list of retrieved items. Once you have found an example of the type of document you are looking for,

Print and post the Search Engine Feature Chart developed by Susan Feldman. The chart provides an overview and command syntax for six popular search engines. You can find the chart at **http://www.infotoday.com/searcher/may/sidebar2.htm#chart**.

Figure 4-8
Type a search term in the
field and click on the
Search button for results.

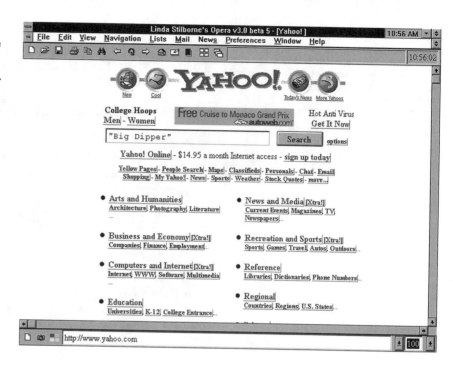

Figure 4-9
Yahoo can quickly pass
your search request on to
other search engines.

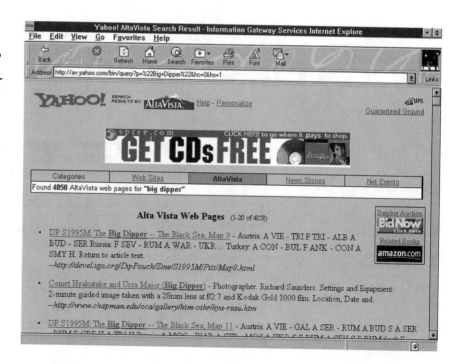

Figure 4-10
HotBot offers a range of searching options, including searching for Usenet newsgroups or searching for images

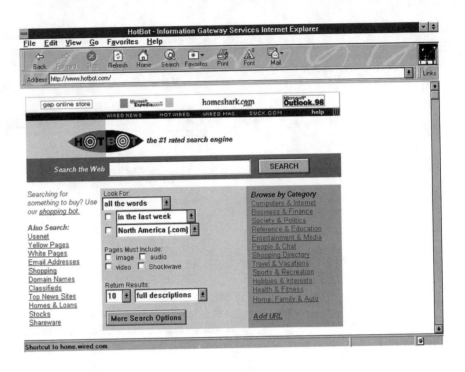

Figure 4-11
Excite includes a "More Like This" option.

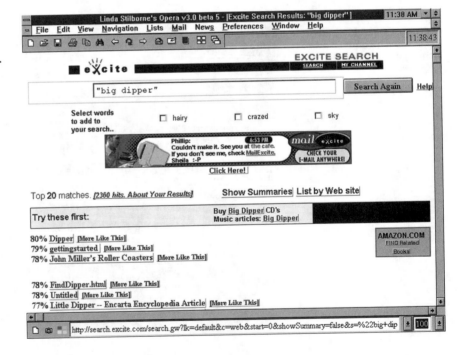

The Teacher's Complete & Easy Guide to the Internet

Excite will let you search for more of the same by clicking on the *More Like This* option.

Infoseek
http://www.infoseek.com

InfoSeek is another popular search engine with the reputation of providing constantly relevant results. A special feature called Imageseek will let you search for pictures. In addition to searching the Web, Infoseek will also let you search for top news stories from several newswire services and a number of U.S. newspapers.

Metasearch tools

Metasearch engines will let you submit a query to several search engines at the same time. This can be very useful if you don't expect to get a lot of results. Some will filter out duplicates and broken links, and while some are slow, others are surprisingly fast. A disadvantage to using metasearch tools is that you are seldom able to refine a search in the way that you can if you are using a specific search engine. In addition, special features, such as lists of related keywords will not be available. A number of metasearch engines are listed on page 101.

Hints for searching the Internet

Finding exactly the information you are looking for on the Internet requires knowledge and persistence, but knowing how to search will give you confidence in having your class use this resource as a learning tool. Here are some points to be aware of:

- **There are a number of different search engines**. Some provide full-text searches of Web pages, while others may index only the first twenty words on a page. That's why search engines sometimes yield wildly different results. Pick two or three search engines and learn to use them well. Be sure to explore the advanced searching techniques and make use of special features, such as the ability to search for news or to save searches. If you don't find what you are looking for using one search engine, try another, or try one of the metasearch tools.
- **Choose keywords carefully; use phrases (in quotes) and combine terms (using a + sign) to narrow your search**. If your search term is too general, you may need to combine it with additional terms in order to find the information you seek. For example, if you were looking for travel information on *Montreal* and used only the keyword Montreal, you would find many files that had nothing to do with travel. If, however, you included the keyword *travel* in your search, you would have a better chance of finding exactly what you were looking for.

- Sometimes you have to go to a site to get information from a database that is available there. Many specialized lists and directories are available on the Net. For example, at Bigfoot (**http://www.bigfoot.com**) you can search for people, and Liszt (**http://www.liszt.com**) helps you find Internet discussion groups. You have to go to the Microsoft site to retrieve information from the Encarta Concise Encyclopedia (**http://encarta.msn.com/ EncartaHome.asp**), or to the University of Texas site for the Perry-Castaneda Map Collection (**http://www.lib.utexas.edu/ Libs/PCL/Map_collection/Map_collection.html**) to locate a map. You can find links to many specialized databases at the Internet Sleuth, which is available at **http://www.isleuth.com/**.

- **Locate a helpful guide.** In addition to the range of subject guides you can find at the Argus Clearinghouse, there are a number of very good lists that have been developed by experienced Internet users. These include John Makulowich's **Awesome List** at **http://www.clark.net/pub/journalism/awesome.html** and John December's Top of the Web **http://www.december.com/web/top.html** as well as these three sites organized by Internet-savvy librarians:

  Where the Wild Things Are: **http://www.sau.edu/CWIS/Internet/Wild/index.htm**

Figure 4-12
Internet Sleuth lets you search many different databases

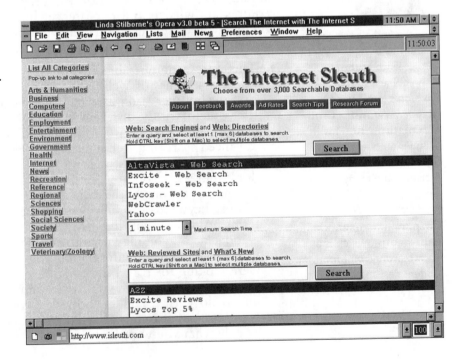

The Teacher's Complete & Easy Guide to the Internet

HINT Looking for a particular reference on a very long page of information? Most browsers offer a tool that will search for a word on the page that is currently displayed. On Netscape, for example, the Find button on the toolbar performs this function.

Librarian's Internet Index: http://sunsite.berkeley.edu/InternetIndex/

Mansfield Cybrarian http://www.mnsfld.edu/~library/

- **Although there is abundant information on the Internet, not everything is readily or freely available.** It helps to have a sense of Internet resources — universities, government and research institutions, schools, museums, community groups and many commercial organizations provide information over the Internet. However, when information has been painstakingly gathered, or when it falls under the realm of traditional publishing, only sam-

CHOOSING THE RIGHT SEARCHING TOOL		
Search engines		
AltaVista	http://www.altavista.digital.com	Fast and comprehensive. Use multiple search terms for the best results.
Excite	http://www.excite.com/	Includes a "More Like This" feature and news search feature.
HotBot	http://www.hotbot.com	Comprehensive; includes a save search feature.
Infoseek	http://www.infoseek.com	Popular and Fast. Relevance weighting and a useful "Fast Facts" area, with links to dictionaries, phone books, etc.
Lycos	http://www.lycos.com/	Well-established and reliable search engine that will let you search Lycos picks for the top five percent of Web sites.
Northern Light	http://sirocco.northernlight.com/	Searches the Web and (for a modest cost) full text articles from over 1800 journals, books, and magazines.
MetaSearch Tools		
Dogpile	http://www.dogpile.com	With Dogpile you can obtain quick results from a number of different search engines.
Metafind	http://www.metafind.com/	Lets you sort results and keep the search engine running in a background window.

| Inference Find | http://m5.inference.com/infind/ | Parallel searching; removes redundancies and clusters the results. |
| All-in-One-Search Page | http://www.albany.net/allinone/ | Provides links to a range of different kinds of search tools. |

Subject Directories

Britannica Internet Guide	http://www.ebig.com/	More than 65,000 sites are rated and reviewed.
LookSmart	http://www.looksmart.com/	Great source for popular interest topics — travel, entertainment, etc.
Magellan	http://magellan.mckinley.com	Includes reviews and ratings.
Librarian's Index to the Internet	http://sunsite.berkeley.edu/InternetIndex/	Selected sites on many general interest topics. Includes descriptions of search tools and lists where to find information on how to search the Web.
Yahoo	http://www.yahoo.com	An established favorite. Be sure to also use Yahoo country indexes, such as Yahoo.ca.
Yahooligans	http://www.yahooligans.com	This subject tree has been designed for children and young adults.

Searching for People

Canada 411	http://www.canada411.cympatico.ca/	Canadian source for phone numbers, e-mail, etc.
Infospace	http://www.infospaceinc.com/	Find phone numbers and e-mail addresses and city information.
The Ultimates	http://theultimates.com/	Twenty-five net services, such as phone directories, travel information, etc. Meta-searching for white pages, e-mail addresses, etc.

Other Useful Search Sources

Deja News	http://www.dejanews.com/	Search Usenet news postings.
Filez	http://www.filez.com	Search for image files and shareware.
Internet Public Library	http://www.ipl.org	Here you can find dictionaries and many full-text sources.

Internet Sleuth	http://www.isleuth.com/	Over 2000 searchable databases on many subjects.
MapQuest	http://www.mapquest.com	Search for road maps.
My Virtual Reference Desk	http://www.refdesk.com/	Multi-purpose reference source—headline news, dictionaries, quick facts, etc.
National Library of Canada's Canadian Information	http://www.nlc-bnc.ca/caninfo/ecaninfo.htm	Good starting point for Canadian information.
News Index	http://www.newsindex.com/	This is a news-only search engine that lets you search for current news stories.
Scout Report Signpost	http://www.signpost.org/signpost/	Over 4100 of the best research and education sources chosen by Scout.

ple files will likely be available, or the material will be available for a cost. *The Encyclopedia Britannica* is on the Internet, but you must pay to access it. Spending time cruising the Net and exploring resources such as Yahoo will help you become familiar with what is and what is not available on the Internet.

- **Remember that one of the very best resources on the Internet is other people.** If you're searching for a specific piece of information, sometimes participants on a listserv or in a newsgroup can be a great help. The FAQs (Frequently Asked Questions) from some of the discussion groups can be useful as well. You can find pointers to these at Yahoo.

GETTING STARTED

... with the World Wide Web

Exercise for Teachers: A Visit to EdWeb

Since the World Wide Web is so vast, here is an exercise to help you get a feel for how you might use the Web in the classroom. You can also take this activity as a starting point if you are planning a teachers' workshop.

EdWeb is a Web site with a mandate to provide a focus for ideas on how the Internet can be used in education.

HINT Internet addresses are constantly changing. If items are not available exactly as described below, hunt around a bit at the site. ▶

Step 1. Use your Web browser to access EdWeb at **http://sunsite.unc.edu/edweb/**. Note that there are a number of options for entering the EdWeb Home Room. Select the location nearest you.

Step 2. Use your space bar to move down the page to get an overview of what's available. A good place to start to explore EdWeb is to access the link for Computers and Kids: Life on the Front Lines. This resource provides case histories and examples of how the Internet is being used in schools. Select a story option and begin to explore. Aim to find examples of projects that might be doable in your classroom.

Step 3. One of the best ways to see how teachers and students are using the Internet is to sample Web pages that have been developed by schools. Return to the EdWeb home page. (You can use your browser's history list to return quickly to a site that you've accessed earlier in a session). Scroll down the page to Related Educational Resources and click on the link titled *Web66 Registry of K12 Schools* on the Web. Now, select an area you'd like to explore. When you have chose a country location, Web 66 presents a "clickable" map, which lets you visually select a state or province that interests you. Listings are grouped by elementary or secondary schools. Sample a range of links to school sites and watch for links to student projects.

Step 4. Return to the EdWeb Home Room page. This time, choose **Page down** and select the *K–12 Educational Resource Guide*. The Guide offers some excellent pointers to additional Internet resources organized by type of resource. One of the best features on this list is the pointers to state-sponsored educational sites. Click on Gophers and World Wide Web Servers. Scroll down (or press the spacebar to page down) and you will see link to federal and state-run Web servers. Be sure to also visit the links to Privately Operated Servers for a descriptive list of many useful sources. Be sure to bookmark your favorites as you explore this site.

A sampling of educational Web sites

The number of Web sites on the Internet is growing at an astonishing rate. In addition to the great number of sites that are of professional interest to educators, more and more schools are developing their own sites on the World Wide Web. The Web has metamorphosed teachers and students alike into successful cyberjournalists. Appendix B contains many curriculum resources on the Internet, and listed below are some particularly noteworthy Web sites that you can sample as a way of familiarizing yourself with the wealth of educational resources on the Internet.

Armadillo This directory of WWW educational resources has been developed for elementary and secondary school teachers and students. It lists resource materials that teachers can quickly access for lesson plans or as supplementary educational resources for students.
http://www.rice.edu/armadillo/Rice/Resources/reshome.html

Artsedge An outstanding resource for arts information, with many links to learning resources.
http://artsedge.kennedy-center.org

AskERIC Virtual Library Here you'll find lesson plans, satellite images, and links to many other educational resources.
http://ericir.syr.edu

Awesome Library for Teachers, Students, and Parents With 10,000 sources, it would be easy to become lost at this site, but there is a helpful alphabetical index and a search engine to help you find things. Many of the resources include brief descriptions. Comprehensiveness and good organization combine to make this a valuable resource for teachers.
http://www.neat-schoolhouse.org/awesome.html

Berit's Best Sites for Children This site points to some excellent resources for elementary and secondary school students aged five to fourteen. The site is organized by general topics that are easy to relate to curriculum areas, including Animals, Astronomy, Dinosaurs, Environment, as well as pointers to elementary schools on the Web.
http://db.cochran.com/li_toc:theoPage.db

Blue Web'n Learning Applications Sponsored by Pacific Bell, this site offers an excellent collection of curriculum-related lessons, activities, projects, and resources. You can browse the content table or search for a topic. You can enter your e-mail address to receive updates.
http://www.kn.pacbell.com/wired/bluewebn/

Busy Teachers' WebSite This site was developed with two goals in mind: to offer teachers direct-source materials, lesson plans, and classroom activities; and to provide an enjoyable and rewarding experience for the teacher who is learning to use the Internet.
http://www.ceismc.gatech.edu/busyt

Carrie's Site for Educators This site offers another useful set of links developed with the educator in mind. Check out in particular the *Internet in the Classroom*.
http://www.mtjeff.com/~bodenst/page5.html

Figure 4-13
Busy Teachers' WebSite

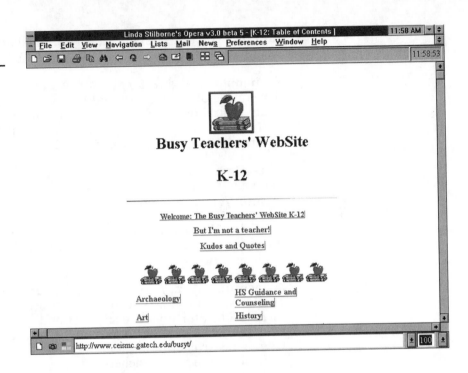

Cisco Educational Archive Links to the NASA SpaceLink, Frog Dissection, and more. This site has a *Virtual Schoolhouse* with a meta-library of elementary and secondary school Internet links. The Classroom area at this site offers educational links by subject. The *What's New* feature at the archive is a useful way to track current resources, and *Schoolhouse NOC* provides information on school networking.

http://sunsite.unc.edu/cisco/edu-arch.html

Classroom Connect Education This is an exceptionally good resource for teachers looking for helpful information on the Web. There is a searchable index of educational links as well as a resource station of online materials for educators and a teacher contact database. The resource station includes an infobot that you can use to obtain an FAQ (and a sample) of Acceptable Use Policies. Classroom Connect also publishes a wonderful newsletter for teachers, *Classroom Connect*.

http://www.classroom.net/

Community Learning Network Contains a well-developed set of links to many K-12 resources from the British Columbia Ministry of Education. Highly recommended.

http://www.etc.bc.ca/tdebhome/cln.html

Connections+ Internet resources, lesson plans and learning activities

for K-12. Includes arts, social studies, language arts and maths and sciences — linked with corresponding subject-area content standards.
http://www.mcrel.org/connect/plus/

Cool Sites for Kids These sites have been selected and evaluated by the American Library Association. Categories include *Reading and Writing, Facts and Learning* and *Just for Fun*.
http://www.ala.org/alsc/children.links.html

CyberDewey If you long for the Internet to be as carefully organized as your local public library, try a visit to this site. The traditional Dewey Decimal library classification system has been used to structure the links.
http://ivory.lm.com/~mundie/DDHC/CyberDewey.html

Cyberspace Middle School An index of interesting interactive multimedia topics and activities on the Web. Each contains a short description of what you will find there. Since this home page began as part of a science program for middle school science teachers, the emphasis is on science. Topics include Astronomy, Geology, Mathematics, and more.
http://www.scri.fsu.edu/~dennisl/CMS.html

D.K. Brown's Children's Literature Web Site An excellent resource for elementary school teachers. The focus here is on children's literature. One teacher states, "This may be the single most useful site for elementary teachers that I have found to date."
http://www.ucalgary.ca/~dkbrown/index.html

Education World Another comprehensive set of links. Here you can search a database of over 50,000 sites. Features include K-12 Schools Online, Regional Resources, Employment Listings, and Events Calendar.
http://www.education-world.com/

Educational Hotlists from the Science Learning Network's Franklin Museum You'll find many valuable resources at the Franklin Institute Science Museum. The hotlists identify Web sites of value to educators. Items are added to the hotlist every day, so you may want to consult this source often.
http://sln.fi.edu/tfi/hotlists/hotlists.html

Eisenhower Clearinghouse for Math and Science A repository for elementary and secondary mathematics and science instructional materials funded by the U.S. Department of Education.
http://www.enc.org

Exploratorium From the Palace of Fine Arts in San Francisco, this site includes hundreds of interactive exhibits on broad subject areas such as color, sound, music, emotion, etc. Elementary and secondary students will find this a fascinating site to explore. Includes a monthly selection of the best science and art sites.

http://www.exploratorium.edu/

Frank Potter's Science Gems Popular resource for science activities and resources by category, subcategory and grade level. Approximately 2000 resources are available.

http://www-sci.lib.uci.edu/SEP/SEP.html

History/Social Studies Web Site for K-12 Teachers The focus for this site is to encourage the use of the Web for learning with a particular emphasis on history and social sciences. History resources are included for American, European and non-Western history and there are sections for diverse populations, including Asian-American, African-American, Native American, and Hispanic.

http://www.execpc.com/~dboals/boals.html

Judi Harris's Network-Based Educational Activity Collection "Sample Curriculum-Based K-12 Educational Telecomputing Projects, Organized by Activity Structures." Activity structures include such things as global classrooms, classroom information exchanges, and telementoring.

http://lrs.ed.uiuc.edu/Activity-Structures/harris.html

Jumbo This site calls itself the "official Web shareware site," and it's an excellent resource for newcomers interested in obtaining shareware and freeware. Just find the shareware you want, and click on the program name to download. The site also offers the Getting Started Kit with instructions on how to install and run programs.

http://www.jumbo.com/

Kathy Schrock's Guide for Educators A classified list of Internet sites. The links are useful for developing and enhancing curriculum and for teachers' professional development.

http://www.capecod.net/schrockguide/

Kids on Campus Hands-On WWW Demonstration The Cornell Theory Center sponsors Kids On Campus, a computer day for area elementary school students, as part of the university's celebration of the National Science Foundation's National Science and Technology Week. Originally designed as part of the computer event, this site pulls together great resources for kids. The Cornell Theory Center also provides excellent gateways for Maths and Sciences, Arts and Social Sciences, and educator information.

http://www.tc.cornell.edu/Edu/CTC/EduK-12.html

KidsWeb Links to great "kid stuff," broken down by broad subject area. Pages are available for curriculum areas including Arts, Literature, Drama, Physics, Environment Sciences, Weather and Meteorology, Mathematics, Geology, History, and Geography. From this page you can also access other collections of Web sites for kids.

http://www.npac.syr.edu/textbook/kidsweb/

Learning Resource Server Developed by the College of Education at the University of Illinois, this is a particularly well-organized site that includes curriculum resources and a range of practical information.

http://lrs.ed.uiuc.edu/lrs/index.html

NASA Spacelink Very good resource for science information and projects.

http://spacelink.msfc.nasa.gov/

Online Educator Weekly Hot List This site is related to a publication called the *Online Educator*. The site gives capsule summaries of new and interesting resources for classrooms and links to the sites so you can sample the ones that may be of interest. Set up a bookmark to this resource so you can sample the offerings on a weekly basis.

http://www.cris.com/~felixg/OE/index.shtml

"Last year I discovered the WWW as a publishing tool and research medium with my Grade 3/4 class. Although I'm on deferred leave this year, I continually find new Web sites and projects that I'm filing for next fall, planning to integrate the World Wide Web into my classroom."

— *Nancy Barkhouse, Teacher, Atlantic View Elementary School, Lawrencetown, Nova Scotia, Canada*

Physics Lecture Demonstrations A must if you are interested in physics. From astronomy to magnetism to waves, this site covers it all.

http://www.mip.berkeley.edu/physics/physics.html

Pitsco's Launch to Educational Resources The Resources for Educators Link at this site provides a comprehensive set of links to a wide range of sources that will interest educators, including funding, projects, technology plans, and special-education links.

http://www.pitsco.com

Quest: NASA K-12 Internet Initiative One of a number of NASA educational resources on the Web, this site is intended to help elementary and secondary teachers fully utilize the Internet as a basic tool for learning. A good resource for information about classroom projects, grants, and international projects such as MayaQuest. Access *Bring the Internet into Your Classroom* to find out more about what's available.

http://quest.arc.nasa.gov/

SchoolNet Canadian-based educational resource with a wealth of useful content, including links to Canadian provincial education networks.

http://www.schoolnet.ca

Teacher Topics The goal of this site is "to make life a little easier for K-12 classroom teachers and students." It provides quick access to elementary and secondary curriculum-based resources. It is organized around common units of classroom study, such as insects, plants, rain forests, and the human body, and includes a hotlist of pointers to additional curriculum resources. You'll be able to identify resources that you can use immediately in units of study.

http://www.asd.k12.ak.us/Andrews/TeacherTopics.html

Teacher's Edition Online This site features lesson plans, a teacher's forum as well as instructions for subscribing to the online newsletter.

http://www.teachnet.com/

Technology-Based Learning Network Canadian resource for using technology for education. The site includes some useful pointers to resources for elementary and secondary students.

http://www.humanities.mcmaster.ca/~misc2/tblca1.htm

UCI Science Education Programs Office An excellent collection of science and math resources on the Web.

http://www-sci.lib.uci.edu

WebSites and Resources for Teachers A collection of sites and resources for classroom use developed by professors of elementary education.

http://www.csun.edu/~vceed009

You Can This is a "must-visit" for grades 3 to 6 (ages eight to twelve).

http://www.beakman.com/

Personal favorites
Use this form to make notes on your own favorite Web sites.

Site: _____

http:// _____

Notes: _____

Site: _____

http:// _____

Notes: _____

The Teacher's Complete & Easy Guide to the Internet

Site: _____

http:// _____

Notes: _____

Site: _____

http:// _____

Notes: _____

Site: _____

http:// _____

Notes: _____

Site: _____

http:// _____

Notes: _____

Summing up

In this chapter we have presented topics to help you become familiar with the Web environment and introduced a number of sources that are particularly useful for teachers. While knowing how to find information on the Net is an important stepping stone to learning, the real goal is to use the Net in a meaningful way in the classroom. In the next chapter, we will discuss practical techniques and resources that you can use to integrate the use of the Web with your goals as a teacher.

5

Bringing the World Wide Web into the Classroom

"Technology is useful as students construct meaning. While [some] contend that the student-teacher relationship is at education's core, I would contend that it is the student-meaning relationship that is at education's core, and that both technology and faculty are tools to build that relationship."

— DIANE WALTON, PH.D. CANDIDATE UNIVERSITY OF OREGON
CHRONICLE OF HIGHER EDUCATION COLLOQUY (POSTED 1/19/98,
3:10 P.M., E.S.T.) HTTP://CHRONICLE.COM/COLLOQUY/98/SKEPTICS/21.HTM

Once you have become confident about using the Web yourself, you will undoubtedly begin to think about some of the ways in which the Web could be used for student learning. In the first three chapters, we provided an overview of the kinds of student projects that use the Web as a learning resource and noted some of the things to think about as you are planning your own projects. In this chapter we will look at several different models for projects that you can adapt for your classroom and we will provide ideas for introducing your students to using the Web as a research tool.

Chapter goals
- ■ **To provide sample exercises to introduce students to the Web**
- ■ **To provide guidelines for evaluating and citing online resources**
- ■ **To offer some examples of Web-based student research projects**
- ■ **To provide a range of ideas for curriculum-based projects**
- ■ **To introduce WebQuests as a model for curriculum-based projects**

The Project Ideas for student activities outlined in this chapter are of three general types.

The *first* are activities to introduce your students to a Web browser and to show them how to find things on the Internet. It is essential that students know how to go about finding the information they need for reports and assignments. This is similar to learning how to use a card catalog to find information in a library. Students will need to know how to search the Net using LookSmart or some other search engine. The Project Ideas that follow contain specific lessons to help students master these skills.

Learning how to navigate the Web can be spread over several lessons. Use your judgment about how much time to spend on navigating activities and which features of the browser will be the most useful to your students. For example, a basic skill would be knowing how to move in and out of a document, but saving a file or viewing source information are skills that can be learned later.

A *second* category of Project Ideas shows students how to use the Internet to complement print-based information for classroom projects. For the most part, the World Wide Web can help teachers greatly extend the research that students do for projects and reports. A study of earthquakes, for example, can extend beyond the culling of print materials in the library to accessing online weather research stations, news reports, and even special sites set up for reporting on earthquakes.

The wealth of resources on the Internet helps students gain skill in evaluating and organizing information. These extensive resources also provide an ideal context for group work. One goal in such a project might be to learn something about earthquakes, but more importantly, the objective is to learn how to locate, sift through, and organize a body of information. We will introduce some valuable Internet research sources such as museums and news media. Being able to evaluate information from the Internet is an important research skill.

HINT
Teaching and Learning on the WWW
http://www.mcli.dist. maricopa.edu/tl/

Maricopa Center for Learning & Instruction (MCLI) has collected over 500 examples of Web resources for learning. At this site you can search for examples of learning activities ranging from sources to supplement a specific lesson to complete courses available on the Web.

Figure 5-1
Using the Internet to research class projects

Many museums, government agencies, and news organizations have compiled resources that you can simply download and use in the classroom. Lots of educational Web sites will point to these resources. Also, check out these sources for lessons plans:

Teachers Helping Teachers, a teacher idea exchange at **http://www.pacificnet. net/~mandel**

The lesson collection at the Awesome Library for Teachers, Students and Parents at **http://www.neat-schoolhouse.org/awesome**

The Encarta Lesson Collection, a free resource of K-12 lesson plans at **http://encarta.msn.com/ schoolhouse/lessons/default.asp**

WebSites and Resources for Teachers **http://www.csun.edu/~vceed009/**

Collaborative Lesson Plan Archive **http://faldo.atmos.uiuc.edu/CLA/**

Guidelines for using the World Wide Web in the classroom

- A good rule of thumb is to avoid pursuing Web project activities that would work just as well without the Web. For example, don't search for poetry resources online if your school library already has several excellent poetry anthologies. Do, however, think about using the Web if you are in search of in-depth, up-to-the minute weather information or an interactive learning resource.

- One of the best ways to organize classroom use of the Web is to set up a series of bookmarks related to your research project that students can use as a starting point. Ask the school librarian for help with this. If your librarian knows how to use the Net, he or she may be able to identify quickly some of the best resources for your project. If necessary, a preconfigured bookmark file can be copied to individual student machines.

- A valuable technique for enhancing learning is to create opportunities for students to share what they have learned. One way to share would be to have students

create a Web page with pointers accompanied by short personal accounts. These can be stored on a local hard drive. Alternatively, you could have students cut and paste information from a Web site, print it, and collect it in a binder that other students can then leaf through.

- Although it is generally preferable to have students use the Web only for specific projects, a number of sites can be used as a resource for gifted students or as an enrichment activity for students who finish classroom work early. You could set up your own page with pointers to safe sites (see Chapter 3), selected kids' sites (such as Berit's Best Sites for Children, Interesting Places for Kids, or B.J. Pinchbeck's Homework Helper), favorite museum sites, or a "site of the week."

- When assigning students Web page projects, warn them that URLs can change. If you are having them investigate particular sites (such as museums on the Net), be sure to have addresses for some back-up sites that stu-

dents can explore if the original sites don't work out. Assign an older student to check site addresses shortly before introducing an assignment to your class.

- Remember that your aim is not to explore everything that's on the Web, but to work with students in uncovering resources that are particularly relevant to your classroom. If Net access is available in the classroom or school library, try featuring a different subject area each month—geography, wildlife, astronomy, government.

- Probably the most important point to keep in mind is that you don't have to know everything about the Internet or the World Wide Web to introduce a Web project to your students. In fact, an ideal way of using this resource is to involve your students in researching sites and then have them share their discoveries with one another. The teacher's role is not to have all the answers, but to delight in and also learn from students' discoveries.

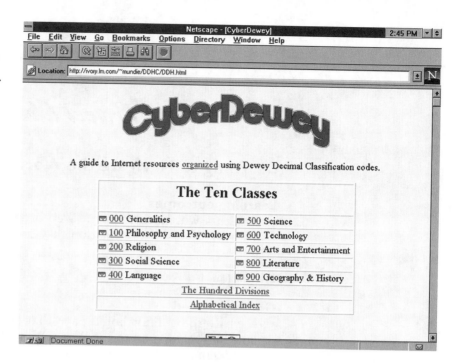

The *third* type of Project Ideas will give you a sense of the range of curriculum possibilities. One of the best ways to organize student work on the Web is to organize student activities and learning goals using a WebQuest. We will describe how WebQuests work and provide a collection of practical ideas that you can use to get students using the Web as a learning tool.

Project Ideas

Learning to Navigate the World Wide Web

Learning outcomes
- Students will learn to use a Web browser and become familiar with the kinds of information they can find on the World Wide Web.

Grade level: 4–8

Getting started
- Identify the default home page that should appear when your students first log on to the World Wide Web. It is simplest to use the default home page that comes with your browser, but if you have been using the Net for a while yourself, you may want to have them go to a different home page or even a customized home page on the local system that you've set up yourself, such as a bookmark page that you have set up in advance.
- Take time to allow students to become familiar with their Web client software. Explain and have them explore the various menu options and buttons for navigation. Show them how to turn the image loading off, and how to load images again as they are needed. Explain the concept of links, and have them sample various links. Point out how the information in the URL window changes as they access different sites.

Developing
- Explain the concept of a URL to your students. You may want to explain how the Internet can be used to access different kinds of resources (e.g., Web pages, software, and audio files). List some examples of URLs on the board. Be sure to include URLs for local files (e.g., *file:///C\/internet/randy.htm* in which the file *randy.htm* is located in the Internet subdirectory on the local C drive).
- Review some of the reasons a URL might not work, reminding students that a server might be down or excessively busy, or that a file might be removed. Be sure to suggest that they try the technique of omitting the filename at the end of the URL if they have trouble accessing a site the first time.

Extending

- Now your students are ready to apply what they have learned. Following is a sample scavenger hunt. In this exercise, students are given a series of specific URLs and will be asked to provide one or more pieces of information from each site. In some cases, they may have to explore to find the required information.

- Finally, students will have an opportunity to search the Net using LookSmart. Be sure to give them ample time to complete the assignment. Accessing each site and having a chance to explore will likely require more than one class session. Instruct them to complete the sheet in a more or less random fashion, so that they are not all trying to access the same site at the same time. Tell them that if they have difficulty accessing one site, they should move on to another and try again later.

The Well-Connected Educator is an online publication from the Global Schoolhouse in which teachers write articles about how they have successfully used technology in their classrooms. Access this resource for ideas, and submit your own at **http://www.gsh.org/wce/**.

Students will need time to explore the Web browser on their own before using it in a class project.

INTERNET LEARNING HUNT

Directions: Complete as many of the items below as you can. In each case, begin by typing the designated URL. Once you access a site, hunt for the information you are asked to provide. If a site you are trying to reach seems to be taking too much time, cancel the connection and return to it later.

1. http://volcano.und.nodak.edu/
   Name a place where a volcano has recently erupted. _____

   _____

   When did this eruption take place? _____

2. http://sln.fi.edu/tfi/virtual/vir-summ.html
   Benjamin Franklin was an expert in many different fields. You can find out about Benjamin Franklin at the Benjamin Franklin Museum. Name two fields in which Benjamin Franklin excelled.

   _____

3. http://www.fws.gov/
   The U.S. Fish and Wildlife Service is one place to find out about animals. Try this link. Look for Wildlife Species Information, and name two species of animals that you can learn about here.

   _____

4. http://www.bev.net/education/SeaWorld/homepage.html
   Next, visit Sea World. The blue whale is the largest animal on earth. What is the record size of a blue whale? (Tip: You will have to look around a bit to find this answer.)

   _____feet _____pounds

5. http://www.hawastsoc.org/solar/homepage.htm
   Find out about our solar system at Views of the Solar System. This information resource tells us that Jupiter has sixteen satellites. Can you name one? _____

6. http://www.sas.upenn.edu/African_Studies/K-12/menu_EduKNTR.html
   This URL is for African Studies WWW Country-Specific Information. Select a country from those listed. Now look for the **World Fact Book** information.

   What country did you select? _____

What is the population for your country? _____

What is the population growth rate? _____

What is the life expectancy? _____

7. **http://www.ipl.org/index.text.html**
   On the Internet, you can get whole books to download and read. The Internet Public Library Reading Room is one place to obtain electronic books. Access this site. Can you find the author of the text titled *Mudfog and Other Sketches*?

   _____

   Name one other title that you can download from this site.

   _____.

8. **http://www.cco.caltech.edu/~salmon/world.heritage.html**
   Here you will find the UNESCO World Heritage list. What heritage site is shared by the United States and Canada? _____

   _____

   Name another heritage site in either the United States or Canada. _____

9. **http://www.isleuth.com/**
   There are a number of places on the Web where you can search for current news stories. The Internet Sleuth is one place to search for news. Access this site and click on news to find out what is available. Select one of the news sources and locate a recent story on weather or the environment.

   What news source did you search? _____

   Write the headline for your story here: _____

   Would you find this news source helpful if you were writing a class report on this topic? _____

10. **http://www.cyberkids.com/**
    You can also find magazines on the Internet. *Cyberkids* is a kids' publication on the Internet. Have a look at a recent issue, and identify a feature article that interests you. Write the title here:

    _____

11. Use the **Back** arrow button on your browser to return to the Cyberkids home page. Now check out the Cyberkids Launchpad

link. Navigate to a site that interests you. Write down the URL and a brief description of the site you've found.

URL: _____

What is this site is about?: _____

Bonus question

Try this question if you have extra time.

12. http://www.excite.com

Excite is one of a number of search engines that will let you search for information on a topic of your choosing. Access the site, then put in the name of your state or province. Click on the word **Search**. Wait for the system to search your topic. List two resources you found that could be helpful if you were doing a school report on your state or province.

Project Ideas

HINT You might want to invite the school librarian to participate in this exercise or suggest ways to expand it.

Searching for Information Online

Learning outcomes

- Students will develop thinking skills related to searching for information electronically.

Grade level: 6–10

Getting started
- Discuss with students some of the ways in which the Internet is the same as, or different from, a library. Here are some points to consider.

LIBRARY	INTERNET
Clear organization by subjects	No clear organization
Subject headings assigned to information	Finding things requires a keyword search
Librarian available to help	No Internet experts—people have to find things for themselves
Librarian selects materials to suit users	Organizations post their own materials; some subjects might be neglected
Resources limited by physical space	Resources almost unlimited (just add new servers)
Information can be out of date	Can include very latest information
Printed format not easily captured	Electronic format easily captured
Sometimes closed when you need it	Sometimes too busy; information may have moved to another site

Developing
- Ask students to think about some of the things they might need to consider when searching for material online. Have them work out the following questions with paper and pencil and share their answers:

  1. List the following topics (or alternatives) across the top of your page:

     animals   weather   politics

Tech Talk

In many computer applications, an asterisk can be used in place of letter characters. The star, or wild card, means "anything can go here."

2. Under each word, give examples of some more specific terms you could use to search for information on the topic (e.g., *Animals: dogs, livestock, or wildlife*).

3. Pick one of the more specific terms and think of some alternative terms you might use to search for information on these (e.g., *dogs: canines; livestock: farm animals*).

4. Take one of your more specific terms and try to think of a term you could combine it with to make it more specific (e.g., *dogs and training; wildlife and habitat*).

- Introduce the concept of truncation (shortening a word to produce more "hits"). Ask students to write down how they would change the word farming to make sure they also find references to farmers and farms (e.g., *farm**).

- Pose this question to your class: *How might you go about finding a resource that would tell you the name of the configuration of stars that looks like a bear?* Ask students to think of some other examples where the computer might be confused about what you're looking for if you enter only one term. Here are some samples to get them thinking: Indian (for information on North American Aboriginal peoples), football (for information about soccer), courts (for information on the legal system).

Extending

- Draw a diagram on the board to illustrate the concept of Boolean searching—that is, using *and, or,* and *not* in a search. Explain that most search engines on the Internet assume that when you include two words in your search you want those words to occur together (e.g., *dog training*).

Figure 5–3
Boolean logic

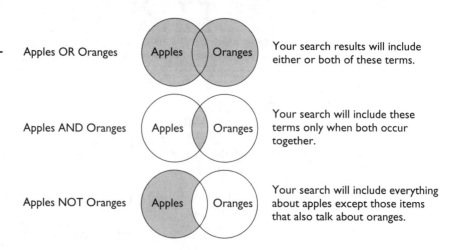

Apples OR Oranges | Apples | Oranges — Your search results will include either or both of these terms.

Apples AND Oranges | Apples | Oranges — Your search will include these terms only when both occur together.

Apples NOT Oranges | Apples | Oranges — Your search will include everything about apples except those items that also talk about oranges.

The Teacher's Complete & Easy Guide to the Internet

- Have students list all the reasons they can think of to explain why they might not be able to find the information they are seeking on the Internet. (Reasons could include a faulty search strategy, spelling mistakes, lack of information, information available only in a specialized database that needs to be searched separately, such as a database that stores full-text magazine articles.)

Analyzing their search strategies helps students to sharpen their reasoning and organizational skills.

"Some teachers who are well versed in HTML (the computer language of the Web) write Web assignments, including information scavenger hunts and Web searches for their classes, and include them on their school's Web pages. I found out, however, that searching for an answer and then having to refer back to a home page for the questions is more time consuming than having the questions printed out and being able to look over the entire assignment. That way, also, you don't have to know HTML, and you'll have a paper that the students can hand in when they are finished."

Jean Johnson in "So You're Finally Online. Now What?"
http://www.gsh.org/wce/jjohnson.htm

Project Ideas

Searching for Information on the World Wide Web

Learning outcomes

- Students will develop skill in locating information on the World Wide Web using Yahoo, Infoseek, and Lycos.

Grade level: 5–9

Getting started

- Ideally, this exercise should be done in conjunction with an actual research project. Alternatively, each student could select a suitable topic for online searching. Be sure to approve student topics in advance to ensure that searching is appropriate and well focused. Sample topics include tundra, rain forests, deserts, lakes, oceans, stars, forests, taiga, grassland, earthquakes, volcanoes, nutrition, wasps, place names, animal species, current events.

At **http://www.classroom.net/classroom/www.html**, you will find pointers to several popular World Wide Web search engines. This site includes a description of various search tools. Print out a copy of the page to use in discussing the different search engines with your class. Ask them to speculate on why there might be so many different ways to search the Web.

The Teacher's Complete & Easy Guide to the Internet

WORLD WIDE WEB SEARCH

1. Access Yahoo at **http://www.yahoo.com**.
   Input your search term(s) in the search window and then click on **Search**.
   (If no matches are found, the Yahoo search will go to an AltaVista Simple Search.)

   How many items did your search return? _____

   List two items that could be helpful for researching your topic.

   _____

   _____

   Be sure to set up a bookmark or write down the URL for any resources that you want to return to later.

2. Now try the search again using Infoseek. Access Infoseek at **http://www.infoseek.com**. Input your search term(s) and click on **Seek**.

   How many items did your search return? _____

   List an item from here that could be helpful for researching your topic. _____

   _____

3. This time search Lycos, which is at **http://www.lycos.com**. At this site, check out Advanced Search to see the ways you can customize your search.

   How many items did this search engine return? _____

   List two items that could be helpful for researching your topic:

   _____

   _____

HINT If you have not found at least two good references at each of the above sites, try your search on Metafind at **http://www.metafind. com/**.

Variations

- (Grades 5–12) Have teams of three or four students each select a different search engine to search for information on the same topic. Ask one student in each group to browse for resources by using a subject tree such as Yahoo or LookSmart at **http://www.looksmart.com**, or by visiting the Librarians' Index to the Internet at **http://sunsite.berkeley.edu/InternetIndex/**.

  Have all students prepare a list of any useful resources they have found, and discuss together which search technique was most useful. Then have them report back to the class.

- (Grades 5–10) You will find a number of places on the Net that offer a range of searching tools from a single site. A particularly comprehensive one is the All-in-One Search Page. This search page includes a selection of tools for searching the World Wide Web and a range of more specialized tools, such as one for searching newsgroups. As an exercise, have students access this site at **http://www.albany.net/allinone/**. Choose a topic that might interest your class, such as nutrition or beluga whales. Assign one Web search engine to each student or pair of students. Have them report their findings to the class. What useful references did they find? Was the search tool easy to use? Was there anything they didn't like about this particular searching tool? Students will want to make note of this page for future projects.

- (Grades 1–4) Develop a list of animals and assign an animal to each student for research. Have students access the AOL NetFind Kids Only search site at **http://www.aol.com/netfind/kids/**. This search engine has a user-friendly interface that younger students will be able to use easily. For younger students, you can enlarge the print size using the browser options settings. Explain how they can type in the name of their animal to retrieve information about it. Have them sample one or two items and write down something they have discovered about their animal. Have students access any of the following sites to obtain more information.

NetVet: **http://netvet.wustl.edu**
Electronic Zoo: **http://netvet.wustl.edu/e-zoo.htm**
SeaWorld Animal Database: **http://www.bev.net/education/**
    SeaWorld/animal_bytes/animal_bytes.html
Yahooligans Animals: **http://www.yahooligans.com/**
    Science_and_Oddities/Animals/

There are also a number of online learning tutorials about animals. Have students try these pages.

All About Bats (from Bat Conservation International):
    http://www.batcon.org
California Gray Whales: **http://www.slocs.k12.ca.us/whale/**
    whale0.html

Recruit a parent volunteer or older student to work with younger students on Web searching.

HINT There are a number of sources for obtaining full-text magazine articles over the Internet. These include:

Northern Light http://www.northernlight.com/
Electric Library http://www.elibrary.com/
CARL Uncover http://uncweb.carl.org

In each case there is some cost involved in obtaining articles, but you can also use these sources to get references to articles that might be obtainable through your local library's interlibrary loan service. School librarians in particular will want to be aware of what's available from these sources.

HINT "Information Literacy and the Net" is an eight-hour staff development course about information literacy and information problem solving. The course engages participants in learning the Research Cycle, and several types of literacy based on Gardner's Seven Intelligences. The course is available from **http://www.bham.wednet.ed/literacy.htm**.

Evaluating online resources

While the Internet is an increasingly important tool for student research, as many teachers are aware, not all of the information is valid. Newspapers and magazines are scrutinized by proofreaders and editors, but the Internet looks a lot like an information free-for-all. Although in some respects this is to be lamented, it also presents an excellent teaching opportunity. Students need to learn to evaluate the quality and accuracy of everything they read—including traditional news sources, the validity of which is sometimes taken for granted.

Students need to learn to evaluate Web sources for such things a currency and objectivity. They also need to be able to determine which sources are likely to be of most value for their projects. Take time to discuss with your students some of the reasons why information on the Web might not be totally accurate. As a group, consider such things as what interest the agency sponsoring the site might have in presenting the information with a particular bias. Ask students their views on whether a site developed by an individual is likely to provide inaccurate information—or may in fact contain more accuracy and detail than information available in the press. When was the material last updated? Can the information presented be verified? Is this information complete or are you left with many questions about the subject? What do spelling mistakes, incorrect grammar, and typographical errors indicate about the validity of the information on that site? Have students use the checklist on the next page to evaluate Web resources for their research projects.

Understanding how bias works is best taught using examples. Create a folder of materials from both newspapers and the Web that illustrate this concept. Have students review the examples and identify statements that they think might not be totally accurate. Have them explain why they feel the information may not be entirely believable.

You can use Metafind (**http://www.metafind.com/**), which sorts references by domain to contrast information on a topic that comes from an educational organization with information from a commercial agency or other group that has an interest in presenting a particular view. You can also access some examples of sites to compare at The Good, the Bad, and the Ugly (**http://lib.nmsu.edu/staff/susabeck/evalexpl.html**) and at Untangling the Web (**http://www.closeup.org/ncss-ex.htm**).

WEB SITE EVALUATION CHECKLIST

1. What topic are you researching?

   _____

2. What is the URL of the Web source you are evaluating?

   _____

3. What is the name of the site?

   _____

4. What is the main purpose for this site?

   _____

5. What group or individual is responsible for this site?

   _____

6. Do you feel that the group/individual responsible for this site is a good authority on the subject you are researching?   YES/NO

7. Are pages at this site easy to load and navigate?   YES/NO

8. Is the information presented in an interesting way?   YES/NO

9. Does the site seem to provide enough information about your topic?   YES/NO

10. Is the information easy to understand?   YES/NO

11. Is the information on this page up-to-date?   YES/NO

12. Does this page lead you to other useful resources for your topic?   YES/NO

13. Is there anything you particularly like about this site? YES/NO

    Describe:

    _____

14. Is there anything you dislike about this site?   YES/NO

    Describe:

    _____

15. Would you recommend this site to another student wanting to learn about your topic?   YES/NO

Project Ideas

Museum Reports

HINT Use these sources to find out more about evaluating Web sites:

Technology in Education at **http://mcrel.org/ connect/ techined.html**

Thinking Critically about World Wide Web Resources at **http://www. library.ucla.edu/ libraries/college/ instruct/critical.htm**

Evaluation Criteria Rating System for Web Sites at **http://www.ala.org/ ICONN/rating.html**

Teaching Students to Think Critically about Internet Resources at **http:// weber.u.washington. edu/~libr560/NETEVAL/**

The Good, the Bad and the Ugly at **http://lib. nmsu. edu/staff/susabeck/eval. html**

Untangling the Web: Guidelines for Researching on the World Wide Web at **http://www.closeup. org/untangle.htm**

This is similar to a book report but with a Web twist. The exercise is designed to help students explore the World Wide Web in a meaningful fashion. The information they collect can become a helpful resource for other students.

Learning outcomes
- Students will explore Internet sites that have a learning focus.
- Students will evaluate Web resources and communicate information to others.

Grade level: 4–8

Getting started
- Museums and science centers offer a wealth of interesting opportunities for learning on the World Wide Web. Any of these might prove to be relevant for a particular unit of study. To find out what is available, have your students prepare museum reports. One site that you can use to visit a number of science centers around the world is **http://www.cs.cmu.edu/~mwm/sci.html**. Access the site.
- Have students each select a science center they would like to visit. Then have them fill in the information sheet that follows and report back to the class.
- Instruct them to design an eye-catching header for their museum report in which they include the name of the museum and a small picture reprinting its theme. If you have a graphics program and a color printer, students might want to download sample graphics from the site to use for their headers.
- File student reports in a binder and make this available as a reference for other students to use in exploring the Web.
- Consider this "class report" strategy for collecting references to other types of sites on the Web, such as a selection of sites with environmental information or some favorite kids' sites. Develop a bookmark or Web page (museums.htm) to help other students easily access sites that have been reviewed favorably.

Link to the Virtual Library Museums Page:
http://www.comlab.ox.ac.uk/archive/other/museums.html

Figure 5-4
Museums on the Internet

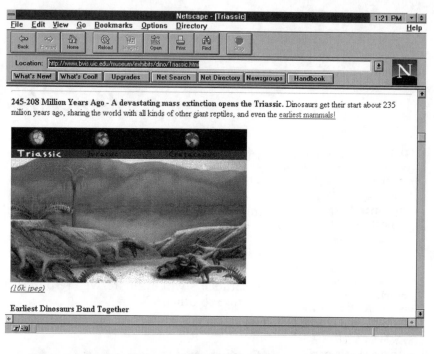

245-208 Million Years Ago - A devastating mass extinction opens the Triassic. Dinosaurs get their start about 235 million years ago, sharing the world with all kinds of other giant reptiles, and even the earliest mammals!

(16k jpeg)

Earliest Dinosaurs Band Together

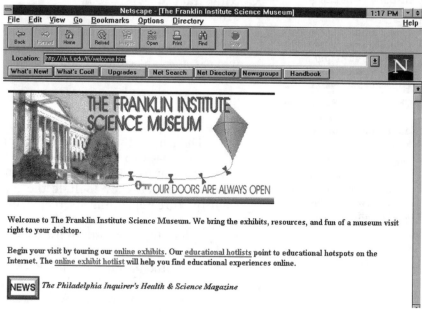

Welcome to The Franklin Institute Science Museum. We bring the exhibits, resources, and fun of a museum visit right to your desktop.

Begin your visit by touring our online exhibits. Our educational hotlists point to educational hotspots on the Internet. The online exhibit hotlist will help you find educational experiences online.

NEWS *The Philadelphia Inquirer's Health & Science Magazine*

MUSEUM REPORT

What is the name of the museum that you visited? _____

_____

_____

What is the URL? _____

_____

What is the focus of this museum? (e.g., art, sea animals, history of computers, insects) _____

_____

Describe a special exhibit or feature at this museum that your classmates might find interesting to explore. _____

_____

_____

_____

_____

Did you find any other resources at this museum that might be helpful if you or one of your classmates were researching a project?

_____

_____

_____

_____

What did you like best about this site? _____

_____

_____

_____

_____

Overall, how would you rate this site? (Circle one)

| Great | Pretty good | OK | Could be better | Could be a lot better |

Variation

- (Grades 1–4): In this activity, students will create a classroom "scrapbook" of a visit to a museum exhibit. Have each student draw a picture of something in the exhibit and write one or two sentences about what they discovered.

Variation

- (Grades 9–10): Have students visit an online museum as a way to further explore a period of history. Invite them to develop a virtual time capsule. They are to visit a museum and select artifacts and works of art or documents that illustrate some aspect of life in that era. They should briefly describe the resource, designate its location on the Net, and explain its historical significance. Examples of sites that could be used for this exercise include: The Vatican Exhibit **http://sunsite.unc.edu/expo/ vatican.exhibit/Vatican.exhibit.html**, The Soviet Archives Exhibit **http://sunsite.unc.edu/expo/soviet.exhibit/soviet. archive.html**, Canada's Digital Collections **http://www.school-net.ca/collections/** and American Treasures **http://lcweb.loc.gov/ exhibits/treasures/trupscale/**.

HINT To find exhibits that your students might like, visit the Hotlist at the Science Learning Network's Franklin Institute (**http://sln.fi. edu/tfi/ jump. html**), or consult the Busy Teachers' WebSite at **http://www.ceismc. gatech.edu/BusyT/TOC.html**.

You can also check the museum links at Yahooligans: **http://www.yahooligans. com/Art_Soup/Museums_and_ Galleries/**.

Copyright

With so much material easily downloadable from the Net, teachers need to be sure that they and their students are knowledgeable about copyright. As a general rule, teachers are permitted to make "fair use" of material for instructional purposes. With print materials, "fair use" (or "fair dealing") often means *limited* use *for classroom purposes only*. This guideline also pertains to text and images available on the Internet. While it may be permissible for a student to use a downloaded photograph of dinosaur remains in a report, a teacher may not, in turn, be able to post the report on a school Web site. Some Web sites intended for educational use post a notice authorizing use for educational purposes. When in doubt about whether material can be downloaded for school use, send a message to the Webmaster or the author of the document informing them of your intended use. It is particularly important to seek permission to copy when material may have some commercial value. One enthusiastic Winnie-the-Pooh fan found himself threatened with legal action when he attempted to establish a Winnie-the-Pooh Web site.

Jamie McKenzie offers a very good discussion of the copyright issue in an article entitled "Keeping It Legal: Questions Arising out of Web Site Management," available from **http://www.from-nowon.org/jun96/legal.html**. A booklet providing information on copyright laws for educators and students in the area of multimedia along with many useful references has been produced by the Consortium of College and University Media Centers (CCUMC). You can obtain a copy from

Executive Office
Media Resources Center
Iowa State University
Ames, IA 50011
(515) 294-8022

Other useful documents include:

The Fair Use Guidelines for Educational Multi-media: **http://www.libraries.psu.edu/avs/fairuse/guidelinedoc.html**

Copyright and K-12: Who Pays in the Network Era by David Rothman: **http://www.ed.gov/Technology/Futures/rothman.html**

A Legal and Educational Analysis of K-12 Internet Acceptable Use Policies by Nancy Willard: **http://www.erehwon.com/k12aup/legal_analysis.html#pac**

and Copyright Tips and Issues: **http://www.siec.k12.in.us/~west/online/copy.htm**

You can access more copyright information from the Stanford University Copyright and Fair Use Site at **http://fairuse. stanford.edu/** and from Ethics and Intellectual Property Resources on the Web at **http://199.233.193.1/cybereng/nyt/ethics.htm**. Useful links on Canadian copyright legislation are available from CanCopy **http://cancopy.com/**.

Having a good understanding of copyright is important for all teachers, since students will look to their teachers for guidance. Unfortunately, copyright legislation is very complex, particularly as the law attempts to grapple with such things as digitized images, networked computers, and distance education. Ask your board to sponsor a copyright workshop for teachers, or work with your school librarian to initiate one in your own school. As a group, teachers can review some of the references above and share ideas on how to deal with specific issues. You may even be able to find a knowledgeable expert who is willing to talk to the group about this issue.

Citing Internet sources

As students make use of the Internet, they should be expected to provide the same level of care with respect to citing sources as they would use when referencing print resources in a bibliography. The difficulty with Internet resources, however, is that material can disappear or change location from one time to the next, so in addition to providing information about the authorship, title, and location of a Web resource, a citation should include the date the material was available at that site.

Although the exact format for citing online sources can vary depending on the reference you consult and the publication characteristics of the item you wish to cite, a basic format you can use for citing Web sites in a bibliography is:

Author Last Name, First Name (if available). "Title of item." Date on the document or date of last revision (if available). [Online] Available: URL, Day Month Year.

Example:
Kronk, Gary. "Comets and Meteors: The Differences." 1997. [Online] Available: http://medicine.wustl.edu/ ~kronkg/index. html, 30 January 1998.

A basic format for citing an e-mail message is:
Sender Last Name, First Name. "Subject Line from Posting." [Online posting] Available E-mail: to@address from from@address, Day Month Year. (In this case, the date is the date the message was sent.)

A succinct guide to formats for citing sources, including useful links to Web sites about citations, is available from Classroom Connect: **http://www.classroom.net/classroom/CitingNetResources.html**. For a more detailed list of rules and examples, you can consult Columbia Online Style: MLA-Style Citations of Electronic Sources at **http://www.cas.usf.edu/english/walker/mla.html**. A list of other sources is available from Pitsco's Launch to Citing WWW Addresses at **http://www.pitsco.inter.net/p/cite.html**.

Using online newspapers and magazines

A major resource for student research projects is available through online newspapers and magazines. With the Internet, students can have access to up-to-the-minute news sources, such as news discussion groups or Web pages set up to follow current events. This provides an excellent opportunity for students to compare different versions of news stories and to examine such issues as how news can be slanted or what kinds of stories are considered newsworthy.

News resources on the Internet can easily be used to track coverage of a story over a period of weeks. For example, students might look at how an election is reported in two different newspapers. Such an activity might be enhanced by accessing discussions within newsgroups dedicated to political issues. Some newspapers and magazines provide archived stories. These can be used to study the events that led up to a story in light of its outcome.

At the Ecola Newsstand (**http://ecola.com**), you will find links to sites for hundreds of newspapers and magazines. Many of the magazines offer archives of past articles. This resource includes English-language magazines from different parts of the world. By browsing sources such as the Ecola Newsstand, you'll discover ways to use online news and magazine stories in the classroom. One magazine recently featured an article on climate change, while another offered a full-text article on animal poaching in the Amazon rain forest. Such topics could easily be tied to the curriculum.

Because the magazines at this site are intended for adults, this is not a good location for students to roam freely, but it is a valuable resource for teachers. Visit the Ecola Newsstand to identify a selection of publications that would be suitable for student research, then have students directly access the magazines that you have selected.

The Electronic Newsstand (**http://www.enews.com/**) is a similar resource, and the CMPA Reading Room provides links to Canadian magazines. The CMPA Reading Room Alphabetical list of magazines is at http://www.cmpa.ca/magindexalpha.html.

A sampling of good Internet news sources

Canoe (Canadian Online Explorer)
A Canadian online news source that issues a daily news update and provides links to top stories from a range of Canadian news media sources.

http://www.canoe.ca/

CBC (Canadian Broadcasting Corporation)
Traditional broadcast sources are another source for online news. Some, such as the CBC, offer programs in an audio format. CBC for Schools is a current affairs audio subscription series.

http://www.cbc.ca

Christian Science Monitor
Full-text version available. Excellent resource for comparison with popular press to illustrate different journalistic styles in news coverage.

http://www.csmonitor.com/

CNN
Source for current news, including complete transcripts of broadcast news.

http://www.cnn.com

Environmental News Network
This is a news service for environmental education and awareness. The Environmental News Daily provides informative articles on a wide range of issues at a good reading level for students. Note that access to some of the information requires a subscription.

http://www.enn.com/

Globe and Mail (Toronto)
Canada's national newspaper.

http://www.GlobeAndMail.ca

JournalismNet
Terrific journalism resources page developed by Julian Sher for professional journalists, but with many useful links for schools. Includes links to news archives.

http://www.journalismnet.com

My Virtual Newspaper
This site offers up-to-date links to newspapers around the world.

http://www.refdesk.com/paper.html

Media Launchpad

This resource was developed to help students and teachers explore the concept of media literacy. "Canada's one-stop website for K - 12 media education resources."

http://www.oise.on.ca/~nandersen/pad.html

The Media Literacy Project

The goal of this site is "to provide a support service for teachers, and others, concerned with the influence of media in the lives of children and youth."

http://interact.uoregon.edu/MediaLit/HomePage

Nando Times

Popular newspaper from Raleigh, North Carolina.

http://www.nando.net

New York Times

An eight-page version of the *New York Times*. This site requires an Adobe Acrobat viewer, which can be downloaded from the site.

http://nytimesfax.com

News Index

This is a news-only search engine. News Index currently indexes over 200 news sources from around the world.

http://www.newsindex.com/

NewsCentral

This site links to a whopping 3200 newspapers around the world, including some student newspapers. Because this site includes newspapers from many different countries, it is a good resource for foreign language studies.

http://www.all-links.com/newscentral/

NewsLink

This source claims to be the most comprehensive news resource on the World Wide Web, and it probably is. It includes pointers to newspapers, broadcast sources and magazines, and an excellent selection of special links. From this source you can also access a news-only search engine.

http://www.newslink.org/

PBS

Online News Hour and a number of exciting learning projects, including electronic field trips.

http://www.pbs.org

Time-Warner's Pathfinder

This resource links to full-text information from *Time* and other

Figure 5-5
Media on the Internet

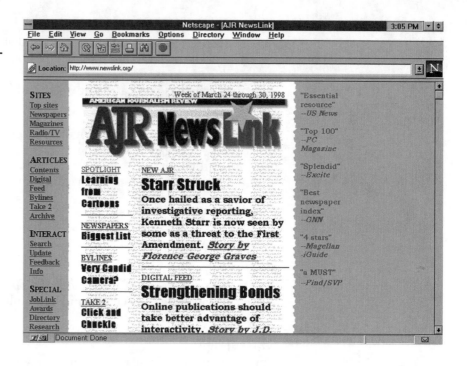

magazines, as well as interactive conferencing with regular featured guests.

> http://www.pathfinder.com

Times Newspapers Ltd.
British news source that includes the *Sunday Times* and many excellent news features. Registration required.

> http://www.sunday-times.co.uk

USA Today
Regularly updated news and a number of useful archives for student research, such as archives of stories on health issues.

> http://www.usatoday.com

Washington Post
This is a very well-respected online newspaper. It includes a supplements feature that provides links to background articles related to current news stories.

> http://www.washingtonpost.com/

The next Project Ideas is intended to help students discover biases in news reporting and to develop analytical thinking skills as they consider what news reports suggest about Russian society and how it differs from their own.

Project Ideas

News from Russia

Grade level: 7–8

Learning outcomes
- Students will use news reports to learn about a foreign culture.
- Students will consider how well news reporting reflects a community.
- Students will develop writing skills as they translate their findings into a letter to a friend.

Getting started
- Have students locate St. Petersburg, Russia, on a map.
- Give students some background on Russia's political history, and take time to discuss what students might already know about life in Russia.

Developing
- Have students access the *St. Petersburg Times* (**http://www.spb.su/times/index.html**), a weekly English-language newspaper from St. Petersburg. While its intended audience is English-speaking people living in Russia, it is nevertheless a good way to give students a glimpse of day-to-day news events in Russia.
- Have all students look at one or two current issues of the newspaper, and have a class discussion in which students are asked to consider how life in Russia is reflected in the news stories. Have them compare the news stories with stories appearing in their own local paper. Discuss in particular how well newspaper reports reflect their communities. This is a particularly interesting exercise, because a look at a foreign newspaper calls into high relief the tendency of all newspapers to focus on "bad news" rather than "good news."
- Next, have students delve into the newspaper's archives. Assign a different issue of the paper to each student. Issues should include feature stories, breaking news, business, commentary, classifieds, and culture. Allow sufficient time for students to examine their assigned issues carefully. If time allows, some students may want to look at more than one issue.

Extending

- As a last step, have students write about their discoveries. Ask them to imagine they are student visitors in Russia. They are writing a letter home and will be using the incidents they read about to communicate to someone who has never been to Russia just what Russia is really like. Emphasize that in their letters students should communicate both the things that are different about Russian issues and those that are similar to news at home.

For a great collection of lessons and activities for teaching about media, visit the Media Awareness Network at **http://www. schoolnet.ca/medianet/**. Also check out the classroom ideas from Maclean's In-Class Progam located at **http://www.mh-educational.com/ macinclass/index.html**.

Online traveling

Part of the value of the Internet is the fact that through it we can reach more than 160 different countries. Tapping into online information from and about countries around the globe will captivate students and stimulate learning. Ideally, students will use online resources to supplement printed material that is available in their classroom or library. The advantage of online resources is that they are wide-ranging and can be kept totally up to date. Learning about another country and compiling a report on it can be relevant to geography, history, and other social studies areas, as well as language studies (e.g., using travel information about France as project resources for French-language studies). You can link to resources for countries around the globe using the Yahoo Regional index at http://www.yahoo.com/Regional/Countries/. You can also use the many travel and geographical information resources available on the Net.

A sampling of Internet travel guides

CIA World Factbook
Published annually in July by the Central Intelligence Agency for the use of U.S. government officials, this is a great resource for factual information about countries around the world. The Factbook can be found at many places on the Internet, such as
http://www.odci.gov/cia/publications/nsolo/wfb-all.htm

City.Net
Comprehensive guide to cities around the world.
http://www.city.net/

Clearinghouse Net
This is a repository for many different subjects. There is a good

Use travel sources to explore a country along with a class project involving students who exchange e-mail with keypals from other countries.

selection of country specific guides. Look for resources under Places and Peoples.

http://www.clearinghouse.net

E-Conflict

The purpose of this site is to eradicate world conflict through cultural understanding. This site pulls together information from a range of sources on the Net to provide a substantial repository of country information.

http://www.emulateme.com/

Galaxy

A substantial collection of travel and country information, this resource includes links to many guides, directories, travel publications, and FAQs for specific countries. This is another meta-index, like Yahoo.

http://galaxy.einet.net
http://galaxy.einet.net/galaxy/Leisure-and-Recreation/Travel.html
http://galaxy.einet.net/GJ/countries.html

Library of Congress Country Studies

This resource offers over eighty-five detailed studies of countries around the world. The reports include information on geography, history, society, culture, and the economy. If hyperlinks for a particular country do not work, use the search engine to retrieve sections of the reports.

http://lcweb2.loc.gov/frd/cs/cshome.html

Map Machine

Country maps, including political maps and physical maps, flags, and other country information from National Geographic.

http://www.nationalgeographic.com/resources/ngo/maps/

Some good travel writing in the form of travelogues can be found at the Yahooligans site. Use this resource to generate ideas for student writing projects or to enhance a geography lesson. Travelogues are available at **http://www.yahooligans.com/ Around_the_World/Travel/ Travelogues/.**

National Atlas Information System (NAIS)

Canadian resource with an interactive mapping tool, a community atlas, a geographical factbook, a place name search, a geography quiz, and more.

http://www-nais.ccm.emr.ca/schoolnet/

Tiger Mapping Service

Census and geographic information for the United States. Students will enjoy looking up place names and being able to zoom in on them on a map.

http://tiger.census.gov/

Washington Post — Travel

This resource provides detailed information about all fifty states and more than 200 countries and territories around the globe.

http://www.washingtonpost.com/wp-srv/style/travel.htm

World Flags

Pictures of flags from around the world, with links to the CIA World Factbook (see above). Students will be intrigued by an index that identifies world flags by their design elements, such as the presence of stars or the inclusion of a natural land feature as part of the design.

http://www.adfa.oz.au/CS/flg/col/Index.html

Figure 5-6
Projects like GlobaLearn help students learn about their own and other countries.

The Teacher's Complete & Easy Guide to the Internet

World Wide Web Virtual Library—Geography
A comprehensive set of pointers to information resources for individual countries, this site has links to other sites such as the Guide to Australia and Information on India.

http://www.icomos.org/WWW_VL_Geography.html

Yahoo Countries
Have students take an imaginary trip and report on sights from around the world. Yahoo points to travel information for specific countries.

http://www.yahoo.com/Recreation/Travel/Regional/Countries/

The following Project Ideas is designed to have students explore the Internet as a way of refining and developing their understanding of Africa and its peoples.

Project Ideas

Exploring Africa Online
Grade level: 5–8

Learning outcomes
- Students will use the World Wide Web to learn about Africa.
- Students will question their assumptions, synthesize their ideas, and express their ideas in writing.
- Students will find information on the Internet and work as part of a team.

Getting started
- Post a map of Africa in your classroom. Have a brainstorming session in which students discuss what they already know about Africa. When information relates to a specific country, pinpoint that country on the map.
- Have students access an Internet news resource, print news source, or print encyclopedia to obtain basic information about Africa.

Developing
- Before attempting further research, have students respond to the true/false questions listed below. Compare answers and discuss. (The online version of this questionnaire is available from **http://www.sas.upenn.edu/African_Studies/K-12/Perceptions_16165.html**.)

Curriculum resources about Africa on the Internet are particularly rich. Pointers to educational resources about Africa are available from **http://www.sas.upenn.edu/African_Studies/K-12/menu_EduBBS.html**

This site offers lesson plans, handouts, and full-text articles for studies in African history, geography, politics, languages, religions, social studies, and culture.

QUESTIONNAIRE: PERCEPTIONS OF AFRICA

True or False?

1. Much of Africa consists of rain forest.

2. Most African economies are based on agriculture.

3. Few modern/technological cities exist in Africa.

4. All Africans are Black.

5. Most African nations are governed by White regimes.

6. Africa has an abundance of mineral wealth.

7. Traditional African religions are prominent in Africa.

8. Africa is a country with Nelson Mandela as president.

9. Africa changed little until its contact with the West.

10. Most African nations received their independence in the 1960s.

11. Africa is the same size as the continental United States.

12. One can see snow in Africa.

13. Most African men tend to marry more than one wife.

14. Africa is a place of great physical danger from wild animals, which roam freely through the countryside.

15. Most African art forms, such as carved masks, would never be used for decoration in an African's home.

16. Divination is a popular form of traditional religion.

17. Drums are the primary form of communication used in Africa.

18. Swahili is a major language spoken in Africa.

19. Most Africans speak several languages.

20. African political and economic affairs have little interest for the rest of the world.

- Use the questionnaire as a springboard for Internet research about Africa. Have the class identify the broad areas of knowledge reflected in the various questions (e.g., geography, people, history, politics, religion, languages, culture).
- Divide the class into pairs or groups of three, and assign a different African country to each group. Each student should take responsibility for researching on the Internet two or more topics identified in the previous step. Their task will be to prepare one or two paragraphs on their area of research. Students may want to begin their research by accessing the Country-Specific Pages available at the University of Pennsylvania African Studies Web Page **http://www.sas.upenn.edu/African_Studies/Home_Page/ AFR_GIDE.html**.

  They should also conduct Web searches using one or more of the search tools that can be found at the All-In-One Search Page (**http://www.albany.net/allinone/**). Invite them to share with their teammates any particularly good resources they locate.

Extending
- As a follow-up, have the class exchange African discoveries. Ask each student to tell the group what he or she has learned about Africa that he or she didn't know before or found particularly surprising.
- Have the class return to the Perceptions of Africa questionnaire and see if any assumptions have changed.

Variations
- (Grades 5–8): Assign student groups to investigate the broad topics identified above for other countries and develop similar reports. For more in-depth reports, select a single country and assign different topic areas for students to investigate.
- (Grades 3–5): Assign each student an African country. Locate the countries on a classroom map. Have students access the African Country-Specific pages and identify just a few key pieces of information for their country: climate, population, capital city, language spoken, etc. Have students record their findings on a chart. When they have finished assembling their data, have them discuss similarities and differences they have discovered among the countries.

Project Ideas

A Potpourri of Web Projects

The goal for many teachers is to get enough of an idea about what's available on the Web to be able to pick up on relevant resources that complement existing curriculum and classroom activities. These project ideas provide some examples of what is available and how to make use of it in the classroom. You will discover more ideas for projects as you explore the sites listed in Appendix B.

- **Book Reports (Grades 4–8).** Have students sample the book reports posted at the Book Nook. Some great lists of good children's books are waiting to be reviewed by kids. Students can select one of these or another of their choosing, write, and submit a review to the Book Nook at **http://i-site.on.ca/ booknook.html.**

- **Studying Bees (Grades 4-8).** Divide the class into teams. Each team should research and be able to identify three different kinds of bees, three foods that depend on bees for pollination, and three different reasons why the bee population is threatened. In addition, each team should develop one "why" question and one "how" question about bees. Have students share their questions (and answers) verbally with the rest of the class, or you can redistribute student questions for further research. Students can use these sources for their research:

  Of Bees, Beekeepers and Food **http://users.aol.com/queenbjan/ primbees.htm**

  Gears **http://gears.tucson.ars.ag.gov/**

  P.O.'s Homepage **http://www.kuai.se/~beeman/**

  Africanized Honey Bees on the Move **http://ag.arizona.edu/ AES/mac/ahb/ahbhome.html**
  (At this site, you will find a list of downloadable activities to extend this lesson.)

- Youth in Action (Grades 8-12). Youth In Action Network provides an opportunity for youth from all over the world to share ideas and come up with solutions to environmental and human rights problems. First, visit the site to get an overview of the kinds of opportunities for social action that are available. You will need to register for the site, and you can register your class as a group. Select a specific area for your class to focus on. For example, in the area of human rights, your class could choose to learn about the rights of indigenous peoples. At the Youth in Action site, you can get background information and Internet resources and organizations relevant to this topic. Read and discuss with your students the ideas presented in the document "An Introduction to Social Action," which is available at the site. Discuss how students can make a difference locally, nationally, or internationally. Review the range of options for taking action — such as developing a petition or writing a letter to the media. As a group, agree on a strategy for taking action. You may prefer to use Youth in Action as an idea generator rather than as a tool for contacting agencies. If so, ask your school librarian to help track down addresses for sending letters to newspapers, local politicians, Congressional representatives, or members of Parliament. **http://www.mightymedia.com/**

- **Windows to the Universe (Grades 4–8).** This is a terrific starting point for students studying the solar system. The site includes teacher resources and an Ask a Scientist link. Have younger students search for the names of the planets and their relative sizes, and record this information on their own handmade charts. Older students can prepare in-depth reports, following relevant links and searching for other information on the Web. **http://www.windows.umich.edu/**

- **Learning about World War II (Grades 7-10).** The SchoolNet Digital Collections offers resource material that can be used to learn about Canada's social, cultural, or natural history. Included in the collections are photographs from Kryn Taconis, an underground photo-journalist during the Dutch Resistance of World War II. In conjunction with a unit of study on World War II, have students visit the site and study the photographs. Discuss what the pictures reveal about the experience of war. Have students assume the role of war-time journalists. Use the photographs as a starting point for writing "news stories" that describe conditions that existed during the war. You will find the Taconis collection at **http://www.schoolnet.ca/collections/english/index.htm**. You will find related material for learning about World War II at these sites:

What Did You Do in the War, Grandma **http://www. stg.brown. edu/projects/WWII_Women/tocCS.html**

World War II Time Line **http://www.historyplace.com/worldwar2/timeline/ww2time.htm**

Grolier Online World War II Commemoration Page **http:// www.grolier.com/wwii/wwii_mainpage.html**

- **Flags of the World (Grades 4–8).** Have students download images of flags from around the world and incorporate them into geography reports. This site provides images of flags from a great many countries with links to additional information about the country.
http://fotw.digibel.be/flags/

- **Solving Math Puzzles (Grades K–12).** MathMagic is a stimulating Web site for kids who like solving mathematical puzzles. Current and past puzzles are posted for different grade levels. Visit the site yourself, or select a student to visit this site and come back with a puzzler to present to the class for solution.
http://forum.swarthmore.edu/mathmagic/

  Another resource for developing math and reasoning skills is 21st Century Problem Solving, a database of problems and solutions for grade school through graduate school. **http://www2. hawaii.edu/suremath/journal.html.**

- **Online Scrap Books (Grades 4–10).** Have students make an electronic scrapbook. First, check out Amy's Amazing Adventure. This site is a creative account of Amy's experience at summer camp. Amy has also identified resources on the Net where a visitor to her Web page can learn more about a topic. The site will generate other ideas for similar classroom projects. The exercise will help develop student skills in writing and Web-based research.
http://sln.fi.edu/camp/camp.html

- **Learning about Energy (Grades 5–8).** Have students identify and discuss the pros and cons of various forms of energy that they are aware of. Next, visit Charlotte's Energy Module at **http://www.swifty.com/apase/charlotte/energy.html**. Have all students read the Introduction and History of Energy sections. Then assign one form of energy to individual students or teams. As a group, create a large chart (or Web page) that lists the various forms of energy described at the site, along with the advantages and disadvantages related to each energy form. List or include as links information sources for each energy form being researched.

  Have students select one form of energy to learn more about and report on. Students can use their knowledge of Web searching and these sources of information to find out more:

  The Energy Story **http://www.energy.ca.gov/education/story/ story-html/story.html**

EnergyNet Resource Page **http://teaparty.terc.edu/energy/template/resource/resource.html**

- **Developing Language Skills through Fables (Grades 1–4).** Students can use the Fluency through Fables site to help develop language skills. Lessons include vocabulary development and comprehension exercises. Have students access the site and read the current fable or an assigned one. Have them complete the exercises online. Then use the discussion questions for an in-class discussion or written exercise. Have them compose a group response to the discussion and select a volunteer to submit your class response for posting at this site.
  http://www.comenius.com/fable/

- **Earth and Sea Investigators Resources (Grades 7–12).** The purpose of this site is to "help teachers prepare to coach students toward effective work in student-designed scientific investigations." An online tutorial introduces students to the process of scientific investigation. The site provides examples of topics and related Internet resources that can serve as starting points for research. Have students work through the tutorials, then use the sample Group Investigation (or similar activity) to apply what has been learned. Students can develop Web pages to share their research.
  http://www.earthsea.org/

- **Creating a Personalized Newspaper (Grades 4–12).** Crayon is an online resource that allows students to create their own version of an online newspaper. The site draws its news items from current Web sites, then mixes and matches them according to your specifications. Allow students to access the site and develop their own customized versions of a newspaper. The newspaper templates the students create can be saved as HTML files. These then can be accessed and read periodically or daily as a way for students to learn about current events. Take a few minutes each day to have students share with the class items from their online newspapers.
  http://crayon.net/

- **Women's History (Grades 7–12).** Students can learn the contributions women have made by visiting the Encyclopedia of Women's History. The entries included in the encyclopedia are all from students. After your students have had a chance to look at this resource, have them share what they've learned with the class. Encourage them to research and submit their own reports to support this project.
  http://www.teleport.com/~megaines/women.html

The Teacher's Complete & Easy Guide to the Internet

- **Learning about Tornadoes (Grades 4–8).** Have students research tornadoes and prepare oral reports for the class. They can find out such things as how tornadoes are formed, where they form, how they are rated, how they die, and what to do if a tornado hits. For comprehensive information on this topic, they can visit the Tornado Web Page:
  http://cc.usu.edu/~kforsyth/Tornado.html

  Other weather-related resources are available from WeatherNet (http://groundhog.sprl.umich.edu/index.html) and Weather Mania (http://www.cameronlaw.com/weather.html).

- **Learning about Hurricanes (Grades 5–8).** The five-part series Storm Science is a resource developed with the elementary student and teacher in mind. You can supplement this resource with recent online news reports on hurricanes or other storms.
  http://www.miamisci.org/hurricane/hurricane0.html

- **Earthweek (Grades 4–8).** Each week, this resource provides a look at the weather on the planet. Have each student select a continent and document the weather phenomenon on that continent for a week. They can then research and report on a weather event they would like to know more about. Use the Earthweek Classroom Companion for more classroom ideas.
  http://www.earthweek.com

- **Geography Studies (Grades 5–12).** Have students develop their own maps based on selected geographical features. The site also offers a Canadian Geographical Names server and a quiz:
  http://www-nais.ccm.emr.ca/schoolnet/.

  Also check out the wonderful set of map resources available from http://www.lib.utexas.edu/Libs/PCL/Map_collection/Map_collection.html.

- **Learning about Maps (Grades 5–10).** Use this resource as an introduction to a map-study unit. Have students access the site to learn about different types of maps and to view examples of each. You can also print parts of this page and use it as a handout for a map-study unit.
  http://loki.ur.utk.edu/ut2kids/maps/map.html

- **Midlink Magazine (Grades 4–8).** This is an electronic magazine for students in the middle grades. Issued bi-monthly, Midlink offers an exciting range of learning activities. It includes written contributions from kids, reports on student Internet projects, and pointers to resources that students will enjoy. Each month features a special theme. Some issues contain examples of student portfolios that have been prepared using largely electronic resources. The magazine is an appealing way for middle

grade students to get involved in online activities, and you can use this resource to generate your own ideas.
http://longwood.cs.ucf.edu/~MidLink/

Kidsworld Online is a similar resource, with stories and artwork by kids: http://www.kidsworld-online.com/

- **Currency Conversion (Grades 4–9).** This excellent Australian resource for learning about currency exchange walks students through the activity step by step. Students can check on currency exchange rates for many different countries dating back to January 1, 1990. They are asked to contribute and compare information on food costs, including the cost of a meal from McDonald's in different countries.
http://www.wimmera.net.au/currcomp/currcomp.html

- **Viewing the Earth (Grades 5–9).** This resource gives students a different perspective on the earth. They can specify longitude and latitude and view locations from the perspective of the sun or moon, and they can see the division between night and day in different time zones. This site also points to some public domain software for downloading.
http://www.fourmilab.ch/earthview/vplanet.html

- **Parts of Speech (Grades 4–6).** Wacky Web Tales is a fun resource that tests students' skill at identifying parts of speech. Students select a story, then fill in parts of speech in the designated fields. They submit their completed forms, and a "wacky" story is returned. (Some teachers may remember this activity as "Madlibs" in pre-computer days.) There are Madlibs elsewhere on the Internet, but this source has an exceptionally clear focus.
http://www.hmco.com:80/hmco/school/tales/

- **Math Puzzlers (Grades 3–10).** A new set of puzzles is offered every week at this resource. Select a puzzle for your class to solve. Then check for the answers each Wednesday when new puzzles and answers to the previous week's puzzles are posted. Puzzles are available for Grades 3/4, 5/6, and 7+. Strong math students may enjoy exploring the math puzzle archives, where previous puzzles are posted along with their solutions.
http://www.eduplace.com/math/brain/

- **Learning about Earthquakes (Grades 7+).** The Internet provides many outstanding resources for learning about climate and geological phenomena. The Earthquake Resource Centre provides links for finding out about earthquakes. From this site, students can access earthquake data and submit their questions about earthquakes to Ask a Geologist.
http://www.comet.net/earthquake/

HINT Check these other sources for more Internet Lesson Ideas:

Blue Web'N **http://www. kn.pacbell.com/wired/ bluewebn/**

Lesson Plans Using Internet Web Sites **http:// www. v o i c e n e t . c o m / ~reevesk/**

Online Educator **http:// ole.net/ole/**

Internet Lessons from UCI **http://www.gse.uci.edu/ Lessons/lessons.html**

K–12 Sources — Lesson Plans **http://www. execpc. c o m / ~ d b o a l s / k - 1 2 . html#TOP**

Ed's Oasis **http://edsoasis. org/Treasure/Treasure. html**

The Well-Connected Educator **http://www. gsh. org/wce/**

Learning@Web.Sites **http://www.ecnet.net/ users/gdlevin/home. html** (primarily for senior high school level)

- **Writing (Grades 5–8).** Have your students contribute something to KidNews. This publication publishes student writing in a number of different categories, including news, sports, feature stories, creative writing, reviews, and personal profiles. Preview the publication and select sections that you would like to have students focus on. Writing can be submitted using conventional e-mail or online using the KidNews Magic Writer. http://www.vsa.cape.com/~powens/Kidnews3.html

"[By contributing to online projects], students can easily become part of a much larger project, while appreciating the uniqueness of their own area. When my class began work on our school Web page, we used it as an extension to the social studies program."

— *Nancy Barkhouse, Teacher, Atlantic View Elementary School, Lawrencetown, Nova Scotia, Canada*

- **Résumé Writing (Grades 9–12).** An extensive list of articles about résumé writing is available from the Archeus Resume Writing Resources site. Have students each read one or two of the available articles and review the tips on résumés and cover letters at the Career Center. Students may discuss and compare findings before developing their own résumés, either for imaginary careers or part-time or summer work.

Archeus Resume Writing Resources: http://www.golden. net/~archeus/reswri.htm

Career Center: http://www.kaplan.com/career/

Figure 5–7
Freezone

WebQuests

Using the Web effectively depends in part on having a good sense of the kinds of learning resources you can find on the Internet. If you have taken time to explore some of the resources we have talked about so far, you have likely found a number of activities that you could use in your classroom. The next step is to develop an effective method for introducing students to useful resources in a way that ensures the learning will tie closely to curriculum. WebQuests provide a model for linking Web-based research and learning outcomes in a practical and engaging fashion. WebQuests as a way of learning on the Internet were first developed by Bernie Dodge, an educational technology professor at San Diego State University. His definition of a WebQuest includes the following description: "an inquiry-oriented activity in which some or all of the information that learners interact with comes from resources on the Internet . . ." In addition, WebQuests can be short term (from one to three class periods), or long term, requiring a week, a month, or even more. The appeal of WebQuests has to do with the fact that they can be adapted for a range of technology environments and many different curriculum areas. In addition, WebQuest projects can easily be used in cross-curricular learning situations.

The basic elements of a WebQuest are:

- An introduction, which provides background information to interest students in the assignment.
- An interesting task.
- Process or steps involved in completing the task.
- Resources to be used. Typically, these are primarily Internet resources, but other sources, such as library resources, can be included.
- Guidance in organizing information and completing tasks.
- Conclusion (what's been learned with suggestions for learning more).

Optional elements can include:

- Group activities/discussion
- Online conferencing (audio or video)
- Motivational context (controversial theme, role playing, real-world environment)
- Creating of a learning "product" online or offline.[1]

WebQuests foster active learning in which the instructional goal is knowledge acquisition and integration. Ideally, the learner will deal with a significant amount of new information, interpreting it through synthesis and analysis and ultimately transforming information into knowledge.

Another appealing feature of WebQuests is that they can readily be shared among teachers, and with some attention paid to keeping them up-to-date, they can be used from one year to the next, so that the value from time a teacher spends developing an assignment is maximized. Some teachers have posted their WebQuests on the Web. A good selection of WebQuest examples for various grade levels is available from Edweb: **http://edweb.sdsu.edu/webquest/ matrix.html**.

The best way to get a sense of how WebQuests work is to look at an example. The following WebQuest about the dangers of tobacco was created by Ginger Nehls of Magnolia Elementary School.

Tips for Developing WebQuests

- Think about real world issues (e.g., political, interest groups, scientific controversies).
- Use real-world roles to motivate (e.g., you are a judge, you are a visible minority).
- Think of a new perspective on an old topic.
- Use imaginative or historical settings.

- Think about topics that interest kids.
- Think about new areas of learning to explore.
- Think about investigative research projects your students have done "off-line." How might these be extended to the Internet in the form of WebQuests?

- Consider a multi-discipline approach.
- Don't forget about opportunities to communicate online.
- Provide imaginative texture as a motivator (e.g., Does the Tiger Eat Her Own Cubs?).

Webquest

Instructional Technology Development Consortium

The Real Scoop on Tobacco

You have been hired by the parents of Icabod, a sixth grade student. They suspect their child of smoking or about to start. He's gone through D.A.R.E. and listened to the lectures of his parents and teachers. However, he thinks they are all just handing him a line. After all, he sees lots of adults smoking and figures it isn't really so bad. In fact, he thinks it's pretty cool. But he might listen to you. After all, you're his peer. That's what his parents are counting on. They've hired you to convince him to quit smoking. To do so, you must show your commitment to the fight against youth using tobacco and create a memorable message for him. Do a good job - it could be a matter of life and death.

The Task

Your client's son doesn't particularly like to read, so you must approach him in a more creative way. He is, after all, much like you, a member of the MTV generation. He'll listen to a rap song; he'll hang a poster in his room. But to earn his respect, you must first demonstrate your knowledge of tobacco and your commitment to fight its use by young people. So here's what you're being paid to do:

- Become an expert about tobacco use and issues surrounding its use.
- Create an ad or poster that visually conveys the message you want to get across.
- Demonstrate your commitment to fight tobacco use by writing a letter to a tobacco company and an editorial for the local paper.
- Get Icabod's attention and give him a memorable message using a music video, skit, or TV commercial.

The Process

1. Determine how you will organize information in your journal. You will use this to record all information and activities throughout the project, including a log of your daily activities, brainstorming questions, notes from research, comments from other students, drafts of project tasks, etc.
2. Conduct research on tobacco and respond to the following questions:
   - What diseases are caused by smoking cigarettes? smoking cigars? chewing tobacco?
   - What influences people to smoke?
   - What keeps them smoking?
   - What are the facts about nicotine?
   - What can you find out about the tobacco industry?
   - Identify and explain the significance of recent court cases involving the tobacco industry.
   - Collect any other interesting or important facts.
3. In your journal, brainstorm the position and supporting facts you will use to convince Icabod to stop smoking.
4. Collect tobacco ads, posters, etc. and analyze them using the following questions:
   1. What graphic design techniques did they use to appeal to you?
   2. What does the ad say directly?
   3. What does it say indirectly (hinting, suggesting)?
   4. Who do you think this advertisement is designed to interest? How does it do this?
5. Based on your research, design an advertisement or poster to convey your message about tobacco use. Consider analyzing any ads aimed at your age level for techniques graphic designers use to attract you. Use these techniques in your ad to promote your position on tobacco use.
6. Spread the word by writing an editorial to your local newspaper making a persuasive statement about one of the issues related to youth using tobacco. To get a feel for style and format of this type of writing, read a variety of editorials published in newspapers or magazines. Does the editorial convince you to agree with the author's position? If so, how was it convincing? If not, why wasn't it convincing? How can you relate this to your task of writing an editorial?
7. Go directly to the source! Write a letter to tobacco companies stating your concerns for their impact on youth. Support with facts from your research and ad analysis.

Page: 1

8. Give a message that'll stick! Determine how you will convince Icabod to quit smoking. Select from the following presentation ideas or propose your own idea. Regardless of your approach, you need to be convincing, relate important facts, and connect with your audience. You can create a:
   - song and a music video for it
   - skit using a scenario related to youth using tobacco
   - TV commercial
9. Prepare a presentation to Icabod and his parents in which you can offer your letters and ad/poster as testimony to your knowledge and commitment. Then deliver your message to Icabod in a way he won't forget!
10. Present your final product to Icabod and his parents on a designated "Youth Against Tobacco" day in your class.

Resources

Below are some sites that will help you accomplish your tasks. Many have links to additional sites. Stay focused on your tasks, however,
and know what you are looking for, or you can waste a lot of valuable time.

Master Anti-Smoking Page is a great resource for links to organizations working to combat the smoking habit. It also provides a way to ask an expert specific questions. You'll need to scroll down quite a bit to find the Anti-Smoking page listed under "Specialty Pages -General Interest".

American Cancer Society is the site specifically targeting tobacco control. It provides facts about smoking cigars and includes a position
statement and cigar fact sheet.

Quit-Net is a site by the Massachusetts Tobacco Control Program with information on how to quit, resources, news items, and great links.

The Learning Trip has easy-to-understand information on the physical reasons people continue to smoke and on nicotine's effects on
various parts of the body.

If Tobacco Ads Really Told the Truth is a fun site showing kids' versions (parodies) of tobacco ads.

Campaign for Tobacco Free Kids includes information about recent legislation (laws) and policies. Be sure to check out the "Kid's Corner". It's written just for you!

Adverse Effects of Smoking has some interesting information - including a picture of a smoker's lung.

Learning Advice

Feedback: Get feedback from at least two other people while each part of your project is still in rough draft form. Have them record their feedback (what's good, suggestions for improvement) in your journal. Record your reaction to their feedback and any changes you made
based on their suggestions.

Writing a song: If you're having trouble designing both the music and lyrics, pick out a catchy tune or a popular song to which you can
rewrite the lyrics.

Performing: Determine whether you would prefer to act out your presentation live or videotape it. If you choose to videotape it, become familiar with the functions of your camcorder, storyboard the presentation, and determine effective shooting techniques.

Evaluation

Use the following questions to evaluate the quality of your work:

- Were you able to put together accurate and current information about the effects of using tobacco?
- Is your journal complete, including notes, feedback from others, log of activities, etc.
- Is your poster creative, appealing, and professional looking?
- Does your skit get your point across? Is it thought-provoking and interesting to watch?
- Is your letter to the tobacco company written in proper form and expressing a clear opinion substantiated by facts?
- Is your editorial to the newspaper written in proper form? Is it persuasive and supported with facts?

Page: 2

Reflection

1. Do you feel this was an effective learning experience? Explain.
2. How did you determine which information was helpful and accurate?
3. If you were doing this activity again, what would you do differently?
4. What suggestions or hints would you offer to future students doing this WebQuest?

Conclusion

What have you learned about the effects of tobacco that you didn't really know before? In what ways has this project affected you and your
opinion about smoking and other forms of tobacco use?

Extension

Find out about smoking laws in your state and city. If there are laws restricting smoking, what are the restrictions? Why do you think these
law were enacted? What impact do they have on you and your community? Write to your council members supporting or urging action.

Notes to the Teacher

Lesson Title: The Real Scoop on Tobacco

Curricular Area: Health

Grade Level: 5-9

Goal/Purpose: To give students the opportunity to apply and make sense of the myriad of information available regarding tobacco and to
be able to personalize it so that the information can aid them to make better decisions regarding their health.

- learn to identify the effects of tobacco on different parts of the body.
- understand the influences that promote drug use including peer pressure, advertising, etc.
- develop and use interpersonal and other communication skills such as assertiveness, refusal, etc.
- become aware of the legal issues concerning tobacco use.
- identify ways of obtaining help to resist pressure to use (or to quit using) tobacco.

   (quoted from the *California Health Framework,* 1994)

Interdisciplinary Connections: Language Arts, Visual and Performing Arts

Length of Lesson: 2-3 weeks

Materials:

- notebooks/journal for note-taking and organization
- magazines full of ads
- newspapers that have a kid editorial section
- names and addresses of tobacco companies
- camcorder (optional)
- tape player/recorder
- poster paper
- markers, glue, etc.

Teacher Resources:

- A List of Tobacco Industry Addresses
- Tobacco BBS (Bulletin Board System) is a free resource center focusing on tobacco and smoking issues. It features tobacco news, information, assistance for smokers trying to quit, alerts for tobacco control advocates, and open debate on the wide spectrum of issues concerning tobacco, nicotine, cigarettes and cigars.

- *Here's Looking at You, 2,000* 6th grade drug prevention program published by Comprehensive Health Education Foundation. Lesson 3 deals with smoking; lesson 4 deals with chewing tobacco; lesson 6 deals with advertising.
- *Microsoft Encarta '95* CD - look under "Smoking."

Prerequisite Learning: students need to be comfortable with the following skills or supported throughout the process:

- cooperative learning skills
- willingness to solicit and consider constructive criticism
- note-taking and organizational strategies
- letter writing skills (format and style)
- ability to identify and target different audiences
- ability to use Internet resources

Suggestions:

1. Organize the students into small groups. Discuss the advantages of dividing up responsibilities. Be clear in what your expectations are for individuals and groups.
2. When presenting this project, provide students with a copy of the project to include in their journal. Conduct a brainstorming session to determine organizational strategies for notebooks, materials, computer use, etc.
3. Conduct small group or whole class sessions throughout the project to provide support on various activities and peer feedback opportunities.
4. Arrange a "Youth Against Tobacco" day in your class/school. Ask administrators or parents to participate as Icabod and his parents and have students present their products. Provide opportunities for students to share their projects beyond the classroom with their school, parents, and community.

Written by <u>Ginger Nehls</u>, teacher at Magnolia Elementary School, Upland Unified School District.

Ideas for WebQuest Learning Tasks

WebQuest activities can range from a simple set of questions that students are to answer using the Internet, to a more involved group assignment culminating in an online debate or publication. At the bottom of the page is a chart of some examples of the kinds of activities that could be the focus of student learning using the WebQuest model.

Where possible, students should share their knowledge over the Net.

WebQuest Resources

Find out more about WebQuests using these sources:

The WebQuest Page
http://edweb.sdsu.edu/webquest/webquest.html

Some Thoughts About WebQuests Overview by Bernie Dodge.

http://edweb.sdsu.edu/courses/edtec596/about_webquests.html

ITDC WebQuests

http://itdc.sbcss.k12.ca.us/curriculum/webquest.html

WebQuest: Searching for China

http://www.kn.pacbell.com/wired/China/ChinaQuest.html

WebQuest: Does the Tiger Eat Her Cubs?

http://www.kn.pacbell.com/wired/China/childquest.html

WebQuest: Planet Earth Expedition

Good example of science topic with research question focus.

QUESTIONS	SUMMARY	PROBLEM SOLVING	CREATIVE WORK	DEFENDING POSITION
open ended	outline	flow-chart	logbook	debate
targeted	concept map	report	journal	essay: compare and contrast
scavenger hunt	text summary	action	student news report	table: pros / cons
data collection	time line	diagram	poem	
table completion			play	
			letter	

http://scoe.shastalink.k12.ca.us/www/telementors/test.html.

WebQuests in Our Future: The Teacher's Role in Cyberspace WebQuest developed by Kathy Schrock

http://www.capecod.net/schrockguide/webquest/webquest.htm

Template for Developing a WebQuest
http://edweb.sdsu.edu/edfirst/TMarch/Web_Template.html

Summing up

In this chapter we have suggested some of the ways that the Internet can be used for student research. While the most dynamic Internet projects include collaboration with students in other classrooms, learning how to use the Internet as a research tool is an essential first step.

In the next chapter we will explain how to develop Web pages. Knowing how to develop Web pages will increase the ability of students to share what they have learned. Although such projects require a higher level of skill than just using the Web to find information, they are particularly exciting activities for students because they give them a way to present their own creative work and research findings to others. It is in designing and publishing their own Web pages that students and teachers will fully appreciate the power of the Internet.

Chapter 6

Developing Web Pages for Learning

"A Language Arts teacher asked me to teach her ninth- and eleventh-grade students how to make a Web page. Several of my student assistants volunteered to teach these kids enough to put a writing project or two online. These projects are not perfect nor very sophisticated, but they do function. It is also our first experiment in electronic portfolios as a means of alternative assessment."

— Currie Morrison, Technology Coordinator, Nathan Hale High School, Seattle, Washington, U.S.A.

Perhaps the most powerful application of Web technology for classrooms is as a publishing tool. With the ability to publish home pages, students can share their work with one another and even make the work they do available to the world. Knowing how to program in HTML (*Hypertext Markup Language*) and to create online learning resources such as WebQuests is a practical skill for teachers and the most exciting part of the Web for many students. *Be aware, however, that HTML programming is not for everyone.* Learning to develop Web pages is not hard, but it can be time consuming and frustrating for those who do not possess a good eye for detail. Many teachers have neither the time nor inclination to master this skill. Don't worry if you fall into this category. Read through this chapter to get a sense of what's involved, then find an eager student to develop pages for you. Using an HTML editor, which we describe later in this chapter, will also greatly simplify the task of creating Web pages.

Chapter goals

- To provide an overview of HTML tagging
- To provide instructions on how to develop a Web page
- To provide guidelines and resources for Web graphics
- To offer some examples of how Web pages can be used in schools
- To provide guidelines and ideas for developing effective school Web pages

"What the Web offers that books, magazines, or videos don't is the opportunity to publish their work for a worldwide audience, which motivates them to write. I wish you could have seen my students last spring creating a Web page for their school. They were so proud!"

— *Karla Frizler, ESL Instructor and Founder, Frizzy University Network (FUN), San Francisco, California, U.S.A.*

Figure 6-1
A secondary school Web page

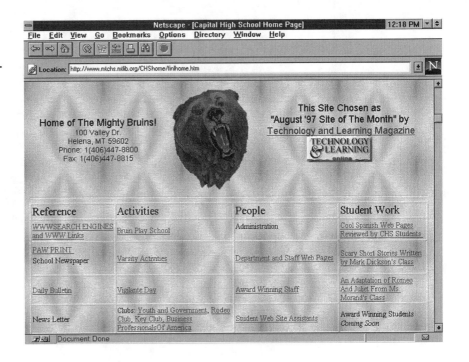

Introduction to HTML

HTML stands for Hypertext Markup Language. Basically, HTML offers a set of tags that tell your browser how to format and display text on a Web page.

You can see how a Web page is constructed by using your Web browser to view what is called the *source document*. In Netscape, after accessing a Web page, click on **View** and **Source**. The cryptic-looking page that is revealed is in fact the Web page you have accessed. It displays the codes that are interpreted by your Web browser. Although a first look at a Web source page can be intimidating, if you take a closer look you'll see that it's not much more than a text document with a series of codes enclosed in brackets. Here's a sample:

```
<HTML><HEAD><TITLE>Online Educator
Samples</TITLE></HEAD>
<BODY bgcolor="#fffff0">
<A HREF="SAFETY.html">[Safety]</A>
<A HREF="OWL.html">[Writing]</A>
<A HREF="NASA.html">[Space]</A>
<A HREF="CUREVEN.html">[Events]</A>
```

```
<A HREF="CYBERJ.html">[Cyberjournalists]</A>
<A HREF="QUAKE.html">[Quake]</A>
<A HREF="GEOG.html">[Geography]</A>
<A HREF="EMAIL.html">[E-Mail]</A>
<A HREF="MUSEUM.html">[Museums]</A><br>
<A HREF="../OEWELCOME.html"><IMG WIDTH=220 BOR-
DER=0 VSPACE=4
SRC="../OEFOLIO.GIF"></A><br> <ADDRESS>A sample
article from our monthly publication
</ADDRESS> <hr NOSHADE SIZE=3> <STRONG>January
1995</STRONG>

<hr NOSHADE>

<H1>Caution and good sense keep Net safe</H1>

<P>Taking your students online will open up a
whole world of educational possibilities. It also
will present them and you with the opportunity to
come in contact with questionable material and
subjects.

<P>The Internet can deliver pictures from Jupiter
and Mars into your classroom, and it can also
bring nudes and other inappropriate photos. You
can download great works of literature and docu-
ments such as the Declaration of Independence into
your classroom computer, and you can just as easi-
ly get instructions on how to build pipe bombs or
mix chemical explosives.
```

If you take a close look at this example, you can discern a combination of the text that appears in the normal viewing of a Web page and a series of tags (which appear in bold type in this example). These tags are just a set of commands that tell your system's browser

- where specific images should be placed:

```
<IMG WIDTH=220 BORDER=0 VSPACE=4
SRC="../OEFOLIO.GIF">
```

- where to display a link to another file:

```
<A HREF="MUSEUM.html">[Museums]</A>
```

- which text to display in a larger font:

  `<H1>`Caution and good sense keep Net safe`</H1>`

- which text to display in bold letters:

  `<STRONG>`January 1995`</STRONG>`

- where to place a hard return (which in Netscape appears as a line across the page):

  `<hr>`

Developing a Web page

Although the source code (as described in the above example) can make Web page development seem very confusing, it is not difficult to create a simple page for student work. Once you have grasped the basics, you can develop a Web page with instructions for an Internet research project and integrate links to the sites you want your students to visit. You can also develop a basic template for student reports that would allow you to display completed student assignments so your students can share their work online. Pages that you have developed can be accessed from a local hard drive. When you are ready to have the public view work that your students have done, transfer your files to a school or district Web server.

These days you will find many pages on the Web with complex features, such as interactive components and heavy-duty graphics. Fortunately, you don't need this to create a functional page. In fact, most teachers prefer simple pages that download quickly and are easy to navigate.

The process for creating an HTML page is to key in HTML tags to any plain text file. You can do this using your word processor. Most newer word processors have incorporated the ability to add HTML tags as a formatting option. It is, however, still important to learn about HTML codes in order to know how to use the range of tags available. Many people find it valuable to learn a few basic HTML tags before trying to develop Web pages using a word processor or other software.

Basic HTML tags

Most HTML tags appear in pairs, and the second tag in a pair includes a slash. (e.g., <H1> </H1>) The first of the two codes is placed at the start of the text you want to format and the second tag is inserted immediately after that text.

Here are a few of the most important tags to know about:

Tech Talk

Use the Save As ... option from the File menu to change a word-processed file into plain text. As you are prompted by the dialog box for a new file name, you will see a small window near the bottom of the screen identifying options for saving the file. Click on the arrow to see the list of options. Selecting Text Only or ASCII Text will delete all the special coding related to your word processor and save the file in text format. If you have added HTML tags to a plain text file, you can re-name the file with an .htm or .html extension that your browser will recognize.

Page formatting tags (These tags identify the different sections of a page and should be included in all HTML documents.)

<HTML> </HTML> These two tags signal the beginning and the end of a Web page.

<HEAD> </HEAD> These tags signal the beginning and end of the document header. The header provides information about a Web page, such as the title of a page and sometimes optional information that is not intended to be displayed.

<TITLE> </TITLE> These tags frame the title of the page. The title of the page displays in the title bar at the top of the browser, rather than on the page itself.

<BODY> </BODY> These tags frame the body of the document. The <BODY> tag appears after the closing tag for the header and can incorporate some document detail, such as the background color information. The closing body tag </BODY> should be included at the very end of the document, and just before the final </HTML> closing tag.

Here is an example of what the above tags would look like in a document:

```
<HTML>
<HEAD>
<TITLE>Assignment — Week 1</TITLE>
</HEAD>
<BODY>
<H1> Web Museum Reports </H1>
This week you will visit a museum on the Web, blah, blah, blah!
</BODY>
</HTML>
```

Text formatting tags

1. Headings
<H1> </H1> This tag tells your browser to display text in the largest size available.
<H2> </H2> This tag will display text in the second largest size available.
<H6> </H6> Font size tags continue up to six; six represents the smallest size.

2. Emphasis
<B> </B> Bold text
<I> </I> Italics

Geekspeak

The Teacher's Complete & Easy Guide to the Internet

3. Line Breaks

You will quickly discover that your browser pays no attention to line breaks unless you change the text size or use one of these tags.

<P> This tag adds a space. Use it to start a new paragraph.

 This tag inserts a line break, so that text is continued on the next line.

<HR> This tag adds a horizontal line as a break in the text.

4. Links

The examples below illustrate how to set up hyperlinks.
To link to another site:

<A HREF="http://www.gsn.org/"> Global SchoolNet </A>

The example above offers a link to the Global SchoolNet site. The URL is enclosed in quotation marks, exactly as illustrated. The URL can include directory and file names as well. Following the reference is any descriptive text you wish to display for the link (frequently the name of the site). *Additional tags can frame the text, such as a size tag (<H2> Global SchoolNet </H2>) or a tag for italics or bold.* The reference is closed with the **</A>** tag.

HINT Try EdWeb's HTML Crash Course for Educators:

http://edweb.gsn.org/ htmlintro.html

- To link to a document on your own server:

<A HREF="assign1.htm">Assignment #1</A>

In this example, the tags are exactly the same as those used in the previous example of a link to a Web site. In this case, the file is on your own server, so only the file name is required. Be sure to include any directory and subdirectory names if the file will not be in the same directory as the Web page you are linking from.

- To link to somewhere else on the Web page you are developing.

<A HREF="#Evaluation">Evaluation </A>

In this example, "#Evaluation" refers to a NAME anchor. A NAME anchor is a tag that you have set up as a reference. The NAME anchor tag looks like this:

<A NAME="Evaluation"> Here are the points you will be marked on. **</A>**

In this case, the text *Here are the points you will be marked on* is not a link, but simply a marked section in the text. Clicking on the *Evaluation* link described above will cause the browser to immediately bounce to this section of the document.

- A link to an e-mail address.

  <A HREF="mailto:president@whitehouse.gov">
  Send a letter to the White House</A>

5. Lists

Lists are an efficient way to include a number of similar items on a Web page. As an example, you could use a list to identify the steps for a science investigation.

<OL> </OL> Use these tags to set up an ordered (numbered) list. The browser will automatically *number* the items designated **<LI>** within the list.

<UL></UL> This set of tags will give you a *bulleted* list.

<LI> Use this single tag to designate the start of each new item in a list.

Format example for a numbered list:
<OL>
<LI> beans
<LI> peas
<LI> cabbage
</OL>

Adding colors and images

I. Background Colors

You can add color to your Web pages by specifying a numeric code for each color you want to include. The numeric codes are hexadecimal values for RGB colors (Red/Green/Blue or #RRGG-BB). If you do not specify colors on your Web page, the browser default colors will apply. The following example adds a background color (BGCOLOR):

<BODY BGCOLOR="#612f75"> The BGCOLOR tag is embedded into the body tag.

You can also specify colors for the text (TEXT) on a page, *links* (LINK), and *followed* links (VLINK):

<BODY BGCOLOR="#ffffff" TEXT="#000000" LINK="#FFOOFF" VLINK="##2F4F2F"> (In this case, the background is white and the text is black. Links are magenta and followed links are dark green.)

Although there is a method for calculating the RGB valuations for colors, it is easier to consult a color palette that provides these values. Many Web site editors (discussed below) include

Tech Talk

Found a Web page with a background color that you like? Check the BGCOLOR numeric code using the View Source option. You can use this option to learn how coding was done for other elements on a page as well. Another BGCOLOR tip is that for simple colors (e.g., white, black, yellow, red, purple, cyan, green) you can replace the numeric code with the word, as in *BGCOLOR ="WHITE"*.

The Teacher's Complete & Easy Guide to the Internet

hexadecimal codes for colors. A number of downloadable "HTML Color Pickers" are available for both Windows and Macintosh computers at TUCOWS (**http://www.tucows.com**). On the Web you can visit the RGB Color Chart at **http://www.phoenix.net/~jacobson/rgb.html** or the The ColorMaker Page at **http://www.missouri.edu/~wwwtools/colormaker/**. At each of these sites, when you select a color the hexadecimal value will be presented.

2. Images

To insert an image use the following tag:

<IMG SRC="sunflower.gif">

To position the image on the page add the ALIGN tag:

<IMG SRC="sunflower.gif" ALIGN=top>

The ALIGN attribute can be top, bottom, middle, left, or right. This attribute will affect how the text flows around the image.

ALT
<IMG SRC="applepicture.gif" ALT="[Apples]">

If you include the ALT= reference in the image tag, visitors to the page who have turned off the image loading feature on their browser will still be able to make sense of the page. Always use the ALT tag for documents that will be accessible outside of the school network.

3. Background images

You can add texture to your page by using a background image:

<BODY BACKGROUND="clouds.gif">

In this example, the browser will duplicate a graphic file called *clouds.gif*, filling the page and creating a tiled effect. Text and images on the page will appear against the tiled background. As with other image files, the image file referenced by the background tag needs to be in the same directory with the Web page, or directory and subdirectory names need to be included in the reference.

Use background textures carefully. Soft, subtle patterns work best. If background texture is too bold, the page will be hard to read. You will find lots of background textures at Texture Land (**http://www.meat.com/textures/**) and at Texture Station (**http://www.aimnet.com/~bosman/TextureStation_Lobby.htm**). For a good collection of backgrounds, buttons, and bars, visit Bull's Backgrounds, Buttons and Bars at **http://www.gbd.com/personal/cbull/back.htm**.

HINT HTML no-brainer: try HomeMaker Online **http://www.kn.pacbell.com/wired/homemaker/**. Type in information about yourself, select a color scheme, and click!

Web graphics

The simplest way to obtain graphics for your Web page is to download them from the Web. For links to many graphics sources, visit these sites:

Barry's Clip Art Server at **http://www.barrysclipart.com/**

Hee Yun's Graphic Collection **http://soback.kornet.nm.kr/~pixeline/ heeyun/graphics.html**

Clipart.com Clip Art Index **http://www.clipart.com/**

Pedago Net — Clip Art Server at **http://www.pedagonet.com/ clipart/clipart.eht**

The Awesome Library Clip Art Page at **http://www.neat-schoolhouse.org/Classroom/Technology/Clip_Art_and_Graphics/Clip_ Art.html**

Web Places Clip Art Review **http://www.webplaces.com/html/ clipart.htm**

You can also search for graphic images by name (cat, Christmas, etc.) at Filez **http://www.filez.com/** and at Clip-art Searcher **http://www.webplaces.com/search/** which provides quick access to the clip-art feature on several different search engines.

When you want to download an image from a Web page, place your cursor over the image and click on the right-hand mouse button (PC), or just hold down the mouse button on a Mac. Then select **Save This Image As.**

Most of the images you will encounter on the Web end in *.gif* or *.jpeg*. Web browsers recognize both of these file formats. The .gif format is commonly used for line drawings and simple images (such as a cartoon image with big blocks of color), while .jpeg is generally used for photographs, paintings, and other images with considerable detail.

Sometimes you may have an image you want to include on a Web page that is in a format other than .gif or .jpeg. To convert other image formats (such as .pict, .pcx or .bmp), you will need a graphics editor. A graphics editor lets you open a graphics file in one format and save it to another format. You can generally also re-size a picture, cut out a section to create a new image, and perform similar editing functions using a graphics editor. Here are some examples of graphics editors (viewers):

Windows:

LView Pro **http://www.lview.com**

Graphic Workshop **http://www.mindworkshop.com/alchemy/ alchemy.html**

Macintosh:

Big Picture **http://www3.sk.sympatico.ca/tinyjohn/**

BME **http://www.softlogik.com/Products/products.html**

You can find these and other graphics image viewers at TUCOWS: **http://www.tucows.com**. TUCOWS is a comprehensive site for Internet software.

If you are planning to create your own graphics, you will need a paint program. A number of good graphics programs are available for both Windows and Macintosh computers. One of the most popular and relatively inexpensive graphics programs for Windows is Paint Shop Pro at **http://www.jasc.com/psp.html**. Another program, Dabbler, is available for both Windows and Macintosh (**http://fractal.com/products/dabbler/**). More expensive (but very popular) programs include Corel Draw and Photoshop.

Finally, if you want to try your hand at creating animated .gifs, try Cell Assembler at **http://www.gamani.com/** or Pro Motion. Pro Motion is a drawing package that lets you create animations as well as still images. You can downlaod a trial version at **http://www. tu-chemnitz.de/~jzi/english/product_info.html**.

HINT A terrifically useful page with pointers to the best sites for Web page development is Lynn's Web Mastery at **http:// www.geocities.com/ Paris/Metro/4870/**. It includes pointers to resources for kids' Web pages.

HTML editors

For many people, having to manually type HTML tags into a document is a form of slow torture. In addition, it's easy to make small typographical errors that can cause havoc on a Web page. The solution is to use a Web page editor.

A Web page editor will allow you to add HTML tags to your Web page using a graphical interface (drop-down menus, point and click, highlight and select). Editors include many useful features, such as the ability to select a background color from a color chart and simplified list creation.

Although most editors cost between US$100 and US$150, most are available as trial versions that can be downloaded from the Web. Some software browsers, such as Netscape Gold, Netscape Communicator, and the newest versions of Internet Explorer, include an HTML editor. If you have one of the latest browsers, you may find that the HTML editing feature is all you need to develop basic Web pages. If you do not have a built-in HTML editor on your browser, try one of these:

Windows

Hot Dog (Sausage Software)
    http://www.sausage.com/
    This is one of the most popular HTML editors. If you are developing a school site, you may want to choose the professional version, which includes a number of site management features.

Homesite (Windows NT 4.0 or Windows 95)
http://www.allaire.com/
Well-designed program for under $100.

FrontPage (Windows 95 or Windows NT)
http://www.microsoft.com/frontpage
This is a powerful and easy-to-use editor, but it requires substantial hard disk space.

Gomer
http://stoopidsoftware.com/
This is a text-based editor, but it is inexpensive (US$20) and easy to use.

Netscape Composer
http://www.netscape.com
This editor provides image format conversion, a built-in spell checker and the ability to create an HTML-based discussion group. In addition, Netscape Composer is free to schools.

Macintosh

PageMill
http://www.adobe.com/prodindex/pagemill/mail.html
Very popular and easy-to use-editor for Macintosh.

BBEdit
http://www.barebones.com
This is a well-liked word-processing program with HTML add-ons.

Claris Home Page
(Also available for Windows 95 and Windows NT)
http://www.claris.com/products/claris/clarispage/clarispage.html
This editor has lots of features for both beginners and experienced Web page developers.

PageSpinner
http://www.algonet.se/~optima/pagespinner.html
Inexpensive editor (US$25) with a number of useful features.

Where to learn more about HTML

There are many excellent resources that you can use to learn more about HTML.
Try these :

Introduction to HTML and URLs by Ian Graham **http://utoronto. ca/webdocs/HTMLdocs/NewHTML/intro.html**

HINT A good place to find out about many different HTML editors is at Mag's Big List of HTML Editors at **http://sdg. ncsa.uiuc.edu/~mag/ work/HTMLEditors/**. Reviews of various editors are available at Carl Davis's HTML Editor Reviews Page: **http://www.techsmith. com/community/html-rev/index2.html**.

HINT If you find a page you like, check out the source code. Print a copy of the page and a copy of the coding display so you can compare the two side by side. Circle or highlight sections of code that you might want to use on your own pages.

The Barebones Guide to HTML http://werbach.com/barebones

The HTML Writer's Guild at http://www.hwg.org/resources/index.html

You can find other HTML Tutorials at The Web Masters Reference Library at http://webreference.com/html/tutorials and at the Web Developer's Virtual Library at http://www.charm.net/~web/.

For a desktop help file, download The HTML Reference Library Windows HLP file. It provides numerous screen shots and examples of HTML. The program is available from http://subnet.virtual-pc.com/~le387818/.

Tech Talk

Using graphics is a great way to brighten up your pages.

Unfortunately, graphic images can also slow down page loading.

Try to keep individual graphics below 50K (particularly on school Web pages that might be accessed outside of the local area network).

You can also "reuse" graphics. If you include several references to the same graphic on your pages, the image needs to be loaded only once. The browser's computer places the image in a computer storage area called a cache and will retrieve the image from there. To find out more about how to manage graphics for faster loading, visit The Bandwidth Conservation Society page at http://www.infohiway.com/faster.

HINT If you plan to make your page available outside of your school, test how it will appear using a number of different browsers. Some browsers are more forgiving than others of mistakes in HTML coding. Also, what appears fine in one browser can be a major eyesore in another.

School Web pages

Once you have learned the basics for putting together a Web page, the challenge becomes figuring out how to use this technology in a meaningful way in a classroom setting.

The Web66 WWW Schools Registry (http://web66.coled.umn.edu/schools.html) provides links to hundreds of schools around the world, broken down by geographic location. Accessing this site and using your Web browser is an ideal way to sample the range of school-produced Web pages. In addition to providing basic information about the school and sample class newspapers, many schools also include class projects, sample school publications, and links to useful curriculum sources that can be used by other teachers. Some provide information about the history of the school or information about the local community.

For a list of examples of the kinds of things that might be good to include on a school Web page, visit Exemplary School Sites at

http://www.techlearning.com/web-schools.shtml

HINT Gleason Sackman maintains the HotList of K–12 Internet School Sites for the U.S.A. You can sample these sites state by state at http://www.sendit.nodak.edu/k12/ http://www.sendit.nodak.edu/k12/

Another good place to sample school Web sites is at the Classroom Web (http://www.wentworth.com/classweb/). Here you can look at school Web pages from many different countries, including Australia, Canada, Denmark, Germany, Japan, Mexico, New Zealand, and Sweden, as well as the fifty states. The pages

Figure 6–2
Schools everywhere are putting their own home pages on the Web.

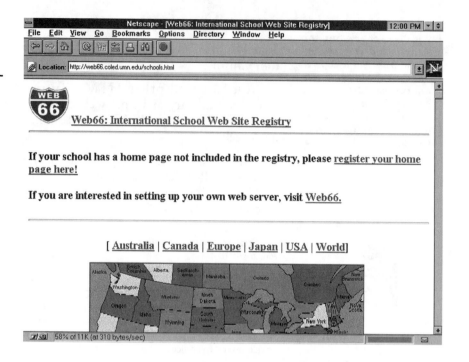

HINT Check the Scout Toolkit regularly for information and links to effective network tools:

http://scout.cs.wisc.edu/ scout/toolkit/

HINT Visit these great Web sites:

Cotton Fields pages (developed by seven-year-olds) **http://www.hipark. austin.isd.tenet.edu/ home/projects/first/ cotton/cotton.html**

Bellingham Public Schools Student Writing and Student Art **http://www.bham. wednet.edu/**

Arbor Heights Elementary in Seattle, Washington **http://www.halcyon. com/arborhts/arborhts. html**

include school projects, student papers, poetry, drawings, class and school information, information about the students' own countries, and, often, links to favorite educational sites.

School Web pages have themselves become a way of contributing ideas to the rest of the world. One class collected Halloween stories from other schools (via e-mail) and developed a Web page based on them. Another class was given the task of identifying useful curriculum-based resources and establishing links that their classmates and teachers or anyone else accessing their site could use. Students can also use the Web to display their own research reports and creative writing or artwork, or they can profile local community services or events.

> "My students are excited and eager both to publish their own work and to see what other kids have done. They think of the Web as some kind of huge 'Just Grandma and Me,' except that they can make the click-places themselves. They love getting e-mail from people who mention seeing their work, and they love sending e-mail to others whose work they like."
>
> — *Clare Macdonald, Computer Teacher, Bernadotte School, Copenhagen, Denmark*

But publishing Web pages is not just a way to broadcast the existence of your school to the world. Web publishing is also a significant classroom learning tool. Central to what students will need to master is how to gather, organize, and present information. Working through an activity that involves organizing a set of links or interrelated pieces of information is directly related to developing analytical thinking skills. Having to gather information from community groups or another class and develop a Web page offers the opportunity to build and refine verbal and written communication skills. Web pages can be the focus for a cultural exchange in which a school in one country teams up with one or more schools in another country to design a collaborative site on a topic of common interest, or as a way of highlighting each nation's history, culture, and diversity.

HINT For additional ideas on developing Web pages in schools, read the online article entitled "Designing School Web Sites to Deliver" from *From Now On Educational Technology Journal* available at **http://fromnowon.org/webdesign.html**. The article offers a good overview of reasons for developing a school Web site. It also includes some very useful links, including a link to the School Web Page Development Guide (**http:// www. massnetworks.org/~nicoley/ schools/**) where you will find detailed ideas for creating Web pages, templates that you can download and adapt for your school, and a great collection of graphics designed just for schools.

Class projects featured on School Web pages can be wide ranging. At Monta Vista High School in Cupertino, California (**http://www.mvhs.fuhsd.org/home.html**), students developed an Internet resources database of useful curriculum materials. Many of the resources they identified were incorporated into Web pages that, in turn, could be used to introduce other students to the Internet. Students involved in the project were expected to locate, evaluate, and describe resources, and to create Internet tutorials and actual lessons, including learning goals, objectives, procedures, and worksheets that a class might use in a computer lab.

While Monta Vista's project may seem to be particularly sophisticated, Web publishing is not just for students in the upper grades. Atlantic View Elementary School posts a Web page developed by a Grade 3/4 class. Topics from these students' Web pages include

- food allergies in children
- winter surfing in the North Atlantic
- Lesley Choyce—local author, musician, publisher, surfer
- Gordon Stobbe, their best-known local fiddler
- report on an in-school performance by Razzmatazz for Kids
- their multicultural folk-dance program
- the participation of some of their students in the Nova Scotia International Tattoo
- autobiographies of the students in the class (Grade 3/4B)
- information about an endangered species that nests in their community.

It is essential to have clear policies and guidelines for school Web pages. Guidelines address technical and design issues as well as questions such as who will contribute to the development of the Web site and how long student work will be kept on the site.

For an overview of school Web issues and an example of a school district policy and a parent permission form for placing student work on the Web, consult the Technology Connection article, "Developing Web Page Policies or Guidelines" at **http://wms.luminet.net/Mary Alice/WebPageGuidlines.**

Figure 6-3

The Cotton Fields project was developed by seven-year-olds at Highland Park Elementary School, Austin, Texas.

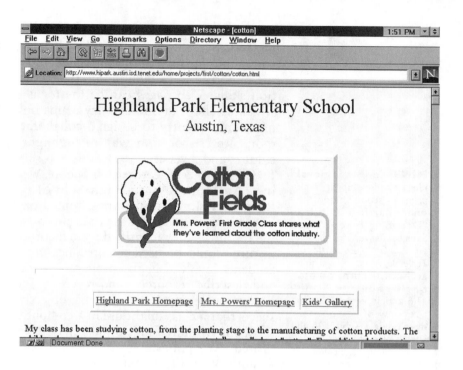

Figure 6-4

This project from Cotton Fields uses a scanned student drawing.

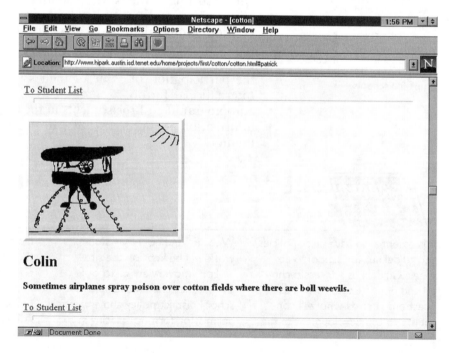

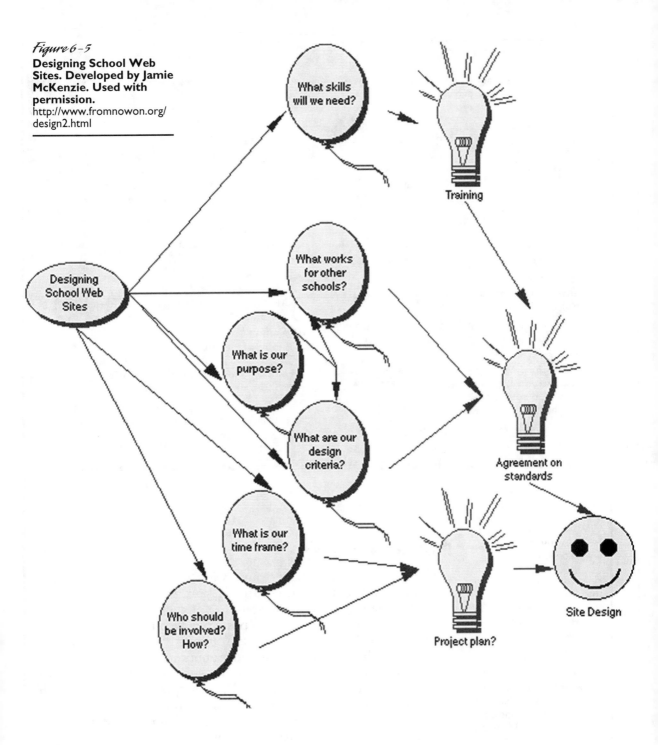

Figure 6-5
Designing School Web Sites. Developed by Jamie McKenzie. Used with permission.
http://www.fromnowon.org/design2.html

What skills will we need?

Training

Designing School Web Sites

What works for other schools?

What is our purpose?

What are our design criteria?

Agreement on standards

What is our time frame?

Who should be involved? How?

Project plan?

Site Design

Tips for Developing School Web Pages

- Think of your Web page first as a communications and public relations tool, and as an information resource second.

- Start small. Develop a Web page of links for a unit of study, or a single page of teacher resources (distribute to teachers on a diskette!).

- Limit what's available at any one time. Use archives to store things as you focus on specific features.

- Don't have too many different things vying for attention: animated .gifs, busy background, many different font changes.

- Don't even think about putting your picture (or the principal's) at the start of your school Web page!

- Style should match content (check out the American Memory Collection: **http://rs6.loc.gov/amhome.html**).

- Think about design! Print Web pages and keep them in a notebook where you can jot down what you like in a Web site and what you don't like.

- Keep the site dynamic. Add new material, and try to develop resources around changing themes. At the same time, try to include something familiar — an established format, consistent banner, etc.

- Develop an archives for older material, in favor of keeping the latest up-front.

- As a general rule, include a brief description with each link you offer. This makes it easier for people to browse your site. It can also save time if access to a machine is an issue.

- When your Web page features something new, print a copy (ideally in color) and post it on a school bulletin board.

- Get others involved! (Kids, teachers, parents, community groups, librarians.) Try to make your site inclusive.

- Use templates for easy, consistent production. Find knowledgeable students to help with more complex tasks.

- Spend some time sampling school sites at Web66: **http://Web66.coled.umn.edu/schools.html**. What do you like? What don't you like? Be sure to register your own school page at Web66.

- Use kids' artwork. Use great art, historical photographs, cave art. Be careful about copyright and seek permission from the student's parents before posting student work on the Web.

- Master the basics of a paint package (Paint Shop Pro or similar graphics package for creating simple graphics).

HINT Use your Web browser to link to the archives site for the WWWedu mailing list: **http://edweb.gsn.org/wwwedu.html**.

Headers are highlighted so that you can quickly find topics of interest. These archives provide an opportunity to tap into an ongoing dialog among teachers who are exploring ways to use the Web in schools. (Even better, you can also simply click on highlighted URLs in a posted message and access the location being discussed. You can also access the archives from the FAQ document.)

Posting Web pages

Although student Web pages can always be accessed as individual files on a local computer, eventually you will want to post your pages for the world to see. If you are not running a server in your own school, it may be possible to post your Web pages on an existing Internet server for little or no cost. You may wish to contact a local university or Internet service provider about hosting your page. You could also use one of several Internet sites that offer posting for schools, including Classroom Web (**http://www.wentworth.com/classweb/**) and Canada's SchoolNet (**http://www.schoolnet.ca**). In Australia, the SchoolsNET site will post home pages for schools (**http://www.schnet.au**). Be wary of commercial agencies that offer free Web page posting. Some will display intrusive advertising to those who visit your page.

HINT Visit the School Web Maker site, which offers basic information about developing school Web sites as well as information on where to post if you don't have a server. **http://edweb.sdsu.edu/ edfirst/SchoolWeb/ SchoolWeb.html**.

Student web projects

A number of resources on the Internet provide a context for students developing Web pages. One example is Global SchoolNet (GSN) (**http://www.gsn.org**), which was originally established in 1984 as FrEDMail. The purpose of this site is to foster the use of telecommunications to promote basic skills (reading, writing, and communications), along with cross-cultural understanding on a global level. Global SchoolNet sponsors a project registry to publicize online projects for schools, as well as several well-designed Internet projects that emphasize student learning.

For the International Cyberfair Contest (**http://www.gsn.org/cf/ index.html**), student teams are invited to develop and publish Web pages in one of eight categories. These categories include Local Leaders, Community Groups and Special Populations, Historical Landmarks, Environmental Awareness, Local Music and Art, making it easy to integrate student Web work into the curriculum. More than 30,000 students from 500 schools in 37 countries have participated in this event. Student projects vary widely. Past entries have ranged from a profile of special populations in Dauphin, Manitoba (**http://www.mbnet.mb.ca/~cdaviso1/cbsummry.html**), to an exploration of local music groups from California's Diablo Valley (**http://cyberfair.gsn.org/woodside**), to a look at the local

Figure 6-6
Environmental Awareness. This project was created by pupils in Vasaövningsskola in Finland.

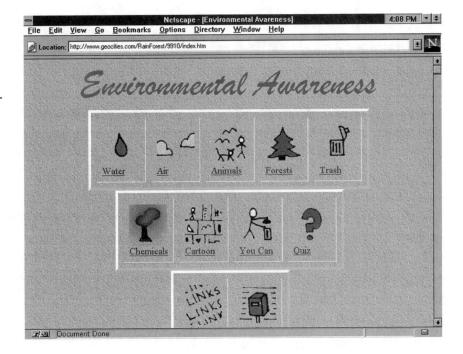

environment from a school in Finland (**http://www.geocities.com/RainForest/9910/index.htm**). One of the most appealing aspects of GSN's Cyberfair is that it motivates students to learn about their own communities.

A similar initiative is ThinkQuest (**http://www.advanced.org/thinkquest/**), which we discussed in Chapter 1. ThinkQuest projects tend to be very sophisticated, reflecting a level of teacher support that may not be available for most student projects. Having your students visit this site to see what has been produced, however, is a good way to motivate them. Your students may have some great ideas of their own about projects that can serve as learning resources for your school. Sample the library of online learning resources created by ThinkQuest student teams at **http://www.advanced.ord/thinkquest/explore/index.html**.

At the Internet Science and Technology Fair (**http://istf.ucf.edu/**), students in middle school and junior high communicate with an online expert to investigate sophisticated technological topics such as AIDS vaccines, soil washing, and semiconductor lasers, and then develop project home pages to capture their research.

The sources listed above provide exciting opportunities for participation, but they can also be used to generate ideas for curriculum-based Web projects. Students and staff at Loogootee Elementary West in Indiana have developed a Web site that features some great student projects. A Grade 2 class at the school studied

HINT You can find out about other opportunities for student projects, many of which include Web page development, at the NickNacks Telecollaborate site: **http://www1.minn.net/~schubert/NickNacks.html**.

Figure 6-7
Fifth-grade students at Fairland Elementary School develop Black history commemorative stamps.

Jean Baptiste Dusable

by Michael

This stamp commemorates Jean Baptiste Dusable. He was the founder of Chicago. Jean was born in Haiti in 1818. He became a fur trader in St. Louis, Missouri. Then Jean moved to Peoria, Illinois, because the British took over St. Louis. The Native Americans help Dusable establish a trading business. During his trading business Jean passed by a place called Eschikagov. So in 1774 he built a cabin there, for his family. Then other people began to move there. The settlement grew and soon became Chicago. That is how Chicago became one of the greatest cities in the U.S.A

The Teacher's Complete & Easy Guide to the Internet

emus; their Web site offers an online quiz that was written by the class, and photographs of the emu eggs waiting to hatch. Third-grade through fifth-grade students developed and posted reports and pictures on endangered animal species. The Loogootee site (**http://www.siec.k12.in.us/~west/west.htm**) also includes steps for designing a curriculum-based Web project and links to other online projects. Fairland Elementary School (**http://www.wam.umd.edu/~toh/Fairland.html**) also posts interesting examples of class projects, including projects done by special needs students. The Fairland site makes available a number of ready-to-use handouts.

> "I just finished a week-long HTML home page project with my eighth graders. We followed a simple recipe that allowed students who had some prior HTML knowledge to forge ahead and add fancier tags. The words were equally important to the coding. Students prewrote what would appear on their page. I noticed far fewer spelling and grammatical errors. The voice and style of their writing was clear. The students were very conscious of the fact that their page might be seen by others even though we do not at this time have Internet connectivity at our middle school. Their enthusiasim was enormous, in part because for them this is *new* information. Students came very early in the morning (7:30 A.M.), worked through their lunch and stayed until 5:30 in the evening to put in extra time. I was exhausted by the end of the week but delighted at the self-directed and collaborative learning that took place."
>
> — *Inez Farrell ionez7@usit.net*

Summing up

The World Wide Web is central to the way in which the Internet is evolving as a tool for learning. Arguably, the Web derives its greatest value as a learning resource from the fact that students and teachers can actively participate in the development of the Web by contributing resources from their own communities and classrooms. For teachers, the ability to develop Web pages will become an increasingly valuable skill.

The chapters that follow describe some additional tools for using the Internet, but likely none of these will match the Web with respect to the impact they will have in the classrooms of today—and tomorrow.

Chapter 7

Communicating Over the Internet

"I think the Internet has the potential to help students realize that they are an integral part of a living, global community. Students in minority cultures can appreciate anew the value of their own culture by seeing it reflected in the interests and questions of others."

— SANDY MCAULEY, SECONDARY PROGRAMS CONSULTANT, BAFFIN DIVISIONAL BOARD OF EDUCATION, NORTHWEST TERRITORIES, CANADA

Although the World Wide Web is an exciting learning technology, some students (and teachers) are almost as enthusiastic about the learning that can happen through electronic mail projects. Electronic mail is a relatively simple technology for sending messages from one computer to another. In schools, students use electronic mail to gather data, connect with experts, communicate with students around the globe, and collaborate on projects. Teachers use electronic mail to keep up to date in areas of professional and personal interest, to exchange ideas and information with colleagues, and to work collaboratively with teachers at a distance. Despite the considerable attention given to the Web by the media, electronic mail is for many the mainstay of the Internet.

This is also an ideal technology for classrooms that have minimal connectivity, such as a single account on the library computer. Through the Internet, with just a simple (even somewhat slow) modem connection and a very basic computer, teachers and students can connect to the world.

Chapter goals

- ■ To provide an overview of electronic mail on the Internet
- ■ To offer an example of how to use an electronic mail software package
- ■ To describe how mailing lists work and provide some examples of lists that would interest teachers
- ■ To explain how newsgroup discussion groups work
- ■ To explore how electronic mail can be used in a classrooom and provide some ground rules for e-mail projects
- ■ To offer some examples of classroom-based electronic mail projects

Electronic mail is the networking vehicle for many Internet inter-classroom projects. You can also use it to communicate with other teachers or subject specialists, to participate in educational discussion groups (listservers), and to subscribe to journals and request articles. You can even use electronic mail to search for and transfer computer files. Despite the many sophisticated tools for accessing information over the Internet, electronic mail is not about information. Rather, it is about human communication. It's a great place for teachers to get started using the Internet. Figure 7-1 shows a typical e-mail message.

If you have not used electronic mail previously, begin by sending messages to yourself to learn the ins and outs of your particular mail software. Try all sorts of variations, including sending attachments. Experiment with setting up a mailing list by entering your

Figure 7-1

A sample e-mail message

```
Message 5/47 KIDSPHERE Mailing List

Date: Tue, 1 Aug 1997 14:41:47 EDT
Subject: Keyboarding Program
To: KIDSPHERE Subscribers
<kidsphere@vms.cis.pitt.edu>
Errors-To: <kidsphere-request@vms.cis.pitt.edu>
Warnings-to: <kidsphere-request@vms.cis.pitt.edu>
Reply-to: <KIDSPHERE@vms.cis.pitt.edu>

Date: Tue, 01 Aug 1997 07:19:10 +0100
From: twinter@ousd.k12.ca.us (Tony Winter)
Subject: Keyboarding Program

Hi Kidsphere,

I am planning to set up a typing program for
grades 4-6 this year in our computer lab and
classrooms. I have been trying to decide on a typ-
ing software program. I am considering three
possibilities. These are Ultra Type, Type! (by
Broderbund), and Type to Learn (Sunburst). I'd
appreciate your recommendations (or other com-
ments).

Tony Winter
Hepburn School
Maplewood, California
```

Communicating Over the Internet

own address a number of times. The advantage of using yourself as a recipient is that you have immediate feedback on whether your procedure worked. After mastering a few basics, you'll be able to communicate electronically with other teachers.

Later, this chapter will explore in detail some of the ways in which teachers can use electronic mail for classroom learning. But first, let's take a broad look at how electronic mail works.

Electronic mail: Overview

To send messages over the Internet, you will need (in addition to a computer that is connected to the Internet) your own Internet mail address and electronic mail software.

Internet mail addresses

If you have purchased an Internet access account from a local service provider, chances are you already have everything you need to send an electronic message. With an Internet account, you will receive, in addition to a place to log on to the Internet, an e-mail address on the Internet computer to which you are connecting. The messages you send out will be identified with this address, and this is the address that others can use to communicate with you. An Internet e-mail address looks something like this:

bscott@uoregon.edu

The format used for addresses on the Internet is essentially:

username@hostname

The first part of this name is the user (you), commonly in some abbreviated form, and sometimes even a number. The second part of the name (after the @ sign) identifies the location of the computer that uses the electronic mail account. Here are some more examples.

anita-gibson@admin.ubc.ca

kwilliam@aol.com

bowenr@sheffield.ac.uk

library@ocicl.ou.utoronto.ca

nhenry@capaccess.org

12345.678@compuserve.com

meyer@educat.hu-berlin.de

If you look at an e-mail address carefully, you can often determine a bit about the location of the account. Following are some clues for reading an e-mail address.

- The final two or three letters in an address constitute the *top-level domain*. In the United States these are commonly descriptive domains that identify the type of institution where the address is located.

Domain	Type
.edu	Educational institution
.com	Commercial organization (used throughout the Internet)
.mil	Military site
.gov	Governmental office
.net	An Internet resource, such as an access provider
.org	Non-commercial organization

- In many instances, an Internet address will end with a two-letter designation for the country in which the account is located.

Domain	Country
.au	Australia
.ca	Canada
.de	Germany
.dk	Denmark
.es	Spain
.fr	France
.il	Israel
.jp	Japan
.ru	Russia
.uk	United Kingdom
.us	United States

- The .us (pronounced "dot U.S.") designation has traditionally not been used in favor of the basic descriptive domains for U.S. addresses, but is becoming more common as elementary and secondary schools connect to the Internet. When the .us appears, it is frequently used in conjunction with a two-letter state code. Here is an example of what an Internet e-mail address could look like for a teacher in Nebraska: **mnichol@esu3.k12.ne.us**

Free e-mail accounts

There are a number of places on the Internet where you can obtain free electronic mail accounts. With a free Web-based electronic mail account, you receive mail messages over the Web, so that you can access mail from a computer in the library and other locations away from your home account. Teachers involved in telecommunications projects may find that free e-mail accounts provide a useful way to manage project mail. Students can obtain individual accounts or you can set up a single account for the project. Web-based mail can also be an advantage if you are currently sharing Internet access with other members of your family. Some services even let you check mail from other e-mail accounts that you may have. The downside is that free e-mail is supported by advertising. In addition, you must be connected to the Internet to manage mail messages. For some teachers the fact that it may be difficult to monitor student accounts is also a concern. Setting up accounts for teams or pairs of students can help to address this issue.

Free electronic mail accounts are available from

Yahoo E-mail: **http://mail.yahoo.com/**
American School Directory: **http://www.asd.com/**
RocketMail: **http://www.rocketmail.com/**
Excite: **http://mailexcite.com**
HotMail: **http://www.hotmail.com/**
Juno: **http://www.juno.com 1-800-654-5866**

Find out about other free e-mail options using the Free E-mail Guide at **http://www.geocities.com/SiliconValley/Vista/8015/ free.html**.

Electronic mail software
Both Netscape (Navigator and Communicator) and Microsoft (Internet Explorer) include an electronic mail feature within their

Figure 7–2

InfoSpace is one resource for finding mailing addresses on the Net.

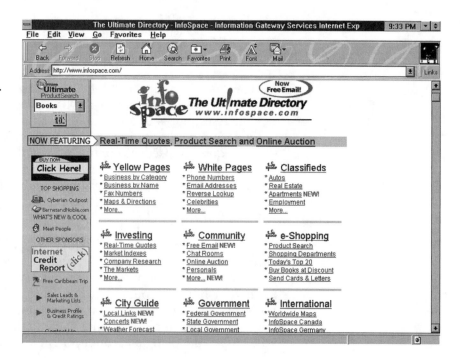

The Teacher's Complete & Easy Guide to the Internet

Finding people on the Net: Use these sources to locate electronic mail addresses, phone numbers, and mailing addresses.

Infospace:
http://www.infospaceinc.com/

Four11:
http://canada411.sympatico.ca/ (Canada)

http://www.Four11.com/ (U.S.)

BigBook: (U.S. addresses including street maps):
http://wwwbigbook.com/

Pitsco's Launch to Finding People
http://www.pitsco.com/p/address.html

Ahoy (Ahoy also looks for home pages.)
http://ahoy.cs.washington.edu:6060 http://ahoy.cs.washington.edu:6060.

HINT Opera (see Chapter 4) lets you set up a link within the software to an electronic mail package of your choice, so, like the browsers with built-in mail packages, the mail function can be called up with a single click.

Internet e-mail packages must be configured with information about your specific mail server. Many products have a wizard-type set-up that will simplify installation; however, you may still need to provide information about your account. You will also need to specify your name and e-mail address. If you are unsure of how to set up your electronic mail software, contact your Internet Service Provider.

browsers. The latest version of each of these browsers offers well-designed, full-featured mail programs. Nevertheless, many people choose to use an electronic mail package that is separate from the browser.

Although the latest offerings from the two corporate giants are very good, many teachers do not have computers that can manage these very large programs.

In a Windows or Macintosh environment, you will have a choice of user-friendly mail packages. The latest versions of many electronic mail programs are designed to work with Web browsers, so that such things as clicking on a URL reference in an electronic mail message will immediately activate your browser. As with Web browsers, you don't have to stick with the product offered by your service provider. A range of options for electronic mail, including downloadable shareware programs, can be found at TUCOWS at **http://www.tucows.com**. Below are some examples of popular electronic mail programs.

Most e-mail programs will allow you to

- send electronic mail to a specified address,
- send one or more carbon copies,
- reply to electronic mail sent to you,
- forward electronic mail,
- set up an address book with "nick names" for addresses you use frequently,
- save messages to a file,
- send enclosures or attachments,
- automatically include a customized signature,
- delete electronic messages, and
- store messages in folders.

POPULAR ELECTRONIC MAIL PROGRAMS

Calipso 2.2	Basic e-mail features. Includes a "bulk mail" feature that will send blind carbon copies (BCC) using a text file of names and addresses.	Available from Micro Computer Systems Inc. at **http://www.mcsdallas.com**
Claris Em@iler 2.0	Runs AppleScripts and handles automated replies.	Available for Macintosh only from Claris **http://claris.com**
Eudora Lite	Very popular shareware package. You can access Andrew Starr's Eudora Site for more information about Eudora: **http://www.amherst.edu/~atstarr/ eudora/eudora.html.**	freeware Available from Qualcomm Inc. at **http://www.eudora.com**
Eudora Pro	Strong mail filter feature and support for multiple e-mail accounts.	Available from Qualcomm Inc. at **http://www.eudora.com**
Juno	This is a bare-bones e-mail client. Its primary recommendation is that it includes a free e-mail service available through dial-up across the U.S.	Available from Juno Online Services 1-800-654-5866 **www.juno.com**
Internet Mail	Basic features, although the interface design is not as effective as that of other packages.	Bundled with Internet Explorer 3.0 **http://microsoft.com**
Netscape Mail	Basic features with an easy-to-use interface.	Integrated with Netscape 3.0. **http://www.netscape.com**
Netscape Messenger	Basic mail functions along with newer features, such as HTML mail and the ability to search messages.	Bundled with Netscape's latest browser, Netscape Communicator **http://www.netscape.com**
Outlook Express	Supports multiple accounts and will filter messages to a specific account. Also supports HTML tagged messages.	Bundled with Internet Explorer 4.0 (Available for Windows 95 or newer.) **http://microsoft.com**
Pegasus Mail 2.53	Well-designed and solidly established electronic mail package. Nice "noticeboard" feature lets you post notices for viewing on a network. Includes the ability to annotate mail you have received.	freeware (printed manual available for US$35) Available from David Harris at **http://www. pegasus.usa.com**

Let's look at how these basic functions work for Netscape Mail, currently one of the most commonly used programs for sending and receiving electronic mail. In addition, you will find that the features detailed below are available for most other mail software programs. Use the Help function as well as online resources to explore the range of features available in your own mail software program.

HINT Many useful links to information about electronic mail software, as well as listservs, newsgroups, and other types of online communications are available from Infinite Ink's Mail News and General Messaging page at **http:// www.ii.com/internet/messaging/** and from John December's Computer Mediated Com-munications site at **http://www.december.com/net/tools/cmc.html**.

Using Netscape Mail

To access Netscape Mail, open the Netscape Navigator browser and click on **Window | Netscape Mail.** You may be prompted for your mail password the first time mail is accessed within an online session. After you log on, new mail messages will be automatically downloaded. You can click on **Cancel** in the logon screen if you don't want to access your messages immediately.

The most frequently used electronic mail functions can be quickly accessed using the toolbar at the top of the Netscape Mail screen. Netscape provides tool-bar (one-click) access that will allow you to

- get new mail
- delete a message
- send a new message
- respond to a message (sender only)
- respond to a message (sender and all recipients)
- forward a message
- move to the previous message
- move to the next message
- print the currently highlighted message.

Sending an e-mail message

1. From within Netscape's mail screen, call up Netscape's message template by clicking on the toolbar icon for a mail message or select **File | New Message** from the menu bar.
2. Key in an Internet mailing address in the window labeled **Mail To:.** If you are just getting started, you can practice by sending messages to yourself.
3. Place your cursor in the **Subject** window and type in a brief subject line. Subject lines will identify messages on the message index screen, so always include a meaningful subject line.
4. Type a message in the space provided below the addressing information.
5. Click on **Options** on the message screen and note the choices for immediate delivery or deferred delivery. Choosing deferred delivery will allow you to compose messages offline and send a batch of messages when you log on. It is not necessary to access the Options screen for each message. Your selection will remain in place as a default until you change it.

6. Click on the **Send** button to send the message. If you have select-
   ed the deferred delivery option, you will need to Click on **File |
   Send Messages** in Outbox to complete delivery.

Receiving messages

1. Check for incoming messages by clicking on the **Netscape | Mail
   File** menu. Select **Get New Mail**.
2. The POP (Post Office Protocol) mail server will request your
   password the first time you request mail after logging on to the
   system. Input your password and click **OK**.
3. Incoming messages are downloaded into your **Inbox** folder. You
   can read your incoming mail by double-clicking on individual
   messages listed in the inbox.

Forward and Reply

1. Ensure that the message you want to reply to is displayed in the
   message viewing frame. Click on **Message** in the menu bar.
2. Note the range of choices for forwarding and responding to messages. The **Reply to All** option will send your response to the
   originator of a message and to other recipients. **Forward Quoted**
   will allow you to add your own comments to a forwarded message. **Forwarded** only messages will be sent to the recipient as a
   mail attachment.
3. You can also use the toolbar icons to respond to or forward a
   message. If you are unsure of how to interpret pictures on the
   toolbar icons, change the icons to text on the **Options |
   Preferences | Appearance** frame.

Storing messages in folders

1. To set up a new folder, click on **File | New Folder**. Next, key in a
   name for the folder.
2. To move messages from your Inbox to individual folders you
   create, click on **Message Move**. Select the folder where you want
   to store the message. Messages can easily be moved from one
   folder to another. You can move a deleted message from the
   Trash into another folder as long as you have not disposed of the
   message. You can also flag messages individually by clicking on
   the left-most dot adjacent to the subject line in the message list.
   Use the edit option to select flagged messages for moving them
   into a folder as a group rather than one at a time.

Deleting messages

1. Highlight the message. Click on the **Trash** icon. This moves the
   message to the **Trash** folder.
2. Don't forget to empty the trash occasionally. Click on **File |
   Empty Trash** Folder.

Tech Talk

You will find that sometimes
messages "bounce" (can't be
delivered). When this happens,
you'll receive a message from
Mailer-Daemon or Postmaster.
The subject line will start with
"Returned mail." If you look
carefully at the header information, you may be able to determine exactly why the message
bounced. *Host Unknown* means
that the computer address cannot be reached. Often that's just
because of a typo you may then
quickly spot. Another possibility
is *User Unknown*. Again, this
could be a typo, but it could also
be that the person you are trying
to reach is no longer at that
location. Occasionally you might
encounter network problems.
For example, a server could be
out of commission. Or you
might run into a "traffic jam,"
which occurs when many systems are set up to resend messages automatically over several
days before giving up.

Address Book

By setting up an address book, you can avoid having to type in a complete address each time you send a message. Instead, you can simply type the nickname, and Netscape Mail will associate this with the correct address.

1. If you have received a message from someone whose name you want to add to the address book, highlight the message, then click on **Message | Add to Address Book**.
2. Fill in a short **Nick Name** for the entry. Once you have added a name to the **Address Book**, you can address messages simply by filling in the designated **Nick Name** in the message **Mail To:** window. You can also select names directly from the **Address Book** by clicking on the **Address Book** icon from within the mail message template.
3. You can edit, add, and delete addresses from the **Window | Address Book** screen.
4. Create mailing lists using the **Item | Add List** menu selection. Once you have set up a mailing list folder, you can use your mouse to drag names from your general list into the mailing list. Set up mailing lists for school committees, parents, and student projects.
5. To send a message to multiple addresses on a mailing list, highlight the list name in your address book. Then click on **File | Mail New Message**.

Signature files

Signature files are automatically appended to outgoing messages. They can lend a bit of distinctiveness to your messages. Many people choose to use humorous or thought-provoking quotes as part of their signatures. Some people also provide their phone number, address, and fax number.

1. Set up a signature file using your word processor, and save the file as *ASCII text* (see Attachments).
2. In Netscape, access **Preferences | Identity**. Use the browse button to locate and insert the subdirectory path and name for the file you have just saved.

Figure 7-3

Signatures lend a distinctive touch to messages and tell something about the sender.

```
Mary Lam, violinist (marylam@aol.com)

    _____    _____
   /      (_)       _____888
  ( {        _   %    _____$&$&$
   _____( )_____/                  888
```

Attachments

This feature enables you to send files that have been prepared earlier in a word-processing application. With a single Internet connection, the **Attachments** feature may be the easiest way to have your students send messages. It's best to avoid attaching messages that include word-processing codes. You can prevent this by saving a file as a text-only (.txt or ASCII) file or rich text format (.rtf), which will preserve basic formatting, such as bold lettering. Usually this just involves investigating the various Save options in your word-processing package. With the text file format, you don't have to worry that the recipients will be unable to read your message because they don't use the same software as you. If you do want to preserve the word-processed format, try sending a test attachment to your recipient. Most newer word-processing packages will recognize files from other popular word processors.

1. To attach a document to an outgoing message, click on the **Attachment** button from within the message template.
2. Select **Attach File**.
3. Select the file to attach from the Windows file listing. Then click on O.K. Repeat the process for additional files that you want to attach.

Tech Talk

Binary files (such as word-processed files) must be coded before being sent as part of an electronic mail message.

Common formats for coding files for transmission include MIME, Uuencode, and Binhex. Netscape and Internet Explorer will code files automatically, but if you are using an older mail package, it may be necessary to select one of the above coding options. You can use MIME as a default, but try one of the others if your recipient is not able to successfully decode the message. Word-processed messages can also be converted to text before sending. You can find out more about file encoding and decoding at The Cross Platform Page: **http://vtginc.com/ebennett/xplat. comp.html**.

Listservers: Discussion groups via e-mail

Joining a listserver (or listserv) is an immediate way to connect with other teachers who are using the Internet. To join a listserver, you need only basic knowledge of how to send an e-mail message and specific information on how to subscribe to any given list.

What is a listserver?

Listservers are special-interest discussion groups available through the Internet. Members post messages, and listserv software redistributes them to all members of a given discussion group. To participate, simply send a subscription message ("subscribe <listserver name> <your name>") to the listserver address (e.g., listserv@msu.edu). Once you've subscribed, you will begin receiving

The Teacher's Complete & Easy Guide to the Internet

messages from the list. You will be able to contribute your ideas and thoughts directly to the group, too, by using the group e-mail address (e.g., edtech@msu.edu).

The term *listserver* is often abbreviated *listserv*. Listserv is the original program developed to handle mailing lists. Today, a number of other programs, such as Listprocessor, Mailbase, Mailserv, and Majordomo, can also be used to manage mailing lists. Because there are variations on the Listserv software, the commands that you send to a mailing list can vary. For example, Majordomo requests your e-mail address, rather than firstname, lastname in the message area of a subscription request. To find out which commands pertain to a given list, contact the listserv address and send a one-word message: *help*.

HINT Once you have subscribed to a listserv, you will receive important introductory information from the list owner. *Save this message!* It may be useful to print the message and keep it in a binder. Whenever you want to suspend your subscription, you will want exact information on how to *unsubscribe*.

Some discussion groups for educators

Here is just a sampling of discussion groups for educators that are available on the Internet. For an extensive list of education listservers, check out Education E-Mail Discussion Lists and Electronic Journals at **http://edweb.gsn.org/lists.html** and Mailing Lists for Teachers at **http://www.kli.org/jquick/mailinglists.html**.

For mailing lists with a scholarly flavor, consult the Directory of Scholarly and Professional E-Conferences by Diane Kovacs, available from **http://n2h2.com/KOVACS/**. The directory includes references to many K–12 education lists, such as **k12.ed.art**. Archives for a number of education discussion groups are available from the AskERIC Education Listserv Archive at **http://ericir.syr.edu/Virtual/Listserv_Archives/**.

ArtsEdNet Talk

Arts education discussion. Archives available from:
http://www.artsednet.getty.edu/ArtsEdNet/Connections/index.html.
Subscription message should read:
subscribe artsednet.
Subscribe to:
artsednet-request@pub.getty.edu

CREWRT-L

Creative writing — how and why creative writing is being taught.
Subscribe to:
listserv@umcvmb.missouri.edu

Edtech

A discussion group for using technology in education. An excellent place to begin appreciating the potential of technology. Subscribe to:
listserv@msu.edu

HINT You can receive hundreds of interesting publications via electronic mail. Although many are also available on the World Wide Web, it may be more convenient to subscribe to an "e-zine" so that new issues regularly arrive in your e-mail box. To find out about many different electronic publications that you can subscribe to or access over the Web, visit John Labovitz's E-Zine list at **http://www.meer.net/~johnl/e-zine-list/.**

You might also want to sample the newest Scout publication called the K.I.D.S. (Kids Identifying and Discovering Sites), which is published by K-12 students as a resource to other K-12 students. You can find out more about the *Scout Report* and K.I.D.S. at **http://scout.cs.wisc.edu/scout/report/indextxt.html.**

Ednet
A discussion group for educational networking. Subscribe to:
listserv@lists.umass.edu.

hilites
Projects ideas, activities, and resources from Global SchoolNet. Subscribe to:
majordomo@gsn.org

IECC (International E-mail Classroom Connections)
A key resource for finding classroom keypals and e-mail projects. Subscribe to:
iecc-request@stolaf.edu

InClass
A Canadian source for educational discussion. Topics focus on subjects of interest to middle and high school teachers. Subscribe to:
listproc@schoolnet.ca

Internet_Invitations-l
Developed for teachers in British Columbia. This is another source for Internet project and keypal information. Subscribe to:
listpro@etc.bc.ca

K12-webdev
A mailing list for K–12 Web site developers.
list@mail.lr.k12.nj.us

K12admin
A discussion group for those interested in school administration. Subscribe to:
listserv@listserv.syr.edu

K12assess-l
Discussion group on assessment in K-12 Subscribe to:
mailserv@lists.cua.edu

K12Opps
Informative list with sites, discussion, and projects.
majordomo@gsn.org

K12small
A forum for education in small or rural schools. Subscribe to:
listserv@uafsysb.uark.edu

Kidlink

The KIDLINK listserv distributes official information about the Kidlink project. Subscribe to:
   listserv@nodak.edu

Kidlit-L

A forum for the discussion of children's literature. Subscribe to:
   listserv@bingvmb.cc.binghamton.edu

Kidsphere

Extremely popular list for elementary and secondary school teachers. Discussions range from queries about marking software, to great Internet project ideas, to instructions on how to make bubbles. The volume of mail on this list tends to be high, but it is a stimulating place to begin using the Internet as a professional tool. Subscribe to:
   kidsphere-request@vms.cis.pitt.edu

Learn-Net

Discussion for new Internet users. Subscribe to:
   learn-net-request@iastate.edu

LM_Net

Busy list focusing on school library media interests. Subscribe to:
   listserv@listserv.syr.edu

LRN-Ed

Support and information for K-12 teachers. Subscribe to:
   listserv@listserv.syr.edu

Middle-L (Middle School)

A discussion group for teachers involved with the middle grades. Subscribe to:
   listserv@postoffice.cso.uiuc.edu

Network_Nuggets-L

Find out about new Net resources. Subscribe to:
   listproc@etc.bc.ca

SchoolNet

General educational focus. One of a number of SchoolNet lists. Subscribe to:
   listproc@schoolnet.ca

SNEtalk-L
General discussion in the area of special needs education. Subscribe to:
>   listproc@schoolnet.carleton.ca

Speced-l
Special education list. Subscribe to:
>   listserv@uga.cc.uga.edu

TESLK-12
Teaching English as a second language in K–12. Subscribe to:
>   listserv@cunyvm.cuny.edu.

Tag-L
Talented and gifted education. Subscribe to:
>   listserv@listserv.nodak.edu

Teacher2Teacher
Teacher discussion, also available as an online forum from
>   http://www.teachnet.com/

Subscribe to:
>   majordomo@teachnet.com

Webtalk
For teachers attempting to develop Web sites and use the Web in their classrooms.
>   majordomo@teachers.net

WWWedu
World Wide Web in education. Archives available from
>   http://sunsite.unc.edu/edweb/wwwedu.html.

Subscribe to:
>   listproc@ready.cpb.org

> "I joined the listserv Kidsphere, and that has opened many projects on various networks to me. Choosing listservs, group conferences, and newsgroups establishes relationships with others who have similar objectives and focus."
>
> — *Stephanie Stevens, Teacher, San Francisco, California, U.S.A.*

HINT A few very busy listserv discussion groups are also made available as newsgroups. Accessing a group as a newsgroup rather than as a listserv keeps your mailbox from filling up with too many messages. Newsgroups are discussed later in this chapter.

Finding other e-mail discussion lists
In addition to subscribing to some general education lists, such as Edtech or Kidsphere, you'll probably also want to locate some lists for specific subject areas, such as biology or geography. You can use the following techniques to find out about many more mailing lists.

- **World Wide Web access**
  Web sources for information about mailing lists include:

HINT Use this resource to find out more about e-mail, including how to start your own mailing list and how to deal with un-solicited e-mail: Everything E-mail at **http://every-thingemail.net/**.

Liszt: **http://www.liszt.com/** (over 24,00 lists)

Tile.Net: **http://www.tile.net/tile/listserv/index.html** (includes lists grouped by host country)

- **E-mail access**

To locate many more lists with an educational focus, as well as lists for other topics, send the following message to **listserv@list-serv.net**

LIST GLOBAL/topic
Sending just the message <list global> without the qualifier (/topic) will retrieve an extensive list of lists.

Newsgroups

For some people, one of the most exciting resources on the Internet are newsgroups. Through newsgroups (or Usenet), you can gain access to over 13,000 discussion groups on subjects ranging from fine arts to outer space. Messages from newsgroups are not sent directly to your mailbox. Instead, messages are posted centrally and you can access recent postings using a newsreader program.

Unfortunately, newsgroups are not an ideal classroom application. Some deal with adult, frivolous, or unsavory subjects, and most groups are unmoderated, so that no one screens messages before they are posted.

This is not to discourage teachers from allowing students to access Usenet newsgroups. However, you should be aware of potential problems and have a good idea in advance about how you want students to use these groups. Newsgroup science discussions or discourse around political issues can stimulate ideas and sharpen students' critical thinking skills.

You will undoubtedly want to access some of these groups in pursuing your own professional and personal interests. Newsgroups for teachers can be a valuable source of ideas. Also, they are less cumbersome than listservs, since messages are posted centrally rather than to your personal mailbox.

Some newsgroups are also available as listserv mailing lists, but many people prefer to access these discussions as newsgroups to avoid having to deal with excess e-mail. You might want to subscribe to listservs for one or two discussion groups that you are keenly interested in and opt for newsgroups for everything else. (Not all listservs are available as newsgroups. Also, there are many newsgroups that won't be available as listserv mailing lists.)

You can access newsgroups by using a newsreader such as WinVn or Free Agent. You can also use the newsreader feature incorporated into your Web browser. Netscape, Internet Explorer, and Opera include a news reader.

Tech Talk

Newsreaders must be set up to access newsgroups from a particular news server. Most often your ISP will provide access to news groups and provide you with the correct settings. In Netscape, the Preferences menu offers an option for configuring Mail and News. The Internet server address for your newsserver should be inserted in the News (NNTP) Server window.

PERSONAL FAVORITES

Use this page to make notes on your own favorite listservs.

Listname: _____

Description: _____

Subscribe to: _____

Listname: _____

Description: _____

Subscribe to: _____

Listname: _____

Description: _____

Subscribe to: _____

Listname: _____

Description: _____

Subscribe to: _____

Listname: _____

Description: _____

Subscribe to: _____

Listname: _____

Description: _____

Subscribe to: _____

Listname: _____

Description: _____

Subscribe to: _____

Newsreaders will let you select for easy viewing those groups that you are most interested in. The newsreader will allow you to view, save, and respond to messages.

Here are some groups of interest to teachers.

alt.education.disabled
alt.education.distance
K12.ed.comp.literacy (computer literacy and applications in the classroom)
K12.ed.tag (for teachers of talented and gifted students)
K12.ed.math
K12ed.soc-studies
K12.ed.art
K12.ed.health-pe (for teachers of health and physical education)
K12 ed.music
K12 ed.business
K12.ed.life-skills
K12.ed.science
K12.ed.special (for teachers of special needs students)
K12.chat.elementary (general bulletin board for youngsters, including keypal listings)
K12.chat.teacher

A number of services will let you "search the news." These are useful for picking up general comments about a topic or finding a resource. Use your Web browser to try the following news search resources. At Deja News use the Interest Finder to search for newsgroups by name.

Deja News: http://www.dejanews. com/
HotBot: http://www.hotbot.com/
Alta Vista: http://altavista.digital. com/

You might consider subscribing to the Global SCHLnet Newsgroup Service. This is a service of the Global SCHLnet Foundation, formerly known as FredMail. FredMail was a well-established conferencing network for elementary and secondary schools. The current Newsgroup Service provides access to listservs and newsgroups that are of most interest to schools and delivers them to a central conferencing area on your network. A modest cost is involved, but you can get a free ninety-day trial subscription. Check this site on the World Wide Web for details:
    http://www.gsh.org/gsn/gsn/schl/index.html.

Accessing Newsgroups
Although this section describes how to access the news using Netscape, other browsers offer a newsreader feature as well. The

steps described below provide a general overview of the procedure for viewing newsgroups.

1. To access news discussion groups in Netscape, click on **Window | Netscape News**. Your default newsserver should be listed as a folder on the left-hand side of the screen.
2. Select the folder, then select the menu item **Options | Show All Newsgroups**. Double click on the folder to view the list of available newsgroups.
3. A list of individual newsgroups along with a number designating the number of unread messages should appear on the left-hand side of your screen. To access conference messages, highlight the name of the newsgroup you want to read. Current messages will be loaded from the server and displayed on the right-hand side of the screen. Note that newsgroup messages are organized by "thread," that is, messages dealing with the same topic are grouped together.
4. Once messages have downloaded from the server, you can now read and respond to them in the same way you would read and respond to electronic mail. Use the **File | New News Message** or the **To: News** button from the news screen to initiate a message to the currently highlighted group.
5. Use **Message | Post Reply** to respond to the whole group or **Message | Mail Reply** to respond individually to the originator of a message.
6. Subscribe to groups you are interested in by clicking on the box adjacent to the name of the group. Messages from these groups will automatically download when you access newsgroups from the server.

Tech Talk

To access an alternative news service in addition to that provided by your ISP, configure a Windows-based newsreader (such as Free Agent) to access one of the public newsservers. Follow these steps:

1. Use your Web browser to download the Free Agent (Windows) newsreader from **http://www.forteinc.com/ agent/ freagent.htm**.

2. Find a public (free) news server near you. There are many all over the world. Find them at **http://www. jammed.com/~newzbot/**.

3. Configure the Free Agent software with one of the public news server addresses. Be sure to select a server with a substantial number of active newsgroups.

HINT Usenet groups for newcomers

news.announce. newusers A good place to learn about Usenet

news.answers Subscribe to this group to access frequently asked questions (FAQs)

alt.internet.services FAQs plus lots of good information about Internet services

Finding out more about Usenet news

You can find out more about Usenet news at the **Usenet Info Center Launch Pad** at **http://sunsite.unc.edu/usenet-i/**. To find out about Usenet newsgroups, send an electronic mail message to **liszter@bluemarble.net** with *news "keyword"* in the body of the message (no subject). The keyword should be the subject of your choice. You can access a list of education newsgroups through EdWeb at **http://edweb.gsn.org/usenets.html**. Once you have identified a newsgroup of interest, click on a link to activate your newsreader, or sample recent messages using HotBot at **http://www. hotbot.com** or Deja News at **http://www.dejanews. com**.

FAQs

FAQs (Frequently Asked Questions) are a great way to get the "facts" about a wide range of topics, including how to use the Internet. You will find FAQs for many different newsgroups at: **http://www.cis.ohio-state.edu/ hypertext/faq/usenet/top.html** and at **ftp://rtfm.mit.edu/pub/faqs/**. Originally, FAQs were associated specifically with newsgroup discussions, but these days FAQ is used to refer to basic information about a topic. Try using one of the heavy-duty search engines, such as AltaVista or HotBot and use FAQ as a keyword along with a topic of interest. Visit the FAQ Finder at **http://ps.superb.net/FAQ/**.

Netiquette: Internet etiquette for students using e-mail

DON'T type your e-mail message all in capital letters. This is considered the electronic equivalent of YELLING AT SOMEONE!

DO use meaningful subject lines on your messages. This helps the recipient to sort through messages quickly or delete those that might not be of interest.

DO try to keep your message to only one subject. This allows readers to decide quickly whether they need to read the message in full. Secondary subjects are easy to miss if the first topic being discussed is not of interest.

DO sign your message with your name, institution, and e-mail address. Not all mail systems allow the reader to see the address in the header of the message. Many e-mail packages will let you set up a signature file that can easily (or automatically) be attached to outgoing mail.

DON'T send short, unnecessary messages to groups (e.g., "I agree!). This increases traffic on the Internet and clutters mailboxes.

DON'T reply to a whole group when only an individual reply is warranted. Be sure to check to see

where a message has been sent from before activating the "reply" function. Some embarrassing personal messages have inadvertently been posted to several hundred people.

DO respect the character of individual newsgroups. After joining a group, follow the messages for a week or two before jumping in with your own comments—particularly if you intend to take issue with the comments someone else has made.

DO use emoticons, or smileys :-). Smileys are used to convey the tone of voice that is absent in e-mail.

Online forums

In addition to listservers and newsgroups, a growing number of discussion groups are published on the Web. These may be called online forums, message boards, or online conferences. You can review current messages and post replies directly on the Web. The downside to forums is that you need to be online to view messages, and posted messages may be quite out of date if a forum is not particularly active. Try these forums:

Teacher Talk at
http://www.mightymedia.com/talk/working.htm

Educator's Forum at
http://www.education-world.com/netforum/

TalkCity Education Center at
http://www.talkcity.com/educenter/

Teacher2Teacher at
http://www.teachnet.com/

Sympatico Forums (These include Teaching and Learning and Ask an Expert Teacher forums) at
http://forums.sympatico.ca

Discovery Channel School Forum at
   http://school.discovery.com/ forum/index.html.

PedagoNet at
   http://www.pedagonet.com/wwwboard/wwwboard.html

Find out about other online conference sites at the Loogootee
Elementary West Teacher Chat page at

   http://www.siec.k12.in.us/~west/edu/chat.htm, HotBot
   http://www.hotbot.com/partners/forumone.html, and at
   ForumOne, http://www/forumone.com/.

Links to e-mail projects and keypal sources are available from these
sites:

GSN Project Registry at
   http://www.gsn.org/pr/index.html.

Classroom Connect Teacher Contact Database at
   http://www.classroom.net/classroom/teachcontact/

NickNacks Telecollaborate at
   http://www1.minn.net:80/~schubert/NickNacks.html#anchor10
   0100

Classroom Connect Teacher Contact Database at
   http://www.classroom.net/classroom/teachcontact/

Pitsco KeyPals at
   http://www.keypals.com/p/keypals.html

Pitsco's Ask an Expert at
   http://www.askanexpert.com/askanexpert/

The Intensive American Language Center at
   http://www.ialc.wsu.edu/Class/eIALC/eresources.html.

e-Mail Classroom Exchange at
   http://www.iglou.com/xchange/ece/ index.html

GETTING STARTED

... with an E-mail Class Project

Guidelines for teachers

Classroom projects built around electronic mail are one of the
principal ways that the Internet is being used in schools. These
projects can range from a simple exchange of personal messages
to sophisticated research and data collection.

The following guidelines can form the basis for many types of e-mail projects. (Be sure to also review the general guidelines for planning a project presented in Chapter 2.) Think of these steps as a framework around which to build your specific project.

Step 1: Establish the scope of the project.
Here are some key questions to consider:

- Will each student have a keypal, or will the class as a group compose messages for transmitting to another class?
- If each student is to have a keypal, will the students all be in the same class, or from different locations? (Note: Collaborating with another class as a group is probably the easiest way to manage student communications.)
- Will your students' keypals be located in another state, province, or country?
- When will the project begin?
- Do you want to establish connectivity based on a particular project or theme (such as global ecology)?
- Do you want the correspondence between students to include specific learning objectives, such as research or data collection?

Step 2: Establish time frames.
Be specific about project phases and deadlines.

Step 3: Advertise your project.
You can use one or more listservs, such as IECC (International Electronic E-mail Connections), K-12 Opportunities, or SchoolNet. You can also post on a more targeted list, such as Middle-L, or a math teachers' discussion group for a project with a math component. Post at least eight weeks in advance. You may need to post more than once. You can also register your project at the Global SchoolNet Registry, a central resource for project posting, at **http://www.gsn.org/pr/index.html**.

Step 4: Communicate formally with the other teachers involved.
Thank them for their participation and state exactly what you hope will be accomplished with the exchange of letters. Be sure to explain any specific instructions you would like followed. This is particularly important if the e-mail exchanges are to be integrated with a data collection project.

Step 5: Ensure that your own students are familiar with the procedures for sending electronic mail.
Posting specific instructions near the computer will help students learn the steps involved. Have them practice sending

teaching tip

A good resource for helping your students learn about effective online communication is "A Beginner's Guide to Effective E-mail," available from **http://www.web-foot.com/ advice/email.top.html**

messages to one another, and walk them through any specific skills they will need, such as saving word-processed files as text or uploading files. Don't forget to cover netiquette, acceptable use, and safety on the Net.

Step 6: Discuss the project with your students.
Encourage them to contribute ideas on how to make it a success. Remind them in advance that they won't all receive responses at the same rate, and explain some of the reasons why messages can be delayed, such as limited access to a computer or occasional network problems.

Step 7: As participants are identified, prepare a reference sheet.
The reference sheet will list who is communicating with whom, along with relevant e-mail addresses. This will be a great help if messages are returned because of incorrect addressing or if a student loses a keypal's address. Post the list and have students check off when their messages have been sent and a response received.

Ten tips for success with e-mail projects

1. Post a list of safety and netiquette do's and don'ts.
2. Have students practice sending messages to one another.
3. Aim for short, frequent messages.
4. Use a classroom map to track where messages are being sent from.
5. Seek out new keypals for any students who are not getting responses after sending two or three messages.
6. Establish time limits for composing student messages, especially if computer time is limited. Also, establish a policy for how long messages will be left on the system before being deleted (e.g., messages could be deleted once a reply has been received).
7. For more complex projects, consider having students work with partners or in small groups.
8. Use helpers, such as parent volunteers or older students.
9. Respond right away to those who offer to participate in your project, whether or not you are able to include them. Those who will be included may wish to seek other projects if participation in yours is limited.
10. Review educator Ron Corio's FAQ, "Regarding E-mail Projects" (use your Web browser to access **http://www.nyu.edu/pages/hess/docs/ronfaq.html**).

Project Ideas

Student Keypals

Learning outcomes
- Students will exchange messages with other students around the globe.

Grade level: 4–12

Getting started
- Send your requests for keypals to IECC (International Electronic E-mail Connections), Kidsphere, SchoolNet, or InClass. Or access and register your project at the IECC World Wide Web site at **http://www.stolaf.edu/network/iecc/**. You will also find a range of keypal sources at Pitsco's Keypal's site at **http://www. keypals.com/p/wwwsites.html**.
- Specify the focus, such as French-language exchange or messaging related to a particular project.

Extending: Snail-mail exchange
Using "snail-mail" can add texture and excitement to an electronic mail exchange, especially if you lack the equipment necessary to scan and upload photos and artwork.

Here are some ideas for a snail-mail exchange:

- Have students exchange class pictures, brochures, school newspapers, or travel brochures.

- Students can create drawings of their homes or neighborhoods and exchange them. Use the pictures as the basis for a classroom discussion about cultural differences.

- Have students create and exchange pictures around a theme, such as holidays, Earth Day, world peace, or helping the poor. Use these pictures as a starter for a class discussion of the chosen topic. The same topic can be used as the basis for the students' electronic messaging or reports.

- Students can select and exchange stories from their local newspapers. Deciding which stories best reflect the students' community can be an interesting class exercise.

If your computer system allows you to create sound files, consider attaching a verbal message to an electronic mail message. This can be particularly enjoyable for younger students; however, do not let the vocal message replace the text message, since composing text messages helps develop writing skills.

Project Ideas

Introducing Friends

This is an easy and interesting project for those new to electronic mail. Students interview a friend and send their interviews via e-mail to students in another class. Then the students receiving the messages respond by introducing themselves. Invite other classes to participate using one of the listservers, or simply co-ordinate with another teacher in your school or another local school.

Learning outcomes
- Students will gain skill in interviewing, writing, and presenting information.
- Students will learn to send e-mail messages.

Grade level: 4–12

Getting started
- Explain to the students that you will be meeting another group of students — but online, rather than in person.
- As a class, brainstorm a simple interview format that students might use with their interview partners. Typical questions might include likes and dislikes, unusual interests or talents, or humorous anecdotes.

Developing
- Allow class time for student pairs to take turns interviewing each other.
- Assist students to use their word processors to write their introductions. Here is one possible format for students to use in developing their messages.

  Paragraph 1: Describe what your friend looks like, and a bit about what he or she likes and dislikes.
  Paragraph 2: Tell about your friend's interests and opinions.
  Paragraph 3: Write an amusing story about your friend.
  Paragraph 4: Describe your friend's strengths and talents.

- If individual student accounts are available for both classes, have students send their introductions to individual students from the other class. Alternatively, students can send or submit their interviews to you for forwarding as a batch to the other class teacher.

- Complete the exchange by having the students in the class receiving the introductions send a reply in which they introduce themselves using a similar format.

Variations

- Devise a template with a list of interview questions. Send them to individual students using electronic mail. Have each student respond to the questions and send the replies back to you. Post or re-distribute the responses for the rest of the class to read.
- Use the format from the Introducing Friends project, but select a partner class from another country. Remind students that their interviews should include some information about the country in which they live. When the message exchange has been completed, have the class discuss some of the things they have learned about the other country from reading messages they receive.

"I have been teaching LD kids for thirty years and have found the computer itself to be the best thing that ever happened for my students' writing. They are much more willing to sit and write, and make corrections because it is so easy. We are using the Internet for keypalling. The students jump at the chance to write someone from another country or state because it gives them a chance to open up and write freely about things they care about."

— *Cliff McCallum, Teacher, Seneca Junior High School, Holbrook, New York, U.S.A.*

Project Ideas

E-mail Surveys and Questionnaires

In this project, students develop a questionnaire based on the topic of personal "favorites."

Learning outcomes
- Students will develop and exchange electronic questionnaires.
- Students will incorporate an existing file into an e-mail message and/or forward a message.

Grade level: 4–8

Getting started
- Have your students discuss and list possible "favorites" for discussion, for example:
  - favorite season
  - favorite color
  - favorite subject in school
  - favorite TV show
  - favorite book
  - favorite place to visit
  - favorite music group
  - favorite food
  - favorite movie
  - favorite sport.

Developing
- Develop a questionnaire listing the selected questions. You can provide an electronic copy of the list to each of your own students; they, in turn, may send the file to each of their keypals. Students will enjoy comparing the responses they receive.

Variation
- Older students may wish to develop a questionnaire focusing on a research topic, such as a survey of students' leisure-time activities, their attitudes about violence on television, or their recycling habits. Suitable topics will flow from curriculum areas.

Extending

- Use the data collected in this project to build a database of responses. Plan in advance how to formulate the questions to simplify data input. Short-answer and multiple-choice responses will be easier to tally than open-ended responses.
- Using database software, collate and analyze the results of the surveys in a math or science lesson.

"E-mail is and will always be the most powerful tool for educators. While it's nice for my students to access information from Web sites, the real power is their being able to contact others in their search. For example, my fourth grade students will soon be looking for information related to gold prospecting. I have found Web sites that have good information, but more importantly, from these sites I've been able to contact gold prospectors who have enthusiastically agreed to field any questions my students may have."

— *Gary Quiring (1995, December 21) "Benefits of Web/E-mail,"*
International E-Mail Classroom Connections.

Project Ideas

Exchanging Research Projects

Learning outcomes
- Using the library and the Internet, students will research a country.
- Students will conduct an online interview (using e-mail) with a student from the country they have chosen to research.
- Students will prepare written reports on their own country and submit them to their keypals for comments.

Grade level: 4–12

Getting started
- Determine which country will be the focus for this project. Use the IECC listserv or Web site to advertise for participants.
- Have the class develop a list of topics to investigate as they learn about the country they intend to research. The list should include standard geographical information such as climate and location, but can also include topics of particular interest to students, such as favorite sports in a country or subjects that are studied in school.

Developing
- If students are able to use Internet tools such as the World Wide Web, they can explore the Internet for information on the country they have chosen.
- Alternatively (or in addition), they can use magazines and books from a local library to conduct their research.
- Once the students have completed their preliminary research, they should develop a list of questions to address to a keypal in the country they are researching. These questions will form the basis of an electronic mail interview.

Extending
- Once students have completed their interviews and written their reports, they should send what they have written to their keypal interviewees for feedback.

Variations

- Students enjoy exchanging their stories and reports with other classes. These can be a report they have completed for a unit of study or a creative writing endeavor.
- Have students put together a "travel guide" on their own country, state, province, or community and exchange them with other classes. This project is most exciting if more than one remote classroom is involved, so that each of the participating classes receives reports from more than one country, province, or state. If your students have access to Web resources, they can use them to research their reports.
- Have students research a current issue or event and create a "newswire" service. First, explain what a newswire service is, and clip some examples from a local newspaper. Then, have students research and prepare their reports. Students from another classroom can look at the reports and select their favorites for a simulated online news broadcast. Learning is enhanced when students have the opportunity to share their thoughts on world issues. Follow this project up with a discussion about the advantages and disadvantages of getting the news from a wire service.
- Join the International Newsday Project at **http://www.gsn.org/ project/newsday/index.html**. This is a student-developed news exchange. Students create a newspaper based on articles that are submitted by students around the world.

Project Ideas

Sharing Book Reviews

The Internet Public Library offers World of Readers where kids can send in reviews of their favorite books. Students are thrilled by the idea of having others read their work. Here's how your students can contribute.

Learning outcomes
- Students will access, over the Internet, book reviews written by other students.
- Students will create their own book reviews for posting on the Internet.

Grade level: 4–8

Getting started
- Visit the World of Readers site at **http://www.ipl.org/youth/ ByteBookie/**. Print a selection of book reviews and discuss them with students. Does the review make them want to read the book?
- As a group, decide what a good book review should contain.

HEY DUDE! FOUND OUT ABOUT IT AT THE BYTE BOOKIE!

Developing
- Have each of the students write a review of a favorite book. Ideally, reports should be written using a word processor and sent to you using electronic mail.
- You can choose to submit all the reports to the World of Reading for posting or select a few class favorites from the group.
- Mail the reports in text file format to **world-reading@ipl.org**.
  Be sure to include:

  Student's First Name
  Student's Age
  Teacher's Name
  Teacher's e-mail

School Name
School Location
School URL
Book Title
Book Author
Text of the book review.

You can also submit reports at
http://www.ipl.org/youth/ ByteBookie/teachers.html
http://www.ipl.org/youth/ByteBookie/teachers.html.

Extending
- Have students share their reviews by reading them aloud or by sending them as an e-mail message to other members of the class.

Variations
- Students in Grades 4–8 can publish their own stories on the World Wide Web by sending them to **Submissions@KidPub.org**. Stories should be sent as individual mail messages (text format) and can include a brief note of introduction mentioning the country or state the message is being sent from in addition to things such as the students' favorite foods, hobbies, and so on. Stories can also be submitted directly onto the Web at **http://www.kidpub.org/kidpub/kidpub-template.html**. For more information, use your Web browser to access **http://www.kidpub.org/kidpub/**.
- Students in Grades 4–12 can exchange e-mail book reviews with another class. Establish a format for the book reviews (similar to the format indicated above). Exchange reviews with a group of students from another school. This activity can be particularly motivating if students exchange reviews with students from another country. Classes should be able to manage a common language at a similar level. Each group should read an author from their own country and write a review that will introduce the work to a class from another country.
- A book rap (for Grades 7–12) is a book discussion conducted by e-mail. Identify the book to be discussed and set a start date for the discussion. Each week a coordinator posts one or more open-ended questions about the book and students respond. A range of different topics focusing on themes, characters, and other aspects of the book can be developed over several weeks.

Figure 7-4

A sample book review

```
Title: MacDonald Hall Goes Hollywood
Author: Gordon Korman
Published: 1991
Publisher: Scholastic
ISBN: 0-590-43941-3
Ages: 8 and up
Name: Darren Romijn
Age: 12 (grade 7)
Acadia Jr. High School
175 Killarney Ave.
Winnipeg, Manitoba
R3T 3B3

Review: This book is about a movie star that comes
to Macdonald Hall (a private school) to make a
film. Bruno tries to get into the movie but the
headmaster bans the students from the movie set.
Bruno won't stop until he gets to be in the movie.
This book was really funny! If you like funny
books you'll definitely like this one!
```

Summing up

While electronic mail is only one of the ways in which the Internet can be introduced into the classroom, it is potentially one of the most versatile. With a little creativity, teachers can use e-mail as an effective tool to achieve learning outcomes in basic skills such as computer literacy and communications, as well as in more specific subjects such as science, geography, or language studies. Through electronic mail projects, students can learn about teamwork and global cooperation.

Advanced users may want to experiment with using e-mail to transfer software, or to exchange graphics, sound, or even multimedia files. But for newcomers, electronic messaging can be wonderfully rewarding. A simple exchange of text messages can dissolve the walls of the traditional classroom and open a door to exploring the world.

The next chapter will look at some additional Internet technologies, including other methods for communicating online.

Chapter

8

Additional Internet Tools

"Physicists at MIT stood by and watched last week as scientists in California used the Internet to manipulate their fusion reactor from more than 3000 miles away .... Stephen Wolfe, the physics operations leader for the trial, said, 'We've shown that it doesn't much matter any more where the physicists and the machines are located, as long as you've got a fast link.'"

— QUOTED IN "THE INCREDIBLE SHRINKING LABORATORY," *SCIENCE, 268* (5207; APRIL 1995), 35.

While more and more applications are being integrated into the World Wide Web, knowing about some additional tools will give teachers a better idea of how the Internet is structured and access to further resources. The applications discussed in previous chapters — the World Wide Web and electronic mail — represent the areas of greatest interest for teachers using the Internet in the classroom. But a number of other technologies, such as FTP, telnet, MOOs, real-time conferencing and online video-conferencing also have a distinctive role to play. In addition, knowing how to set up your browser to accept plug-ins and helper applications, and being aware of Web utilities, such as offline browsers, will help you use the Web environment more effectively. While a Web browser on its own will go a long way toward meeting your needs, you can extend what you are able to do over the Web by knowing about other applications.

Consider, as an example, the fact that you cannot access a computer on the Internet via the World Wide Web if that location is not actually running a Web server. There are some interesting and useful bulletin board services (BBSs) — some school boards actually operate their own bulletin board services — but to use these effectively over the net, you may need to use an application called telnet. Similarly, a teacher may negotiate with a local university to have a class use a specialized piece of software. But if the software is not available on a Web server, gaining access to the software would require the use of *telnet*. Passing a piece of software or an information file from one computer to another requires the use of FTP (*File Transfer Protocol*). And if you would like to have your students carry on a real-time dialog with another class, you might be interested in doing this through a MOO.

Because so many Internet processes have gravitated to the Web, some would claim that these technologies are disappearing. Certainly, as more agencies integrate their services onto the Web, an application such as telnet is not used as frequently as it used to be.

The Teacher's Complete & Easy Guide to the Internet

But in a university environment, using telnet is how many people hop from their network computer to a computer elsewhere on campus. With distance learning on the rise, you could be doing just this from home. Because the process of accessing files using FTP is commonly done with a Web browser, many people view it as just another part of the Web; however, FTP as a separate application is still important for uploading files.

As some of the established technologies start to grow cobwebs, shiny new applications, such as streaming audio and streaming video gain in popularity. Again we are reminded that the Internet is in a constant state of flux. This chapter will look at some old and some new Internet technologies. You can use this chapter for background and find out more when you want to explore how these technologies can be used in the classroom.

Chapter goals

- ■ **To explain the basic process for obtaining files using FTP**
- ■ **To identify some file types and explain the concept of file compression**
- ■ **To identify how and where to locate software over the Internet**
- ■ **To explain the basic telnet process**
- ■ **To provide an introduction to a couple of ways to "chat" in real time over the Internet**
- ■ **To provide basic information about real-audio**
- ■ **To provide a general introduction to Internet video-conferencing using CU-SeeMe**
- ■ **To offer basic information about other Web plug-in applications**
- ■ **To introduce offline browsers**

Some of the tools included in this chapter are somewhat more complex than the World Wide Web. If you are a novice computer user, read each section carefully to determine how useful the feature is likely to be in your own classroom and how much technical detail there is to master. If the technique being described looks complicated, find a knowledgeable friend to walk you through it the first time you attempt to use it. Because these tools are less important than e-mail and the World Wide Web, you can take your time learning about them.

FTP

FTP is the process used to transfer files from one computer to another, and it can be an extremely powerful and useful application. You can use FTP to obtain updated versions of some of the Internet tools you are currently using and to obtain new viewers for your Web browser. FTP may also be a way for you to access useful shareware or freeware (such as learning software, marking programs, or information files). If you have direct Internet access, you might even use FTP to transfer files from your local machine to another machine on the network.

Although your Internet access provider may have supplied software specifically designed for transferring files (e.g., Fetch or WinFTP), it is possible — and much easier — to transfer these files using Netscape, Opera, or a similar Web browser. The procedure involves simply designating the URL for the FTP site, just as you did for accessing a Web (**http://**) site. (You may recall from Chapter 4 that a URL for an FTP site looks something like: **ftp://nic.umass. edu**.)

Some Web pages include links to FTP sites. Selecting one of these links brings up a list of files and directories at that site. In this way, you may already have been navigating FTP sites. Clip art resources and sites for obtaining software are commonly made available as FTP sites, rather than as Web sites.

For many people, it may not be necessary to go beyond the FTP navigation that is available through Web pages. The information in this chapter will give you a precise procedure for downloading files, and an idea of some things to watch for when navigating such sites.

FTP using a Web browser

Here are the steps for retrieving a file from an FTP site using your browser.

- **Step 1.** Clear the Location/URL window and type in the URL, which in this case begins with **ftp://**. When you press enter, your browser will retrieve an actual directory of files from the remote site. If the reference is to a folder, you may see an icon that looks like a folder. File names will include the size of the file and whether it is compressed. (Compressed files are those that have been "shrunk" to make them easier to transfer and store. This concept is explained in detail later in this chapter.)

- **Step 2.** Scroll through the list to find the directory or file you would like to access. Then simply click on the file name to retrieve it. If the file is a text file, it will be displayed on the screen just as a normal file would that might be a part of a Web page. Other types of files, such as large-image files or PostScript (special printer) files, will display only if you have preconfigured your browser with an appropriate viewer (discussed later in this chapter). In some cases, clicking on the file results in an **Unknown File Type** box being displayed.

- **Step 3.** The Unknown File Type dialog box gives you three options: **Save to Disk, Cancel Transfer**, or **Configure a Viewer**. In most instances, you'll want to Save to Disk. Simply click on this option to initiate the save.

Figure 8-1
A file directory at an FTP site

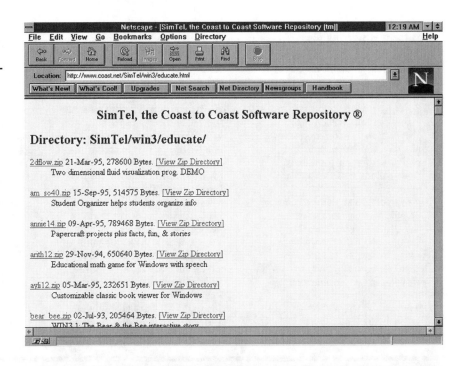

Figure 8-2
Should the Unknown File Type dialog box appear, click on one of the options.

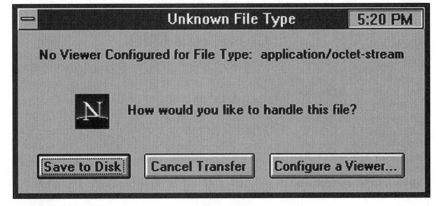

Tech Talk

An ASCII file is a text-only file, i.e., a readable file that contains no special characters or formatting codes. The file extension for an ASCII file is .txt. Binary files can be either files that perform a task (such as a software application) or they can be specially coded files, such as word-processed files or compressed files.

Tech Talk

Be sure to scan any downloaded files for viruses before running them on your system. If you don't currently have antivirus software on your computer, ask a local software dealer about obtaining some. McAfee's Viruscan is a popular program that scans for viruses on a PC, while Disinfectant is available for the Macintosh. Another type of program prevents viruses before they become active (e.g., FluShot for the PC, Gatekeeper for Macintosh).

To find out more about computer viruses, access the FAQ at **http://www.dmu.ac.uk/~rpandit/virhelp.html**.

Compressed files

HINT To get a complete list of all file compression/ archiving methods and programs to decompress them, use FTP to access the following site, and retrieve the file called compression: **ftp://cso.uiuc.edu directory:pub/ doc/pcnet/compression**. This document also tells you where to go to get the proper software for decompressing. You can also locate a number of programs for decoding and decompressing files at TUCOWS: **http://www.tucows.com./**. The files are listed under *Compression* Utilities.

While it is relatively easy to download uncompressed text files, sooner or later you will need to deal with a compressed file. These are files that have been "shrunk" using a software program in order to save disk space or to speed up the time required for transfer. There are many different programs that can be used to compress files. The key is to identify and obtain the particular type of software you need to decompress the type of file you have at hand.

One type of compressed file you will commonly see is *zipped* files. These have a .zip extension. To "unzip" these, you will need a shareware program called PKUnzip. This is available at **http://www.pkware.com**. Sometimes you will see the file automatically included with a group of zipped files that need to be unzipped. The latest version of PKUnzip includes a "wizard" that will walk you through the process for unzipping files.

Other programs for unzipping files include WinZip, available from **http://www.winzip.com/**. In the Macintosh world, compressed (.sit) files can be unpackaged using Stuffit Expander or Stuffit Lite. Stuffit can be found at **http://www.aladdinsys.com**.

Common file formats

The kind of file you are dealing with can usually be identified by its *file extension*, or the letters following the file name. For example, a document prepared in WordPerfect might have the file extension *.wp*. Here are some common file extensions.

.txt	Text or ASCII file	.wav	Sound file	.sea	Macintosh compressed file that unpacks itself when you double-click on it
.exe	Executable file; performs a task when you double-click on it. Sometimes it will unpack other files.	.au	Sound file		
		.mpg	Moving picture file		
		.uue	File that has been coded for transfer through e-mail	.arc	DOS compressed file
. ps	PostScript file (must be printed on a PostScript printer)			.zip	Zipped file
		.hdx	BinHex; a Macintosh compressed file	.tar	Unix file
				.Z	Unix compressed file
.gif	A photo or picture file				
.jpg	Another type of graphical file	.sit StuffIt	Macintosh compressed file	.gz	Unix compressed file

Figure 8-3
Finding files using Filez

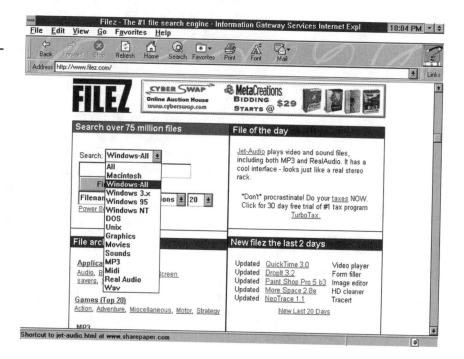

GETTING STARTED

... with Finding files

Although finding a file you're searching for at an FTP site sometimes requires that you have the exact file name, you can sometimes locate files on a topic just by entering a name that makes sense. In this exercise, you can try this technique and learn how to search for files at Filez.

Let's say that you're searching for an image file of Van Gogh's painting, *Sunflowers*.

- **Step 1.** Use your Web browser to access **http://filez.com**.

- **Step 2.** Ensure that the window under the Find button reads *Filenames & Descriptions*. Click on the selection arrow in the window labeled "Search." This window offers a range of searching options. Select *graphics* to search for graphics files.

- **Step 3.** Type the word *sunflowers* in the window adjacent to the *Find* button. The last window will let you designate the maximum number of matching items to list. You can leave this as the default value of twenty listings. Click on *find*. The next screen will return a selection of sunflower images.

- **Step 4.** Click on one of the sunflower links in .gif or .jpg format. On the resulting screen, Filez will provide a direct link to the download locations for the specific file you have selected. From here you can retrieve the file by clicking on the file name again. If there is more than one site where the file is available, select the FTP site nearest you. If a server does not seem to be responding, choose another one.

- **Step 5.** When your browser successfully accesses the file, the image will display on your computer screen. To save the file to your local hard drive or diskette, place your cursor over the image and click on your right mouse button. Use your right mouse button to select the **Save Image** option from the menu.

- **Step 6.** Saved images can be re-sized or changed to another format using an image viewer or graphics software (see Chapter 6).

HINT Have students use this technique to search for pictures to include in their reports or Web pages, but remember that image files will not be available for all topics.

Sites for downloading software and educational resources

The following list describes sites where you can find software programs and other shareware or freeware that can be downloaded. Math tutors, typing programs, or lessons can all be downloaded for printing. Remember that shareware programs are offered as a way to let you try before you buy. If you plan to use a shareware program on a regular basis, be sure to pay the licensing fee. Licensed use of shareware programs is generally very reasonable.

Explorer
This site offers a collection of downloadable education resources for maths and sciences. The resources include instructional software programs. You can browse through the curriculum areas to find out what is available.
http://explorer.scrtec.org/explorer/

WinSite
This is a major computer shareware site for Microsoft Windows Software, with over 300 Mb of public domain software and shareware. You will find a good selection of programs for educators, including math tutors, marking programs, and more.
http://www.winsite.com

Jumbo
Plan to visit this site when you have time available to explore. This site offers over 250,000 shareware programs and links. The best places to explore for useful learning resources are in the Homework Helper section or the Jumbo Kids area. Homework Helper includes pointers to downloadable electronic books.
http://www.jumbo.com

EASI (Equal Access to Software and Information)
If you are working with students with disabilities, visit this site for the latest information about adaptive technologies. The K-12 resource includes some pointers to math and science tutorial programs that may be of general interest.
http://www.rit.edu/~easi/k12.html

Download.com
This site includes an Education area and a Kids area, along with a number of other specific topics. If you browse in these areas, you will be able to pick out the "most popular," "newest titles," and the "topics" within each category.
http://www.download.com

Gatekeeper

This is a large site with files on a wide variety of subjects. The pub directory contains over thirty subdirectories and includes resources ranging from maps to full-text books.

ftp://gatekeeper.dec.com

Internet Information

A range of resources about the Internet, including FAQs (Frequently Asked Questions) from Usenet newsgroups.

ftp://rtfm.mit.edu/pub/

Educational Software Institute

This is an important resource for finding out about educational software. From this resource, you can browse for software by curriculum area and by computer platform (Window, Macintosh, etc.) Registered users can order many of the software programs online. Registration is free and there are frequent free software offers for members.

http://www.edsoft.com

Soulis' Suggestions for Internet Solutions

This is yet another source for useful free and inexpensive programs. This site includes Apple and Unix freebies as well as such things as free e-mail sources and links to a number of international shareware sources.

http://www.lyra.simplenet.com/msw/indax.html

Virtual Software Library

This site has an excellent list of sources for freeware (freely redistributable software) along with links to many large shareware collections.

http://www.cfcl.com/free/archives/P/VSL.html

Macintosh Archives

A number of excellent FTP sites for Macintosh computers include HyperCard stacks, modem software, graphical tools, and QuickTime software and movies. Look in the Mac subdirectory.

ftp://mac.archive.umich.edu

Online Books Page

Extensive collection of full-text book resources from Carnegie Mellon University.

http://www.cs.cmu.edu/books.html

Bob Bowman's Guide to Free Educational Technology

Educational freeware, online tutorials, how-to-guides, freeware graphics, downloadable Spanish course from the Embassy of Spain, etc. — free, free, free!

http://www.user.shentel.net/rbowman/

Educational Technology Resource Center

This is another interesting resource with links to some downloadable resources. Emphasis is on science and math resources. Most are suitable for higher grades.

http://www.thomson.com/pws/canit/canit.html

HINT Chez Mark's Mac Picks regularly reviews the newest and the best Macintosh shareware. It is available from **http://www.ualberta.ca/~mmalowan/Picks.html**. A directory of Macintosh sites and a Macintosh search engine are available from a site called *macinsearch.com* located at **http://www.macinsearch.com**. Check out these Macintosh sources as well:

Macintosh Educator's Site
http://www.hampton-dumont.k12.ia.us/web/mac/default.html

Macintosh Internet Resource Database (MacIRD)
http://host.comvista.com/Internet.tfm

MacFixIt
http://www.macfixit.com/
The Low End Mac (for teachers who have not managed to purchase the latest PowerBook).
http://www.mactimes.com:80/lowend/

The Macintosh Resource Page
http://www.macresource.pair.com

MacWorld
http://macworld.zdnet.com/

Hypercard Heaven
http://members.aol.com/hcheaven/index.html

Download one of these useful learning programs that you can find listed at Keystone High School at **http://www.keystonehighschool.com/shareware/**

Demo of 3D Molecular Modeling Set:
vsepr115.zip

Astronomy Planetarium Simulator:
hubble19.zip 410 KB

Crossword Puzzle Creator:
cwe32.zip 802 KB

Educational Physics Program:
phys116.zip 2337 KB

Math Game for Windows:
arith12.zip 635 KB

Math and Science Program:
pleasr11.zip 215 KB

Memory 2:
memory2.zip 5625 KB

Word Search Puzzle Creator
Cross11.zip 162 KB

PERSONAL FAVORITES
Use this page to make notes on your own favorite download sites.

Site: _____

Description: _____

Note files: _____

Site: _____

Description: _____

Note files: _____

Site: _____

Description: _____

Note files: _____

Site: _____

Description: _____

Note files: _____

Site: _____

Description: _____

Note files: _____

Site: _____

Description: _____

Note files: _____

Site: _____

Description: _____

Note files: _____

The Teacher's Complete & Easy Guide to the Internet

HINT RFC (Request for Comment) files are usually technical documents. However, there is one that may be of interest to teachers looking for background information on the use of the Internet in Schools.RFC1941 (Frequently Asked Questions for Schools) is available at **http://ds.internic.net/ds/dspg1intdoc.html**.

Big IBM mainframes require their own special form of telnet, known as tn3270. There are not many of these on the Internet, but it is useful to know about this just in case you're trying to log on to one.

Telnet

Telnet is the application that lets you navigate anywhere on the Internet and log on to remote computers. Although telnet is not used nearly as frequently as it used to be, there remain some resources that are simply not available any other way. One common use for telnet is to log on to a computer where you have a second account. Some teachers may have a school account and a separate personal account with an access provider. On a business trip or on your summer vacation, find someone who is willing to log you on to their account so that you may telnet to your home account and not have to dial in by long distance. Some special Internet services, such as MOOs, are still available only through telnet. (MOOs are described later in this chapter.)

To use telnet, you will need some type of telnet client software. It is possible to telnet using a Web browser, but only if you have set up a telnet helper application in advance. In this case, when you put in the URL for a telnet site, your telnet client will be automatically activated. Once you've finished the telnet session, you will be returned to your Web browser.

In most instances, when you want to run telnet, you would call up your telnet client as a separate application. The main thing that a telnet client will do for you is to allow your smart computer to pretend that it is a dumb terminal. If you configured your own communications software, you may recall the term *terminal emulation*. Large mainframe computers generally require you to "dumb down" your personal computer before they will recognize you. Some common terminal emulation types are VT100, VT102, ANSI, and TTY. On the Internet, VT100 is the most frequently used terminal emulation, so you will probably want to set this as a default on your telnet software.

Your access provider should have given you a copy of some sort of telnet software. In a Macintosh environment, you can use Better Telnet or Nifty Telnet; in Windows, you may use CRT, WinTelnet, QVT/Term, or another of the available telnet clients. If your service provider has not provided you with telnet software, you can obtain this from Stroud's Consummate Winsock Applications Page at **http://www.stroud.com** or from TUCOWS at **http://www.tucows.com**. With any telnet program, you will use the basic menu choices to configure the software and access a site. Remember that you will need to be logged on to your service provider for these applications to work.

The basic information needed for a telnet session is:

- the *address* for the site that you want to connect to (e.g., compuserve.com to telnet to a CompuServe account)
- the *logon information* for the site. This could be your name and

password for a personal account, or it could be a public logon, such as *bbs* on a telnet site that has been set up for public access.

Gophers

This once very useful Internet tool was developed in 1991 at the University of Minnesota. The name is derived from the gopher mascot for the University's Golden Gophers athletic team. Happily (and not coincidentally), the name also describes exactly what Gophers do — they "go fer," or retrieve, information from the vast resources on the Internet. For many types of information, Gopher's method of presenting information — that is, in hierarchical lists — was admirably efficient.

Now, however, most agencies in North America that originally set up Gophers no longer strive to keep Gopher information up to date, and instead make their information available on the Web. Sometimes you may find a Web page that points to a Gopher. When this happens, your browser will handle the connection automatically. Gopher menu choices will be displayed as hyperlinks, and you can navigate by clicking on the link to the item you want to access. A URL for a Gopher site starts with *gopher://*. If you are given a URL reference for a Gopher site, you can access it using the same technique you use to access a Web site.

Real-time discussion on the Web

MOOs

MOO stands for *Multi-user Object-Oriented*. It is a text-based, virtual environment for real-time discussion. MOOs are another example of an older or more established Internet technology.

Because MOOs are text-based, they can seem cumbersome and unnatural compared with the World Wide Web. Another reason MOOs can be challenging to master is that they usually rely on the metaphor of an actual physical location, so that one MOO might include a "foyer," a "study hall," a "lounge," or a "grassy knoll." In order to join in the conversation, you first need to find your way around. Finally, there is the issue of your identity as you enter a MOO. Even though you can often log on as a guest, some MOOs present you with a series of questions—such as what you would like to be called during your visit. (Made-up names are not considered a problem here; in fact, MOO culture encourages you to assume a "character.") Some MOOs will ask you to identify your gender (though the choices frequently include "neutral" and even "royalty"!). Once you have managed to log on to a MOO, you need to use a set of cryptic commands to move about and make yourself heard. Because of the arcane command structure required to interact with others inside a MOO, many teachers will not be motivated to explore this tool. But MOOs have many staunch supporters and there are a number of MOOs specifically focused on education.

The advantage of a MOO over a normal "chat" type of discussion or real-time conference over the Net is that it allows for the imaginative construction of a virtual world. Students involved in MOO projects have an opportunity to gain both language skills and programming skills. One teacher who has used a MOO to help students improve their writing skills pointed out that students must learn to use language much more precisely in a MOO environment, where the usual auditory and visual clues are not available.

Students learn to express themselves clearly, to consult directly with tutors, and generally to "think on their feet." On some MOOs you can even establish your own learning space (known as "digging a new room"). Students can work with teachers to design a project and to manage the group consultation process.

> "Teachers should help students create personally meaningful tasks before the MOO is accessed, to be followed up with an assessment of outcomes. As an example, language learners might decide what topics they want to discuss with native speakers, then later report to the class what they learned, who taught it to them, and what Web sites support their findings."
>
> — *Lonnie Turbee, Educational MOO: Text-Based Virtual Reality for Learning in Community. ERIC Digest. ED404987 Mar 97*
> *http://www.ed.gov/databases/ERIC_Digests/ed404987.html*

Tapped In is another MOO that operates over the Web. It has been developed for shared teacher professional development. Teachers can use this environment for sharing knowledge or collaboration with other teachers. You can visit Tapped In almost any time to get a sense of how to participate. Check the Tapped In events calendar to find out about scheduled discussion topics and online guests. Tapped In is at **http:// www. tappedin. org/**

Such learning experiences can be rewarding. But teachers planning to use a MOO with students should expect to spend at least fifteen hours familiarizing themselves with the MOO environment. Additional hours will be necessary to plan to manage the experience in the classroom. Students need careful preparation, including instructions about MOO netiquette.

One very active MOO with more than several hundred users is available on Canada's SchoolNet. SchoolNet has also developed a Web interface to the MOO that offers some of the functionality of an actual MOO. Other educational MOOs include Connections MOO, a place for teachers and students to interact; the Athena Academy, a tutoring environment for K-12 students; Le MOO Français for practicing conversational French; Mundo Hispano for Spanish language learning and even a university called Diversity University. You can find out about these and other educational MOOs at Educational Virtual Reality Sites located at **http://www.cris.com/~angus1/links.html**. Other good resources for learning about MOOs are:

The Lost Library of MOO (**http://lucien.berkeley.edu/moo.html**)
A link library of manuals, tutorials, and research papers about MOOs; The Educational Technology: Educational VR (MUD) sub-

page (**http://tecfa.unige.ch/edu-comp/WWW-VL/eduVR-page. html**); and Diversity University (**http://www.du.org/**), which provides general MOO information and hosts meetings for educational projects and groups.

Most MOOs require the use of telnet, but if you just want a simple introduction to a real-time chat environment you can visit the SchoolNet Web version of a MOO at **http://www.schoolnet.ca/ moo/**. If you want to try logging on to an actual MOO, the best advice is to read everything displayed on the screen very carefully. If necessary, read it twice. Also, read through the general instruction guides that are frequently available on the Web sites that support individual MOOs.

HINT While MOOs can provide a useful learning experience, MUDs and MUSHes (*Multi-User Shared Hallucinations*) are unsuitable for classroom use. Teachers need to be aware that these areas exist online. Once you have introduced students to the techniques for using a MOO, be sure that they respect your rules.

Basic MOO commands

Connect guest A common logon. You may need to type this in rather than wait for a login prompt.

@quit To log off

@who To see who is currently logged on and in which room, within the MOO, they are located

@join <character name> To join a character you have found by using the @who command. This can be a quick way to navigate to a room.

look You can use this command to figure out where you are and what is around you. You can also type **look <object>** to obtain a description of some meaningful item in the room. If the object might convey information, you can type **read <object>** (e.g., **read newspaper**).

@go To go to a particular area. You can often navigate using directions, such as **@go north**.

" Use a quotation mark to precede anything you want to say to the group in your room.

say This command is the same as the quotation mark in some MOOs.

whisper"<message>" to <character name> Use this command if you want to speak only to one person in the room.

page <character name> "<message>" To talk to someone who is not in the room you are in

help For general help

help index To view a list of items for which help is available

Be aware that commands can differ slightly from one MOO to the next. The most user-friendly MOOs give you specific prompts at the bottom of each screen to help you move elsewhere. Most MOOs also offer an online tutorial, so watch for these.

HINT MOOs are easier to use with a MOO client (such as TinyFugue for Unix) rather than straight telnet. To find out about clients that run on your platform, access the MUD/MOO Client FAQ at **http://www.cs.okstate.edu/~jds/ mudfaq-p2.html**.

"One student who became interested in our MOO expressed a wish to recreate her family's cabin in the mountains, complete with the treehouse and paths that are so dear to her. Her descriptions are beautiful testaments to her love for her family cabin. Now, anyone who logs on to our MOO can see them, and she can show off 'her' place while 'talking' to visitors."

— *Andrew Smallman, Director, Puget Sound Community School, Seattle, Washington, U.S.A.*

Other chat environments

There are a number of other ways to have real-time discussions online. Services such as AOL and CompuServe sponsor Web-based chat sessions. The Time-Warner Pathfinder service and Yahoo feature regular guest speakers in Web-based chat sessions. IRC (Internet Relay Chat) "channels" allow real-time conversation with people from around the globe. Unlike MOOs, however, most of them currently do not offer significant value for educators. Chat group discussions traditionally have not had an educational focus and they are not easily monitored.

One notable exception is customized computer-to-computer communications that you can set up using the latest communications software products. Web-phone technology allows actual voice conversations if your computer is equipped with speakers and one of the Internet phone software products, such as WebPhone or Freetel. Netscape Communicator and the latest version of Internet Explorer allow you to connect in real time to other people on the Web. If you are not using either of these browsers, you can use a number of other software products to communicate online, such as PowWow, ICQ, or Sticky Notes. PowWow includes a number of interesting features for educational applications, including a whiteboard, an easy mechanism for exchanging files, and the ability to cruise the Web as a group. Discussion groups can range from two users up to seventy-five. For users set up to receive sound, PowWow allows voice communications, although even with a 28.8 modem, conversations can be a bit distorted.

In a school context, real-time chat software programs, such as PowWow, can be used to support a student collaboration project, as a way for a class to communicate with an invited guest expert or as a "fun" finish to an e-mail exchange.

HINT For a real-time class exchange that does not require much set up, try E-mail Classroom Exchange — CHAT http://www.iglou.com/xchange/cgi-bin/Conferences/ecelive.cgi.

teaching tip

Set up an online challenge with another class. Arrange to study a novel, unit of history, or science topic in parallel with another class. Agree on basic concepts to be mastered. With the other teacher, develop a set of short-answer quiz questions to be issued "online" using PowWow. Have teams of two students from each school ready to respond to the questions. Rotate teams, so that as many students as possible have a chance to participate. The team with the most correct answers wins.

Even with clever software in place, real-time communications can quickly become unmanageable without careful planning. PowWow offers a New PowWow Users Community that you can join to become comfortable using this software before attempting to use it with your class.

You might also consider inviting a group of interested teachers within your school board to experiment with using PowWow. Eventually you may find that communicating online is a practical way to have a meeting with colleagues from other schools. PowWow is available at: **http://www.tribal.com/powwow**. You can find out about a range of other chat software and Web-phone products at TUCOWS **http://www./tucows.com** and at the Dave Central software archive at **http://www.davecentral.com/sitemap.html**.

CU-SeeMe

CU-SeeMe is a software program that can be used for video-conferencing over the Internet. CU-SeeMe allows simultaneous conferencing with more than one site. With some versions, participants can exchange text and slides. Best of all, CU-SeeMe is available free. Ultimately, video-conferencing over the Internet will be a major means to deliver distance education courses.

For the time being, however, this type of application is, for many schools, a luxury. That's because video-conferencing requires specialized equipment. While the conferencing software is free, you will

Figure 8-4
CU-SeeMe video-conferencing

The Teacher's Complete & Easy Guide to the Internet

also need a microphone, a video camera or camcorder, and a frame grabber (a piece of equipment that connects the video camera to the computer). Once this connection is in place, whatever is captured in the lens of the camera is digitized and transmitted to the computer. You will also need a direct connection to the Internet, and your modem must transmit data at 14.4 kbps or faster.

CU-SeeMe runs on both Macintosh and Windows platforms. With this software, you will have the option to send and receive video or just receive.

Here are specific hardware and software requirements for desktop video-conferencing using each of these platforms.

Windows
To receive only:
- 386SX processor or higher
- Windows 3.1 running in Enhanced Mode
- Windows Sockets-compliant TCP/IP stack
- a 256-color (8-bit) video driver at any resolution (640x480, 800x600, 1024x768, or higher).

To send and receive:
- 386DX processor or higher
- Windows 3.1 running in Enhanced Mode
- Windows Sockets-compliant TCP/IP stack
- a 256-color (8-bit) video driver at any resolution (640x480, 800x600, 1024x768, or higher)
- video capture board that supports Microsoft Video for Windows (see below)
- a video camera to plug into the video capture board.

Macintosh
To receive only:
- Macintosh platform with a 68020 processor or higher
- System 7 or higher operating system (it *may* run on system 6.0.7 and above)
- ability to display 16-level grayscale (i.e., any color Mac)
- an IP network connection
- MacTCP
- current CU-SeeMe application
- Apple's QuickTime, to receive slides with SlideWindow.

To send and receive:
- the specifications to receive video, listed above
- QuickTime
- a video digitizer (with VDIG software) and camera.

The simplest way to establish a video-conferencing setup for your school is to purchase a complete video-conferencing package from an appropriate vendor. You can download a free copy of the CU-SeeMe software from the Web page for the CU-SeeMe Project (**http://cu-seeme.cornell.edu/**) or obtain an enhanced version from White Pine Software (**http://www.cuseeme.com/**). Another very good source for information about CU-SeeMe is Michael Sattler's Web page (**http://baby.indstate.edu/msattler/sci-tech/comp/CU-SeeMe/**).

Once you have obtained the necessary hardware and software, you can connect to a site that is currently sending. CU-SeeMe send sites are also called reflectors, and the video segments are called *events*. One early event that received considerable press was a Rolling Stones concert. Other events have included online interviews with politicians, poets, and scientists. Teachers should begin to think about how they might use this technology to have classrooms interact across the Net.

> "One of our elementary schools will be setting up video-conferencing for a first-grade student who will be having cancer treatments after Christmas. She will not be able to physically be part of the class the rest of this school year, but will be rejoining them in second grade. While she is being tutored at home, she will still be able to communicate with her classmates, maintain friendships, and be part of the class discussions using CU-SeeMe."
>
> — *Janet Barnstable, Communications Resource Teacher, Percy Julian Junior High School, (Oak Park, Illinois) in Classrooms Without Walls http://www.wpine.com/edu/eduBarnstable.html.*

HINT To find out about school-related CU-SeeMe events and a directory of schools that use CU-SeeMe, access

http://www.gsn.org/cu/index.html.

To find out about other video-conferencing options, visit

The Videoconferencing Site at

http://www.video-conferencing.com.

Streaming audio

Streaming audio is a term for sound files that play as they are downloading. RealAudio is an example of streaming audio. RealAudio provides broadcasts over the Internet that are similar to radio broadcasts — except that you can select exactly what you want to listen to, when you want to listen to it. With RealAudio you can sample a CD or catch a radio interview. *The Christian Science Monitor* and ABC news offer RealAudio broadcasts, the CBC offers special real-audio programming for schools, and some distance learning lectures are beginning to become available in RealAudio format. Although listening to a rock concert as it is being broadcast requires a very fast connection to the Internet, with even a 14.4-baud modem you will be able to download files and play them at your convenience.

To listen to RealAudio, you must download and install a RealPlayer that plays both RealAudio and RealVideo. This helper application is available free from:

http://www.real.com/

Sites featuring RealAudio commonly provide a link to the player. In addition to the player, you will require, at a minimum:

- 486/33-MHz DX with 4 MB RAM (or Macintosh equivalent)

Although the RealPlayer plug-in will play both audio and video, streaming video requires a faster modem and more powerful computer. For detailed information about the requirements for playing both audio and video, access the RealPlayer System Requirements information at **http://www5.real.com/ products/player/sysreq.html**.

You will find other kinds of audio files on the Web, in addition to streaming audio. If you encounter a *.wav* or *.au* file, you can play the file as long as you have installed the appropriate type of helper application.

You can test a wide range of helper applications at the WWW Viewer Test Page: **http://www-dsed.llnl.gov/ documents/ WWWtest.html**. Use this site to ensure that new viewers are working properly.

- 2 MB hard disk space
- sound card
- speakers
- 14.4-baud or faster modem connection (faster for music and higher-quality sound).

Broadcast radio on the Internet is not extensive, but like everything on the Net, it is growing. Teachers will soon be able to access an increasing number of news and educational broadcasts from around the world. Try these sites to sample some of the RealAudio broadcasts that are currently available:

Exploratorium Learning Studio
http://www.exploratorium.edu/learning_studio/

AudioNet
http://www.audionet.com/

National Public Radio
http://www.npr.org

CBC Radio
http://www.radio.cbc.ca/

Monitor Radio–RealAudio
http://www.csmonitor.com/audio/audio.html

INFOSEARCH Broadcasting Links
http://www.broadcastinglinks.com/

To find out more about how to use RealAudio and what's available, visit the Real Audio home page: **http://www.real.com**.

Other helper applications

RealAudio is one example of an application that requires special software to play on your computer. But there are many others. Sooner or later you will arrive at a site where valuable information is packaged in a file format that your browser doesn't know how to display. When this happens, you need special software called a viewer or "plug-in." Many of these are used to play multimedia, but there are others designed to let you pay for things electronically, or view a document in a special format, such as a map.

One of the most useful plug-ins is a viewer for .pdf files. PDF stands for *Portable Document Format*. School boards, departments of education, and government agencies commonly provide information in .pdf format. This format is particularly suitable for long documents that are also available in print. With .pdf, you can make a document available online in the same format that it was originally published in (headlines, columns, graphics, etc.) — rather than having to convert the document into a Web page using HTML.

HINT If you want to sample a .pdf document, visit the Explorer site at **http://explorer.scrtec.org/explorer/**. This site offers a lot of useful curriculum material in .pdf format. You can also download back issues of *Speaking of Teaching*, a newsletter on teaching at **http://www-ctl.stanford.edu/teach/speak-menu.html**.

A .pdf version of the *Scout Report*, a popular publication providing regular updates of new Web sites for educators, is now available. The format makes it easy to print and post this useful publication in the school library. The publication is available from **http://wwwscout.cs.wisc.edu/scout/report/pdf/**.

PDF can help prevent illegal copying of material, and it ensures that a document will look the same regardless of which browser — or which computer platform — you are using. The *New York Times* delivers the **TimesFax** service (**http://www.nytimesfax.com**) over the Net using Adobe Acrobat portable document format, which is the most commonly used .pdf format.

PDF files require the use of a helper application known as a PDF viewer. These viewers are usually free. Most sites that provide information in PDF format also provide a link to the viewer you will need. Usually, you need only click on the viewer link to download it to your own computer. Then, just install the viewer as a helper application (described below).

Take time to explore the viewer's features, such as increasing the size of a display for easier reading. Editing features will vary. For example, although a PDF viewer will generally allow you to view and print a document, you may not be able to cut and paste from it.

You can find out more about Adobe Acrobat files at:

Adobe Acrobat
http://www.adobe.com

Software developers are always launching new applications requiring plug-ins and making them available via the Internet. You will find an extensive list of plug-ins at Browserwatch (**http://**

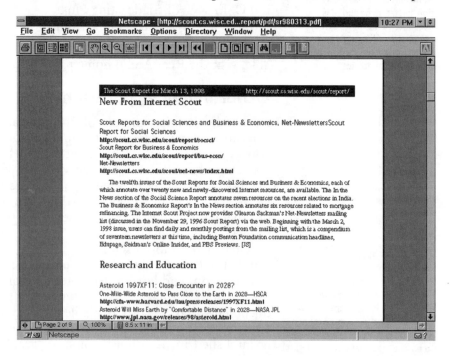

Figure 8-5
Portable Document Format preserves the original look of a document.

browserwatch. internet.com/plug-in.html). If you are downloading one of the newer versions of Netscape or Internet Explorer, you will have the option of downloading many different viewers at the same time. Be cautious about downloading too many viewers, as they will gobble up space on your hard drive and take up computer memory.

You will probably only need a small selection of viewers. We have already discussed some of the most commonly used viewers — Quicktime for video, a player for RealAudio, and the Adobe Acrobat Reader for .pdf files. Shockwave is a common viewer for multi-media applications that may combine graphics, animation, and streaming sound. Shockwave is available from **http://www.macromedia.com/shockwave**.

You will also encounter the term VRML. This acronym stands for Virtual Reality Markup Language and refers to a technology that provides three-dimensional Web pages. There are a number of different plug-ins for viewing three-dimensional space. The Cosmo Player at **http://cosmo.sgi.com/player** and WorldView at **http://www.intervista.com/products/worldview/index.html** are examples.

Installing viewers

Once you've learned to set up one viewer program, it's easy to add new plug-ins for other types of files as your needs change.

To link the Netscape browser to a helper application, follow these steps:

Step 1. From the **Options** menu, select **General Preferences | Helpers**.

Step 2. From the list displayed in the window, click on the file type for which you will be adding a helper application. Note that some applications already read **Browser** in the Action column. This means that the Netscape browser will display the file directly, so you won't need to set up a separate application.

Step 3. The name of the file type you've selected will appear in the smaller file extensions window. At this point you can click on **Browse** and locate the viewer or helper on your hard drive. Once you have selected a viewer to use, click on **OK**. The next time you call up that particular type of application, Netscape will recognize the file type by its extension and automatically launch the application you specified.

This procedure will be slightly different on a Macintosh computer and for other browsers, but the basic process is similar. In essence, you are telling your browser where on your hard drive to find a particular helper application.

Offline browsers

It can sometimes be useful to download Web pages and associated graphics for viewing offline. You may want to do this if you are planning a demonstration or want students to have access to a site without having to worry about whether a connection is down. Downloading a site, however, takes time, and occasionally it may be necessary to rename URL references within a Web page to ensure that the page displays properly. A reference to a graphic that was originally in a particular subdirectory on a remote server will not be accessible with the same subdirectory reference once the graphic has been downloaded to your hard drive. Basically, capturing sites offline is not something you will want to do often, but when you do want to capture a site, you can do so using an offline browser. As with other downloading, be sure your use of an offline browser falls within the guidelines "fair use" or "fair dealing" — or get permission.

HINT Saving more than one or two levels — a level is a page plus links off the page — of a site can result in an excessive number of links being accessed and downloaded, and many may not be relevant to your purpose. Saving one level at a time is a good policy.

You can capture Web sites offline using any of the following products. Offline browsers commonly cost between US$40 and $60.

Web Whacker

This popular offline browser will let you organize saved pages into categories.
  http://www.ffg.com

AnaWave WebSnake

A good offline browser for Windows 95. This one includes a wizard that will walk you through the process and let you download your bookmarks.
  http://www.anawave.com/websnake/

Summing up

Because the Internet is constantly developing, there will undoubtedly be other kinds of software available for audio- or video-conferencing on the Internet. If you feel that some of the applications discussed in this chapter are too challenging for a novice to tackle, be reassured that none of them are necessary to make good use of the Net. It's worth repeating that the real power of the Internet is as a tool for human communication, and although such applications as MOOs and CU-SeeMe are interesting technologies for classroom learning, much can still be accomplished with a simple e-mail connection. Telnet and FTP will allow you to access some additional Net resources, but most users will probably find that the World Wide Web provides sufficient access to the resources that will be most useful to schools.

9 Bringing the Internet into Schools

> "I think that the way to a teacher's heart is through the students. I doubt any teacher who sees the interest, the motivation, the skills, and the excitement in her or his students can long resist taking what, here in Quebec, we call 'le virage technologique' — 'the technology turn.'"
>
> — CHRISTIANE DUFOUR, TEACHER, SMALL SCHOOLS NETWORK, QUEBEC, CANADA

Because so much of a teacher's work is done after school hours, you are likely to find that you want to be connected to the Internet from both home and school. In order to access the many wonderful things the Internet has to offer, you need a computer, a modem, and a connection to the Internet. Once you have a connection, you will use the Internet for much more than schoolwork. You can find the latest news, take an online course, get up-to-date travel information, or communicate with colleagues, friends, and family.

If you are in the fortunate position of having Internet access through an already established school- or system-based infrastructure, getting connected may be as simple as turning on your computer and clicking on an icon or selecting from a menu. If not, you will need to deal more directly with the hardware and software required to get connected, whether at home or at school. Your school will be faced with such questions as, How many phone lines, computers, and modems do we need? Where should they be located? Who will monitor students as they use the Internet?

Change is rarely easy. School administrators, librarians, computer teachers, and classroom teachers all face the challenges of implementing this new technology. Problems are inevitable; in fact, we can't learn without them. When teachers discuss using the Internet in education, the hurdles of time, money, motivation, and technical training are mentioned time and again.

This chapter explores several different kinds of Internet connections and examines some of the ways in which schools are overcoming barriers that restrict Internet use. Although each school has different needs and resources, examining the various models described here will help you with technological and resource management decisions. This chapter will help plan for change in your school and will suggest some sources of funding to help make that change a reality.

■ **To examine options for connecting to the Internet**
■ **To provide guidelines for Internet implementation planning**
■ **To examine teacher training opportunities and procedures**
■ **To explore sources of funding**

What is a connection?

Remember that the Internet isn't a place or a thing; it is a network of computers linked together. You want to become a part of this global communications network in order to communicate with others and gain access to resources and information. Although approximately twenty million people use the Internet in some fashion, many have limited access, and many others use only e-mail. For educational purposes, you want to take advantage of the full range of resources available. The kind of connection you establish determines, to a great degree, both the type and format of the information that you and your students can access. This, in turn, affects learning outcomes for students. In order to plan for your integration of Internet resources into the curriculum, consider the kind of connection that will best suit your needs and the costs of the equipment and services that are required.

If your school is already connected, you can skip the next couple of pages. Still, it's useful to know how the connection works and why certain things may be possible while others aren't. Your students will certainly want to know! Or, you may wish to consider upgrading your existing connection.

Types of connections
There are many ways of connecting to the Internet. The most popular ways are:

- dialing into a large computer that is on the Internet
- joining an online service such as the Microsoft Network, CompuServe, America Online, Sympatico, or Prodigy
- connecting your computer directly to a local area network (LAN) whose server connects to an Internet host
- establishing a SLIP/PPP connection with an Internet service provider.

Each kind of connection has specific advantages and disadvantages. The following pages explain in greater detail all these ways of connecting.

Dialing into another computer
Many people get indirect access to the Internet by using a modem to dial in to a large computer (host) that is itself on the Internet. Your

computer becomes a terminal that communicates with the host computer. Community freenets allow Internet access of this kind. When you log on to the central computer, you use its programs to navigate the Internet.

Joining an online service

Commercial services such as the Microsoft Network, CompuServe, America Online, Sympatico, and Prodigy offer online banking, shopping, dating, entertainment, and connectivity to the Internet. Using these services in schools where students spend many hours online can be expensive, but they have been designed to be user friendly. Most of these services offer their own interface to the Internet, which can help reduce the learning curve for teachers and students. America Online offers a wide variety of educational resources, such as live classes, homework assignments, contests, awards, conferences for teachers, and complete graphical Internet access. Classroom Prodigy is a special version of the Prodigy online service designed for use in schools. It includes a bulletin board, craft ideas, an online encyclopedia, an art gallery, quizzes, current events, creative writing exchanges, and more. The Microsoft Network is an online service built into Windows 95. You can join directly using a modem and your Windows 95 software. The Microsoft Network offers full access to Internet facilities and e-mail, with different pricing plans from which to choose.

Commercial services vary in cost, and several cost options are available. For example, you might pay between US$20 and US$30 per month for ten hours of online time, or get a nine-month subscription with twenty-five hours of online time per month for about US$400. For specific details, contact the services directly. Be sure to ask which services are offered, as some offer only e-mail and may add personal message charges. Others may add surcharges for specific features. The best advice is to devote some time to exploring each service before joining. Look for current articles in computer magazines such as *PC World* or *MacUser* comparing the most recent offerings of the major commercial providers. Joining an online service is the easiest way to connect to the Internet, but it may not be the cheapest or the most inclusive. However, these companies are competing to make complete access for consumers easy, cheap, fast, and reliable.

Connecting through a LAN

Large organizations such as universities, school districts, and corporations purchase high-speed, high-volume direct connections to the Internet. They make use of these connections by developing ways in which hundreds of their users at a time can share that single high-speed central connection. Users may be physically dispersed

HINT For a comparison between direct dial-up options and LANs in schools, read "Internet Access for Educators: Options, Solutions and Costs" by Bob Avant and Keith Rutledge (**gopher:// SJUVM.stjohns.edu/00/ educat/nebraska/ neb-inf-0022.nebraska**).

throughout many buildings in laboratories, offices, and classrooms. Everyone is then connected by some technical means to a central server that controls the Internet connection.

Similarly, in many schools, all the computers in the school are connected on a local area network (LAN). By connecting a modem to the LAN, every computer on the network has Internet access. This is a complex way of connecting to the Internet, and explaining it in detail is beyond the scope of this book.

Despite the complexity and expense of installing and maintaining an Internet connection through a LAN, most large schools have or will select this option because it provides such generous and complete access for students and teachers.

> "Our school has a large lab of sixteen computers directly connected to the Internet. The library has its own network, which is hooked into our Internet pipeline. Our goal is to have one computer in every room directly connected. The staff has already trained in Net use and has access to the lab for that purpose."
>
> — *Jamie Boston, Librarian, Birch Lane Elementary School, Davis, California, U.S.A.; quoted in* Classroom Connect, *May 1995*

Two technologies are presently being considered for quicker Internet access: cable modems and ADSL (asymmetrical digital subscriber lines). With a cable modem, you gain access to the Internet through your local cable company. ADSL comes from the phone companies on a private line. These options are currently more expensive than telephone modems, and thus are not widely used. Future telecommunications through a seamless, high-speed, universal system will be convenient, fast, and powerful.

Establishing a SLIP/PPP connection

You can also get full Internet access by establishing a SLIP/PPP connection. You will see the acronyms SLIP (*Serial Line Interface Protocol*) and PPP (*Point-to-Point Protocol*) used interchangeably, although there are subtle differences between them. SLIP is the older of these two technologies and is now almost obsolete. The important thing is that a SLIP/PPP account gives you a temporary direct connection to the Internet from home or school. To get an account, you'll need to sign up with a company called an Internet service provider. Service providers charge a startup fee in the US$30 to US$50 range plus monthly charges, usually about US$20 to US$30. The service provider will supply the basic software you need and help you to get connected if you run into problems. Once you have your SLIP/PPP connection, you can run Internet client software directly from the hard drive of your computer. This means you can use either the simplest or the most advanced Web browser available, according to your needs and the amount of memory in your computer. To open your Internet connection, whether at home or at school, you simply dial in to your service provider.

Selecting a service provider

Look for lists of service providers in computer magazines, business magazines, Internet books, phone books, and newspapers. A large number of providers are available, and they offer a wide variety of subscription plans.

Once you register with a provider, you are assigned an Internet address, like a phone number, which others use to communicate with you. If you've ever had to change your phone number, you know how inconvenient *that* is. The same is true of your Internet address, so selecting a reliable, stable provider from the huge number available is important. Consider the following factors.

What computer do I need?

You don't need a particular type of computer to connect to the Internet, nor do you need to reserve a computer solely for this purpose. Chances are you'll be using an existing school or home computer that you also use for daily tasks such as word processing and desktop publishing. Old, low-memory machines such as an Apple IIe or 386 PC will do the job, but very slowly. In general, if you are using this type of equipment, you will be limited to low-volume, text-oriented activities. Don't expect your students to be able to access the multimedia features of the World Wide Web on these machines. They may also become frustrated at the slow pace at which the screen displays changes when commands are issued. With instructional time at a premium, many teachers are understandably reluctant to have students spend an hour locating a small amount of information that might have been obtained more easily from a book, video, or phone call. On the other hand, if your learning goals relate to communicating with e-mail or simply learning to use text-based Internet menus, older technology is adequate. However, if your students have more sophisticated computers with Internet access at home, you may find them less than enthusiastic using these slower machines.

If you are buying a new computer, consider a multimedia Pentium PC, or a Macintosh PowerPC. Such attributes as the amount of available RAM (Random Access Memory) and the size and speed of the hard drive inevitably have an effect on your computer's performance on Internet tasks. As a general rule, you will want sixteen to thirty-two megabytes (Mb) of RAM. As the Internet rapidly expands its offerings, we will need faster, more powerful computers with more storage space to take full advantage of its multimedia features. In other words: *Buy the best machine you can afford, and don't be disappointed when it becomes rapidly outdated.*

Tech Talk

Remember that phone lines can be "tone" or "pulse." Most people today have tone dial service, but if you live in a rural area you may have pulse. When installing your modem, be prepared to specify your dialing service - as well as any special codes you need to use (such as dialing 9 for an outside line). For example, if you must dial 9, you would type in your modem's protocol using a comma to indicate a brief pause in the sequence. Thus, typing "9, 1-800..." instructs your modem to pause briefly after dialing the 9. For a longer pause, insert two commas.

Figure 9-1
What you'll need for cruising the Internet

	Slow	Acceptable	Good Performance
Computer			
PC	386	486	Pentium
Macintosh	680040	PowerPC 603	PowerPC 604
Operating system			
PC	Windows 3.1	Windows 95	Windows 95
Macintosh	7.5.1	7.5.3	Open Transport
Hard Drive	100 MB	810 MB	1–2 GB
RAM	8 MB	16 MB	32 MB
Modem speed	14,400 bps	28,000 bps	33,600 bps or ISDN

HINT If it's not possible to purchase a new computer, consider upgrading your current system. You can add memory to your CPU and a second hard drive for less money than it would cost to buy a new computer. Your local dealer can inform you of the range of options for upgrading.

It's wise to stick with the type of computer, either PC or Macintosh, that is prevalent in your school, since each type requires its own brand of Internet software. Most people don't want to buy, install, or learn to use two different species of hardware and software.

What software do I need?

To dial in to an indirect connection, you need only basic communications software on your computer. Most new computers come with a communications package, and all modems come with software. Works packages such as ClarisWorks and Microsoft Works include communications software. Many shareware programs are also available at little cost. Once your modem has connected to the host, you use the host's software for your Internet navigation and tasks. This software can include an e-mail package, telnet (to connect to other computers), and FTP (to get files from other computers); but these tasks can now all be accomplished through your Web browser. We have discussed some of the options available for Web browsers and e-mail in Chapters 4 and 7. In Chapter 8, you found out more about telnet and FTP.

With a direct connection, on the other hand, your computer is part of the Internet and the network applications you need must run on your own computer. You need two types of software — the first to establish your connection and the second to navigate the Internet. Your service provider or your school computer expert should handle all this for you, but here's a very brief explanation.

The Internet's computer language is called TCP/IP (*Transmission Control Protocol/Internet Protocol*). TCP/IP software lets your computer "talk" to other computers on the Internet. In other words, it governs the way packets of information are broken up, packaged, labeled, transmitted, and received. Once your Internet connection is open and the TCP/IP software begins to work, you are ready to navigate. At this point you need a Web browser. Most people currently use either Netscape or Microsoft Internet Explorer, though the Opera browser may be another choice for schools. Both of these browsers include access to the World Wide Web as well as a range of resources such as FTP, telnet, a newsreader, and e-mail.

Most service providers have Web sites that give away all the software you'll need. Download it from the site and install it on your computer. This is generally not a difficult process, though there are lots of instructions to follow and it may take several hours. Alternatively, you can usually pick up the software from the service provider or have it mailed in the form of diskettes or a CD-ROM.

If you're an advanced Internet user, you may be the person installing and configuring TCP/IP software. In the Windows 3.1 and NT environment, obtain a shareware program called Trumpet Winsock. Windows 95 has built-in (32-bit) Winsock. You can access a helpful file that explains TCP/IP access with Windows 95 at **http://www.windows95. com/connect/tcp.html**. In the Macintosh platform, you will need a copy of the program called MacTCP (which is included in System 7.5 and later operating systems) and SLIP/PPP software such as MacPPP or InterSLIP. In order to configure your TCP/IP software to work with your SLIP/PPP connection, you'll need to get the following information from your service provider:

• your login user name and password

• the access phone number you'll be using
• your Internet Protocol (IP) number, which is the address of your machine
• the IP address of the domain name server you are assigned to use
• the IP address of the gateway machine used to handle e-mail and Usenet newsgroups
• the maximum packet size to use in your connection
• any other technical information, such as subnet mask address, that your service provider wants you to use.

You'll also need this information if you plan to create a dial-up connection to your own Internet service provider using the built-in TCP/IP feature of Windows 95. The help menus provided within Windows 95 will walk you through this process step by step.

Services offered

What do you want to do on the Internet? What do you want your students to be able to do? Make sure the service offers the Internet features you want.

Cost

For many users, this is the first consideration. Ask for detailed fee schedules, and spend some time examining and comparing different packages. Usually, the charge depends upon the services you use and the amount of time you spend online. Many services have a flat-fee monthly rate for a given number of hours (from US$15 to US$35 for thirty hours per month or more) and surcharges if you exceed the designated limit per month. Others charge a basic fee plus an hourly rate based on the exact amount of time you spend online. Thus, one provider's rate might be better for people who spend a lot of time online, but not as good as another's for those who spend less time. Reasonable cost is nice, of course, but as with many other things in life, you are likely to get what you pay for from an Internet service provider.

Access

Access relates to cost if there is no local number for the service you want to use. Find out how you would connect — via a local call, a long-distance call, or a 1-800 number. Long-distance charges can add up quickly. Don't assume that a 1-800 number is free, either; you'll pay for it through a surcharge. For home or school use, a local number is best. If you travel frequently, find out if the provider has local numbers in other major cities. Many do. Access also relates to the number of lines and modems the service has. How often will you get a busy signal when you dial in? You can ask the provider for their user-to-line ratio, and you can ask others who use the service if they ever have trouble getting connected.

HINT The number of phone lines that an Internet access provider controls is very important. Ideally, a provider should offer an account/line ratio of not more than 10 to 1. Commercial vendors should also offer at least 28,800 baud access, but be aware that rural phone lines don't always accommodate higher speeds.

Customer assistance/technical support

This might be the most important factor for beginners and even experienced users. Find out the answers to these questions.

• Does the service provider supply some help documentation?
• Do they staff a help desk?
• During what hours is assistance available? (evenings? weekends?)
• Is there an extra monthly charge for help?
• When you call, do you get a machine or a person?
• How quickly do they respond to requests for help?

The best way to get an honest, unbiased answer to these questions is to talk to someone who uses the service.

Track record
New service providers used to pop up frequently and some were short lived for a variety of reasons. Others suffered from technical problems that caused their system to shut down more frequently than users liked. A history of reliable service can be a sign that a provider is here to stay; these days the large companies tend to take the lion's share of the market. Look in computer magazines and periodicals for Internet provider performance surveys, and talk to colleagues and friends who have been on the Net for a while.

Software
What software will you need to do what you want to do? Access providers should give you a package of software (on a diskette or CD-ROM with clear instructions for loading) or a dial-in number that gives you access to the software for downloading. If you have a preference for a particular browser, ask if that's the one they will be providing to you. Some providers will tell you that everything you need is available on the Net — but unless they tell you exactly *how* to get it, choose another service. When you connect to a commercial online service, you may need a special software package. Sometimes this is an added cost, and you might prefer to use your own communications software. Check with the provider to find out if your software will work.

Models for schools

The Cadillac model: all computers in the school connected
Imagine that your students can access the Internet whenever they need to from any computer in the school. All the computers are connected to a LAN, which in turn is connected to the Internet. This kind of flexibility allows students virtually unlimited access to information and the ability to communicate worldwide. Information passes quickly in text or graphical form over a high-speed, dedicated data line. In every unit you plan, you can include a component that requires students to use the Internet. They can e-mail peers and experts in different fields, search for information, and telnet to remote sites to find particular documents. They can download pictures, video clips, and sound clips to include in their multimedia projects. Any project described in this book is easy to manage — the possibilities are endless.

The standard sedan model: Internet terminals in various locations in the school
Some schools have several phone lines, each with a modem-

HINT A good source for school networking information with practical advice on getting schools connected is the Schoolhouse Networking Operations Center at **http:// sunsite.unc.edu/cisco/ noc/index.html**.

equipped computer, located around the school. In this case, school equipment dedicated primarily to Internet use might include

- two or more computers with modems
- two or more dedicated phone lines
- communications software (which often comes with your computer, and much can be obtained free of charge from the Internet itself)
- Internet access through a service provider, commercial online service, or even a community freenet (costs will vary, according to your choice).

Although students may have to leave the classroom, they can still have easy Internet access provided that the number of terminals is adequate for the student and teacher population of the school. Other schools have several modems but are limited to only one phone line. If your class is online and another unknowingly tries to connect, you'll be disconnected in the midst of your work. To avoid this inconvenience, you can obtain an inexpensive "line-in-use" indicator light from your local hardware store, although some modems don't draw enough power down the line to activate the light.

In our experience, we see most terminals located in the school library/resource center and the computer lab. This configuration allows each class structured Internet use for an hour or so per week but makes it difficult to integrate activities into the curriculum in a seamless, natural way. This model also works best with older students, where teacher supervision is not an issue. With younger students, the most useful location for a terminal is in the classroom. You'll need to plan for individuals or pairs of students to move freely to wherever the terminals are located at the times that they need them. The cooperation and teamwork of all staff members helps to make this work. A schedule might be needed, especially in larger schools, so that all classes get a fair share of time. You'll also have to arrange for someone to be available to assist these students as they work, especially at first. Often, the librarian or computer teacher can be available. Parent volunteers and student experts are also invaluable.

If you are fortunate enough to have phone jacks in each classroom throughout the school, you might consider putting one or more modem-equipped computers on carts and creating a rotating schedule for their use. Modems on wheels allow access in the classroom, where you can use the technology most effectively to meet your educational goals. Depending on the type of connection you have, students may be able to access graphics or may be limited to text only. You can plan your Internet activities accordingly.

"The Internet becomes a valuable tool when it is accessible to the greatest number of students. It is difficult to find a location (when you have only one shared phone line) to allow all students supervised access. The computer room is supervised only when there is a class in attendance; the library is run by volunteers on a part-time basis. Each classroom needs its own access."

— *Debra Killen, Teacher, Chelsea School, Chelsea, Quebec, Canada*

The economy model: one computer, one modem, one phone line

This is an excellent, inexpensive way to get started. All you need is

- a computer
- a modem
- a dedicated phone line
- communications software (which often comes with your computer, and much can be obtained free of charge from the Internet itself)
- Internet access through a service provider, commercial online service, or community freenet (costs will vary, according to your choice).

The installation of a dedicated phone line in your classroom or school library is often the biggest hurdle. Your school's parent council or a local business might be willing to cover installation costs or monthly charges. If you have to depend on using one of the school's existing lines, you'll probably be limited to after-school connections, since most schools need all their lines during school hours. In this case, students can compose their e-mail messages during class, and you can send them after school. In one school, the after-school com-

---

Start small if necessary

"It is not necessary to spend a lot of money to bring the Internet to a school. Even a very inexpensive 2400 baud modem could do for a start. Since high-speed data transmission isn't essential for small quantities of text, one of your school's older, slower computers could be recycled to become your Internet computer. Next, find out if you'll need to install a separate phone line. As this can be expensive, see if there is a way you can operate your modem over the school's regular phone lines. Often, it's possible to get an outside line by dialing 9 first. You'll also need a communications program. We opted for shareware. We selected Z-Term (Mac). It is an excellent program, costs about $50, and has served us well. Finally, you'll need a dial-up service to connect you with the Internet. If your community has a Freenet like Ottawa, then you can dial the local Freenet number and access the Internet without incurring base utility charges. If not, you'll need to shop around for a commercial Internet provider. Hourly rates make more sense for schools doing many high-volume data transfers. A school does not need many Internet connections. Most student work on an Internet project is done offline using existing school resources. Material developed on word processors can quickly be uploaded or downloaded. In our school, only one of our computers connects to the Internet. While two or three more would have made things easier, we've been able to manage the complexities of our Internet projects without difficulty. If you have only one or two computers that connect to the Internet, you should think about where to put these machines. Our school finally decided upon the library. That way, the Internet computer could be available to everyone in the school."

— Doug Walker (1994) The Grassroots Program, Canada's Schoolnet **http://www.school-net.ca**, 01/10/97

---

puter club has the task of sending and receiving e-mail twice each week and distributing it the next morning.

> "We used school funds to purchase a modem and hooked it to the existing computer in the classroom. When I approached the parent council, they were excited about the idea and immediately agreed to install a dedicated phone line in the classroom and pay the monthly phone bills out of the profits from their fund raisers."
>
> — *Bob Benning, Principal, Convent Glen Catholic School, Orleans, Ontario, Canada*

Because only one computer can access the Internet at a time, curriculum integration is somewhat limited. Whole-class e-mail projects are a good way to take advantage of this setup. By pairing students at the computer and using cooperative learning groups, you can also maximize usage. Hopefully, every student would get an opportunity to use the Internet in a classroom project at least once each term.

Checklist for connectivity

You're ready to "surf" the Internet when you have

- a modem of sufficient speed to sustain your work (28, 800 bps or faster), unless you are connected through a LAN
- a personal computer and monitor of sufficient resolution for the text and graphics activities you wish to carry out
- a telephone line or high-speed data line
- a connection to the Internet in one of the ways described in this chapter
- instructions from your service provider on how to make and sustain a connection
- software to use once connected
- your service provider's customer service telephone number, should problems arise.

The Teacher's Complete & Easy Guide to the Internet

Project Ideas

Cybernauts Only

Learning outcomes
- Students will participate in an Internet club.
- Students will exchange messages with keypals.
- Students will explore World Wide Web sites and share their findings.

Grade level: All

Getting started
- Invite students to join an "Internet Club."
- Establish a time for weekly meetings.
- Select a general topic for meetings, such as space, animals, weather, or countries.

Developing
- Have students select more specific subtopics, identify some World Wide Web sites, and set up bookmarks.
- Share sites at the next meeting.
- Compile a list of sites for school use.
- Have students exchange electronic messages with keypals to get more ideas for their topics.

Extending
- Have students compose messages offline, on another computer, and bring their messages on diskette to the weekly meetings, where they can upload them.
- As responses are received between meetings, you can simply print them for distribution at the next meeting.

School implementation planning

The planning process gives school communities an opportunity to develop a vision of what they want their school to become and to plan the steps in getting there. A well-developed strategic school plan for implementing or expanding Internet use addresses current equipment and its present utilization, how and why these technological learning resources and their management need to be improved, who will be responsible for which aspects of the improvement, and how the school will evaluate its progress. Planning for curriculum and staff training are crucial elements too often ignored. Planning committees can include administrators, teachers, parents, and students. The committee will require help from individuals with curriculum, technological, and administrative expertise. Key issues should never be decided without consultation with others.

A good plan includes

- the names and contact information of committee members
- a brief philosophy and mission statement
- a list of anticipated beneficial student outcomes
- the planned integration of the technology across the curriculum
- proposed changes to current technology and its usage
- a hardware/software purchase plan, including proposed time of acquisition, cost, and sources of funding
- a detailed budget that includes costs of teacher training and support materials such as student learning guides, paper, duplication, and computer disks
- strategies to address upgrades, obsolescence, and maintenance
- the source and cost of ongoing technical and professional support
- the role of each person involved in the implementation, and timelines for their actions
- an explanation of how the project will sustain itself over time
- a description of how the project will be evaluated, including review dates.

HINT An excellent resource for overall technology planning is *The Switched-On Classroom*, a technology planning guide developed for the public schools of Massachusetts, U.S.A. This 250-page book outlines a twelve-step technology plan and implementation process, describes case studies of successful technology implementation, and includes an extensive listing of resources to help schools in their strategic planning efforts. It can be found at the World Wide Web site **http://www.swcouncil.org/switch2. html**. Other good examples and guidelines for technology planning are located at

The British Columbia Ministry of Education at **http://edub057.educ. gov.bc.ca/**

Pitsco's Launch to Technology Plans at **http://www.pitsco.com/p/ techplans.html**

Everyone should understand that a good plan is not static: it is always being adjusted to take advantage of changes — in technology, in resources, and in teacher expertise. Since the plan will probably be used to solicit funding, it must be easy to understand. Thus, keep technical and educational jargon to a minimum. Prepare a brief summary as a handout. It's a good idea to have a catchy name and a student-designed logo for your package. If you have an opportunity to present your plan in a format other than print, try to use the very technology that you are advocating.

Training

Motivation

As a teacher who has chosen to read this book, you must already be motivated to learn more about using the Internet in your classroom or school. You may now be wondering: How can you excite and motivate your colleagues to join you?

When asked what moved them to get involved in using the Internet in their classrooms, many teachers cited the availability of accounts at low (or no) cost, either through discounts from vendors, local or national grants, or pilot projects. Such advantages tended to trigger acquisition and implementation. Some teachers mentioned that their prior involvement with computers made using the Internet a natural evolution. Others found that a personal interest (such as planning a vacation, researching a hobby, or communicating with a family member) got them started on the Internet. In many cases, the enthusiasm of a friend, relative, fellow teacher, or student provided the motivation; a team approach eased the learning curve. The availability of a central resource, such as Canada's SchoolNet, Global SchoolNet, or EdWeb, was also helpful. Most importantly, all the teachers' comments reflected excitement and enthusiasm about the educational possibilities of the Internet.

> "Our school district purchased thirty accounts and distributed them to personnel who were willing to volunteer twelve to fifteen hours of training time to the project. Its success has made some other teachers wish they had invested the time. The initial group will train others in Internet usage."
>
> — *Carol Willard, Teacher, Troy Junior High School, Troy, Missouri, U.S.A.*

Training yourself

A common response from teachers when they see the educational possibilities of the Internet is "This looks great, but there's so much to learn. Where do I begin?"

Start by examining the opportunities within your own school. Once you are committed to becoming Internet literate, look for learning partners and mentors among your colleagues. It's more fun, and more productive, to learn in collaboration than in isolation. Many schools hold inservice sessions, both during the day and after school. "Brown bag" meetings held during the lunch period offer an opportunity for users to share experiences, frustrations, and discoveries. You can save time by sharing lists of educational sites among colleagues who have visited them.

> "We [twenty to thirty teachers] got together for Internet training using an LCD panel two separate times for four weeks, two hours a week. Our librarian did the training and each week provided us with practice activities that forced us to use our newly acquired skills. It was a great experience, and humbling, too. We felt 'dumb' at times, just as our students sometimes do when we present them with new information."
>
> — *Carol Willard, Teacher, Troy Junior High School, Troy, Missouri, U.S.A.*

Your school and/or district probably has resource people who can assist you in a variety of ways. Ideally, resource people would be located in your own school so that they are available when needed. However, with the realities of today's shrinking budgets, this isn't always possible. Reach out for whatever services are available from these resource people, such as

- offering workshops for groups of teachers, parents, and/or students
- working cooperatively with you and your students on a project
- finding useful Internet sites to fit your curriculum
- putting you in touch with a focus group of interested teachers in other schools
- helping with technical problem solving
- recommending resource books, training manuals, and magazines
- providing lists of conferences and courses
- arranging a visit to another school or site.

> "We have given demonstrations to entire staffs as an introduction to the Internet. We have also given workshops for small groups of teachers who are interested in learning more about the Internet. This approach has worked well because it allows us to offer more one-to-one help. In addition, I have also been busy helping teachers who want to be connected at home. I go to their homes, set up their computers, and give them one-to-one tutoring. . . . Teachers who are comfortable enough to connect at school and at home will in turn help others in their own schools."
>
> — *Bonnie McMurren, Stony Mountain Elementary School, Stony Mountain, Manitoba, Canada*

Many school districts have established their own bulletin board system. Though these may not have Internet access, you can use such local bulletin boards to learn and practice the skills of sending and receiving e-mail, uploading and downloading files, general navigation, and netiquette. They also provide forums through which you can exchange resources and ideas with other teachers. And there are Internet-related discussion groups you can join. Other districts and states have established Web sites that assist teachers with curriculum matters as well as facilitating communication between peers and community organizations.

> "Our school board features a mobile computer lab, the Micromobile. It travels from school to school, offering students and teachers opportunities to learn and use computer skills in a state-of-the-art facility. . . . Each school now has an Internet account and a Net manager — a teacher who is given a computer to take home for the summer to get comfortable with the Net. The Net manager then becomes an on-site trainer for other staff. We also have a school board BBS that provides access to, and help with, Internet and other computer-related topics."
>
> — *Peter K. McLeod (1995, June 22), "Training." Classuse@schoolnet.carleton.ca*

Some Canadian provinces and U.S. states offer training courses to assist their teachers in acquiring various computer competencies. These are often free of charge. For example, Utahlink, the state network, provides Internet training for all levels from beginners to advanced courses designed for technology specialists. You can look at their training calendar at **http://www.uen.org/utahlink/**.

University courses in educational technology, including the Internet, are numerous today. Many of them focus on practical classroom applications. The advantage of taking a course during the school year is that you can try out new strategies immediately in your own classroom. Your local high school may offer evening and/or weekend courses focusing on a specific software package such as Netscape or a particular skill such as creating Web pages. These are very useful, as they tend to be brief, inexpensive, hands-on, and student centered.

> "One teacher from each school that has Internet access was sponsored for an Internet course for new users, offered through the University of Calgary. Weekly assignments forced us to practice what we had learned. After five sessions we each had to present our project. This was excellent because each of us took on something entirely different. It gave us ideas for student projects and provided us with a list of resources that we could use in the classroom."
>
> — *Sharon Lewis, Teacher, Red Deer, Alberta, Canada*

HINT When you attend a computer conference, look for sessions that focus specifically on classroom use for the age of students you teach. That way, you'll come away with ideas to try in your classroom right away. If you're a beginner, avoid highly technical sessions.

Conferences such as those offered by the International Society for Technology in Education (ISTE), the National Education Computing Conference (NECC), and the Educational Computing Organization of Ontario (ECOO) offer sessions for both beginners and advanced Internet users.

Several education-related agencies offer training for teachers, for a price. This may take the form of workshops, seminars, or courses, on or off line. Visit these Web sites for more details.

Forefront Curriculum

Forefront Curriculum offers a great variety of seminars for K–12 educators and administrators throughout the United States. They will come to your school site and conduct seminars tailored to meet your specific curricular needs. Their recent seminars include Internet Basics for K–12 Educators, Creating a Classroom Web Site, Intermediate Internet for Educators, Walking the Web with Special Ed, Internet Curriculum Club, Internet Basics for Administrators, One Computer in the Classroom, Internet Basics for Librarians, Technology in the K–12 Classroom, Child Safety on the Net, Improving Instruction with the 'Net, and Net Integration for Science Educators.

http://www.4forefront.com/seminar.html

Global SchoolNet Foundation

Global SchoolNet Foundation offers training opportunities such as Internet Applications and Guided Practice, Making and Managing Global Learning Projects, Designing and Publishing Your Own School WWWeb Pages, and Designing On-line Courses. Fees are based on the duration of the workshop. The Online Internet Institute is a collaborative project between Internet-using educators, proponents of systemic reform, content area experts, and teachers desiring professional growth.

http://www.gsn.org/teach/pd/index.html

Some private agencies, such as Internet service providers and computer stores, also offer short workshops and longer training sessions. Though they may not deal specifically with educational applications of Internet resources, they can introduce you to general Internet tools and allow hands-on practice time.

Many teachers prefer to schedule their Internet training in a more flexible manner. You don't have to leave home to learn how to use the Internet; you can access distance education courses, tutorials, reference books, and Internet guides on the Internet itself.

Here are some of the many useful starting points on the World Wide Web. As you visit these sites, bookmark any you'd like to have your students or colleagues use.

Andy Carvin's HTML Crash Course for Educators

If you want to learn about how Web pages are made, this will get you started. The tutorials are easy to follow — great for beginners to HTML, the language of Web publishing.

http://edweb.gsn.org/htmlintro.html

Atlas to the World Wide Web

This is a good place to learn about the Web.

http://www.rhythm.com/~bpowell/Atlas/toc.htm

Beginners Central

A top site for newcomers to learn about the Internet.

http://www.digital-cafe.com/~webmaster/begin00.html

Charm Net Learning Page

This provides links to books, tutorials, and hint sheets for Internet learning as part of the home page for the Charm net service provider in Baltimore, Maryland.

http://www.charm.net/learning.html

Electronic School Tour

Take a guided tour of the World Wide Web with the Electronic School. Developed specifically for educators, this site offers many educational resources, including the Library of Congress and the Louvre. This is also a good place to sample such sites as AskERIC and the Cisco Systems Meta-library of elementary and primary school Internet links.

http://www.electronic-school.com/surf.html

Getting Technologically Savvy

Learn about online technologies. Topics include Internet searching, newsgroups, and listservs.

http://204.98.1.1/di/savvy.html

HTML Goodies

Joe Burns offers tutorials, HTML primers, free images, scanning service, video service, an archive file of frequently asked questions and much more.

http://www.htmlgoodies.com/

Internet Island

An entertaining and informative Internet tour for beginners of all ages.

http://www.miamisci.org/ii/default.html

Internet School Networking (ISN)

The goal of this site is to list the questions most commonly asked about the Internet by elementary and secondary school educators, and to provide pointers to sources that answer those questions. It is directed at teachers, school media specialists, and school administrators who have recently connected to the Internet, who are accessing the Internet via dial-up or means other than a direct connection, or who are considering an Internet connection as a resource for their schools.

http://www.cusd.claremont.edu/www/people/rmuir/rfc1578

Internet Tourbus

Archives for a popular e-mail course about the Internet. When you subscribe, you receive information via e-mail about useful sites.

http://www.worldvillage.com/tourbus.htm

John December's Web Site

John December is a well-known author and speaker who has extensive experience in Web development, publishing, and research. His site is intended for both beginning and experienced Internet users. It has pointers to resources to help you learn about and use the Internet and the Web, master the art of Web development, and understand the significance of the online world.

http://www.december.com/works/

Learn the Net

A comprehensive guide to the Internet, including help with digging for data; using search tools, mailing lists, and databases; exchanging files; and developing Web pages.

http://www.learnthenet.com/english/thetools/map.htm

Microsoft Library; Internet resources

This is a well-organized Internet guide that includes help for beginners.

http://library.microsoft.com/nethelp.htm

Oz-TeacherNet

This site is a starting point for Australian teachers who want to use the Internet for professional development and curriculum purposes. The project team will assist in developing online resources and tools for events and discussion.

http://owl.qut.edu.au/oz-teachernet

Figure 9-2
Oz-teacher Net is a model of professional development based on creating opportunities for teachers to talk, share, and gain help while participating in curriculum projects using telecommunications.

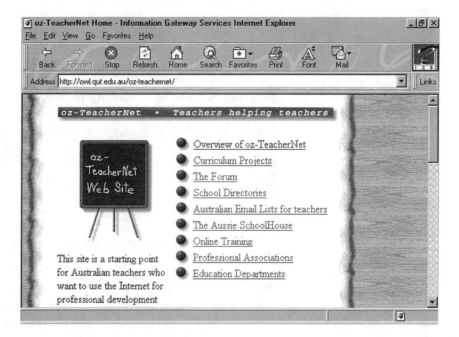

The Teacher's Complete & Easy Guide to the Internet

PD Rosetta Stone
This site is dedicated to professional development with lots of great links to organizations and events, resources, staff developers, and help with using the Internet.

http://fox.nstn.ca/~psmith/throsetta.html

Quest: Home of NASA's K-12 Internet Initiative
This site includes many links for finding online training on the Net, along with curriculum-related resources, technology planning, and funding.

http://quest.arc.nasa.gov/net-learning.html

University at Albany Libraries
You'll find online tutorials on topics such as how to connect to the Internet, evaluating Internet resources, choosing a Search Engine, and navigating the World Wide Web with Netscape.

http://www.albany.edu/library/internet/

Yahoo's listing of Internet guides
Start here for links to all sorts of online learning materials.

http://www.yahoo.com/computers_and_Internet/Internet/Infor
mation_and_Documentation

> "The Internet is like an elephant: you can eat it, but you have to take it one bite at a time!"
>
> — *Christiane Dufour, Teacher, Small Schools Network, Quebec City, Quebec, Canada*

Figure 9-3
Internet Island: an Internet tutorial

Training others

Many different staff development strategies have been tried with mixed success. Staff development does not mean pouring information into teachers' heads or training them in a few technical skills, but rather providing meaningful contexts for learning, emphasizing collaborative problem solving and personal expression, and placing the learner at the center of the learning experience. Teachers, like their students, must see the relevance of what they are to learn or they are not interested. Thus, the Internet needs to be both understood and used in relation to its relevance to curriculum. Once its educational applications are apparent, teachers are motivated to take the time to learn how to use it.

Teachers teaching one another is one of the most successful professional development strategies. This might involve freeing one teacher to work as a teacher-trainer in another teacher's class for a given length of time. The teacher-trainer can assist by observing what goes on in the class, working with students and the teacher to learn a new skill, and suggesting ways in which that teacher could try to integrate the technology. This is valuable because it occurs within the "real" situation of the teacher, who can feel more comfortable knowing that help is at hand and thus may be more inclined to explore new ideas.

HINT The Internet Training site at **http:// www.december.com/ cmc/info/internet-training.html** contains links aimed at instructors who provide Internet training, including lesson plans and resources.

If you are training other teachers, offer them a choice of opportunities to see the Internet in action, so that they can select the presentation that best fits their timetable.

You'll need to have a computer system available after school for teachers' use, with a co-trainer to attend when needed. Offer specific topic sessions, and build Internet awareness activities into scheduled meetings. After a brief introduction to the Net, encourage people to browse on their own. Stay close by to answer questions and give suggestions. Find out each teacher's interest, and then locate sites on the Internet that pertain to them. Show each teacher how he or she might use the Internet in the classroom — and remember what it was like for you when you were just beginning. Experienced users may accept such inconveniences as dropped lines or unavailable sites, but small irritations can be big roadblocks for people who are new to this technology.

> "I believe in 'just in time' training — that is, teaching people to use tools as they relate to projects they want to do now. Teaching Internet tools in the abstract is too overwhelming. But handing teachers a specific tool to do something they want to do makes learning easier."
>
> — *Christiane Dufour, Small Schools Network, Quebec City, Quebec, Canada*

Teachers who have had experience with Internet training courses recommend the following strategies.

The Teacher's Complete & Easy Guide to the Internet

- Ensure each pair of teachers has their own computer.
- Tie training to practical classroom needs.
- Be diverse in the activities you select, as not everyone responds with equal enthusiasm to the same activities.
- Reinforce learning by having teachers complete a project in conjunction with their training.
- Pair teachers with others in the school who are knowledgeable about the Internet.
- Create a few successful "pockets of good practice" within a school, even if this necessitates concentrating resources in a couple of early adopters rather than attempting to get everyone going simultaneously.
- Provide hands-on experience. The only way to learn something is to do it.
- Ensure a low instructor-to-student ratio to allow for individual assistance.
- Plan short instructional sessions followed by lots of practice time.
- Schedule ongoing training over a period of time rather than a one-shot inservice.
- Allow some release time from classes in order to pursue professional development whenever possible.
- Visit other schools to compare practices.
- Reward participants with certification or a recognized credit of some sort.

HINT A sample workshop for librarians interested in learning about the World Wide Web can be found at **http://www.wolinskyweb.com/hand1.htm**. This site includes a handout entitled *101 Sites to See.*

Staying current

With the pace of change today, it's a continuing challenge to keep up to date. The Internet is no exception; in fact, it's the fastest growing technology around. The Internet is always changing. We

HINT One great way to stay current is to look at what other schools around your country and around the world are doing. For an international listing of school sites, see the Web66 Schools Registry at **http://web66.coled.umn.edu/schools.html**. An example of an individual school that always seems to have a lot to offer is Loogootee Elementary at **http://siec.k12.in.us/~west/west.html**.

asked some teachers how they keep abreast of new developments. Here are their suggestions.

- Read magazines such as *Internet World, Web Week, Net Guide,* and *Leading and Learning with Technology.*
- Use the Internet as often as possible. Explore on your own, and do searches of topics that interest you.
- Subscribe to listservs that discuss issues relevant to technology in education, such as those listed in Chapter 6.
- Take a distance education course on the Internet.
- Have discussions with other teachers and individuals already involved in using the Internet.
- Search for tools or help to answer questions about practical needs that arise.
- Use the buddy system.
- Get involved in assisting other teachers to take advantage of the potential of the Net.
- Devote some time each day to surfing the Internet in order to discover new sites that might be useful at school. When a URL is recommended, view the site immediately, and if you like it, add it to your bookmarks. (Then, of course, share your bookmarks with others!)

Funding

In today's economy, money matters more than ever. But this is a good time to be seeking funds for Internet projects. In the United States in 1997, for example, we are seeing the beginning of a massive effort to accomplish President Clinton's goal of wiring every classroom and library in the country to the Internet, an initiative supported by government leaders, corporations, communities, and nonprofit organizations. With the emphasis on educational reform, global communications, and technology, you'll find there are a variety of sources of funding available. Designate several members of your planning team to pursue funding opportunities. Consider local community businesses, large corporations, private foundations, charitable organizations, provincial/state government agencies, and national projects that support technology in education.

The responsibility for finding sources of funding generally rests with your school administration and the school board or district. If you don't presently have Internet access, ask a local service provider or university to allow you to use their account for a demonstration to administrators. Once they see the World Wide Web in action as a learning tool, they will be more likely to pursue funding.

The best way to convince the decision makers of the educational benefits of the Internet is to have students demonstrate their learning and excitement. Invite trustees, parent councils, administrators, and

HINT Kid Wide Web: A Guide to the Internet for Teachers is a Danish site that illustrates some ways in which kids are using the World Wide Web today. The international nature of its links makes this an excellent site to show to decision makers. Visit it at **http://www.algonet. se/~bernadot/teachers/ teachers.html**.

Internet videos

The National Center for Education Statistics in the Office of Educational Research and Improvement at the United States Department of Education has released a seventeen-minute video targeted at school administrators entitled "Experience the Power: Network Technology for Education." It uses interview clips of students, teachers, and policy makers in the United States to educate about what the Internet is and to encourage support for the use of telecommunications in primary and secondary schools. For a copy of the video contact:

National Center for Education Statistics
555 New Jersey Ave N.W., R.410 C
Washington DC 20208-5651 USA
Phone: (202) 219-1364, Fax: (202) 219-1728

The NASA NREN (US National Aeronautics and Space Administration National Research and Education Network) K–12 Initiative has produced an eleven-minute video describing the benefits to schools of using the Internet. The video is entitled "Global Quest: The Internet in the Classroom," and it tells the story through interview clips with students and teachers who have experienced the power of computer networking. For a copy of the video contact

NASA Central Operation of Resources for Educators (CORE)
Lorain County Joint Vocational School
15181 Route 58 South
Oberlin, OH 44074 USA
Phone: (216) 774-1051, x293/294, Fax: (216) 774-2144

The fee for the video is cost plus shipping and handling. You may make a copy yourself by taking a blank copy to the nearest NASA Teacher Resource Center or by taping from NASA Select television. For information on the NASA Teacher Resource Center Network or on NASA Select, log in to NASA at **http://www.nasa.gov/NASA_home-page.html**.

community leaders to attend school technology fairs. Show them videos and slides of students at work using the Internet, and try to maintain a high profile for your technology projects. Collect a file of clippings about educational use of the Internet, and reserve a bulletin board for displaying current magazine and newspaper articles.

School fund raising

Many schools raise money for their projects through such efforts as fun fairs, technology fairs, school plays, bake sales, plant sales, math-a-thons, garage sales, and barbecues. You might not think of making a lot of money this way, but one school in San Francisco managed to raise nearly $100,000 in a year by preparing and selling hot lunches! An active, enthusiastic parent group can accomplish great things.

Corporate funding

Many large companies set aside funds specifically for community and educational projects. In the United States, these funds are often distributed through nonprofit foundations. In Canada, they are

HINT You can find ideas for alternative sources of funding in the *Grassroots Funding* Journal, available from

GFJ
P.O. Box 11607
Berkley, CA 94701 USA

The Grass Roots Fundraising Book: How to Raise Money in Your Community, by Joan Flanagan, is a book of practical advice and comprehensive information available for US$11.95 from Contemporary Books, Inc.

usually controlled by the Community or Public Affairs Branch of the national office of the corporation. In both cases, you'll find formal selection policies and application procedures.

Your first step is to list all the corporations in your area that might be interested in your project. Technology-related corporations are the most likely choice, particularly telecommunications companies; but don't limit yourself. Remember that the benefits to learners are the driving force, not the technology itself. Your community library may have a reference guide to corporate funding that includes contact information. The magazine *Classroom Connect* also includes a monthly section on U.S. grants and funding sources and ideas.

Once you've identified possible sponsors, the next step is to find out what types of projects they support and what types of donations they provide. Ask them to send their application procedures and funding guidelines, then pare your list down to the top ten. Don't make the mistake of thinking that just because a project contributes to good public relations it will automatically be attractive to the company. Ideal prospects are those in which your project matches the stated objectives of the corporation's giving program and/or a senior executive has an interest in your project and will be an advocate within the corporation. Corporations generally prefer to donate to schools in their local area and may be more willing to contribute products or services than cash. You might approach them for donations such as telephone lines, equipment, or technical expertise. Corporate sponsors also tend to prefer to be the only ones of their kind involved in a specific project, so if you obtain significant funding from one source, don't solicit funds from competing companies in the same field.

Develop a succinct summary of your project, one or two pages long. Consider establishing levels of sponsorship, each with a set amount — for example, founding sponsors, $1000; major sponsors, $500; contributing sponsors, $100. Explain in your application how the sponsors will be given credit for their assistance. After clearing prospects with your school principal and board/district supervisors, communicate directly and personally with appropriate corporations. In large corporations, you'll want to talk with a specific person, often called the "giving officer." Use the name of any company executives who you know to support your project. After submitting your proposal, follow up and offer to provide further information or to do a more detailed presentation. If you are successful in securing a sponsor or receiving a grant, stay in close contact with your donor. Forward progress reports, news articles, and results. Invite company representatives to visit your school and see the project in action.

Some smaller hardware and software companies may give in-kind donations or offer reduced costs to schools. In-kind donations might include use of training facilities, printing and copying, surplus equipment, personnel for technical advice, or planning expertise. Don't hesitate to approach your school's parent community for assistance from local businesses, both large and small. Parents are often your best connections and are more than willing to assist when your planned initiative directly benefits their own children.

HINT For a detailed overview of the solicitation process, take a look at the article entitled "Steps of the Solicitation" at **http://cyberadvantage.com/krueger/Steps.html**.

So far this year, AT&T has offered $11,275,082 in cash grants to educational institutions to fund projects that demonstrate effective and innovative uses of technology to support families, schools, and communities. There are no specific deadlines — grant proposals are considered as they are received and awarded as long as funds are available. The URL for the guidelines is **http://www.att.com/foundation/guide.html**. The grants are awarded regionally, so you will need to contact the AT&T regional contributions offices in your area. Their contact information is listed at **http://www.att.com/foundation/contrib.html**. You can also contact: AT&T Foundation at:

32 Avenue of the Americas
24th Floor; New York, NY 10013
Phone (212) 387-4801

The program is open to all accredited public and private elementary and secondary schools as well as accredited public and private two- and four-year institutions of higher education and educational nonprofit organizations in the fifty United States, the District of Columbia, Puerto Rico, and all U.S. territories. The AT&T Learning Network Grants Program focuses on the use of technology, not on the equipment and infrastructure necessary to support that use. AT&T Learning Network grants will not fund requests that are exclusively for the purchase of computers, modems, wiring, or other infrastructure needs. Instead, the program provides resources to help families, schools, and communities understand how to use technology.

Business-education partnerships

Establishing a business partnership is different from asking a business for a grant or donation. True business-education partnerships are cooperative relationships in which partners share values; human, material, or financial resources; and roles and responsibilities, in order to achieve desired learning outcomes. For example, a local Internet service provider might give your school reduced access charges if teachers enroll in their training courses.

> "...Employers and educators support business-education partnerships that:
> - enhance the quality and relevance of education for learners;
> - mutually benefit both partners;
> - treat fairly and equitably all those served by the partnership;
> - provide opportunities for all partners to meet their shared responsibilities toward education;
> - acknowledge and celebrate each partner's contribution through appropriate forms of recognition;
> - are consistent with the ethics and core values of all partners;
> - are based on the clearly defined expectations of all partners;
> - are based on shared or aligned objectives that support the goals of the partner organizations;
> - allocate resources to complement and not replace public funding for education;
> - measure and evaluate partnership performance to make informed decisions that ensure continuous improvement;
> - are developed and structured in consultation with all partners;
> - recognize and respect each partner's expertise;
> - identify clearly defined roles and responsibilities of all partners; and
> - involve individual participants on a voluntary basis."
>
> — *The Education Forum, Conference Board of Canada (1995), "Ethical guidelines for business-education partnerships."*

Partnerships can be formed with individual companies, colleges, and universities, or with groups of individuals representing several related businesses. For a school, the benefits of forming a business partnership might include leadership from experts in a particular technology, gifts or loans of equipment, opportunities for student internships, and/or the provision of support services. You'll find that many of the grants and award programs available today require evidence of one or more business partnerships. Here are some tips for finding a potential business partner.

- Identify companies in your local area and companies whose products you are already using.
- Explore personal contacts, such as parents within your school.
- Find out as much as possible about potential partners and their needs.
- Establish credibility by showing people from the business community some of the great things that are already happening in

HINT The Apple Education/Business Partnership Program enables businesses that have established relationships with educational institutions to purchase hardware and software for their school partners at discount prices. Price lists and order forms are available in the Apple Education Resource Guide; call (800) 800-APPL to find out where to obtain a copy. For additional information about the program, call (800) 793-EDUC.

HINT "Grant Proposal Development: An Educator's Guide" provides basic knowledge of grant writing for US$3 from the Massachusetts Field Center for Teaching and Learning, University of Massachusetts at Boston, Harbor Campus, Boston, MA 02125. "Tips for Writing Grant Proposals" is free from the Association of Supervision & Curriculum Development, 1250 North Pitt Street, Alexandria, VA 22314; (703) 549-9110.

your school through the use of technology. Proposals in which the school raises a portion of the money and the business matches the amount raised are often successful.
- Generate as much publicity as you can for your venture. Try to establish your school as an innovative leader. Everyone likes a winner.
- Provide a detailed plan of your project and its benefits to all parties.[2]

Government grants and awards

Individuals and schools can apply for government-sponsored grants and awards at both the national and provincial/state levels. The 1997 U.S. federal budget contained nearly $57 million for Challenge Grants for Technology in Education, a 50 percent increase from the previous year, and Congress also approved $200 million for the first year of the Technology Literacy Challenge Fund in 1997.

The U.S. Department of Education (ED) awards grants and contracts to schools, school districts, researchers, and others to implement new methodologies, research effective practice, and implement educational reform. The department's World Wide Web site (**http://www.ed.gov**), offers documents explaining the grants and contracts processes and rules. Follow the link, Money Matters. The section "What Should I Know About ED Grants?" is designed to de-mystify the grants process within the Departmentdepartment. The "Guide to U.S. Department of Education Program" provides, in concise form, the information necessary to begin the process of applying for funding from individual federal education programs. It includes a brief description of each of the department's more than 200 programs, specifies who is eligible to apply, and gives the office and telephone number to contact for more information. This Web site features the latest announcements about funding opportunities, as well as the department's "Combined Application Notice," which lists upcoming grant competitions. In some cases, the application packages are available for downloading. Alternatively, you can get this information by writing to:

U.S. Department of Education
Office of Educational Research and Improvement
555 New Jersey Avenue, NW, Room 214
Washington, DC 20208-5725

You may have heard a lot lately about the "E-rate." A recent updating of the communications law, signed by President Clinton in February 1996, extended "universal service" to schools and libraries. Universal service means that telecommunications compa-

HINT ED Board is a computer bulletin board of information about U.S. Education Department grants and contracts, including those from the Office of Educational Research and Improvement (OERI). It is available twenty-four hours a day by modem (no access fee); dial (202) 260-9950 and use settings of (8N1). More information can be obtained from ED Board, U.S. Department of Education, 400 Maryland Avenue SW, ROB3, Room 3616, Washington, DC 20202; (202) 708-8773.

Federal programs granting funding for technology include:

- Chapter 1
  Compensatory Education Programs Section, U.S. Dept. of Education
  400 Maryland Avenue SW
  Washington, DC 20202
  Phone (202) 219-2000

- Field-initiated Studies
  FIS are grants for education research projects, including basic applied research, inquiry with the purpose of applying tested knowledge gained to specific educational settings and problems, development, planning , surveys, assessments, evaluation, investigations, experiments, and

demonstrations in the field of education and other fields relating to education. The U.S. Department of Education, Office of Educational Research and Improvement has awarded over $8.8 million for 47 forty-seven grants under the FY 1996 Field-Initiated Studies Educational Research Grant Program. Grant recipients included universities, state departments of education, school districts, research institutions, a childrenís hospital, and one individual. The awards cover a broad range of topics.
http://www.ed.gov/offices/ OERI/FIS/index.html

- Star Schools program:
  U.S. Department of Education,

Office of Educational Research and Improvement
555 New Jersey Avenue NW
Washington, DC 20208
Phone (202) 219-2116

- National Science Foundation
  Several programs that provide grants for technology, with an emphasis on mathematics and science. NSF's Application of Advanced Technologies Program supports research, development, and demonstration of state-of-the-art computer and telecommunications technologies in education. Call or write the NSF at 1800 G Street NW, Room 233A, Washington, DC 20550; Phone (202) 357-7492.

The Teacher's Complete & Easy Guide to the Internet

nies must provide affordable services to schools and libraries. Schools can receive discounts for installation and services provided after January 1, 1998. All K–12 schools are eligible for the discounts, which apply to the installation and continuing costs of all commercially available telecommunications services, Internet access, and internal connections, including telephones. To be included, you must submit a school or district technology plan that includes clear goals and realistic strategies for integrating technology, including professional development and an evaluation process, along with proof that you can pay for the portion of the rates not provided by the Universal Service Fund. The Schools and Libraries Corp. (SLC), administrator of the E-rate program, has a detailed policies/procedures document available for all schools and libraries who have yet to develop an approved plan; those with approved plans already in place (such as plans developed for Goals 2000 or state technology initiatives) will not need to create new plans. For a copy of the Technology Plan Policies/Procedures, call toll-free (888) 203-8100. At the time of writing, critics of the recently established E-rate are trying to pull the plug on this program. The E-rate is in serious jeopardy due to legal, political, and financial problems. A campaign has been launched to save the E-rate. To find out what you can do to help, check out **http://congress.nw.dc.us/e-rate/e-rateZ. html.**

Although education is not the direct responsibility of the federal government in Canada, schools can apply for government grants and awards sponsored by other federal departments. You can find out about these in the *Handbook of Grants and Subsidies of the Federal and Provincial Governments for Non-Profit Organizations.* The aim of this document is to keep citizens informed of all governmental assistance available. Funding opportunities include Education and Research, Cultural Affairs, Health and Social Services, and Employment and Development. The handbook and monthly updating service are available from:

Canadian Research and Publications Centre (CRPC)
33 Racine
Farnham, PQ J2N 3A3
(Phone: In Quebec, 1-800-363-8304. In all other provinces, 1-800-363-1400.)

Don't limit yourself to grants specifically designated for technology. Be creative in showing how the Internet will benefit at-risk, disabled, gifted, and workplace preparation programs. The time spent in writing a proposal is well worth it. Once you have prepared one funding application, you can easily modify it to meet the criteria of others. Apply well in advance of the anticipated launch of your initiative, and be patient as you wade through the red tape and bureaucracy.

HINT Industry Canada's Computers for Schools Program ships used federal government computers to Canadian schools that have requested them. Some businesses and provincial governments have also joined this "pass the PC" program. Companies including Air Canada, Canadian National, Voyageur Colonial Bus Lines, and Canadian Tire cover the cost of collecting, repairing, and distributing the computers.

America Online, Inc., is launching an Interactive Education Grants Program under the newly created AOL Foundation. The grants will be awarded to teachers, education leaders, parents, and other community leaders who develop innovative and creative ways to apply the online medium in ways that enhance student learning. A special emphasis will be placed on proposals that reach socio-economically disadvantaged children and communities. In addition to the grants, AOL plans to provide assistance and online support for selected Interactive Education Grant recipients. For more information contact Jill Stephens, Corporate Outreach Director, America Online, 22000 AOL Way, Dulles, Virginia VA 20166; Phone (703-) 265-1342), or send an e-mail to AOLGrant@aol.com.

Most state and provincial departments of education have recently created funds for technology initiatives. There are too many to list here, and they change yearly, so contact your local school district or school board to get the details of these programs for your area. You can also find extensive lists of links to sources of grants and funding at:

- The Pitsco Technology Education Web at **http://www.pitsco.com**
- NASA's Grants and Other (People's) Money at **http://quest.arc.nasa.gov/top/grants.html**
- Online Grant Resources at **http://www.siec.k12.in.us/~ice/grants.html**
- US West Connected Schools Program, the Bursar at **http://www.uswesthomeroom.cm/pages/bursar.html**

Private grants, awards and contests

Some computer companies and education-related businesses offer grants and awards of various kinds. At the following sites, you can enter a contest while contributing to a collection of exemplary classroom practices.

Teacher's Choice
Enter a Web site in a contest, explaining how you use it for teaching and learning and how it combines content and the Internet. All approved entries go into The Well Connected Educator's database with your name attached so you get credit for the find and a chance to win the contest.

http://www.gsh.org/wce/choice.asp

Encarta Lesson Collection
Share an original lesson of which you're especially proud. The best lessons are published on the Web site, and the authors win valuable prizes.

http://encarta.msn.com/schoolhouse/lessons/introedit.asp

Compaq's Teaching with Computer Technology Grant Program

Enter by submitting a success story about how technology has been used in the classroom. The three best entries from each state win a $1000 grant. Winning entries are posted to their Web site to inspire other schools around the country.

http://www.compaq.com/education/alliances/contest.html

International Society for Technology in Education (ISTE)

Each year since 1991, the Special Interest Group on Telecommunications (SIG/Tel) of ISTE has sponsored a contest for educators using telecommunications networks for innovative classroom practices. Winners are invited to share their work at two major conferences and the winning entries are published in ISTE's publication, the *Journal of Online Learning*. Winners also receive valuable prizes that facilitate telecommunications in their classroom, such as software, modems, robotics, and magazine subscriptions.

http://www.iste.org

The NetDay concept involves selecting a particular day on which volunteers from business, the parent community, and teaching and administrative staffs work together to get schools wired. Through volume discounts and corporate sponsorships, network kits are available at a reduced price to participating schools. NetDay has been very successful in many parts of the United States. At the NetdDay site (**http://www. netday.org**) schools can register, volunteers can sign up, and you can find reports and helpful tips from past participants.

Authentic learning can occur when students are involved in raising funds for their own classroom and school. Global SchoolNet offers free software and other prizes for correctly answering their question of the month. Answers to all questions are located within the Global SchoolNet WWW archive, so it's also a good way to become more familiar with this site, which has a lot to offer both students and teachers. (**http://www.gsn.org/teach/contest/index. html**) Think Quest Junior, launched in 1997 and modelled after the senior version, is for grades 4–6 students. Students work in teams, coached by their teachers, to build Web-based educational materials that will help other students of the same age. For example, a team of students might create an entry that will introduce other students to the team's favorite books or that shows how the human digestive system deals with a peanut butter and jelly sandwich as it travels through the body. Those who create the entries learn as they collaborate within their team, focus on what will interest other students, and then plan and build their entries. More than $500,000 in cash, computer, and networking awards go to the winning teams of students, coaches, and their schools. (**http://www. advanced.org/ tq-junior**)

Time

One of the challenges to using the Internet most often articulated by teachers is finding time. They need time to

- learn Internet tools
- teach their use to the students
- find appropriate usable resources relating to the curriculum

- collaborate with other teachers on how to use the Internet in the classroom
- implement a project, given many user groups and limited access to computers
- re-think well-worn teaching strategies.

"I believe the biggest challenge is time and training. We must first learn how to use the technology. Then we must fit it to our curriculum in meaningful and appropriate ways. Next, we need to figure out how best to teach our students the power of the tool. We must also cut down the amount of 'surfing' time, and devise ways to move right into classroom use."

— *Dave Lehnis*

You don't have to master Internet tools before you start using the Net with your students. The overview provided in this book and some hands-on experience are all you need. Your ongoing training should focus on specific project needs. Rather than head out on your own, join an existing project such as those described in Chapter 2. Start small. If you run into a problem, you'll find that help is easy to get from the project leaders.

Nor do your students have to master many Internet tools before they begin. They'll learn to use the Internet within the context of their projects. This is authentic learning for a purpose. Arrange training for a few students, and then let them take the lead in training others so that you can move into the role of facilitator. Let parents, teachers-in-training, or older students work with small groups on the Internet while you manage the rest of the class.

"An ironic downside is that [the students] would rather be on the Net than in the book or attentive to the teacher. So we change the teaching style, relinquish the direct power role, and become facilitators of their learning. I think 'what's wrong with the schools today' boils down to too much teaching and not enough learning."

— *Elizabeth S. Dunbar, Teacher, Baltimore City College High School, Baltimore, Maryland, U.S.A.*

The solutions to the challenge of finding time to locate useful resources on the Internet do not lie solely with the teacher. Such institutions as Canada's SchoolNet and its equivalents organize material in such a way as to make it easy for a teacher to find curriculum-related material and entry-level projects. When you begin, adopt a favorite general site, such as Canada's SchoolNet, EdNet, Global SchoolNet, Classroom Connect, or EdWeb, and stick with it rather than spending a lot of time sifting through the huge volumes of information on the Internet. You'll find that your horizons will broaden naturally as time passes and you become a more experienced user. One of the great benefits in collaborating with other teachers is the time saved by sharing specific useful sites among the group. You'll also save time by using the CD that accompanies this

book, which provides a wide variety of specific, reliable educational sites.

Rather than viewing Internet use as an add-on to your already heavy burden of curriculum, use it to replace more traditional methods. When you carefully document the learning outcomes you expect from your Internet project, you'll see how it accomplishes the goals of other activities you might have done in the past. As soon as you're confident that students will learn as well as or better than in the past, abandon the old in favor of the new. You can also use your Internet resources as an alternative to more traditional tools. For example, in a research project, have some students use books as information sources while others use Internet resources. In a project requiring communication, have some students use telephone or postal services while others use e-mail.

Summing up

With effort, creativity, and commitment, you can find the time, money, resources, and equipment you need to get connected and travel the information highway with your students. You will find yourself less isolated, better informed, better equipped with skills for today and the future, and empowered to be a knowledge builder. Because the educational reform movement advocates change and encourages schools to use new technologies such as the Internet, there are literally thousands of funding sources available for technology-related projects. The energy and inspiration you need will come from the collaboration and support of colleagues, students, parents, and the community.

Beyond the Classroom Walls

"Professionally, I see the chance to help my students experience the world outside rural Kansas. I see the chance to share ideas in forums I never thought possible; to gather information that's not in any local library; and to help others who might never have found the answers to their questions without such a wide base to draw from. Teachers often feel isolated. The Internet makes us a community that doesn't have to meet at any set time in a world that seems over scheduled already."

— HEDDI THOMPSON, TEACHER, CHASE COUNTY ELEMENTARY SCHOOL, COTTONWOOD FALLS, KANSAS, U.S.A.

The world of telecommunications is truly expanding learning beyond the confines of the traditional classroom. The Web is a fantastic resource for students that lets them search and research from home and find more information than we would have ever dreamed possible a few years ago. Of course, finding information is only one small piece of the research process; knowing what to look for and what to do with it once it's found are important skills usually taught within the school. Homework help on the Web tends to focus around research, but there are also places for drill and practice of basics, to sharpen problem-solving skills, and to get answers to specific questions. For parents who teach their children at home, the Web is a valuable link to resources, curriculum, and other parents who have chosen this route. The Internet has contributed immensely to the growing field of distance education, as it allows for interactive, multimedia, online courses. The formerly limited learning opportunities and isolation of those who are institutionalized, homebound, or living in remote locations are now overcome by new technologies.

Chapter goals

■ **To illustrate some resources available on the Internet that can help students with day-to-day homework and projects**
■ **To describe ways that the Internet assists with homeschooling**
■ **To examine the development of distance learning on the Internet**

Homework helpers

Web sites specific to homework are popular these days. A simple search will reveal thousands of homework helper sites, posted by individuals, schools, libraries, and some private companies. One of

Figure 10-1

**B.J. Pinchbeck's
Homework Helper**

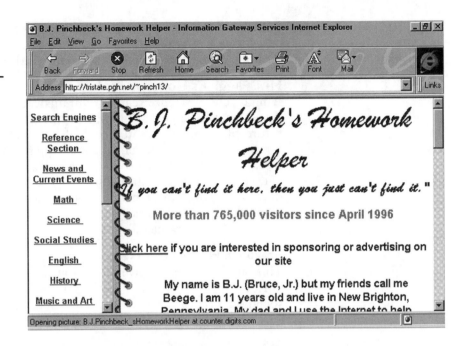

the most well-known is B.J. Pinchbeck's Homework Helper
(**http://tristate.phg.net/~pinch13/**). Beege is a ten-year-old from
New Brighton, Pennsylvania, who has compiled, with the help of
his dad, more than 430 sites on the Internet that can help you find
any information that you need. The reference section is particularly
useful.

Here are just a few of the many other homework helpers available:

Buelah the Beagle
Links to sites in many subjects: mathematics, science, language,
geography, social science, history, health and safety, the arts, music,
physical education, and even free time.
http://www.fmmarinette.com/homeworkhelpre.htm

Educational Talent Homework Helper
Links to dictionaries as well as math sites and research tools.
http://www.uark.edu/~trio/homework.html

Homework Helper: Animals Around The World
This is a mega list of various links to animal information on alligators, tapirs, raptors, llamas, and many more.
http://www.walib.spl.org/youth/html/hmwork.html

Kids' Place Homework Helper
In addition to research sources and a link to Kidopedia, Glen's

Links leads you to a very extensive set of education-related links, everything from automobiles to zoos.

http://magnet.temple.k12.tx.us/meridith/mkids/mhelper.html

Mrs. Fliegler's Homework Helper

A high school science teacher will answer questions, but she is getting so many requests that she is having trouble keeping up. Her future plans are to create areas of her Web site to include science fair information, frequently asked questions for different science disciplines, and an area to help elementary school teachers with science demonstrations and lessons. In addition, she is working to develop a program at her school for advanced science students to help answer e-mail questions.

http://www.trabuco.org

Staroute Homework Helper

This site has an extensive collection of links in the following categories: language, library, health and safety, science, mathematics, social science, the arts, music, physical education, and free time.

http://www.staroute.com/kids.html

States Homework Helper

The American states are listed in alphabetical order, each with several further links to various kinds of information, making research simple.

http://ainet.com/scfl/hhstates.htm

StudyWeb

The object of this site is to assist anyone doing research to find information easily. The categories are sorted according to the approximate appropriate grade level, which makes them valuable tools for teachers looking for lesson plan and curriculum ideas as well as for students doing research assignments. The information for each topic also notes the presence of downloadable or printable images for use as visual aids for school reports or projects.

http://www.studyweb.com

Suffolk Web Homework Helper

This is a comprehensive site with links to biographies, calendars and events, countries, states and flags, dictionaries, encyclopedias, English grammar/style, population and statistics, maps, news, time, weather, quotations, science and math.

http://www.suffolk.lib.ny.us/youth/homew.html

The Shakespearean Homework Helper

The Shakespearean Homework Helper is a site to assist high school students and teachers learn more about Shakespeare.

http://members.aol.com/liadona2/shaketop.html

Commercial companies have entered the homework domain also. Infonautic's Homework Helper, launched in March 1995 on Prodigy's online service, is an online educational information service. Homework Helper is designed to complement school-directed studies, or simply to satisfy natural curiosity about current events, literature, or science. Its reference library incorporates more than 100 newspapers, 400 magazines, 2,000 books, 18,000 television and radio transcripts, thousands of color photographs and maps, and several encyclopedias and almanacs. Students retrieve information by asking questions in plain English, and documents are returned to the questioner in order of relevance. For example, a search for "Who said, 'Et tu Brute'?" will yield citations to an encyclopedia article about Julius Caesar, the full text of Shakespeare's play, and common references and allusions from newspapers, magazines, and other sources. Students can also narrow the search to particular dates, authors, subjects or publications, as well as confine it to materials appropriate to a certain reading level. Homework Helper is currently available to Prodigy subscribers for a monthly fee of US$9.95. It is also available as a stand-alone subscription product for US$9.95 a month. To subscribe to Homework Helper, call 1-800-831-1440, ext. 762. Prodigy members can access Homework Helper by typing "Jump:Homework Helper."

Not only are there resources available that can help students with day-to-day homework, the Web is also a great source of information for projects and essays on any imaginable topic. At the simplest level, students can find information in online encyclopedias such as Microsoft Encarta, which is a free abridged version of the multimedia CD-ROM product. Most of the other CD-ROM encyclopedia publishers — e.g., Grolier, Compton's and Britannica — have more complete versions available — for a price, which ranges from about US$30 to US$85 per year. These online subscription encyclopedias provide traditional content plus Web links. Britannica's content is the most adult oriented, thus not really appropriate for elementary school students.

Sites such as Canada's SchoolNet (**http://www.schoolnet.ca**) provide links to selected resources by subject geared to school-age children. The National Atlas on SchoolNet lets students create customized theme maps that can be printed and included in a project. The Discovery Channel (**http://www.discovery.com**) and Sympatico

Online encyclopedias:

**http://www.encarta.
msn.com/EncartaHome.asp
http://www.gme.grolier.com**

**http://www.comptons.com
http://www.eb.com**

(**http://www1.sympatico.ca**) are also worth looking at for student project information on various topics, though you may have to search a bit to find what you are looking for. Another useful homework and project resource site is Yahooligans! (**http://www.yahooligans.com**), the children's version of the popular Yahoo index. It filters out clearly adult material, and students can search using the tree-structure subject index or with a keyword search. The Homework Answers subheading takes you to a variety of sites that may assist with school assignments; it also includes five dictionaries and an Ask-an-Expert section. Research-It (**http://www.iTools.com/research-it/research-it.html**) includes dictionaries, thesauruses, and translators. Here a student can look up quotations, find maps on the Web, and search factbooks. Flashcards for Kids (**http://www.wwinfo.com/edu/flash.html**) is a place for students who need extra help with addition, subtraction, multiplication, and division facts. They can select the level of difficulty and whether they want to keep score. The problem of the week sites described in Chapter 2, when used with parent assistance, are also helpful to students who require extra practice.

HINT You can do a word search on any of Shakespeare's plays at the Complete Works of Shakespeare at **http://www.the-tech.mit.edu/Shakespeare/works.html**. You can find an entire "clickable" table of periodic elements at **http://www.the-tech.mit.edu/Chemicool**.

At Yahoo's Elementary school homework site (**http://www3.znet.com/yil/content/mag/9709/schoolelementary.html**) you'll find a list of what they consider to be the best homework resources online for students in elementary school. One starting point (the best place to begin research) and one homework helper (the best place to practice a skill, solve a problem, or get an answer to a specific question) are provided for each of the subjects, reading, writing, and arithmetic.

The Info Zone, produced by the Assiniboine South School Division (**http://www.mbnet.mb.ca/~mstimson/**), focuses on links to help students with the research process. It's organized in the categories of wondering about something, seeking information, choosing information, connecting useful information you have found, producing information of your own in a new form and judging the entire process and your product. This site is also an excellent resource for teachers.

Plagiarism

Although the Internet is a great research tool, teachers need to be cautious about the possibility of students taking material from the Internet and submitting it as their own. In some ways, powerful search engines make it easier than ever to track instances of plagiarism. Unfortunately, there are also a number of businesses on the Internet that sell term papers to desperate students. This type of cheating is not new. Indeed, one agency claims to have been operating for over twenty-five years! However, with the Internet, the agencies involved in this business become more visible.

The Teacher's Complete & Easy Guide to the Internet

One way to avoid having students tempted to use these services is to incorporate unique elements into an assignment that are hard to duplicate generically, such as insisting that a literary analysis be done from the point of view of a character in the story. Teachers should also be aware of these agencies that sell term papers:

Other People's Papers
http://www.OPPapers.com/

Essays and Term Papers
http://www.azalea.net/personal/candyman/essay.htm
(includes a list of other places to obtain term papers)

Evil House of Cheat
http://www.cheathouse.com/

One Stop Research Paper Shop
http://members.tripod.com/%7ETexasTwister/

Academic Term Papers
http://www.termpaperassistance.com/2wrdsmain.htm

Homeschooling

For some students, learning at home involves a lot more than homework. These are students whose families have, for one reason or another, decided to join the homeschooling movement. For an increasing number of students, home is where the classroom is. In the United States, the number of students being taught at home has increased from roughly 18,000 in the late 1970s to an estimated 800,000 today (some claim the figure is closer to one million). In Canada, there are approximately 50,000 students learning from home today — up from a meager 2000 in the 1970s.

There are many different reasons why parents choose to homeschool. Some seek this option for religious reasons, while others feel that their children will benefit from a high level of individualized instruction that is simply not possible in schools. A child may have a chronic illness that prevents her or him from attending school. An Ottawa family has gone the home school route to allow them to embark on a two-year sailing venture around the world. They are able to send and receive e-mail from anywhere in the world using an Innarsat satellite dish.

In many ways the Internet is radically changing the nature of learning at home. On the Internet, home schoolers can connect to courses, online tutors, and learning services. Once isolated in their own communities, such students can now participate in live online discussion groups, projects, and activities with other children being schooled at home. NovaNet Campus is an example of the learning services now available to home schoolers. NovaNet is an educational

Parents choose to home-school for many different reasons.

software company located in Tuscon, Arizona. The Nova Net Campus (**http://www.learnonline.com/lol_novanet.htm**) makes available over 1200 computer-based lessons in subjects for students in grades 4–12.

School boards have also recognized that they too have a role to play in the burgeoning homeschooling arena. The New Directions in Distance Learning is a British Columbia virtual school offering Kindergarten to Grade 12 programming to residents of the province. In Ontario, the EDEN project is a consortium of school boards offering courses online. The Virtual School for the Gifted is an Australian school offering courses on challenging topics, such as Existentialism. Home schoolers are also supported by many private agencies and community schools. The Puget Sound Community School facilitates online conferencing and student exchanges through their online education program. Their target student population is high school students who are not formally enrolled in schools. The Keystone National High School is specifically designed for home schoolers.

> "Puget Sound Community School is unique. We don't have a school site; instead, we hold classes in libraries, community centers, and other public places. All our students have dial-up Internet accounts from their home (we help families without computers to get them). We do a lot online; besides our MOO, students also create their own home pages, and a team of students creates home pages for local organizations in exchange for free meeting space."
>
> — *Andrew Smallman, Director, Puget Sound Community School, Seattle, Washington, U.S.A.*

Home schoolers, whether or not they subcribe to formal online courses, are among the most active educational users of the Internet. Many of the Web sites set up by home school families are interesting places to visit, both to get a closer look at the home-schooling movement, and to locate many carefully selected learning activities. Here are some homeschooling sites worth visiting:

Anne's Ultimate Homeschool List
From this Manitoba Homeschool page, you can access well-anno-tated pointers to organizations, curriculum, essays, articles, guides, special needs, readings, resources, alternative education, religious education, catalogs and textbooks, correspondence schools and cur-riculum providers, chat groups, magazines, organizations, books, and more.

   http://www.flora.org/homeschool-ca/test/anne.htm

Canadian Home Schooling Resource Page
This site features links to all Canadian provincial and territorial sites, a chat room, access to the Canadian Homeschool Mail List and the Association of Canadian Home-Based Education as well as links to all sorts of other homeschooling sites and pages published by home schooled students.

   http://www.flora.org/homeschool-ca/

Jon's Homeschool Resource Page
This site is a good one to start with. It is the work of Jon Shemitz, who has created a site so extensive that it's hard to imagine a resource he's missing. He has pointers to various FAQs, research on homeschooling, newsgroups, legal resources, mailing lists, local sup-port groups, organizations, resource lists for several states, and much, much more.

   http://www.midnightbeach.com/hs/

Homeschool Zone
Here you will find pointers to curricula, support, materials and ideas, resources for special needs children, ideas for writing, newlet-ters, marketing outlets, and books as well as a home school calendar and home school chat area.

   http://www.caro.net/~joespa

The Caron Family's Homeschool Homepage
During their four years of homeschooling, this family has discovered many great resources available on the Internet. Their home page includes answers to some common questions about homeschooling, 800+ links to home-education resources on the Internet, help with finding curricular materials, books, magazines, and software on the

Web, homeschooling and television links to networks and programs suitable for home school use, resources for the home schooled high schooler looking ahead to college, and links to their own family's pages plus local Maine resources. You can also join the The Homeschool Webring from this site.

http://www.mint.net/~caronfam/index.htm#options

The Homeschooling Zone

This is a growing resource for people in the homeschooling community and also for people whose children are in traditional public and private schools and who are looking for more resources. The Zone has links to homeschooling support group listings, the Homeschooling Yellow Pages, a list of home education people (with Web sites), Canadian resources and homeschooling organizations. There are links to Cable in the Classroom (Discovery Channel, the Learning Channel, the History Channel, and Biography) resources, the PBS Homepage, which links you in turn to all of the Web pages of all of the PBS shows like "NOVA" and "Newton's Apple" and The Weather Channel's "The WeatherClassroom"

http://ourworld.compuserve.com/homepages/JoeSpataro/home-skool.htm (you may need to put an :80 after the com).

The Teel Family's Homeschool Page

A wonderful site constructed by a homeschooling family in Alaska. Includes software reviews, educational information, links to online curriculum and pages from the kids in the family.

http://www.alaska.net/~mteel/homesch/homeschl.html

Distance Education

An area that has seen even more growth in recent years than homeschooling is distance education. While the Internet is a relatively new medium for delivering distance education courses, distance learning is not a new phenomenon. Indeed, correspondence courses were first developed by universities in the middle 1800s. In the 1930s, radio broadcast became a prevalent medium for delivering distance education, and many of us are familiar with educational television. But interest in distance education has increased considerably since the introduction of Internet technologies. The Internet offers a new medium for instructional delivery that has the potential to go much beyond the earlier one-way instructional delivery systems.

In addition to providing an easy and inexpensive vehicle for providing lessons, the Internet makes it possible to create dynamic learning communities in which participants can ask questions and exchange ideas. Learning environments available through telecommunications technologies may soon match a level of interactivity previously available only in face-to-face learning situations.

Teachers are interested in distance learning for several reasons. In some small or remote schools, distance learning is a way to provide students with access to courses that cannot be offered locally, often because the low enrollment would not justify the cost. With distance education, advanced students can be given the opportunity to reach ahead by taking a university course while still in high school. Arrangements such as these allow schools to continue to offer challenging opportunities to their students, even as budgets for special programs are shrinking.

Some teachers are already involved in developing and delivering distance education courses. They may be dealing with students in a non-traditional school setting (such as the homeschoolers described above), developing online training materials for a commercial agency, or they may be using the Internet or other telecommunications technology to present a course to students located at another school. Many more teachers are taking advantage of the range of opportunities that distance learning offers for professional development or pursuing personal interests.

A significant number of colleges and universities now offer some form of distance education. In one example, CU-SeeMe video-conferencing has been used to allow supervisors of technology teacher education to observe student teachers. A course on electronic networking for educators from the University of New Brunswick included asynchronous communications using Web-based conferencing and synchronous chat rooms for weekly discussions of assignments. A physiology course from Mount Royal College in Alberta featured Shockwave (multi-media) presentations with explanations provided using clips. In an Educational Science and Technology course at the University of Twente in the Netherlands, students learn to design and develop multimedia products for learning-related use and work in groups to carry out collaborative projects. Currently more than 2500 distance education courses are available over the Internet, many offered by accredited institutions. University and college course online offerings range from Baroque art to calculus, from criminology to bee keeping.

Although distance education has grown more quickly at the post-secondary level, a growing number of agencies are now offering high school courses online. Even a few elementary school level

HINT For a lengthy list of college courses available online, visit the Internet University at **http://www.caso.com**.

subjects have appeared on the Internet, most of them intended for homeschoolers.

There are also courses that you can take for free. Most of them will not be available for credit, but enrolling in a free course can be informative, fun, and one way to experience an online learning environment. Free or very inexpensive courses are available from: The Internet Free College at **http://www.aavstudio.com/ifc/** and Spectrum Virtual University at **http://www.vu.org/**.

It is not difficult to understand why interest in distance education is growing. Increasingly, the Web is allowing us to overcome

HINT Examples of agencies offering high school courses online:

The GDCI Virtual High School (Ontario)
http://www.virtualhighschool.com

North Dakota Division of Independent Study
http://www.dis.dpi.state.nd.us

The Virtual High School Cooperative Project
http://vhs.concord.org/

CyberSchool
http://cyberschool.4j.lane.edu/

Electronic High School (Utah)
http://ehs.uen.org

Indiana University Extended Studies
http://www.extend.indiana.edu/

The EDEN Project (Ontario)
MindQuest (Minnesota)
http://www.mindquest.blooming-ton.k12.mn.us/

Figure 10-3
The Virtual High School Cooperative Project

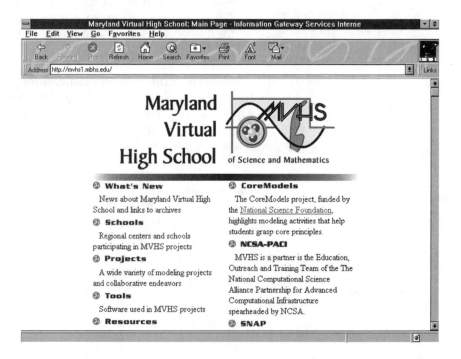

The Teacher's Complete & Easy Guide to the Internet

the barriers of time and space in teaching and learning. Agencies offering courses at a distance have the potential to reach non-traditional students (such as students in the workplace), and students from around the globe. With the Internet, once the infrastructure for course delivery is in place, learning modules can be created relatively inexpensively and updated easily. Even textbooks are appearing in electronic format.

The technologies used for course delivery and interactivity can include:

- basic electronic mail
- electronic mail for text-based lessons, online tutoring, and submitting assignments
- listserver or other group conferencing environment for class discussion and learning circles
- Web-based tutorials in print or multi-media format
- downloadable tutorials as text, .pdf, or multi-media files
- real-time, interactive discussion or simulations using MOOs, PowWow, or other chat technology
- streaming technologies — audio or video for delivering lectures and demonstrations
- CU-SeeMe video-conferencing — for collaboration and interactivity.

HINT Links to a range of development tools, including Lotus Learning Space, TopClass, and WebCT, is are available from Web-based Course Development Tools at **http://www.distance-educator.com/coursdev.html.** Also check out the Integrated Distance Learning Environments listed at the TeleEducation NB at **http://direwolf.teleeducation.nb.ca/distanceed/default.cfm**.

In addition to these individual technologies that are commonly used for distance education, a number of products, such as Lotus Learning Space, TopClass, and WebCT from the University of British Columbia, attempt to provide a complete environment for course delivery and collaborative learning.

Using these environments, students can access lessons and supplementary resources that can be presented through a range of different media; they can interact with an instructor and with other students, and they can share work that they have done. Some products also track student progress, and test performance and levels of participation in group discussions.

Currently, one of the drawbacks of distance education over the Internet is that, despite advances in the technologies available for learning, much of it is text-based. Even when institutions are set up for more sophisticated forms of delivery, such as video-conferencing, the students may not be. Another issue that has proved challenging is how to effectively test online. In many cases, students are required to go to a proctored location for testing.

For these and other reasons, some teachers still have reservations about the effectiveness of distance education. At this particular juncture, some distance education courses are not very effective, while others are excellent. In this respect, they are not much different from traditional instructor-led courses. One particularly interesting and often cited study is entitled the "No Significant Difference" Phenomenon (**http://tenb.mta.ca/phenom/ phenom. html**). In his paper, Thomas L. Russell, director of the office of Instructional Telecommunications at North Carolina State University, reports on the results of 248 research reports, summaries, and papers that compared a range of different teaching methodologies. The studies date back to a 1928 study that compared the levels of achievement attained by college level correspondence students with those of classroom students. Their conclusion — and the conclusion of all of the other studies in the report — is that there is no significant difference between these groups. Some of the studies compare two different technologies. Again, in each case no significant difference was found in the performance levels of the groups under study.

Experts argue about what conclusions should be drawn from Russell's study, but many educators feel that this research paper confirms that the method for delivering educational content matters less than the thought that goes into instructional design and the ability of the learning environment to respond to individual learner needs. Because of the inherent competition for students that exists in a global marketplace, it is likely that, over time, many high-quality distance education programs will be accessible over the Internet.

These sources will help you to learn more about distance education on the Internet:

Online Distance Education FAQ
The Online Distance Education FAQ from the University of Houston provides an excellent overview of distance education, many links, and a special section devoted to Web-based training. It is located at:
> http://129.7.160.115/COURSE/DISTEDFAQ/Disted_FAQ.html

Distance Education Resources from TeleEducation New Brunswick
This is a valuable distance education directory of resources. The site provides links to papers and reports, conference proceedings, information on integrated distance learning environments, resources for developing Web-based distance education courses, as well as pointers to other important sources for distance learning information.
> http://direwolf.teleeducation.nb.ca/distanceed/default.cfm

Institute for Distance Education (University of Maryland)
Links to many general distance education resources, including resources for K–12.
> http://nova.umuc.edu/~erubin/de.html

Jason Merry's Canadian Distance Education Directory
Links to resources for each province as well as links to many distance education guides and resources in the United States. There is a special section devoted to Internet delivery.
   http://is.dal.ca/~jmerry/dist.htm

Al Lepine's Higher Education and Distance Learning Site
There are so many distance education information resources on the Net, that it is difficult to select only a few to recommend. This one is nice because it includes links to alternative education sources and accreditation resources.
   http://members.tripod.com/~lepine/

University of Wisconsin Distance Education Clearinghouse
This site provides information on distance education programs, courses, and technologies. Although this resource focuses on distance education in Wisconsin, the clearinghouse includes a useful selection on definitions and introductory materials. If you are new to distance learning, this is a good place to browse.
   http://www.uwex.edu/disted/home.html

World Lecture Hall
Only some of the courses here are totally online. Other listings are for classroom-based courses that make use of the Internet to deliver course materials, such as course syllabi, assignments, lecture notes, exams, class calendars, multimedia textbooks. For many teachers, offering one unit of study or some component of a course online is a good way to explore online technologies.
   http://www.utexas.edu/world/lecture/

Heritage Online
Distance education courses specifically for K–12 educators.
   http://www.hol.edu/

Web-Based Instruction Bookmarks
If you want to know more about offering a course online, this site includes many valuable links to resources about technology options, development tools, and research. This site also includes links to course listings and instructional design resources.
   http://www.awbl.com/id/links.html

Some Thoughts About How to Offer a Course Over the Internet
This is another good starting point for learning about course development.
   http://www.edgorg.com/course.htm

Distance Learning: A Guidebook for System Planning and Implementation

"This guide is intended for a wide audience, including people in K–12 education, higher education, business, and government who are responsible for planning and/or managing a distance learning system."

http://www.indiana.edu/~scs/dlprimer.html

Distance Education at a Glance...

This is another good introduction to distance education from the University of Idaho. There are fourteen guides in all; they discuss topics such as instructional television and strategies for learning at a distance. This resource includes as Guide #12 *Distance Education and the WWW.*

http://www.uidaho.edu/evo/distglan.html

New directions

There is no doubt that the world of education is changing in ways that few of us would have envisioned just a few years ago. The trend toward homeschooling and distance education will probably continue to grow, but these alternative approaches to learning will not replace classroom-based education, which for most students still affords the richest environment for learning. Yet many things about how learning happens in the classroom undoubtedly will change.

What will schools look like in the twenty-first century? We cannot predict this exactly, but as we plan for the future, it helps to have some idea of current trends. Some of the most pervasive trends in educational reform of the 1990s include

- inclusion of all learners
- students taking responsibility for their own learning
- a shift from all students learning the same things to students learning different things individually
- learning outcomes and performance assessment
- education for global stewardship facilitated by communications technologies
- collaboration, communication, and the integration of visual and verbal thinking
- the changing role of teacher from expert to facilitator, mentor, and partner in learning.

These changing parameters give us some vision of schools in the years ahead.

Imagine the role that technology, and specifically the Internet, can play in helping to integrate these trends into daily learning. It's not technology that will *create* change in education, but rather the

PERSONAL FAVORITES

Use this page to make notes on your own favorite distance education sites.

Site: _____

Description: _____

Note files: _____

Site: _____

Description: _____

Note files: _____

Site: _____

Description: _____

Note files: _____

Site: _____

Description: _____

Note files: _____

Site: _____

Description: _____

Note files: _____

Site: _____

Description: _____

Note files: _____

Site: _____

Description: _____

Note files: _____

power of technology that will *allow* teachers and students to make necessary changes.

Through the power of telecommunication, traditional hierarchies are broken down and education becomes the responsibility of *communities* of learners — students, teachers, and parents. Students now have access to a wide variety of information resources. They can be more involved in designing learning outcomes as part of functioning teams in which people change roles all the time, just as they do in the real world. This kind of teamwork sees students assuming leadership roles as well as being part of the team.

As we approach the excitement and challenge of exploring the educational potential of the Internet, we have the opportunity to be lifelong learners, and by doing so we set an example for the students with whom we work. Communication and collaboration skills are enhanced when both students and teachers are engaged in authentic learning.

Much experimentation is required to figure out the practical aspects of transforming teaching and learning, and it is sometimes difficult not to be overwhelmed by the technology itself. Improvements happen not suddenly, but over time. Continuous reflection and evaluation are critical to the process of change. At some point, teachers will undoubtedly view the Internet as an integral tool for professional growth and learning. Today, our challenge is not to master it, but rather to discover what is most important and most useful for learning, and how to reorganize classroom practices to take advantage of these aspects.

The Internet is a dynamic environment that can sweep students into a world of constant change. In the midst of this dynamic activity, integrative techniques such as metacognition and reflection will help teachers to establish the islands where students can pause, think about, and share their learning experiences.

"It all seems amazing: to be able to send messages halfway across the world with the press of a single button; to get national news before most of the world does; and to meet some of the people who made that possible. Just to be able to sit in this room and type on these computers is a privilege, but to understand what's happening, and how we're doing this, is magnificent. I think that the Internet has influenced me.... When I watch the news on TV, I get all the information I want, but do I really understand it all? On the Internet, when friends tell me the news in words that I can understand, it doesn't just sound like pieces of a puzzle that don't seem to fit together; all the pieces join as one ....

"When my computer teacher asked what I will demand in the future, I started thinking.... I will expect more in middle school and in high school. I will expect to be able to communicate with anybody in the world. I will demand to continue to challenge and encourage us, and I will want the future to be even better than the present."

— *Meredith Geremia, Student, Grade 6, West Windsor Plainsboro*
Upper Elementary School, Plainsboro, New Jersey, U.S.A.

The Teacher's Complete & Easy Guide to the Internet

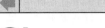

Glossary

Anonymous FTP   One of the Internet's main attractions is its openness and freedom. FTP (File Transfer Protocol) Internet sites let you access their data without registering or paying a fee.

Archie   A search tool that helps you locate information stored at hundreds of anonymous FTP sites around the Internet.

ASCII (Ask-ee)   *American Standard Code for Information Interchange*, plain text without formatting that's easily transferred over networks. (Got a question? Just ASCII.)

Backbone   The main communication line that ties computers at one location with those at another. Analogous to the human nervous system, many smaller connections, called *nodes* or *remote sites*, branch off from the backbone network. (Don't slip a disk!)

Bandwidth   An indication of how fast information flows through a computer network in a set time. Bandwidth is usually stated in thousands or millions of bits per second. See Ethernet.

Baud   Unit of speed in data transmission; maximum channel speed for data transmission.

Bit   The basic unit of data. It takes eight bits (a byte) to represent one character (e.g., a letter or number) of text.

Bounce   Return of e-mail that contained a delivery error.

Bozo filter   A program that screens out unwanted and irritating incoming messages. (Both messages and filter can be breaches of netiquette.)

Byte   The memory space required for storage of one character — eight bits.

kilobyte (KB) = 1,024 bytes of data
megabyte (MB) = 1,048,576 bytes
gigabyte (GB) = 1,000 megabytes
terabyte (TB)= 1,024 gigabytes

CCITT   The Consultative Committee for *International Telegraph* and *Telephone* makes technical recommendations concerning data and telephone communications systems.

CD-ROM   Compact *Disk* Read-Only *Memory*. CD-ROM can hold the equivalent of 1,500 floppy disks. It is the most popular carrier of interactive multimedia programs that feature audio, video, graphics, and text.

Chat and Talk   A chat program lets you electronically "converse" online with many people simultaneously. A talk program is like a personal telephone call to a specific cybernaut — only in text. See IRC (Internet Relay Chat).

CIX   Commercial *Internet* e*X*change, a group of companies providing a range of specialized services, such as financial data, for a fee.

Client   A desktop personal computer that communicates with other PCs and larger computers, called *servers* or *hosts*.

Client/server computing   Combining large and small computers in a network so data are readily available when and where they are needed. For example, in a retail store, information is collected from customers at point-of-sale terminals. Then it is directed to a server in the store and forwarded to a larger enterprise server for inventory management and other functions.

CNRI   Corporation for *National Research Initiatives*, an organization that is exploring different ways to use a national information highway.

Computerphobe   Someone who is afraid of using computers. (Now, who could that be?)

Copyright   The legal right granted to a copyright owner to exclude others from copying, preparing derivative works, distributing, performing, or displaying original works of authorship of the owner. Copyrighted works on the Internet are protected under national and international laws. Examples of copyrighted works include literature, music, drama, pictures, graphics, sculpture, and audiovisual presentations.

Cybernaut   Someone who explores the vast world of cyberspace where only the brave dare venture.

Cybernetics   In 1948, Norbert Wiener coined this term to describe the "entire field of control and communication theory, whether in the machine or in the animal." *Cyber-* has become a popular prefix for many Internet terms: cyberlingo, cyberwonk, cybercast. (What hath Norbert wrought!)

Cyberspace   Word coined by William Gibson in his 1984 sci-fi novel, *Neuromancer*. Refers to all the sites that you can access electronically. If your computer is connected to the Internet or a similar network, then it exists in cyberspace. Gibson's style of fiction is now called *cyberpunk*.

Daemon   Web software on a UNIX server; a program running all the time in background, providing special services when required.

Dedicated line   A telephone line that is leased from the telephone company and used for one purpose. In cyberspace, dedicated lines connect desktop systems to servers.

DES   The *Data Encryption Standard* represents a set of criteria for providing security for transmitted messages. Standards like this lay the groundwork for electronic commerce over the Internet.

Dial-in connection   A way to access a computer on the Internet using a PC, telephone line, and modem. Slower than connecting directly to the Internet backbone, but provides accessibility from many sites and does not require specialized equipment.

Domain   The system of organizing the Internet according to country or type of organization, such as educational or commercial. For instance, an educational institution such as The Franklin Institute Science Museum in Philadelphia, USA would have ".edu" as a suffix to its domain name (sln.fi.edu). Other typical suffixes include ".com" for commercial organizations and ".org" for non-profit groups.

Domain Name System (DNS)   The scheme used to define individual Internet hosts.

Download   When you transfer software or other information from the Internet to your PC. *Upload* refers to transferring content to a server from a smaller computer or a PC.

E-mail   Electronic mail. The term has several meanings: the network for sending messages; the act of sending a message electronically; and the message itself. It all comes down to using a computer network to send electronic messages from one computer user to another. Fortunately, all the electronic junk mail you receive is environmentally friendly since it generates no paper—unless you print it.

Electronic commerce   Buying and selling products and services over the Internet.

Ethernet   (Not an illegal fishing device.) A common type of network used in corporations. Originally limited to 10 million bits of information per second, technical improvements have raised Ethernet bandwidth (how fast information flows through a computer network in a set time) to 100 million bits of information per second—in concept, enough speed to transfer the entire contents of the *Encyclopaedia Britannica* in one second.

E-Zine　A Web-based electronic publication.

FAQ　List of *Frequently Asked Questions* (and answers) about a particular topic. FAQs can usually be found within Internet discussion groups that focus on specific topics. Read FAQs before asking a question of your own—the answer may already be waiting.

Finger　A program that provides information about someone connected to a host computer, such as that person's e-mail address.

Firewall　A mechanism to keep unauthorized users from accessing parts of a network or host computer. For example, anonymous users would be able to read documents a company makes public but could not read proprietary information without special clearance.

Flame　Rude or ludicrous e-mail. Advice: Don't reply to flames, just extinguish them by deleting.

Freenet　A community computer network, often based on a local library, that provides Internet access to citizens from the library or sometimes from their home computers.

FTP　*File Transfer Protocol* is a program that lets you transfer data from an Internet server to your computer.

Gateway　A system that connects two incompatible networks. Gateways permit different e-mail systems to pass messages between them.

Geek   A person who is so involved with computers and the so-called "virtual world" as to have only a tenuous hold on the real world. (But then again, what is reality?) Similar terms: nerd, propeller head, and techie.

Gigabyte   A unit of data storage that equals about 1,000 megabytes. A CD-ROM holds about two-thirds of a gigabyte (650 million bytes). That's enough space to hold a full-length motion picture. (Don't forget the popcorn.)

Gopher   A system that uses menus and special software on host computers so that you can more easily navigate around the Internet. The area of navigation is referred to as *GopherSpace*. See Jughead and Veronica.

GUI   *Graphical User Interface*, software that simplifies the use of computers by letting you interact with the system through graphical symbols or icons on the screen rather than coded commands typed on the keyboard. Microsoft Windows and the Apple Macintosh operating systems are the two most popular GUIs.

Hacker   The best reason of all to put up a firewall. Originally some of these pranksters breached computer security systems for fun. Computer criminals have created chaos on computer networks, stealing valuable data and bringing networks down for hours or days. See DES (Data Encryption Standard).

Home page   Document displayed when first accessing a Web site.

Host   A server computer linked directly to the Internet that individual users can access.

Hotlists   Frequently accessed URLs (*Uniform Resource Locators*) that point to Web sites. Usually organized around a topic or for a purpose, e.g., a hotlist of museums on the Web.

HTML   *HyperText Markup Language*; the codes and formatting instructions for interactive online Internet documents. These documents can contain hypertext, graphics, and multimedia elements, including sound and video.

Hypermedia   Multimedia and hypertext combined in a document.

Hypertext   An electronic document that contains links to other documents offering additional information about a topic. You can activate the link by clicking on the highlighted area with a mouse or other pointing device.

Information Highway   Also referred to as I-Way, Internet, Infobahn, Autostrada, National Information Infrastructure (NII), Global Information Infrastructure (GII). The network is currently "under construction" to make existing computer systems more efficient at communicating and to add new services, such as electronic commerce, health information, education, polling—just use your imagination.

Infrastructure   The base on which an organization is built. It includes the required facilities, equipment, communications networks, and software for the operation of the organization or system. But most important, it includes the people and the relationships that result.

Internet   An interconnection of thousands of separate networks worldwide, originally developed by the U.S. federal government to link government agencies with colleges and universities. Internet's real expansion started recently with the addition of thousands of companies and millions of individuals who use graphical browsers to access information and exchange messages. See Mosaic.

InterNIC   The *Inter*net Network Information Center. This NIC is run by the U.S. National Science Foundation and provides various administrative services for the Internet.

IP   *Internet Protocol* is the communications language used by computers connected to the Internet.

IRC   *Internet Relay Chat*, a software tool that lets you hold keyboard conversations. See Chat and Talk.

ISDN   The *Integrated Services Digital Network* defines a new technology that delivers both voice and digital network services over one "wire." More important, ISDN's high speed enables multimedia and high-end interactive functions over the Internet, such as video-conferencing.

Jughead   A system that lets you restrict your search of GopherSpace to a particular area. See Gopher.

Knowbots   An intelligent program or "agent" that you can instruct to search the Internet for information about a particular subject. While still in their infancy, these agents are the focus of intense software research and development.

LAN   *Local Area Network*, a collection of computers in proximity, such as an office building, that are connected via cable. These computers can share data and peripherals such as printers. LANs are necessary to implement client/server computing since the LAN allows communication to the server.

Listserv; Listserver   An electronic mailing list used to deliver messages directly to the e-mail addresses of people interested in a particular topic, such as education.

The Teacher's Complete & Easy Guide to the Internet

Luddite Person who believes that the use of technology will diminish employment.

Lurking The practice of reading about a newsgroup in order to understand its topics and tone before offering your own input.

Mbone *M*ulticast back*bone* is an experimental system that sends video over the Internet.

MIME (*Not* Marcel Marceau.) *M*ultipurpose *I*nternet *M*ail *E*xtensions, an enhancement to Internet e-mail that lets you include non-text data, such as video and audio, with your messages.

Mosaic This sophisticated, graphical browser application lets you access the Internet World Wide Web. After the introduction of Mosaic in 1993, the use of Internet began to expand rapidly.

Multimedia Multiple forms of communication including sound, video, video-conferencing, graphics, and text delivered via a multi-media-ready PC.

Net surfing The practice of accessing various Internet sites to see what's happening. (A whole new world for the Beach Boys!)

Netiquette Standards of behavior and manners to be used while working on the Internet. For example, a message in ALL CAPS can mean the sender is shouting.

Network People connected via computers to share information.

Newbies Newcomers to the Internet.

Newsgroup The Internet version of an electronic discussion group where people can leave messages or post questions.

Newsreader A program that helps you find your way through a newsgroup's messages.

Newsserver A computer that collects newsgroup data and makes it available to newsreaders.

NFS The *N*etwork *F*ile *S*ystem lets you work with files on a remote host as if you were working on your own host.

NNTP *N*etwork *N*ews *T*ransport *P*rotocol, an extension of TCP/IP protocol; describes how newsgroup messages are transported between compatible servers.

NSFNet Large network run by the U.S. National Science Foundation. It is the backbone of the Internet.

Packet A collection of data. Packet switching is a system that breaks data into small packets and transmits each packet independently. The packets are combined by the receiving computer. (Danger! We may have crossed over into geek-space.)

Point Of Presence (POP)   A method of connecting to an Internet service locally. If a service company has a POP in your area, then you can connect to the service provider by making a local call. POP is also used for *Post Office Protocol*.

Postmaster   The person at a host who is responsible for managing the mail system.

PPP   *Point-to-Point Protocol* connects computers to the Internet using telephone lines; similar to SLIP, but not as widely used.

Protocol   Rules or standards that describe ways to operate to achieve compatibility.

Public domain software   Computer programs you may use and distribute without paying a fee. *Shareware* is distributed at no cost, but you are expected to pay the author a fee if you decide to keep and use it.

Resource hog   A program that eats up a large amount of network bandwidth.

Router   A device that acts as a traffic signal to direct data among different networks. Routers often have enhanced processing capabilities that enable them to send data on an alternative path if one part of the network is busy.

Server   Equivalent to a host, a machine that works with client systems. Servers can be anything from PCs to mainframes that share information with many users.

Service provider   A company that provides a connection to the Internet.

SIG   *S*pecial *I*nterest *G*roup. (Also nickname of Wagnerian opera hero.)

SLIP   *S*ingle *L*ine *I*nternet *P*rotocol is a technique for connecting a computer to the Internet using a telephone line and modem. Also called Serial Line Internet Protocol. See PPP.

Smiley   Manipulating the limited potential of keyboard characters to show goodwill, irony, or other emotions with a "smiley face." There are a number of text-based effects, for example, (–: and ;–).

SMTP   *S*imple *M*ail *T*ransport *P*rotocol, the Internet standard for transmitting electronic mail messages.

Sneakernet   The 1980s way of moving data among computers that are not networked, by storing data on floppy diskette and running the disks from one computer to another. (Very good for the cardiovascular but not the information system.)

SNMP   *Simple Network Management Protocol* is a standard of communication of information between reporting devices and data collection programs. It can be used to gather information about hosts on the Internet.

Spamming   Indiscriminately sending a message to hundreds or thousands of people on the Internet, e.g., unsolicited junk mail. Not good netiquette.

Streaming   Audio, video, and text available for viewing on your computer even as it is in the process of downloading to your system from a Web site.

T1   Telecommunications lingo for digital carrier facility used to transmit information at high speed. (T1 is to the Web what passing gear was to the '64 Cadillac.) If you want to turbocharge your network backbone, many companies are expanding to the even faster T3 service.

TCP/IP   *Transmission Control Protocol/Internet Protocol*; communication rules that specify how data are transferred among computers on the Internet.

Telnet   Software that lets users log on to computers connected to the Internet.

Token ring   Featured on LANs (Local Area Networks) to keep control messages (tokens) moving quickly among the users.

UNIX   Software operating system that provides the underlying intelligence to Internet servers. Mosaic and other browser programs have helped increase Internet usage by hiding the complexities of UNIX from the average cybernaut.

URL   Abbreviation for *Uniform Resource Locator*, the Internet addressing system. (What's your URL?)

Usenet   *User Net*work, an array of computer discussion groups, or forums, that can be visited by anyone with Internet access.

Veronica   Program that lets you explore GopherSpace. *Jughead* restricts your search of GopherSpace to a particular area.

Virus   Destructive computer program that invades by means of a normal program and damages the system.

WAIS   *Wide Area Information Servers* search through the Internet's public databases for specific information. For instance, you could locate information about a particular medical breakthrough by searching through the research libraries of teaching hospitals connected to the Internet.

Web site   A sequence of related Web pages normally created by a single company or organization.

Webster   Habitué of Web sites and other cyberplaces.

White Pages   Because they remind people of the old telephone book, services that list user e-mail addresses, telephone numbers, and postal addresses.

Winsock   *Win*dows *Sock*et, an extension program designed to let Windows applications run on a TCP/IP network.

Worm   This computer program replicates itself on other systems on the Internet. Unlike a destructive virus, a worm passes on useful information. (Maybe we're fishing too deeply.)

WWW   The World Wide Web is a hypertext-based collection of computers on the Internet that lets you travel from one linked document to another, even if those documents reside on many different servers.

Sample Acceptable Use Policy

Internet Use Agreement for K–12 Students, Lafayette County School District and Mississippi Center for Supercomputing Research
April 12, 1995
Please read this document carefully before signing.

I. Introduction

Internet access is now available to students and teachers in the Lafayette County School District (LCSD) through access to computing facilities at the Mississippi Center for Supercomputing Research (MCSR). We are very pleased to bring this access to the LCSD and believe the Internet offers vast, diverse, and unique resources to both students and teachers. Our goal in providing this service is to promote educational excellence in schools by facilitating resource sharing, innovation, and communication.

II. What Is the Internet?

The Internet is an electronic highway connecting thousands of computers all over the world and millions of individual subscribers. Students and teachers have access to:

- electronic mail communication with people all over the world;
- information and news from national and international research institutions (e.g., NASA) and the opportunity to correspond with the scientists at these research institutions;
- public domain software and shareware of all types;
- discussion groups on many topics ranging from Chinese culture to the environment to music to politics;
- many on-line University Library Catalogs, the Library of Congress and ERIC.

With access to computers and people all over the world also comes the availability of material that may not be considered to be of educational value in the school setting. LCSD and MCSR have taken precautions to restrict access to controversial materials. However, on a global network it is impossible to control all materials, and an industrious user may discover controversial information. We firmly believe that the valuable information and interaction available on this worldwide network far outweigh the possibility that users may obtain material that is not consistent with the educational goals of the District.

III. Terms and Conditions

Internet access is coordinated through a complex association of government agencies, and regional and state networks. The smooth operation of the network relies upon the proper conduct of the end users who must adhere to strict guidelines. These guidelines are provided so that you are aware of the responsibilities you are about to acquire. In general this requires efficient, ethical and legal use of the network resources. If a LCSD user violates any of these provisions, his or her account will be terminated and future access could be denied. Violations of this agreement will be referred to appropriate school officials for disciplinary action. Violations of state or federal law will be referred to the appropriate law enforcement agency. The signatures at the end of this document are legally binding and indicate parties who signed have read the terms and conditions carefully and understand their significance.

Parents: *It is important that you and your child read this agreement and discuss it together. When your child is given a login ID and is allowed to use the computers it is extremely important that the rules are followed. As a parent, you are legally responsible for your child's actions. You are responsible for supervision of your child's Internet use when not in a school setting.*

A. Acceptable Use

The use of your account must be in support of education and research and consistent with the educational objectives of the LCSD and MCSR. Use of other organizations' network or computing resources must comply with the rules appropriate for that network. Transmission of any material in violation of any U.S. or state regulation is prohibited. This includes, but is not limited to: copyrighted material, threatening or obscene material, or material protected by trade secret.

B. Privileges

The use of the Internet is a privilege, not a right, and inappropriate use will result in the cancellation of those privileges. (Each student who receives an account will be part of a discussion with a LCSD faculty member about the proper use of the network.) MCSR officials will deem what is inappropriate use, and their decision is final. Also, MCSR officials may close an account any time as required. LCSD officials may request MCSR to deny, revoke, or suspend specific user accounts. MCSR expects the co-signing teacher to monitor the student accounts for which he or she is responsible. This may include random checks of files and/or e-mail to determine whether the accounts are being used in a manner that is consistent with this agreement. Students accepting MCSR accounts consent to such monitoring.

C. Responsibilities

You are expected to abide by the generally accepted rules of network use. These include (but are not limited to) the following:

- Do not use the network for any illegal activity (e.g., violating copyright or other contracts, gaining illegal access or entry into other computers).
- Do not use the network for financial or commercial gain.
- Do not interfere with the proper operation of MCSR systems and networks, as well as systems and networks accessible through the Internet.
- Do not use your account or the network in such a way that you would disrupt the use of the facilities by other users.
- Do not use MCSR computing and network resources in a wasteful or frivolous manner (e.g., tying up resources with computer-based game playing such as MUD, sending trivial or excessive messages, downloading excessively large files).
- Do not use an account owned by another individual.
- Do not share your account with another individual.
- Do not reveal your personal address/phone number or the personal address/phone number of a colleague.
- Vandalism will result in cancellation of privileges. Vandalism is defined as any malicious attempt to harm or destroy data of another user, Internet, or any of the above listed agencies or other networks that are connected to the Internet backbone. This includes, but is not limited to, the uploading or creation of computer viruses.
- If you feel you can identify a security problem on the Internet, you must notify a system administrator or your District official. Do not demonstrate the problem to other users.
- Respect the privacy of other individuals.
- Files/data belonging to others are to be considered private property unless explicit authorization is given by the owner of the files.
- Be polite. Do not be abusive in your messages to others. Use appropriate language. Do not swear, use vulgarities or any other inappropriate language.

MCSR and LCSD make no warranties of any kind, whether expressed or implied, for the service that is provided. MCSR and LCSD will not be responsible for any damages you suffer. This includes loss of data resulting from delays or service interruptions caused by its own negligence or your errors or omissions. Use of any information obtained via the Internet is at your own risk. No guarantee of complete privacy is made. LCSD specifically denies any responsibility for the accuracy or quality of information obtained through MCSR facilities.

IV. Agreement to Comply

User: *I understand and will abide by the LCSD/MCSR Internet Use Agreement. I further understand that any violation of the regulations above is unethical and may constitute a criminal offense. Should I commit any violation, (1) my access privileges may be revoked and (2) school disciplinary action and/or appropriate legal action may be taken.*

Specifically, the co-signing teacher has discussed each of the following points with me.

_____ Accounts for high school students are viewed as a privilege, not a right.

_____ Accounts are to be used for educational and research purposes only, consistent with educational objectives of LHS and MCSR. Misuse will result in loss of the account.

_____ MCSR asks that the co-signing teacher monitor high school accounts, including e-mail, to see that the accounts are being used for the stated purposes. For this and other reasons, e-mail is not private. Violations that may lead to revocation of the account include:

_____ Playing MUDs or other network intensive games, or using IRC

_____ Downloading excessively large files

_____ Sharing password with anyone besides the co-signing teacher

_____ Subscribing to inappropriate newsgroups

_____ E-mail correspondence inappropriate to educational purposes

_____ Any activity posing potential risks to myself or others

_____ Harassing other users (e.g., with unwanted e-mail messages)

_____ Illegal activity

_____ Revealing my or another's home address/phone number

_____ Vandalism of accounts or systems

_____ Using abusive, vulgar, or other inappropriate language

_____ Activities that would violate LHS handbook policy

_____ Failure to report known security problems

_____ Any other inappropriate use or misuse of the account

_____ MCSR officials will deem what is inappropriate use, and their decision is final. Accounts are monitored, and use of the account implies agreement to such monitoring. MCSR may close an account at any time for violations.

I understand the conditions for keeping this account.

User Name: _____

Signature: _____

Date: _____

Parent or Guardian: *(Parents/guardians of K–12 student users must also read and sign this agreement.) As the parent or guardian of this student, I have read the Internet Use Agreement. I understand that this access is designed for educational purposes. LCSD and MCSR have taken precautions to eliminate controversial material; however, I also recognize it is impossible for LCSD and MCSR to restrict access to all controversial materials, and I will not hold them responsible for materials acquired on the network. Further, I accept full responsibility for supervision if and when my child's use is not in a school setting. I hereby give permission to issue an account for my child and certify that the information contained on this form is correct.*

Parent or Guardian's Name: _____

Signature: _____

Date: _____

Sponsoring Teacher: *(Must be signed if the applicant is a K–12 student) I have read the Internet Use Agreement and agree to promote this agreement with the student. Because the student may use the network for individual work or in the context of another class, I cannot be held responsible for the student's use of the network. As the sponsoring teacher I have instructed the student on acceptable use of the network and proper network etiquette (see checklist).*

Teacher's Name: _____

Signature: _____

Date: _____

Curriculum Links:
Online Resources

Introduction

The following list is a selection of some of our favorite links to curriculum resources on the Internet. Although the list is not comprehensive, it provides a sampling of curriculum resources available in a range of specific subject areas. You will find these and hundreds of other wonderful resources on the CD-ROM that accompanies this book.

While the thought of exploring hundreds of Internet resources is not a task for busy teachers, the brief listing included here can serve as a quick reference to the kinds of sites available, and it will help you pinpoint the topic areas that will be of most interest to you, such as Mathematics or Science — Hands-On Activities. Once you have an idea of the kinds of sites you would like to explore, use the CD-ROM to easily access these and many more. Be sure also to check the many curriculum and general resources included in the text. Some of the very best resources are identified in the text as favorite sites, or along with project ideas. In addition to the specific links to curriculum subject areas, this list and the CD-ROM include listings of special needs resources on the World Wide Web, additional sites for kids, and additional sites of professional interest to teachers.

Take your time exploring and think about how the individual sites might be useful for your students. If you bookmark your favorites, you can easily return to them. You can also print a Web page from a site as a visual reference, and make notes on how you could use the site in your teaching.

How to Use This Appendix

Following is a list of the curriculum area resources included in this Appendix.

1. Aboriginal Native Education
2. Art
3. Astronomy/Space
4. Biology/Life Sciences
5. Careers
6. Chemistry

7. Computers
   7.1 E-mail Help Links
   7.2 Tutorials
   7.3 The Internet and World Wide Web
   7.4 Integrating Computers
   7.5 Technical Information

7.6 Searching Tools
7.7 Video Conferencing
8. Dictionaries, Glossaries, and More
9. English
9.1 Language
9.2 English Literature
10. The Environment
11. ESL and Non-English Languages
12. Geography
13. Geology/Earth Science
14. History and Current Events
15. Kids Links
15.1 Kids with Computers
15.2 Kids with Others
16. Mathematics

17. Music
18. News and Media
18.1 News
18.2 Media
19. Physics
20. Special Needs
21. Science
21.1 Hands-On Activities
21.2 Resources
22. Especially for Teachers
22.1 Curriculum, Assessment, Evaluation
22.2 Lesson Plans
22.3 General Sites for Teachers

1. Aboriginal Native Education

Aboriginal links to Internet resources about Aboriginal peoples around the world. This huge collection includes maps of reserves, treaty information, newsgroups, art, and human rights issues.
www.io.org/~jgcom/aborl.htm

Assembly of First Nations. The official Web site of the Assembly of First Nations has links to other sites so that every aspect of aboriginal life is covered.
www.afn.ca/

First Nations Page. This big site, especially designed for Native youth and educators, is a wonderful resource. It supports common tribal backgrounds in southern Canada and the northern United States
www.fdl.cc.mn.us/~isk/canada.html

Native American Curriculum Resource Guide. Visit this site for its extensive bibliography. (Choose American Association for the Advancement of Core Curriculum, then Curriculum Resources, then Native American Studies.)
gopher://mercury.cair.du.edu/00/gophers/public_policy/

Native Web. The Indian Resources site, maintained by Will Karkavelas, offers over 700 wellorganized international referencelinks to sites concerned with Native America.
www.nativeweb.org/listing.phtml

2. Art

Arts Sites for Educators. This is the place for art educators. Regularly updated, it covers all of the arts on the Web and will e-mail updates to sites to help the busy teacher.
www.ceismc.gatech.edu/busyt/art.html

ArtsEdge. This major site for art education materials was established and continues its development under a cooperative agreement between the John F. Kennedy Center for the Performing Arts and the National Endowment for the Arts (with additional support from the U.S. Department of Education).
http://artsedge.kennedycenter.org/artsedge.html

ArtsEdNet. You'll find teaching and learning materials, including art images. The resources are organized so that ArtsEdNet visitors can easily find the sort of information they want.
www.artsednet.getty.edu/

The Incredible Art Department. The site has links to elementary and secondary school art departments, lessons, museums, and art magazines. It's an excellent resource for art teachers that includes lessons, art site of the week, pet peeves, and much more.
www.artswire.org/kenroar/

Inside Art. This online game explores a painting from the inside out. During an art museum tour, you're sucked into a vortex and find yourself inside a mystery painting. Your only hope of escape is to answer the questions "Who? What? Where? How?"
www.eduweb.com/insideart/d4.html

KinderART. The creators of this handy teacher resource have combined their backgrounds in education and the visual arts to develop a site to meet the needs of busy teachers. An absolutely wonderful find!
www.kinderart.com/lessons.htm

Michael's Kid's Club Online! From the well-known craft store, this Michael's Web site is devoted to kids and features lots of neat projects and arts and crafts ideas! This is a resource to share with your fellow teachers, especially the Art teacher!
www.michaels.com

Princeton HS Virtual Museum. An interactive set of lessons for high school students makes art fascinating and fun! Students explore paintings, art objects, and architecture to learn more about world and American history, literature, and the creative arts.
www.prs.k12.nj.us/Schools/PHS/History/World_History/

3. Astronomy/Space

Astronomy Cafe. "The Web site for the astronomically disadvantaged" was developed by a professional astronomer. It provides unusual information about the research scene, data collection, and anatomy of a published research paper, Ask-an-Astronomer, and software suitable for science fair or classroom projects.
http://www2.ari.net/home/odenwald/cafe.html

NASA *Today@NASA.gov*. This is NASA's outlet for daily updates to its activities. It includes press releases, many student-related activities, Internet happenings, and information on upcoming missions.
www.hq.nasa.gov/office/pao/NewsRoom/today.html

Nine Planets. Here's an excellent site to find information on astronomy: planets and moons, spacecraft, astronomical names, a glossary of technical terms and proper names, and a chronology of space discovery.
www.seds.lpl.arizona.edu/nineplanets/nineplanets/nineplanets.html

Quest: NASA's K12 Internet Initiative. NASA's educational outreach program includes Passport to Knowledge, a series of interactive projects designed to stimulate student learning about space.
http://quest.arc.nasa.gov

Sea and Sky: The Sky. This site has lovely gallery photos, an informative tour of the solar system, links, a Challenger memorial, and Java games. Very well put together, it's an all around beautiful site.
www.seasky.org/sky.html

The Space Educators' Handbook. This interesting site uses science fiction to help teach about space technology and scientific laws. You can download the software version (Mac and Windows) of the Space Educators' Handbook. The site also includes a collection of Quicktime movies and other surprises.
http://tommy.jsc.nasa.gov/~woodfill/SPACEED/SEHHTML/

4. Biology/Life Sciences

Access Excellence. Access Excellence is a national education program that puts high school biology teachers in touch with other teachers and scientists. This excellent resource for biology teachers and students contains online mysteries and other interactive resources
http://outcast.gene.com/ae/

Cells Alive. This is a great site to see cells in action. The topics (Anatomy of a Splinter, When a Cell Commits Suicide, This Strain Kills White Blood Cells, and others) have descriptions of each step of

their process, and animated gifs and Quick Time movies to see actual cells!
www.cellsalive.com/

Dinosaurs in the Kangaroo Crypt. Enter the Kangaroo Crypt and take an extraordinary adventure through 4 billion years of Australia's evolution. Covering more than 20 palaeontological time periods this multimedia experience tells the story of Australia's early flora and fauna development.
www.cascadeint.com/htm/product/01665.htm

The Natural History of Genes. Learn how enzymes digest food, or how an arm is genetically different from a leg. This thorough site explores DNA and genetics in the real world, with excellent sections on hands-on experiments and teacher activities.
http://raven.umnh.utah.edu/

Sea and Sky: The Sea. This is a great site with a gallery of wonderful photos, information on all kinds of reef animals, links, and Java games such as a word search, a crossword, and a slider.
www.seasky.org/sea.html

Seeds of Change Garden. The site is the result of the Smithsonian Institution's Natural Partners Initiative and was created by the New Mexico State University College of Agriculture and Home Economics. There are garden activities for all seasons, recipes, and lots of wonderful information about the origins of food crops.
http://horizon.nmsu.edu/garden

5. Careers

Quintessential Career and Job Hunting Resources Guide. This comprehensive, well-organized job search site offers cover letter and resume advice, job and career sites (with great reviews), a step-by-step guide to job-hunting on the Internet, a marketability test, interviewing help, and more.
www.stetson.edu/~rhansen/careers.html

Showing the Children of Today, the Possibilities of Tomorrow! The site contains a description of educational career awareness video programming from Takeoff Multimedia. With a career library of over 125 career fields, the Takeoff collection offers something to satisfy every student's interest.
www.iwc.com/careertv/

So You Want to Be a.... You can access actual informational interviews with professionals from different industries. Learn about career paths, job responsibilities, industry trends, little known facts, best and worst job features, and much more.
http://student.studentcenter.com/inside/bea/bea.htm

6. Chemistry

Chemicool Periodic Table. The clickable periodic table gives in-depth information on each element and is the most complete periodic table seen on the Web to date.
http://thetech.mit.edu/~davhsu/chemicool.html

The Chemistry Place. You've found an excellent chemistry Web site to supplement your course. An outstanding team of educators collaborate to provide you with interactive Web activities for your students; art and animations to enhance your lectures; links to a collection of appropriate Web sites; research news, and much more.
www.chemplace.com/

WebElements from the College of Chemisty UC Berkeley. On the clickable periodic table, find the atomic weight for beryllium or gallium or any element. It's an excellent chemistry resource.
www.cchem.berkeley.edu/Table/index.html

7. Computers

7.1. E-mail Help Links

An Educator's Guide to Email Lists. The Prince Edward Island Department of Education presents an easy-to-read "How to" for educators.
www.gov.pe.ca/educ/listserv.html

Keypals! This is the ultimate site for finding a keypal, or making a connection with a class in another country! This Web page contains many links in helping you get started in setting up keypals for your class.
www.keypals.com/p/wwwsites.html

Lizst. If you're wondering if an e-mail discussion group exists about a particular topic, try this useful directory of mailing lists. Enter any word or phrase to search over 32,000 listserv, listproc, majordomo mailing lists and independently managed lists from nearly 900 sites.
www.liszt.com/

7.2. Tutorials

Beginner's Course in the Net. BCK2SKOL presents a beginner's course in the Net and its various tools targeted toward librarians and other information professionals.
http://web.csd.sc.edu/bck2skol/bck2skol.html

Computer Skills for Integrated Learning Teacher Resources. This site contains a description of resources that provide technology-integrated units for single-subject and cross-curricular work.
www.ozemail.com.au/~linkidea/resource.html

Get Connected to Learning Using the Internet. What is ICONnect? Developed especially for school library media specialists, teachers, and students, ICONnect offers anyone the opportunity to learn the skills necessary to navigate the Information Superhighway.
www.ala.org/ICONN/index.html

Internet Island. If you want to learn how to use the Internet in a classroom, start here. Internet Island is designed to be a safe environment where novice Internet users learn and practice navigation skills.
www.miamisci.org/ii/

7.3. The Internet and World Wide Web

Armadillo's K12 WWW Resources. You'll find one of the most comprehensive collections of board policies and acceptable use policies along with many articles on issues such as censorship and filtering. Armadillo also contains resources covering networking projects; educational databases and lesson plans; learning and instruction; and grant resources. The site also lists great Internet resources for each of the major curriculum areas.
http://chico.rice.edu/armadillo/Rice/Resources/reshome.html

Best Information on the Net. This is a nicely organized and comprehensive list of selected sites. You'll find pages for hot topics such as affirmative action, drug issues, and human rights, as well as many Internet guides and resources.
www.sau.edu/cwis/internet/wild/index.htm

Classroom Connect. The site presents a rich assortment of good information to support the Internet-ready teacher and school. One excellent list of resources listed by school subjects and topics is GRADES+. Classroom Connect also offers resource station; searching; classroom Web — a listing of school Web sites; and a teacher contact database.
www.classroom.net/

Finding Information on the Internet...A Tutorial. Getting started? This is a good introduction to the Internet and has great strategies for searching.
www.lib.berkeley.edu/TeachingLib/Guides/Internet/FindInfo.html

ICONN. Online Internet Courses and Information for School Librarians. Developed especially for school library media specialists, teachers, and students, ICONnect offers anyone the opportunity to learn the skills necessary to navigate the Information Superhighway.
www.ala.org/ICONN/

Internet Information Gateway for Educators. From Planet K–12.

This vast site of wonderful resources is a onestop information shop for teachers of all subjects.
www.planetk12.com

LETSNet. Learning Exchange for Teachers and Students through the Internet (LETSNet), designed for the K12 classroom, contains a collection of teaching units with online student activities that incorporate reading, writing, and research skills.
http://commtechlab.msu.edu/sites/letsnet/noframes/Subjects/la/

NetAdventure. You'll find challenging activities for middle and high school students at this site. Each weekday they post a new topic such as Fibonacci numbers or Monarch Migrations. Every NetAdventure has three interesting challenges, starting with one most 12-year-olds could master in an hour to one that would challenge even the most advanced kid.
www.concord.org/netadventure/

The Online Internet Institute. This results-driven organization offers professional development workshops to help students and teachers improve classroom achievement.
http://www.oii.org/

Pitsco Educational Technology Web Site. At this first-rate resource for teachers, click on "one stop Internet resource for teachers" to access an excellent set of links to curriculum resources, grant information, acceptable use policy information, and much more.
www.pitsco.com/p/resource.html

Premier Tracks. You'll find a collection of K–12 Web-based lessons for a variety of subject areas created by SCR*TEC's TrackStar. To use this tool, teachers enter a list of Web site addresses, annotations, and questions for TrackStar to organize them into an interactive, online, ready-to-use lesson.
www.4teachers.org/premier/

The Spider's Apprentice. Search the Web more efficiently. Check out this site to learn the principles of smart searching. Find ratings and analyses of popular search engines, too.
www.monash.com/spidap.html

ThinkQuest Junior. In this exciting contest for students in grades 4–6, teams, coached by their teachers, build Web-based educational materials for their age group and submit them for evaluation.
www.advanced.org/tqjunior/

Web 66: A K12 WWW PROJECT. A project of the University of Minnesota's School of Education, this server sets out to: help K-12 educators learn how to set up their own World Wide Web Internet

servers; link K-12 WWW servers and the educators and students at those schools, and help K-12 educators find and use K-12–appropriate resources on the WWW.
http://web66.coled.umn.edu/

7.4. Integrating Computers

Consortium for School Networking. "CoSN is a nonprofit organization formed to further the development and use of telecommunications in K12 education." Visit the site to locate articles on the use of technoloty in schools and the latest information on the E-Rate.
http://cosn.org

EdWeb. An educational resource guide specifically written for K–12 use, the guide focuses on the interconnection of education reform and information technology and provides numerous examples of how networking and computers have affected and will affect the classrooms of today and tomorrow.
http://k12.cnidr.org:90/

Global Campus. The creators describe the site as "a collaborative multimedia database containing a variety of educational materials such as images, sounds, text, etc. to be used for nonprofit, educational purposes."
www.csulb.edu/gc/

Harnessing the Power of the Web: A Tutorial. This material from Global SchoolNet Foundation focuses on student preparation and lesson planning.
www.gsn.org/web/index.html

Internet Classroom Projects. This huge site with links to all subjects includes classroom project ideas for teachers, broken down by subject area. A must stop on the highway.
www.ket.org/Education/IN/projects.html

Mid Continent Regional Educational Laboratory. Take advantage of Technology Connections, which "provide some of the best online resources available to help educators, administrators, and parents answer common questions and solve problems related to the implementation and use of technology in education."
www.mcrel.org/connect/tech/index.html

NickNacks Telecollaborations. This site is updated monthly and features projects for class participation, and subject-specific Web links for students and teachers. A great site — bookmark it!
http://www1.minn.net:80/~schubert/Edhelpers.html

United Nation's Cyber School Bus.
Designed for students and teachers everywhere, the site carries pro-

jects and resources about the United Nations and the world we all share. An outstanding site that can be used by all learners.
www.un.org/pubs/cyberschoolbus

7.5. Technical Information

Multimedia Mania. Here's a contest for students and teachers who use multimedia in the classroom. HyperSIG (Multimedia Special Interest Group of the International Society for Technology in Education) invites you and your students to dazzle your global peers by creating dynamic multimedia projects that relate to any class or coursework.
http://www2.ncsu.edu/unity/lockers/project/midlinknc/mmania.how.html

7.6. Searching Tools

The Spider's Apprentice. Search the Web more efficiently. Check out this site to learn the principles of smart searching. Find ratings and analyses of popular search engines, too.
www.monash.com/spidap.html

7.7. Video Conferencing

Videoconference Resource Center. This promising site is hoping to become an open forum for videoconferencing professionals and interested parties.
www.videoconference.com/

Videoconferencing for Learning. Pac Bell's info on using videoconferencing for distance learning includes links to related directories.
www.kn.pacbell.com/wired/vidconf/index.html

8. Dictionaries, Glossaries, and More

Dictionary.com. More languages, more dictionaries and more of what you've asked for.
www.dictionary.com/

Encyclopedia.com. This free encyclopedia includes over 17,000 articles from the *Concise Columbia Electronic Encyclopedia*, Third Edition. The articles are generally short but most include links to related topics.
www.encyclopedia.com

Human Languages Page. Searchable dictionaries, grammar guide, and tutorials for over 20 languages.
www.june29.com//HLP/

The Internet Sleuth. Track down all kinds of information. The site offers access to over 1500 searchable databases. Visit the Reference area for a selection of dictionaries and encyclopedias.
www.isleuth.com/

MetaSearch Engines — Teaching Library Internet Workshops, University of California, Berkeley. In a metasearch engine, you submit keywords in its search box, and it transmits your search simultaneously to most of the popular search engines and their databases of Web pages. Within a few seconds, you get back a compilation of results containing matching sites from all of the search engines queried.
www.lib.berkeley.edu/TeachingLib/Guides/Internet

My Virtual Reference Desk. This online reference source has a Fast Facts section with sources for finding out about population, weights and measures, plus a search engine for a multitude of online dictionaries and glossaries.
www.refdesk.com/

OneLook Dictionaries. Use this site to search over 200 dictionaries on the Internet.
www.onelook.com/

Researchit. You'll find Roget's Thesaurus, a translator, map resources, Merriam Webster and rhyming dictionaries, CMU pronouncing dictionary and language identifier, a biographical dictionary, area codes and phone directories, a currency converter, UPS and FedEx package tracking, and more!
www.iTools.com/researchit/researchit.html

The Wordsmyth English Dictionary-Thesaurus. This claims to be the only integrated English dictionary and thesaurus in electronic form! It has 50,000 headwords with definitions, pronunciations and examples, providing exact synonyms and similars (near synonyms).
www.lightlink.com/bobp/wedt/

9. English

9.1. Language

A+ Research and Writing. This step-by-step guide for high school and college students will take them through the process of writing a research paper from getting the assignment to gathering the information and writing the paper.
www.ipl.org/teen/aplus/stepfirst.htm

English Education and the Internet. In this collection of Internet resources of interest to English educators and teacher educators, the goal is to offer a site that contains essential references to major edu-

cational resources on the Internet so busy teachers can find what they need quickly and safely.
www.mindspring.com/~fordp/pasha/Home.html

Inkspot Resources for Young Writers. Officially part of Debbie Ridpath Ohi's superb Inkspot site for writers, Inkspot Resources for Young Writers features an excellent collection of how-to articles, author interviews, publication opportunities, and other useful resources for young writers
www.interlog.com/~ohi/inkspot/young.html

Inkspot. This award-winning site, maintained by Debbie Ridpath Ohi, is a writer's best friend on the Internet. Inkspot offers a well-organized and comprehensive index that addresses every writing issue.
www.interlog.com/~ohi/inkspot/

LinguaCenterGrammar Safari. This site is designed for bold students of English who would like to broaden their horizons by leaving the safe confines of the grammar book and venturing out into the unruly jungle of real-world English usage.
http://deil.lang.uiuc.edu/web.pages/grammarsafari.html

The Mind's Eye Monster Exchange. The curriculum projects are WinStar For Education's solution for integrating Internet technology into the current core classroom curriculum. Each project has been mapped to the New York State Standards for Learning and has proven to meet many areas in a way that is fun and exciting for the kids.
www.win4edu.com/mindseye/

Vocabulary.com. Here at Vocabulary University, you are able to participate in free vocabulary puzzles to enhance vocabulary mastery. Register, complete 12 sessions (learning 144 words), and you earn your diploma!
www.vocabulary.com./

9.2.   English Literature

Alex. Alex is a comprehensive catalog of books and other works that enables users to find and retrieve the full text of documents on the Internet. It currently indexes almost 1,800 books and shorter texts by author, title, subject, language, and year of publication.
www.lib.ncsu.edu/stacks/alexindex.html

Carol Hurst's Children's Literature Site. This is a collection of reviews of children's books and ways to use them in the classroom. You can look them up by title, author, type, or age, and browse them in categories such as curriculum area, subject, and theme.
www.carolhurst.com/

Children's Literature — Resources for Teachers. This is a good starting point for any language arts teacher. You will find book awards, publishers, and authors, illustrators, and a multitude of other links. This is an outstanding site with links to resources and lesson plans with a focus on reading and literature.
www.ucalgary.ca/~dkbrown/rteacher.html

CyberGuides. These are supplementary units of instruction based on core works of literature, requiring students to use the World Wide Web and are meant to be used as collections of Web-searching activities that lead to a student product. They may be used in a classroom with one computer, connected to the Internet.
www.sdcoe.k12.ca.us/score/cyberguide.html

Pizzaz!... People Interested in Zippy and Zany Zcribbling. Created by Leslie Opp-Beckman, the site provides creative writing lessons and activities with royalty-free student handouts. The site features explanations of various kinds of poetry from limericks to haiku to quatrains.
http://darkwing.uoregon.edu/~leslieob/pizzaz.html

Researchpaper.com. Here's a great resource for those needing inspiration. The site has tips and ideas to help with your writing. The site even includes a chat room so you can talk to other students. The topics index is searchable and there's also a writing center, research center, and chat.
www.researchpaper.com/

Weblit. The Internet is still waiting for a perfect literary index. Until one is developed, you should check out Weblit. Its simple design and four-star site rating system put most of the best author and poet sites at your fingertips.
www.rust.net/~rothfder/weblit.html

Writers In Electronic Residence (WIER). This site links Canada's writers to Canada's schools. The writers join classrooms electronically to read and consider students' work, offer ideas, and guide discussions between students.
www.wier.yorku.ca/WIERhome/

10. The Environment

An Amazon Adventure. A wonderful site! Students from elementary, junior high, and high schools created the majority of this site and the results were checked for accuracy.
http://168.216.238.53/amazon/

Arctica. The site, an Access Excellence Science Mystery sponsored by Genentech, Inc., can be completely downloaded for use off the Internet. A breathtaking Web site.
www.gene.com/ae/arc/

Blue Ice: The Food Web. You can visit Antarctica to learn of the fascinating interrelationship between the animals of the Antarctic and their environment. This is a program packed with information and daily activities.
www.onlineclass.com/BI/BIsub_web.html

Boreal Forest Watch (BFW). BFW is an educational outreach program for the Boreal EcosystemAtmosphere Study (BOREAS). It involves 9–12th graders in conducting real research as part of their educational experience. BFW takes place in the boreal ecosystem region of northern Saskatchewan, Canada.
http://www.bfw.sr.unh.edu/html/files/bfwinfo.html

Carolina Coastal Science. This innovative, inquiry-based, science resource utilizes the interactive technologies of the World Wide Web to explore science in coastal Carolina. It has been created based on the goals stated in the National Science Education Standards.
www.ncsu.edu/coast

Explores! World Headquarters. Not just a site for teachers or students, this site has a great deal of information about weather. If you are a teacher or student, check out the excellent K–12 section.
http://thunder.met.fsu.edu/explores/explores.html

Journey North. One of the best and most successful online science learning communities for K–12 students, this site engages students in a global study of wildlife migration and seasonal change.
www.learner.org/jnorth/jnorth.html

MayaQuest '98: Mysteries of the Rainforest. This outstanding long-term project provides meaningful interactions between students around the world and the MayaQuest team. Subscribe to get biweekly updates and reports that include glorious images and stories about real people met along the way.
www.classroom.com/mayaquest/default.html

Mississippi Adventure. Rivers of Life. Mississippi Adventure engages grades 3–12 students in an interdisciplinary exploration of one of the world's greatest river systems.
www.onlineclass.com/ROL/ROLsub.html

Sierra Club. The club is a nonprofit member-supported, public-interest organization that promotes conservation of the natural environment by influencing public-policy decisions. Test your scientific sleuthing in "River of Venom," the new science mystery from Access Excellence.
www.sierraclub.org/

WeatherNet. This is the Internet's premier source of weather information, providing access to thousands of forecasts, images, and the

largest collection of weather links.
http://cirrus.sprl.umich.edu/wxnet/

World Wildlife Fund. This organization works to fight environmental pollution and support endangered species. Get the latest environmental news and read special features on protecting species and habitats.
www.panda.org/

11. ESL and Non-English Languages

C. B. Putnam's Home Page. The site has been created for Foreign Language Teaching on the Internet. Resources with teaching activities.
www.ea.pvt.k12.pa.us/htm/programs/departments/modlang/putnam/putnam.htm

Dave's ESL Cafe. Visit this site for ESL/EFL students and teachers from around the world.
www.pacificnet.net/~sperling/eslcafe.htm

English as a Second Language (BLN). The site is sponsored by Online Bilingualism and Language Network (BLN) and provides links to relevant ESL resources for students and teachers. Click on The Balance: Students' Pages to take a London tour, practice your English online, and read students' stories.
www.rmplc.co.uk/orgs/bln/esl.html

12. Geography

Amazon Adventure. Follow a New Zealand traveler as he reports back on a nine-week trip to the Amazon and other destinations in South America. Schools are encouraged to participate.
http://vif27.icair.iac.org.nz/

Atlapedia Online. A virtual world almanac of planetary proportions, Atlapedia Online provides facts and vital stats for every country on the globe, and it's free. The simple, alphabetized index lets you click a letter, choose a country and get its geography, climate, people, religion, language, history and economy.
www.atlapedia.com

Earthrise. This database of Earth images was taken by astronauts from inside the space shuttle. Users can search the image database by keyword or by clickable topographical and political maps.
http://earthrise.sdsc.edu/

The Gakkos Website. Gakko is the word for "school" in Japanese. This site provides a mix of lessons from teachers and experts and

students' experiences in their own words. The goal is to give an entertaining educational experience, and it succeeds.
www.gakkos.com/

GeoGame. This unique, upcoming e-mail project helps students learn geographic terms and how to read and interpret maps, and increases awareness of geographical and cultural diversity.
www.gsn.org/gsn/proj/geog

Geography. This is The Mining Company's Geography section. If you'd like someone who loves geography to precede you on the Net, picking out the best sites and describing them, you've hit the jackpot.
http://geography.miningco.com/

Geography — GeoMystery Project. Students can brainstorm what is unique about where they live. They create drawings or take photos of the place, then add captions. Through a successive series of clues, participants will attempt to locate each school.
www.hern.hawaii.edu/hern96/pt053/GEOMYstery/geomys.html

GeoNet Game. "A fun new geography game based on the national geography standards," GeoNet offers low and high bandwith versions as well as easy and hard questions in many categories. Part of Houghton Mifflin's Education Place.
www.hmco.com/hmco/school/geo/index.html

The Great American Landmarks Adventure. The National Park Service, The History Channel, and The American Architectural Foundation offer 3,000 years of U.S. history through word and picture.
www.cr.nps.gov/pad/adventure/landmark.htm#olds

Himalayas — Where Earth Meets Sky. A culmination of collaboration among three high school students and their coaches from separate continents, the project forms an entry in ThinkQuest (1997), an annual contest that challenges students to use the Internet as a collaborative teaching and learning tool.
http://library.advanced.org/10131/

Internet Resources for Geography and Geology. This is a great geography resource. Choose from a dozen topics including world geography, government resources, and teaching helps.
www.uwsp.edu/acaddept/geog/resour.htm

Make a Map of Canada with NAISMap. This site is really cool! Make a map of Canada (or parts of Canada) with your choice of detail. You can select to have the rivers illustrated, or the seismic zoning, or your choice of 28 other items.
http://ellesmere.ccm.emr.ca/wnaismap/naismap.html

Map Resources from StudyWeb. This very extensive listing is updated regularly.
www.studyweb.com/geo/geograph.htm

Mapmaker, Mapmaker, Make Me a Map. This is an entertaining page, geared for kids, that explains maps. The author explains how Will Fontanez, a cartographer, goes about making maps when he gets a request.
http://loki.ur.utk.edu/ut2kids/maps/maps.html

Mapping the World by Heart. David Smith can teach middle school children to do just that: to draw a map of the world with all the countries named entirely from memory!
http://world.std.com/~mapping

National Geographic Online. In addition to its famous features on individual cultures, National Geographic offers a wide range of options including talk, answers to your geography questions, and scenic drive information with lodging, maps, and even car games. A great site.
www.nationalgeographic.com/

Seven World Wonders. The list of the Seven Wonders of the Ancient World was originally compiled around the second century B.C. Each wonder has been beautifully reconstructed, including attractive graphics, detailed description, historical background, and location, all woven together with helpful hypertext references.
http://pharos.bu.edu/Egypt/Wonders/Home.html

World Surfari. Each month World Surfari takes you to a different country. This site has colorful images and lots of information on the country they are focusing on.
www.supersurf.com/

13. Geology/Earth Science

AskaGeologist. Do you have a question about volcanoes, earthquakes, mountains, rocks, maps, ground water, lakes, or rivers? Each message goes to a different USGS earth scientist.
http://walrus.wr.usgs.gov/docs/askage.html

Interactive Multimedia Educational Resources. The Penn State College of Earth and Mineral Sciences has established this site to provide access to a series of interactive multimedia educational resources for teaching introductory earth science. Highly recommended!
www.ems.psu.edu/Earth2/E2Top.html

NJNIE Curriculum Page. New Jersey Networking Infrastructure in Education (NJNIE) Curriculum Page contains several curriculum

modules, related to earth science, plus many excellent links.
http://njnie.dl.stevenstech.edu/curriculum/currichome.html

Volcano. This Web site delves into the study of volcanoes both on Earth and on other planets. It contains information about currently erupting volcanoes; photos and video clips; classroom activities; and a searchable database of volcanoes.
http://volcano.und.nodak.edu/vw.html

14. History and Current Events

American Immigration Home Page. The page was started as a part of a school project for a 10th-grade American History class. It has evolved into a treasure trove of information about the immigrant experience.
www.bergen.org/AAST/Projects/Immigration/

American Memory.
Loads of primary source material from broadsides to early documents, photographs, audio, and film can be found at American Memory. Multimedia material relating to American culture and history.
http://lcweb2.loc.gov/

Ancient World Web. Bookmark this site for excellence. The Ancient World Web, created by Julia Hayden, is a master index to Internet sites "discussing, spotlighting, or otherwise considering the Ancient World."
www.julen.net/aw/

Biography. You can search over 20,000 short biographies from the Cambridge Dictionary of Biography.
www.biography.com/

Flints and Stones: Real Life in Prehistory. The British Museum of Antiquities takes kids on a virtual trip to the Stone Age in this appealing site, which also relates ancient history to today's world, making it more real.
www.ncl.ac.uk/~nantiq/menu.html

Frontier Girl—Laura Elizabeth Ingalls. The site contains a brief menu to subject pages, a full A–Z index, "The Story of Laura's Life" with lots of links, and for younger readers, "The Log Cabin in the Big Woods."
http://webpages.marshall.edu/~irby1/laura.htmlx

The Heritage Post Interactive. This wonderful site offers stories from Canada's historical past. The story of Canadian aviation is available here as well as information on *The Bluenose* and the Water Pump, a

Canadian-designed hand pump used in poorer countries for drawing water. Well worth the time to check it out.
http://heritage.excite.sfu.ca/hpost_e/ipost2/default.html

Horus. This is the first Egyptian Web site for kids. It is bilingual (Arabic and English) and contains more than 300 pages of information and illustrations covering Egypt's 7,000 years of civilization (Ancient, Coptic, Greco-Roman, Islamic and Modern).
www.horus.ics.org.eg

Mr. Donn's Ancient History Page. Mr. Donn teaches ancient history to sixth graders in Maryland. This impressive site offers his own units on Ancient Greece and Mesopotamia (detailed daily lessons, activities, a unit test) plus wonderful teaching resources he's gathered on a dozen ancient cultures including Egypt, Rome, China, Africa, Aztecs, etc.
http://members.aol.com/donnandlee/index.html

The Mythos: Zeus Speaks! This interactive 12-week project explores Greek mythology. It's a great place to do Ancient History via writing and drama.
www.onlineclass.com/Mythos/mythos.html

The North American Quilt. Be part of a great virtual exploration of this wonderful continent, researching your local communities to learn more about the land, the earth systems, and the people.
www.onlineclass.com/NAQ/NAQhome.html

OLD NEWS. What a unique way for kids to learn about history! This site is in a newspaper format and has stories about old news — the *Titanic,* a 1900 hurricane, Sitting Bull, Harriet Tubman, etc.
http://ourworld.compuserve.com/homepages/OLDNEWS/oldnews. htm

This Day in History. Although mainly American in its content, this site provides a list of important happenings for each day, as well as a list of birthdays, music, etc. Choose the month and day to learn about events that happened throughout history.
www.historychannel.com/today/

You Be the Historian. Here's a fun way to explore American history by looking at artifacts. The site asks visitors to "figure out what life was like 200 years ago for Thomas and Elizabeth Springer's family in New Castle, Delaware."
www.si.edu/organiza/museums/nmah/notkid/ubh/00intro.htm

15. Kids' Links

15.1. Kids with Computers

Berit's Best Sites for Children. This is a directory of more than 400 sites for kids, categorized and rated. Learning sites, games, chat ses-

sions, and more are available, plus a list of links to other directories of kids' sites.
www.cochran.com/theosite/ksites.html

Bonus.com. What a great site! It uses Java to open up a separate window that kids can use to navigate the site easily, and there's a Parents and Teachers path as well. Bonus.com offers 900 activities, some linked and some original.
www.bonus.com/

Kids Food Cyber Club. The site is rated "Among the Best" with 23 out of 25 points by Nutrition Navigator, a rating guide for nutrition Web sites!
www.kidsfood.org/

KidsWeb: A World Wide Web Digital Library for School Kids. The site, which links to the arts, the sciences, social studies, and more, is very simple to navigate, and contains information targeted at the K–12 level. Each subject section contains a list of links to information that is understandable and interesting to schoolkids.
www.npac.syr.edu/textbook/kidsweb/

Moose. In this virtual community for kids online, kids can "build" things in their community. It helps them help others get started. What they're really learning to do is object-oriented programming. Wow!
http://asb.www.media.mit.edu/people/asb/moosecrossing/

15.2. Kids with Others on the Internet

Children's Express. The site is created "by children for everybody." With a wealth of news from six news bureaus, it's packed with content. You can also participate in an electronic round table, submit your own story ideas, answer polls, and respond to articles.
www.ce.org/

Digital Education Network (DEN). Six DENs let students obtain up-to-date information, learn, and practice their skills in such areas as math, news, writing, and the Internet.
www.actden.com/

International Kids' Space. This interactive, educational site helps kids learn about science, transportation, animals, the Internet, and more. Kids perform musical pieces and present their artwork, poems, and stories in Kids' Space.
www.kidsspace.org/

16. Mathematics

The Annenberg/CPB Math and Science Project. This organization has funded more than 40 projects to improve K–12 math and science

education. These projects educate and support the key groups of adults that have a hand in changing the way math and science are taught.
www.learner.org/content/k12/

The Center of Excellence for Science and Mathematics Education (CESME). This site offers a variety of math resources including classroom-related and professional-development information. You can find a sample lesson on the history of mathematics and computer spreadsheet applications developed by teachers.
http://192.239.146.18/

Eisenhower National Clearinghouse. ENC is a one-stop gateway for math and science resources. Search the catalog or check out the Digital Dozen, a monthly list spotlighting great Web sites to visit.
www.enc.org/

Fractory. An Interactive Tool for Creating and Exploring Fractals is an educational site designed by students that lets you design your own fractal and learn about their uses and the mathematics used to generate them.
http://library.advanced.org/3288/

The Largest Known Primes. If you or your students are fascinated with prime numbers, you'll love this site. It gives information about prime numbers and the largest primes that have been generated.
www.utm.edu/research/primes/largest.html

The Math Forum. The information and projects offered at this site are devoted to geometry and to math education. For teachers, The Math Forum offers electronic news groups, articles on math education, learning, and research, math workshops, resources, and more.
http://forum.swarthmore.edu/

MathMania. For stories, tutorials, and activities all related to mathematics, give this site a try. Topics covered by MathMania include graph theory, knot theory, sorting networks and finite state machines.
http://csr.uvic.ca/~mmania/

Mathworld Interactive. Join an online community of students working on math challenges! Since 1991, this successful community has offered its participants a new math challenge every nine weeks.
www.mathworldinteractive.com/

Mighty M&M Math. This will help you teach fractions and percentages in a motivating and mouthwatering way. Using bags of M&M's, it answers these questions: What is the percentage of each color? Are the percentages similar worldwide?
www.iphysique.com/school/

Pi Mathematics. A multidisciplinary project designed around the concept of pi, involving math, history, English, and problem-solving skills, this site is designed for grades 5-8 and guides students in discovering the approximate value of pi, using measurement data, formulas, and various problems and activities. Pi Mathematics also offers a downloadable movie and software as inclass resources.
www.ncsa.uiuc.edu/edu/RSE/RSEorange.html

Suzanne's Math Lessons — Math Forum Web Units. Cover many different aspects of math using this wonderful site of creative units ready for application in your classroom.
http://forum.swarthmore.edu/alejandre/

This Is MegaMathematics! Under the auspices of the Los Alamos National Laboratory, MegaMath attempts "to bring unusual and important mathematical ideas to elementary school classrooms so that young people and their teachers can think about them." Some of these very interesting projects would be fun for older students as well!
www.c3.lanl.gov/megamath

17. Music

Internet Resources for Music Teachers. Cynthia Shirk, a music teacher, has compiled a list of links that are useful to teachers. A special feature on the page is the Music Box of Sound and Software with complete downloadable music compositions in QuickTime format.
www.isd77.k12.mn.us/resources/staffpages/shirk/music.html

K12 Resources for Music Educators. This site has many resources and links for music educators and students in all levels of education.
www.isd77.K12.mn.us/resources/staffpages/shirk/cindys.page.K12.link.html

18. News and Media

18.1. News

ABC Hourly News Report. You'll get real audio updates every hour. The site does require you to register, but it's free.
www.prognet.com/contentp/abc.html

CBC: Canadian Broadcasting Corporation—Canadian Arts, Information, and News. Information, downloadable radio programming, including selected archived material dating back to 1965.
www.cbc.ca

18.2. Media

Cyberspace Film School and Movie Web. This is an online resource

center and educational facility. Learn how to produce a film, find an agent, direct your first feature, or sell your script.
www.hollywoodu.com/

Discovery Channel Online. An amazing Web site, it's packed with information about what's on the Discovery cable television channel as well other unique content. Very well designed.
www.discovery.com/

Electronic Elementary. ELink magazine is a nonprofit, educational project that highlights interactive projects and creations of elementary grade students around the world (for ages 5–12).
www.inform.umd.edu/UMS+State/MDK12_Stuff/homepers/emag

Media Literacy OnLine Project. This is probably the best place on the Web for resources related to the influence of media in the lives of children, youth, and adults.
http://interact.uoregon.edu/MediaLit/HomePage

MediaFinder. They say, "If it's in print, it's here." They offer search tools in a number of print media categories such as catalogs, newspapers, and magazines. Thousands of periodicals list their subject, subscription, and circulation information in summary for your perusal.
www.mediafinder.com/

19. Physics

Computer as Learning Partner (CLP) Project. The site provides a one-semester integrated energy curriculum unit teaching the physical science topics of heat, light, and sound to eighth-graders.
www.clp.berkeley.edu/CLP.html

Physics Lecture Demonstrations. If you are interested in physics, this site is a must! From astronomy to magnetism to waves, the site covers it all.
www.mip.berkeley.edu/physics/physics.html

Science at Home (Los Alamos National Laboratory). This is a collection of physical science activities developed to demystify science for adults and children while fostering scientific inquiry and analysis.
www.lanl.gov/temp/Education/Contents.html

20. Special Needs

disABILITY Information and Resources. This great list of Internet resources on disabilities was developed by Jim Lubin, who is a C2 quadriplegic, completely paralyzed from the neck down and dependent on a ventilator to breathe. The pages are meant to serve as a

resource to provide useful information; therefore, they do not contain a lot of useless, pretty graphics, which take a long time to load.
www.eskimo.com/~jlubin/disabled.html

LD Online. This site offers a wealth of information regarding learning disabilities and Attention Deficit Disorder. You can be kept up-to-date on current events, locate help nationally and by state, participate in discussion groups, and more. What a find!
www.ldonline.org/index.html

Sarah's Special Needs Resource Page. This Australian site has been designed for educators (and other interested people, not in the least parents!) in the area of special education. It has many creative and innovative activities: original art and craft activities; reviews of software she has used in the classroom, and strategies for getting the most out of the programs; information on using the IntelliKeys and related software in your classroom, with activities to download.
www.bushnet.qld.edu.au/~sarah/spec_ed/

SNOW (Special Needs Opportunity Window). This is *the* site for special education resources. A central goal of the project is to foster an online community of educators, organizations and special needs students, who share common interests.
http://snow.utoronto.ca

Special Needs Network. Resources for parents, teachers, schools, and other professionals dealing with special needs education. The network supports a number of valuable discussion groups focusing on special needs issues.
www.schoolnet.ca/sne/

21. Science

21.1. Hands-On Activities

Canadian Young Inventors' Fair Page. *It's Cool to Be Creative!* says the page of the Canadian Young Inventors' Fair Society, a not-for-profit registered B.C. society dedicated to forming invention fairs across Canada and helping teachers learn to teach innovation to our young adults.
www.ideas.wis.net/cyif.html

Eduzone Science Tips. This site has everything a science teacher needs. Highly recommended.
www.eduzone.com/tips/science.htm

Hands on Science Centers Worldwide. They have the greatest Web sites and here they all are, all at once. Take it slow, there is so much to see and do, don't get overloaded!
www.cs.cmu.edu/~mwm/sci.html

The K–8 Aeronautics Internet Textbook. This site is an electronic multimedia text, teachers' supplement and student workbook to be used over the Internet with the World Wide Web. For a study of the science of aeronautics at a level elementary and middle school students and their instructors can easily understand.
http://wings.ucdavis.edu/

Kit and Kaboodle. Students in grades 3, 4, and 5 can learn science concepts as they tackle real-world problems through this highly interactive, online curriculum.
www.kitkaboodle.org

NYE Labs Online. Bill Nye, the Science Guy, brings science to life by describing fun experiments kids can do with things around the house, helping them understand complex scientific theories.
http://nyelabs.kcts.org/

Professor Bubbles—Official Bubble Homepage. Don't be fooled by those "unofficial" bubble homepages. This is the "official" one and with a name like "Professor Bubbles" you'd better believe him.
http://bubbles.org/

Science Is Fun. Learn through home science activities, presentations, videos and home experiments. Among the home experiments on offer is the rather interesting sounding "bending water." A superb site that delivers what its title suggests.
http://scifun.chem.wisc.edu/scifun.html

The Tech Museum of Science. This online scientific playground for kids and adults is a great way to learn about how technology affects our lives. The interactive exhibits are a delight.
www.thetech.org/

21.2. Resources

Ask Dr. Science. This is a great site! You can ask scientific questions and participate in e-mail discussion with Dr. Science. People Magazine OnLine and InFinet nominated it as "Cool Site of the Year"!
www.drscience.com/

Center for Excellence for Science and Mathematics Education (UTM). The mission of the CESME is to encourage and support the improvement of science and mathematics education at all levels. To further that goal they have uploaded 40 physical science activities in Word (Mac) and WordPerfect (Windows) format, spreadsheet templates, and activities written to make use of existing freeware and shareware.
http://cesme.utm.edu/

Mad Scientist Network. The site contains questions and answers on a huge range of scientific topics. If you don't find the answer you're looking for already here, be sure to ask a question of the mad scientist.
http://medinfo.wustl.edu/~ysp/MSN/

New Scientist Planet Science. This is a vast and wonderful site by Britain's *New Scientist* magazine. It presents a guide to science sites on the Net, including personal recommendations.
www.keysites.com/keysites/hotspots/hotspots.html

Ontario Science Centre. You'll need Shockwave to get the most out of this site, which offers a number of hands-on science experiments online. An excellent application of the best in Web technology to further learning.
www.osc.on.ca/

ScienceNet. This site includes a monthly feature and a link to an episodic science mystery for kids; a searchable bank of reviews of science sites, categorized by topic; standards-based classroom activities; an Internet help section; and a discussion board.
www.sciencenetlinks.com/science/approved_math.shtml

Whelmers. You'll find five new science activities, each month, which have been aligned with the National Science Education Standards.
www.mcrel.org/whelmers/

The Why Files. The site covers "science behind the news." The Why Files, a product of the National Institute for Science Education, is an effort to illuminate the science, math and technology that lurk behind the headline news.
http://whyfiles.news.wisc.edu/

22. Especially for Teachers

22.1. Curriculum, Assessment, Evaluation

The Big Six Information Management Skills by Michael B. Eisenberg and Robert E. Berkowitz. Big Six is a systematic approach to information problem solving applicable to any classroom in which students conduct research.
http://ericir.syr.edu/big6/bigsix.html

Content Knowledge. The site contains standards in math, science, history, geography, and other fields, and information on how to interpret and implement them.
http://mcrel.org/standardsbenchmarks/

MidContinental Regional Educational Lab. The Midcontinent Regional Educational Laboratory (McREL) consists of three affiliated entities but they share a common mission: to make a difference in

the quality of education and learning for all through excellence in applied research, product development, and service.
www.mcrel.org

TERC — The Regional Alliance Hub. TERC houses articles, curriculum, and project reports organized by key topics in education reform: Assessment Equity | Evaluation of Systemic Reform Mathematics Professional Development | School Reform | Science | Standards and Curriculum | Technology.
http://ra.terc.edu/alliance/HubHome.html

22.2. Lesson Plans

CanGuide. This is a database of current K–12 curriculum guidelines and resource documents approved for use in each province and territory across Canada.
www.oise.on.ca/canguide/

Curriculum Units by Fellows of the Yale-New Haven Teachers Institute. The site consists of hundreds of teaching units prepared by dozens of teachers on scores of themes.
www.cis.yale.edu/ynhti/curriculum/units/

ENC — Eisenhower National Clearinghouse for Math and Science. This site provides teachers with ways to increase their effectiveness with lessons, activities, articles, and the highlighting of 13 outstanding sites every month.
www.enc.org/

Lesson Plans for Technology. Technology 'Nformation for Teachers (T'NT) is a database of over 225 technology-related lesson plans developed by Florida teachers for grades 4–12.
http://fcit.coedu.usf.edu/tnt/

Library in the Sky. Provided by Northwest Regional Educational Laboratory (NWREL), the site contains hundreds of K–12 lesson plans for a variety of curricular subjects.
www.nwrel.org/sky/

Outta Ray's Head. The site has lesson plans with handouts for writing and literature for grades 7–12.
http://www3.sympatico.ca/ray.saitz/lessons3.htm

The Teacher's Internet Use Guide. The intent of this site is to walk teachers through a four-step process of creating their own Internet-based lessons that are aligned with state standards (in this case, Texas) and that have an assessment piece.
www.rmcdenver.com/useguide/index.html

22.3. General Sites for Teachers

Amazing Picture Machine. This searchable index of Internet graphics will help you find images for your lessons. Supporting a wide variety of topics from historical photos to science diagrams, the site also includes lesson ideas and search tips.
www.ncrel.org/ncrtec/picture.htm

AskERIC's Collections (Educational Resources Information Centre). The site includes AskERIC, an Internet-based question-answering service for teachers and others involved in education, and AskERIC Virtual Library (resources for education).
http://ericir.syr.edu

Firn (Florida Information Resource Network). The Web site offers instructional resources that seem to provide access to almost everything related to curriculum and teaching.
www.firn.edu/instruct.html

Going to a Museum? A Teacher's Guide. The guide was written and compiled by teachers and students in the "Museums and Education" course at the University of Virginia Curry School of Education, and offers a collection of lesson plans and resources for field trips to specific museums.
http://curry.edschool.virginia.edu/curry/class/Museums/Teacher_Guide/

Just for Teachers. This is a collection of premier sites for teachers. It's from Knowledge Source, which also offers a "Just for Librarians" and "Just for Kids."
www.sirs.com/tree/teach.htm

Kathy Schrock's Guide for Educators. This highly rated resource is a guide that provides annotated hotlists for teachers in a variety of subject areas. The information is presented clearly and the lists are comprehensive.
www.capecod.net/Wixon/wixon.htm

The Kindergarten Connection. Be sure to show this site to the kindergarten teacher! Ideas, lessons, projects and many links concentrating on the kindergarten curriculum.
www.kconnect.com

ShURLy. Although designed as a Web directory for students, this is an excellent place to locate topical resources by grade level.
http://learningedge.sympatico.ca/shURLy/boom.htm

Pathways to School Improvement. Visit this well-designed site, which looks at critical issues in education and provides extensive research-based materials in a user-friendly format.
www.ncrel.org/sdrs/pathways.htm

Sympatico Learning. Sympatico offers a number of well-designed sites aimed at students, teachers, and parents. These can be accessed through Sympatico's regional home pages.
www.sympatico.ca

Teacher Pathfinder: An Educational Internet Village. The Schoolhouse at this site provides a well-organized list of resources for assessment, arts, language arts, mathematics, and physical education.
http://teacherpathfinder.org/

WWW4teachers. The site provides a space where educators can encounter new ideas about technology's role in education, express their opinions and share experiences, get and give moral support, and be inspired and educated by other teachers' narratives about using technology in educational settings.
www.4teachers.org/

Bibliography

Chapter 1:

Grau, Isidro, IV and Judy Bartasis. Utilizing the World Wide Web to Advance Student Education into the 21st Century. **http://129.7.160.115/INST5931/paper.html#SLC eval,** November 20, 1997.

Learning Theory, **http://www.etc.bc.ca/tdebhome/inservice/itpd/pedagog.html,** November 20, 1997.

Matte, Armand. Marsville: An Educational Odyssey Through Science and Technology. *The Reporter,* Fall 1997, pp. 31–34.

Rogers, Al. Living the Global Village. *Electronic Learning Magazine,* May/June, 1994, pp. 28–29.

Rowe, G.R. Educating in the Emerging Media Democracy. *Educational Technology.* September, 1994, pp. 55–58.

Strommen, Erik F. and Bruce Lincoln. Constructivism, Technology, and the Future of Classroom Learning. **http://www.ilt.columbia.edu/k12/livetext-nf/docs/construct.html,** November 20, 1997.

Tapscott, Don. *Growing Up Digital: The Rising of the Net Generation.* McGraw-Hill, 1997.

Chapter 3:

Drawbacks of Filtering Software. *From Now On,* Vol. 5 No. 5 March/April, 1996 **http://www.pacificrim.net/~mckenzie**

Planning Your Own Project. *Educational Network of Ontario,* **http://www.enoreo.on.ca/students/success.htm**. June 12, 1997.

Protecting Our Children from the Internet and the World. *From Now On,* Vol. 4 No. 10 June, 1995 **http://www.pacificrim.net/~mckenzie**

Rogers, Al, Yvonne Andres, Mary Jacks, and Tom Clauset. Telecommunications in the Classroom: Keys to Successful Telecomputing. *The Computing Teacher,* 1990, Vol. 17 No. 8, pp. 25–28.

Chapter 9:

Forefront Curriculum: Internet Training and Curriculum Development for K–12 Educators **http://www.4forefront.com/home.html** June 3, 1998.

Murray, Chris. Eight Great Steps to Getting Corporate Support, **gopher://cwis.usc.edu:70/00/Librar...chers/Corporate_Funding/8steps.txt** May, 1994.

Panepinto, J. The Year of the Web. *Family PC,* March 1997.

Teachers, Educational Computing and Professional Development, Education.Au, Limited, **http://www.educationau.edu.au/archives/crt/index.htm** June 3, 1998.

Notes

Chapter 3:

1 Morsund, D. (1994). What is the "information superhighway"? *The Computing Teacher*, 22 (3).

2 Heide, A. & Henderson, D. (1994) *The Technological Classroom: A Blueprint for Success.* Toronto: Trifolium Books.

Chapter 9:

1 Harris, J. (1994, October). Teaching teachers to use telecomputing tools. *The Computing Teacher,* 60–64.

2 Heide, A. & Henderson, D. (1994) *The Technological Classroom: A Blueprint for Success.* Toronto: Trifolium Books.

Index

ABC, 234
aboriginal native education Web sites, 307
Academic Term Papers (Web site), 279
acceptable use policies (AUPs), 47, 68, 70, 72-75, 106, 133
access providers. *See* Internet service providers
accounts, Internet, 66, 184, 253
ACEKids (Web site), 154
acronyms, e-mail, 202
address books, e-mail, 187, 191
addresses, e-mail, 102, 184-87
administration, school, 194
Adobe Acrobat
   files, 236
   Reader, 237
ADSL (asymmetric digital subscriber line), 242
Africa, 143-46
Africanized Honey Bees on the Move (Web site), 147
Ahoy (Web site), 187
All About Bats (Web site), 126
Al Lepine's Higher Education and Distance Learning Site (Web site), 287
All-in-One Search Page (metasearch engine), 101, 126, 146, 220
AlphaSmart Pro keyboard, 63
AltaVista (search engine), 93, 96, 101, 201
alt.internet.services (newsgroup), 201
American Library Association, 106
American Memory Collection (Web site), 178
American Treasures (Web site), 132
America Online (AOL), 231, 240-41, 270
   NetFind Kids Only (search engine), 126
Amy's Amazing Adventure (Web site), 149
AnaWave WebSnake (offline browser), 238
Andrew Starr's Eudora Site (Web site), 188
Andy Carvin's HTML Crash Course for Educators (Web site), 256

animals, 126, 275
Anna's Ultimate Homeschool List (Web site), 281
anthologies, online, 39
Anthology of Internet Acceptable Use Policies, An, 74
antivirus programs, 66, 219-20
AOL. *See* America Online
Apple Education/Business Partnership Program, 267
Arbor Heights Elementary (Web site), 174
Archeus Resume Writing Resources (Web site), 153
Arc of the United States, The (Web site), 65
Argus Clearinghouse (subject tree), 94-95
Armadillo (Web site), 105
art, 20, 34, 108
   Web sites, 308
Artsedge (Web site), 105
ArtsEdNet Talk (listserver), 193
arts education, 193
ASCII files, 165, 219
Ask a Composer (e-mail site), 34
Ask a Curator (Web site), 34
Ask a Dinosaur Expert (Web site), 34
Ask a Doc! (Web site), 34
Ask a Geologist (Web site), 34
Ask a Librarian (Web site), 34
Ask a Meteorologist (Web site), 34
Ask a Musician (Web site), 34
Ask a Naturalist (Web site), 45
Ask a Volcanologist (Web site), 34
Ask a Woman Artist (e-mail site), 34
Ask Dr. Internet (Web site), 34
Ask Dr. Math (Web site), 34
Ask Dr. Tooth (Web site), 34
AskERIC (Web site), 105, 193
Ask Kids! (Web site), 34
Ask the Eco Expert (Web site), 45
assessment, 194
Assiniboine South School Division, 99, 278
astronomy, 148
   Web sites, 309
asymmetric digital subscriber line (ADSL), 242

AT&T, 265
Athena Academy (MOO), 229
Atlantic View Elementary School, 175
Atlas to the World Wide Web (Web
site), 256
attachments, e-mail, 183, 187, 192, 206
audio, 16, 217, 234-35, 238, 285
AudioNet (Web site), 235
Aunt Annie's Craft Page (Web site),
154
AUPs. *See* acceptable use policies
Avant, Bob, 242
awards and grants, 266-71
Awesome Library for Teachers,
Students, and Parents (Web site),
105, 170
Awesome List (Web site), 100

Bandwidth Conservation Society, The
(Web site), 173
Barebones Guide to HTML, The (Web
site), 173
Barry's Clip Art Server (Web site), 170
Bat Conservation International, 126
BBEdit (HTML editor), 172
BBSs. *See* bulletin boards, computer-
bees, 147
Beginners Central (Web site), 256
"Beginner's Guide to Effective E-mail,
A" (online document), 205
Bellingham Public Schools Student
Writing and Student Art (Web site),
174
Berit's Best Sites for Children (Web
site), 70-71, 105, 132
Berkeley Public Library (Web site), 95
Better Telnet (telnet program), 227
Beulah the Beagle (Web site), 275
bias, 127, 138
BigBook (Web site), 187
Bigfoot (Web site), 100
Big Picture (graphics editor), 171
Big Sky Telegraph (computer bulletin
board), 16-17
binary files, 192, 219
biology Web sites, 309-10
B.J. Pinchbeck's Homework Helper
(Web site), 275
Blue Web'n Learning Applications
(Web site), 105, 153
BME (graphics editor), 171
Bob Bowman's Guide to Free

Educational Technology (Web site),
224
Bobby (Web site), 65
bookmarks, Web browser
creating, 86, 89, 114
managing, 71, 89-92, 116, 238
uses for, 71, 89, 129, 132, 251, 262
Book Nook (Web site), 147
book reports, 39, 147, 213-15
Book Reports (Web site), 39
books, full-text, 224
Boolean searching, 122
*Bring Business & Community
Resources into Your Classroom: A
Handbook for Educators* (NEA),
267
Britannica Internet Guide (subject
tree), 94, 102
Brown, Jeff, 31
browsers. *See* offline browsers; Web
browsers
Browserwatch (Web site), 82
bulletin boards, computer, 7, 15, 216,
254-55
Bull's Backgrounds, Buttons and Bars
(Web site), 169
business-education partnerships, 266-
67
Busy Teachers' WebSite, 105-06, 132
button bars, 87
Buy Nothing Day: Be a Consumer
Hero! project, 35-37

cable modems, 242
CACI (Children Accessing
Controversial Information) (listserv-
er), 76
California Gray Whales (Web site), 126
Calipso 2.2 (e-mail program), 188
Canada, 33, 102-03, 148
Canada 411 (Web site), 102, 187
Canada's Digital Collection (Web site),
132
Canadian Department of the
Environment (Web site), 45
Canadian Home Schooling Resource
Page (Web site), 281
CANARIE/SchoolNet 1997 Internet
Treasure Hunt (Web site), 51
CanCopy (Web site), 134
Canoe (Canadian Online Explorer)
(Web site), 136

Career Center (Web site), 153
career Web sites, 310
Carl Davis's HTML Editor Reviews
    Page (Web site), 172
CARL Uncover (Web site), 127
Carnegie-Mellon University, 224
Caron Family's Homeschool
    Homepage, The (Web site), 281-82
Carrie's Site for Educators (Web site),
    105
CBC (Canadian Broadcasting
    Corporation), 234
  Web sites, 136, 235
Cell Assembler (graphics program), 171
censorship. See safety and security,
    Internet
Centennial Regional High School, 50
Center for Democracy and
    Technology, 76
Central Intelligence Agency, 140
Charlotte's Energy Page (Web site), 45,
    149
Charm Net Learning Page (Web site),
    257
chat, Internet, 15, 229, 231-32, 285.
    See also Multiuser Object-Oriented
chemistry Web sites, 311
Chez Mark's Mac Picks (Web site), 225
Children and Adults with Attention
    Deficit Disorders (Web site), 65
Children's Express (Web site), 40
children's literature, 107, 195
Christian Science Monitor, The, 234
  Web site, 136
CIA World Factbook (Web site), 140
Cisco Educational Archive (Web site),
    106
citing of Internet sources, 20, 49, 134-
    35
City.Net (Web site), 140
Claris Em@iler 2.0 (e-mail program),
    188
Claris Home Page (HTML editor), 172
classroom, the
  e-mail in, 215-17, 231, 238, 249
  FTP in, 216, 238
  Internet in, 6-27, 51, 58, 216-17,
    238, 247-50, 253, 260-61, 263,
    271-73, 288, 290
  MOOs in, 216, 229
  real-time Internet communication in,
    216, 231-32

  telnet in, 216, 238
  World Wide Web in, 196, 216-17, 238
  See also classroom projects
Classroom Connect, 49, 106, 272
  newsletter, 106, 264
  Web site, 95, 106, 135, 203
classroom projects, 15-16, 18-19, 27-
    77, 112-61, 175, 181-83, 194, 203-
    15, 229, 231, 250, 273
  ideas for, 112-13, 115-26, 129-32,
    138-40, 143-53, 206-15, 251
  See also publishing, student; Web
    pages, school; Web pages, student
Classroom Web (Web site), 173-74, 178
Clearinghouse Net (Web site), 140-41
Clever Games for Clever People (Web
    site), 43
client/server technology, 79-81
climate, 152
Clinton, Bill, 13, 262, 268
Clipart.com Clip Art Index (Web site),
    170
Clip-art Searcher (Web site), 170
Close Up Foundation, 115
CMPA Reading Room (Web site), 135-
    36
CNN (Web site), 136
Collaborative Lesson Plan Archive
    (Web site), 114
ColorMaker Page, The (Web site), 169
Columbia Online Style: MLA-Style
    Citations of Electronic Sources
    (Web site), 135
commercial online services, 240-41,
    247-49
communications programs, 231-32,
    244-45, 247-50
Community Learning Network (Web
    site), 106
Compaq's Teaching with Computer
    Technology Grant Program (Web
    site), 271
Complete Works of Shakespeare (Web
    site), 278
compressed files, 218, 220
CompuServe, 15, 231, 240-41
computer
  selecting a, 243-44
  Web sites, 311-15, 324-25
conferencing, 15-16, 216-17, 232-34,
    238, 261, 283, 285. See also real-
    time Internet communication

Connected to the World/The Teddy Bear Exchange project, 40-43
connections, Internet, 239-50
Connections+ (Web site), 106-07
Connections MOO, 229
Consortium of College and University Media Centers, 133
constructivist learning, 8
Conway, John, 43
cookies, Internet, 87
Cool Environmental Sites (Web site), 45
Cool Places for Kids (Web site), 154
Cool Sites for Kids (Web site), 107
cooperative learning, 55-56, 62, 250
copyright, 20, 49, 133-34, 170, 178
"Copyright and K-12: Who Pays in the Network Era" (Rothman), 133
"Copyright Tips and Issues" (online document), 133
Corel Draw (graphics program), 171
Corio, Ron, 205
Cornell Theory Center, 108
Cosmo Player (VRML viewer), 237
Cotton Fields (Web site), 174, 176
course development tools, 285
crafts, 154
Crayon (Web site), 150
Creating Your Own World Wide Web Page with Claris Home Page (Web site), 50
CREWRT-L (listserver), 193
Cross Platform Page, The (Web site), 192
CRT (telnet program), 227
currency, 152
current events, 20
  Web sites for, 323-24
CU-SeeMe (video-conferencing program), 232-34, 238, 283, 285
CU-SeeMe Project (Web site), 234
CyberDewey (Web site), 107, 115
Cyberdog (Web browser), 82
CyberSchool (Web site), 284
CyberSitter (filtering program), 68
  Web site, 69
Cyberspace Middle School (Web site), 107
Cyberspace Treasure Hunt (Web site), 50

Dabbler (graphics program), 171
Dauphin (Manitoba), 179

Dave Central software archive (Web site), 232
DeafWorld Web (Web site), 64
Deja News (Web site), 102, 199, 201
dentistry, 34
Department of Education (United States), 107, 263, 267-68
  Web site, 268
"Designing School Web Sites to Deliver" (online article), 175
"Developing Web Page Policies or Guidelines" (online article), 175
Diablo Valley (California), 179
dictionaries
  online, 101-03, 278
  Web sites for, 315-16
dinosaurs, 19, 34
Directory of Scholarly and Professional E-Conferences (Kovacs), 193
disabled students. See special-needs students
Discovery Channel (Web sites), 203, 277
discussion groups, 15-16, 20, 25, 100, 254, 279. See also forums, online; listservers; newsgroups
Disinfectant (antivirus program), 219
distance education, 217, 232, 234, 256, 262, 274, 282-88
Distance Education at a Glance... (Web site), 288
Distance Education Resources from TeleEducation New Brunswick (Web site), 285-86
Distance Learning: A Guidebook for System Planning and Implementation (Web site), 288
Diversity University
  MOO, 229
  Web site, 230
D.K. Brown's Children's Literature Web Site, 107
Dodge, Bernie, 154, 160
Dogpile (metasearch engine), 101
Download.com (Web site), 223
downloading
  files, 218-20, 234, 254
  graphics/images, 20, 87-88, 116, 132, 170, 173, 238
  software, 66, 220, 223-25, 245
  Web pages, 82, 84, 86-88, 238
driving, 49

Dr. Jim's Virtual Veterinary Clinic
(Web site), 34
Dr. Solomon's Online (Web site), 220

earth, the, 152
Earth and Sea Investigators Resources
(Web site), 150
Earthquake Resource Centre (Web
site), 152
earthquakes, 34, 152
Earthweek (Web site), 151
EASI (Equal Access to Software and
Information) (Web site), 223
Ecola Newsstand (Web site), 135
E-Conflict (Web site), 141
ED Board (computer bulletin board),
268
EDEN Project, 280
Web site, 284
EdNet, 272
listserver, 194
Ed's Oasis (Web site), 153
Edtech (listserver), 15, 193
education, and technology, 6-14, 26-
27, 110, 112, 193, 262
Educational Computing Organization
of Ontario (ECOO), 255
educational resources, 105-10, 113-14,
223-25, 241, 257-59, 286-88
Educational Software Institute (Web
site), 224
Educational Talent Homework Helper
(Web site), 275
Educational Technology: Educational
VR (MUD) subpage (Web site),
229-30
Educational Technology Resource
Center (Web site), 225
Educational Virtual Reality Sites (Web
site), 229
Education E-mail Discussion Lists and
Electronic Journals (Web site), 193
Education Network of Ontario, 199
Education World (Web site), 107
Educator's Forum (Web site), 202
EdWeb (Web site), 103, 155, 167,
201, 253, 272
8-minute HTML Primer, The (Web
site), 50
Eisenhower Clearinghouse for Math
and Science (Web site), 107
Electric Library (Web site), 127

Electric Postcard, The (Web site), 30
Electronic Frontier Foundation, 74
Electronic High School (Web site), 284
electronic mail. *See* e-mail
Electronic Newsstand (Web site), 135
electronic postcards, 30
electronic process writing, 39
Electronic School Tour (Web site), 257
Electronic Zoo (Web site), 126
E-LINK Magazine (Web site), 40
e-mail, 7, 15, 26, 197, 240-41, 243-44
access to, 46
accounts, 66
acronyms, 202
address books, 187, 191
addresses, 102, 184-87
attachments, 183, 187, 192, 206
citing, 134-35
classroom use of, 15-16, 18-19, 28,
31, 46, 55, 182-83, 194, 203-17,
238, 249
deleting, 187, 189-90
in distance education, 285
emoticons, 201-02
etiquette, 201
free, 185-86
in Internet training for teachers, 261
learning to use, 183-84
overview of, 184-88
programs, 186-92
receiving, 187, 189-90, 254
saving, 187, 190
sending, 187, 189-92, 204-05, 254
signature files, 187, 191, 201
uses of, 15-16, 18-19, 182-83
and Web browsers, 82-83, 86, 186-
92, 197, 245
See also keypals; listservers
eMail Classroom Xchange (Web site),
28, 203, 231
emoticons, 201-02
Encarta Concise Encyclopedia (Web
site), 100
Encarta Lesson Collection (Web site),
114, 270
Encyclopedia Britannica, 103
Encyclopedia of Women's History
(Web site), 150
encyclopedias, online, 277
energy, 45, 149-50
EnergyNet Resource Page (Web site),
150

Energy Probe (Web site), 45
Energy Story, The (Web site), 149
English
  as a second language, 196
  Web sites for, 316-18
Envirolink (Web site), 45
environment, the, 45-46, 136, 147-48
  Web sites for, 318-20
Environmental Awareness (Web site),
  179-80
Environmental Careers (Web site), 46
Environmentally Friendly Community
  project, 44-46, 55
Environmental News Network (Web
  site), 136
Environmental Organization Web
  Directory (Web site), 45
Environmental Solutions at HYPER-
  LINK (Web site), 46
E-rate program, 268-69
ERIC documents on business-educa-
  tion partnerships, 267
Essays and Term Papers (Web site), 279
Ethics and Intellectual Property
  Resources on the Web (Web site),
  134
etiquette. See netiquette
Eudora (e-mail program), 86, 188
Evaluation Criteria Rating System for
  Web Sites (Web site), 129
Evergreen Foundation (Web site), 46
Everything E-mail (Web site), 197
Evil House of Cheat (Web site), 279
Excite (search engine), 96, 98-99, 101
Exemplary School Sites (Web site), 173
exhibits, online, 19-20
"Experience the Power: Network
  Technology for Education" (video),
  263
Exploratorium (Web site), 107-08, 235
Explorer (Web site), 223, 236
E-Zines, 194

fables, 150
Fairland Elementary School (Web site),
  180-81
"Fair Use Guidelines for Educational
  Multi-media, The" (online docu-
  ment), 133
Family Planet House of Cards (Web
  Site), 30
FAQ Finder (Web site), 201

FAQs. See Frequently Asked Questions
favorites, Web browser. See bookmarks, Web browser
Federation of Ontario Naturalists, 45
Feldman, Susan, 96
field trips, online, 19, 37-38, 137
file formats, 170, 220-21, 235
files
  Adobe Acrobat, 236
  audio, 234-35
  binary, 192, 219
  compressed, 218, 220
  downloading, 218-20, 234, 254
  PDF, 235-37
  RFC, 227
  searching for, 220-22
  text, 165, 219-20
  viewers for, 217-18, 235-37
  zipped, 220
File Transfer Protocol (FTP), 15-16,
  85, 216-19, 222, 224, 238, 244-45
Filez (Web site), 102, 170, 220-22
filtering programs, 68-70, 76
flags, 142, 149
Flanagan, Joan, 263
Flashcards for Kids (Web site), 278
Flat Stanley Project, 31-33
Fluency through Fables (Web site), 150
FoolProof (Web site), 69
Forefront Curriculum (Web site), 255-56
Forum One (Web site), 203
forums, online, 202-03. See also dis-
  cussion groups
fossils, 20
Four11 (Web site), 187
frames, Web page, 86
Franklin Institute Science Museum, 34,
  107
Frank Potter's Science Gems (Web
  site), 108
Free Agent (newsreader program), 200
Free E-mail guide (Web site), 186
freenets, 7, 46, 241, 248-49
Freetel (communications program), 231
freeware, 108, 218, 223-24
Freezone (Web site), 153-54
French, 229
Frequently Asked Questions (FAQs),
  60, 103, 201
From Now On Educational
  Technology Journal, 175
FrontPage (HTML editor), 172

FTP. *See* File Transfer Protocol
funding, 59, 239, 249-50, 252-53, 262-71, 273

Galaxy (Web site), 141
galleries, 20, 38
games, 25, 43, 50
Gatekeeper (Web site), 224
GDCI Virtual High School, The (Web site), 284
Gears (Web site), 147
geography, 140-43, 149, 151
  Web sites for, 320-22
geology, 20, 152
  Web sites for, 322-23
Getting Technologically Savvy (Web site), 257
.gif (file format), 170-71
gifted education, 196
global classrooms, 31
GlobaLearn (Web site), 37-38, 142
Global Grocery List Project, 11
Global Kids Commons (Web site), 29
"Global Quest: The Internet in the Classroom" (video), 263
Global Schoolhouse
  Teacher's Choice (Web site), 270
  Well-Connected Educator, The (online publication), 117, 153, 270
Global SchoolNet Foundation (GSN), 194, 253, 272
  Web site, 179-80, 199, 203-04, 256
global village, 6, 10-11
Globe and Mail (Toronto) (Web site), 136
Gomer (HTML editor), 172
Good, the Bad, and the Ugly, The (Web site), 127, 129
Gopher, 17, 85, 228
Graffa, David J., 82
Graham, Ian, 172
"Grant Proposal Development: An Educator's Guide" (Massachusetts Field Center for Teaching and Learning), 267
grants and awards, 266-71
graphics editors, 170-71
graphics/images
  accessing, 248
  and copyright, 133
  creating, 171, 178
  downloading, 20, 87-88, 116, 132, 170, 173, 238
  printing, 132
  saving, 87, 132, 170
  searching for, 98-99, 102, 220, 222
  in Web pages, 169-71, 175
graphics programs, 171, 178, 222
Graphic Workshop (graphics editor), 170
Grassroots Funding Journal, 263
Grass Roots Fundraising Book: How to Raise Money in Your Community, The (Flanagan), 263
Greenpeace (Web site), 46
Grolier Online World War II Commemoration Page (Web site), 149
GSN. *See* Global SchoolNet Foundation

Handbook of Grants and Subsidies of the Federal and Provincial Governments for Non-Profit Organizations (Canadian Research and Publications Centre), 269
Hee Yun's Graphic Collection (Web site), 170
Helfrich, Paul M., 34
Heritage Online (Web site), 287
Highland Park Elementary School, 176
hilites (listserver), 194
history, 108, 150
  Web sites for, 323-24
history feature, Web browser, 86, 88, 92-93
History/Social Studies Web Site for K-12 Teachers, 108
HomeMaker Online (Web site), 169
home pages, Web browser, 71, 84, 87-89, 99, 116
homeschooling, 274, 279-84, 288
Homeschooling Zone, The (Web site), 282
Homeschool Zone (Web site), 281
Homesite (HTML editor), 172
homework, 274-78
Homework Helper (information service), 277
Homework Helper: Animals around the World (Web site), 275
Honolulu Community College, 19
HotBot (search engine), 96, 98, 101, 201, 203, 220

Hot Dog (HTML editor), 171
HotList of K-12 Internet School Sites
    for the U.S.A. (Web site), 173
hotlists, Web browser. *See* bookmarks,
    Web browser
HTML. *See* HyperText Markup
    Language
HTML editors, 162, 168-69, 171-72
HTML Goodies (Web site), 257
HTML Reference Library Windows
    HLP file, The, 173
HTML Writer's Guild, The (Web site),
    173
Hubert, Dale, 31
human rights, 147-48
hurricanes, 151
Hypercard Heaven (Web site), 225
hyperlinks, 79-80, 84, 86-87, 116,
    167-68, 178
hypermedia, 79
hypertext, 79-80
HyperText Markup Language (HTML),
    50, 86, 162-73, 235, 256-57
Hytelnet (Web site), 228

ICQ (communications program), 231
IECC. *See* International E-mail
    Classroom Connections
Illinois State Geological Survey, 34
images. *See* graphics/images
InClass (listserver), 194, 206
Indiana University Extended Studies
    (Web site), 284
individual activities, 56
Industry Canada
    Computers for Schools Program, 269
    Web site, 46
Inference Find (metasearch engine),
    101
Infinite Ink (Web site), 189
information collection projects, 33, 35-
    37, 55
information exchanges, 23, 40-43
"Information Literacy and the Net"
    (staff development course), 127
INFOSEARCH Broadcasting Links
    (Web site), 235
Infoseek (search engine), 99, 101, 124
InfoSpace (Web site), 102, 186-87
InfoZone (Web site), 99, 278
Inkspot Web (Web site), 39
inQuiry Almanack (Web site), 154

Institute for Distance Education
    (University of Maryland) (Web
    site), 286
Institute of Physics (Naples), 19
Intensive American Language Center,
    The (Web site), 203
Interesting Places for Kids (Web site),
    154
International Cyberfair Contest, 179-
    80
International Dyslexic Association
    (Web site), 64
International E-mail Classroom
    Connections (IECC)
    listserver, 194, 206, 211
    Web site, 206, 211
International Newsday Project (Web
    site), 212
International Society for Technology in
    Education (ISTE), 255
    Web site, 271
Internet
    citing sources on, 20, 49, 134-35
    classroom use of, 6-27, 51, 58, 216-
        17, 238, 247-50, 253, 260-61, 263,
        271-73, 288, 290. *See also* class-
        room projects
    compared with a library, 121
    connecting to, 239-50
    evaluating sources on, 127-29
    finding time for, 271-73
    as an information resource, 20-21, 25
    overview of, 7-8
    planning school implementation of,
        252-53
    questions about, 34
    as a research tool, 92, 112-13, 127,
        160-61
    as a revolutionary force, 6-7, 10
    safety and security, 49, 66-76, 205
    searching of, 91-104, 121-26
    student training in use of, 48-51, 272
    teacher training in use of, 252-62
    and the World Wide Web, 15, 48
"Internet Access for Educators:
    Options, Solutions and Costs"
    (Avant and Rutledge), 242
Internet.com (Web site), 85
Internet Driver's License program, 49
Internet Explorer (Web browser), 81-
    82, 244-45
    bookmarks in, 89-90

e-mail program in, 82, 186-88, 192, 245

file viewers for, 237

help menu in, 91

HTML editor in, 171

newsreader program in, 82, 197, 245

obtaining, 81-82, 245

real-time communication with, 231

toolbar in, 81, 88

Internet Filter for Windows, The (Web site), 69

Internet Free College, The (Web site), 284

Internet Information (Web site), 224

Internet_Invitations-l (listserver), 194

Internet Island (Web site), 257, 259

Internet Lessons from UCI (Web site), 153

Internet Mail (e-mail program), 188

Internet Public Library, 34
Web site, 102, 213

Internet Relay Chat (IRC), 44, 231

Internet School Networking (ISN) (Web site), 257

Internet Science and Technology Fair (Web site), 180

Internet service providers (ISPs)
e-mail access through, 46
e-mail programs supplied by, 187
FTP programs supplied by, 218
Internet access through, 240, 242-50, 262, 266
newsgroup access through, 197, 199-200
obtaining software from, 245, 247
as school Web page hosts, 178
selecting, 243, 245-47
telnet programs supplied by, 227
training offered by, 256, 266
Web browsers supplied by, 81-82, 187, 247
Web pages of, 87
See also commercial online services

Internet Sleuth (Web site), 100, 102

Internet Tourbus (Web site), 257

Internet University (Web site), 283

InterSLIP (communications program), 245

Introduction to HTML (Web site), 50

Introduction to HTML and URLs (Graham), 172

IRC (Internet Relay Chat), 44, 231

ITDC WebQuests (Web site), 160

Jacobson, Russ, 34

Jason Merry's Canadian Distance Education Directory (Web site), 287

Jay Barker's Online Connection (Web site), 246

John December's Web Site, 100, 189, 258, 260

John Labovitz's E-zine list (Web site), 194

Jon's Homeschool Resource Page (Web site), 281

JournalismNet (Web site), 136

Journal of Online Learning, 271

.jpeg (file format), 170

Judi Harris's Network-Based Educational Activity Collection (Web site), 108

Jumbo (Web site), 108, 223

Juno (e-mail program), 188

K12admin (listserver), 194

K12assess-l (listserver), 194

K12.ed.life-skills (newsgroup), 16

K12.ed.soc-studies (newsgroup), 16

K12.lang.art (newsgroup), 16

K12Opps (listserver), 194

K12Pals (listserver), 28

K12small (listserver), 194

K-12 Sources—Lesson Plans (Web site), 153

K12-webdev (listserver), 194

Kathy Schrock's Guide for Educators (Web site), 108

"Keeping It Legal: Questions Arising out of Web Site Management" (McKenzie), 133

keypals, 8, 28-30, 47, 141, 203-06, 208-09, 211, 251
locating, 28-30, 194, 206, 211

Keypals: Classroom to Classroom Connection (Web site), 29

Keystone High School, 280
Web site, 225

keywords, 99

Kidlink
listserver, 195
Web site, 29, 195

Kidlit-L (listserver), 15-16, 195

KidNews (Web site), 153

K.I.D.S. (Kids Identifying and

Discovering Sites) (online publication), 194
KidsCom (Web site), 154
Kids on Campus Hands-On WWW
    Demonstration (Web site), 108
Kidsphere (listserver), 15, 195-96, 206
Kids' Place Homework Helper (Web
    site), 275-76
KidsSource OnLine (Web site), 64
KidsSpace (Web site), 154
KidsWeb (Web site), 108, 154
Kidsworld Online (Web site), 152
Kid Wide Web: A Guide to the Internet
    for Teachers (Web site), 263
Kovacs, Diane, 193

language skills, 150
LANs (local area networks), 56, 240-
    42, 247
learning, models for, 14
Learning@Web.Sites (Web site), 153
Learning Disabilities Association of
    America (Web site), 64
Learning Disabilities Association of
    Canada (Web site), 64
Learning Disabilities Home Page, The
    (Web site), 64
learning-disabled students. See special-
    needs students
learning outcomes, 53-54, 58-59, 154,
    215, 240, 266, 273, 288, 290
  for project ideas, 116, 121, 124, 129,
    139, 144, 206-07, 209, 211, 213, 251
Learning Resource Server (Web site),
    109
Learn-Net (listserver), 195
Learn the Net (Web site), 258
"Legal and Educational Analysis of
    K–12 Internet Acceptable Use
    Policies, A" (Willard), 133
Le MOO Français, 229
Lengel, Jim, 50
lesson plans, 49, 105-06, 110, 114,
    144, 153, 276
Lesson Plans Using Internet Web Sites
    (Web site), 153
Librarian's Index to the Internet (Web
    site), 101-02, 126
libraries, school, 195
Library of Congress Country Studies
    (Web site), 141
lifelong learning, 23, 27, 51, 290

links. See hyperlinks
List, The (Web site), 246
listservers, 28, 47, 60, 192-97, 262
  advertising classroom projects on, 204
  advertising for keypals on, 30
  in distance education, 285
  as an information resource, 103
  joining, 28, 192-93
  locating, 193, 196-97
  See also discussion groups
Liszt (Web site), 100, 197
literature, children's, 107, 195
Little Planet Times, The (Web site), 40
LM_Net (listserver), 195
local area networks (LANs), 56, 240-
    42, 247
Loogootee Elementary School (Web
    site), 49, 180-81, 203, 262, 270
LookSmart (subject tree), 94, 102,
    117, 126
Lost Library of MOO, The (Web site),
    229
Lotus Learning Space (course develop-
    ment tool), 285
Louvre, 20
Low End Mac, The (Web site), 225
LRN-Ed (listserver), 195
LView Pro (graphics editor), 132, 170
Lycos (search engine), 94, 101, 124
Lycos Top 5% Sites (subject tree), 94
Lynn's Web Mastery (Web site), 171
Lynx (Web browser), 82, 91

MacFixIt (Web site), 225
macinsearch.com (Web site), 225
Macintosh Archives (Web site), 224
Macintosh computers, 225, 237, 243-44
  antivirus programs for, 219
  communications programs for, 245
  and CU-SeeMe, 233
  FTP sites for, 224
  graphics editors for, 171
  graphics programs for, 171
  HTML Color Pickers for, 169
  HTML editors for, 172
  shareware for, 225
  Stuffit file decompression program
    for, 220
  telnet programs for, 227
  Web browsers for, 81-82
Macintosh Educator's Site (Web site),
    225

Macintosh Internet Resource Database (MacIRD) (Web site), 225
Macintosh Resource Page, The (Web site), 225
Maclean's In-Class Program (Web site), 140
MacPPP (communications program), 245
MacTCP (communications program), 245
MacUser, 241
MacWorld (Web site), 225
Madlibs, 152
Mad Scientist Network, The (Web site), 34
magazines, 23, 39-40, 127, 135-38, 151-52, 262
Magellan (subject tree), 94, 102
Magnolia Elementary School, 155
Mag's Big List of HTML Editors (Web site), 172
mailing lists. *See* listservers
Mailing Lists for Teachers (Web site), 193
Makulowich, John, 100
Mansfield Cybrarian (Web site), 101
Map Machine (Web site), 141
MapQuest (Web site), 103
maps, 100, 103, 141-42, 151
Maricopa Center for Learning & Instruction, 113
Marlo (Web site), 30
Marsville project, 19, 31
  Web site, 19
Massachusetts Institute of Technology, 30
mathematics, 34, 43-44, 107, 110, 149, 152, 223, 225, 278
  Web sites for, 325-27
MathMagic (Web site), 149
MathSoft Puzzler (Web site), 44
MayaQuest project, 21-23
McAfee (corporation), 219
McKenzie, Jamie, 133, 177
McLuhan, Marshall, 6
MDaemon (e-mail program), 189
Mecklermedia, 85
Media Awareness Network (Web site), 140
Media Launchpad (Web site), 137
Media Literacy Project, The (Web site), 137
media Web sites, 327-28
medicine, 34
MegaMath (Web site), 44
mentors, 33, 63, 253
  student, 19, 44, 57, 63
Metafind (metasearch engine), 101, 125, 127
metasearch engines, 99, 101
Michael Sattler's Web page (Web site), 234
Microsoft (Web sites), 95, 100, 258
Microsoft Network, 240-41
Middle-L (Middle School) (listserver), 195
Midlink (Web site), 39, 151-52
MindQuest (Web site), 284
Ministry of Culture (France), 20
Ministry of Education (British Columbia), 106
  Web site, 252
MIT Media Lab, 70
modems, 239-40, 242-44, 246-50
Monitor Radio—RealAudio (Web site), 235
Monta Vista High School (Web site), 175
MOOs. *See* Multiuser Object-Oriented
Mount Royal College, 283
Mrs. Fliegler's Homework Helper (Web site), 276
MUD/MOO Client FAQ, 230
MUDs (Multi-User Dungeons), 230
multimedia, 62, 79, 91, 235, 237, 243, 283
Multimedia Greeting Cards (Web site), 30
Multiuser Object-Oriented (MOOs), 216, 227-31, 238, 285
Mundo Hispano (MOO), 229
Municipalities on the Web (Web site), 46
Museum of Paleontology (online exhibit), 20
museums, 38-39, 129-32
MUSHes (Multi-User Shared Hallucinations), 230
music, 34
  Web sites for, 327
My Virtual Newspaper (Web site), 136
My Virtual Reference Desk (Web site), 103

NandoTimes (Web site), 137
NASA, 263
  Web sites, 109, 259, 263, 270
National Association of Partners in
  Education (NAPE), 267
National Atlas Information System
  (NAIS) (Web site), 142
National Center for Learning
  Disabilities (Web site), 63-64
National Center for Missing and
  Exploited Children, 76
National Centre to Improve Practice in
  Special Education through
  Technology, Media and Materials
  (Web site), 64-65
National Education Computing
  Conference (NECC), 255
National Geographic, 141
National Library of Canada's
  Canadian Information (Web site),
  103
National Public Radio (Web site), 235
National Science Foundation, 268
Native American culture, 34
natural history, 34
Naujokaitis, Dalia, 35
navigation bars. *See* toolbars, Web
  browser
NCSA's HTML Primer (Web site), 50
Nehls, Ginger, 155
NetDay, 271
netiquette, 49, 201, 205, 229, 254
NetNanny (filtering program), 68
  Web site, 69
Netparents (Web site), 76
Netscape (Web browser), 81-82, 244-45
  bookmarks in, 89-90
  default home page in, 89, 99
  downloading images with, 132
  e-mail program in, 82, 186-92, 197,
  245
  file viewers for, 237
  help menu in, 91
  HTML editor in, 171
  newsreader program in, 82, 197,
  199-200, 245
  obtaining, 81-82, 245
  real-time communication with, 231
  toolbar in, 81, 88, 101
  using FTP with, 218
  viewing Web page source code with,
  163

Netscape Composer (HTML editor),
  172
Netscape Mail (e-mail program), 188-
  92
Netscape Messenger (e-mail program),
  188
Netscape search page (Web site), 95
NetShepherd (Web site), 69
NetVet (Web site), 126
networking, educational, 194
Network_Nuggets-L (listserver), 195
New Directions in Distance Learning
  (virtual school), 280
news, 103, 127, 135-39. *See* also
  newspapers
  Web sites for, 327-28
news.announce.newusers (newsgroup),
  201
news.answers (newsgroup), 201
NewsCentral (Web site), 137
newsgroups, 15, 60, 103, 135, 197, 201
  accessing, 82, 85-86, 197, 199-201,
  245
  categories of, 200
  classroom use of, 197
  FAQs for, 201
  and listservers, 196-97
  searching, 95, 98, 102, 126, 199
  URLs, 85
  See also discussion groups
News Index (Web site), 103, 137
NewsLink (Web site), 137
newspapers, 23, 39-40, 95, 99, 135-
  38, 150, 212. *See also* news
newsreader programs, 82, 197, 199-
  200, 245
New York Times
  TimesFax service, 236
  Web site, 137
NickNacks Telecollaborate (Web site),
  180, 203
Nifty Telnet (telnet program), 227
North Dakota Division of Independent
  Study (Web site), 284
Northern Light (search engine), 101,
  127
"'No Significant Difference'
  Phenomenon" (Russell), 286
NovaNet Campus (Web site), 279-80
November, Alan, 12-13

Oba, Sachiko, 34

Oceans of the Earth (online exhibit), 20
Odyssey of the Mind (Web site), 43
Of Bees, Beekeepers and Food (Web
    site), 147
offline browsers, 82, 87, 216, 238
One Stop Research Paper Shop (Web
    site), 279
Online Books Page (Web site), 224
Online Distance Education FAQ, 286
Online Educator (Web site), 153
Online Educator Weekly Hot List
    (Web site), 109
online writing lab (OWL), 19
On Numbers and Games (Conway),
    43
Opera (Web browser), 82-89, 91, 93,
    187, 197, 218, 245
Other People's Papers (Web site), 279
Otterburg, Susan, 267
outcomes, learning. *See* learning out-
    comes
Outlook Express (e-mail program), 188
OWL (online writing lab), 19
Oz-TeacherNet (Web site), 258

Pacific Bell, 105
PageMill (HTML editor), 172
PageSpinner (HTML editor), 172
Paint Shop Pro (graphics program),
    171
Palace of Fine Arts (San Francisco),
    107
paleontology, 20, 34
parents, 23, 51, 62-63, 178, 254, 273
    and fundraising, 249-50, 262-63,
    265-66
    homeschooling by, 274, 279-82
    on Internet implementation commit-
    tees, 252
    and Internet safety and security, 66-
    68, 70, 72-73, 75
    as volunteers, 49, 57, 62, 126, 205,
    248, 271-72
parts of speech, 152
passwords, Internet, 66-67
PBS (Web site), 137
PC World, 241
.pdf (file format), 235-37
PD Rosetta Stone (Web site), 259
Pedago Net (Web site), 170, 203
Pegasus Mail 2.53 (e-mail program),
    188

people, searching for, 100, 102, 187
Perry-Castaneda Map Collection (Web
    site), 100
pets, 34
phone numbers, searching for, 101-02,
    187
photography, 20
Photoshop (graphics program), 171
physics, 19, 109
    Web sites for, 328
Physics Lecture Demonstrations (Web
    site), 109
Pine (e-mail and newsreader program),
    189, 199
Pitsco's Ask an Expert (Web site), 33,
    203
Pitsco's Launch to Citing WWW
    Addresses (Web site), 135
Pitsco's Launch to Educational
    Resources (Web site), 109
Pitsco's Launch to Finding People
    (Web site), 187
Pitsco's Launch to Keypals/Penpals
    (Web site), 29, 203, 206
Pitsco's Launch to Technology Plans
    (Web site), 252
PKUnzip (file decompression pro-
    gram), 220
plagiarism, 278-79
planets, 148
*Plans & Policies for Technology in
    Education*, 74
plug-ins, Web browser, 81, 86, 216,
    234-37
Portable Document Format (PDF) files,
    235-37
P.O.'s Homepage (Web site), 147
postcards, electronic, 30
PowWow (communications program),
    231-32, 285
    Web site, 232
Problem of the Week (Web site), 44
problem-solving activities, 25, 43-44
Prodigy, 240-41, 277
Project Gutenberg, 34
projects, classroom. *See* classroom pro-
    jects
Pro Motion (graphics program), 171
publishing, student, 15, 23, 39-40, 79,
    174-75, 179. *See also* Web pages,
    student
Puget Sound Community School, 280

Purdue University, 19
push technology, 15
puzzles, 149, 152

Questacon (Web site), 20-21
QuickLink Explorer (bookmark utility), 91
Quicktime (video player), 237
quizzes, 25, 43
QVT/Term (telnet program), 227

Reader's Digest, 94
RealAudio, 16, 234-35, 237
  Web site, 234-35
RealPlayer (audio and video player),
  234-35
real-time Internet communication, 216,
  231-32, 285. *See also* conferencing
RealVideo, 234
Recreational Software Advisory
  Council on the Internet (RSACi), 76
"Regarding E-mail Projects" (Corio),
  205
Research-It (Web site), 278
Researchpaper.com (Web site), 99
resources
  educational, 105-10, 113-14, 223-25,
    241, 257-59, 286-88
  text-based, 20
résumés, 153
RFC (Request for Comment) files, 227
RFC1941 (Frequently Asked
  Questions for Schools), 227
RGB Color Chart (Web site), 169
right mouse button, 86-87, 132, 170
Rothman, David, 133
Russell, Thomas L., 286
Rutledge, Keith, 242

Sackman, Gleason, 173
SafeSurf (Web site), 69
safety and security, Internet, 49, 66-76,
  205
San Diego State University, 154
Sandi Goldman's Classroom Corners,
  95
Santa Barbara Museum of Natural
  History, 34
saving
  e-mail, 187, 190
  graphics/images, 87, 132, 170
  Web pages, 82, 87

scavenger hunts, 22, 50-51, 117-20
SchoolNet, 253, 272
  FTP site, 16
  listserver, 195, 206
  MOO, 229-30
  Web site, 109, 148, 178, 230, 277
School Partnerships Handbook
  (Otterbourg), 267
SchoolsNET (Web site), 178
School Web Maker (Web site), 179
School Web Page Development Guide
  (Web site), 175
school Web sites. *See* Web pages, school
Schrock, Kathy, 160
science, 20, 34, 107-08, 110, 150, 180,
  223, 225, 276
  Web sites for, 329-31
science centers, 129
Science Learning Network's Franklin
  Institute (Web site), 107, 132
Scout Report (online publication), 194,
  236
Scout Report Signpost (Web site), 103
Scout Toolkit (Web site), 95, 174
scrapbooks, online, 149
Search Engine Feature Chart, 96
search engines, 76, 92-99, 122, 124-
  26, 137, 170
Search Engine Watch (Web site), 95
searching
  for discussion groups, 100
  for e-mail addresses, 102, 186-87
  for files, 220-22
  for graphics/images, 98-99, 102, 220,
    222
  the Internet, 91-104, 121-26
  newsgroups, 95, 98, 102, 126, 199
  for news stories, 95, 99, 103
  for people, 100, 102, 187
  for phone numbers, 101-02, 187
  for road maps, 103
  for shareware, 102, 220
  for software, 220
SeaWorld Animal Database (Web site),
  126
Shakespeare, William, 276, 278
Shakespearean Homework Helper, The
  (Web site), 276
shareware, 102, 108, 187, 217-18,
  220, 223-25, 244-45, 249
Shareware Shop (Web site), 220
Shemitz, Jon, 281

Sher, Julian, 136

Shockwave (multimedia viewer), 237, 283

signature files, e-mail, 187, 191, 201

.sit (file format), 220

Skinner, B.F., 8

SLIP/PPP (Serial Line Interface Protocol/Point-to-Point Protocol) connections, 240, 242-43, 245

smileys, 201-02

Smithsonian Institution, 20

SNEtalk-L (listserver), 196

social action projects, 44-46, 147-48

social science, 20, 108

software
  antivirus, 66, 219-20
  communications, 231-32, 244-45, 247-50
  downloading, 66, 220, 223-25, 245
  filtering, 68-70, 76
  searching for, 220
  TCP/IP, 244-45
  See also freeware; shareware

solar system, 148

Some Thoughts about How to Offer a Course over the Internet (Web site), 287

Some Thoughts about WebQuests Overview (Dodge), 160

Soulis' Suggestions for Internet Solutions (Web site), 224

source code, Web page, 86, 163-65, 168, 173

Soviet Archives Exhibit, The (Web site), 132

Spanish, 229

Speaking of Teaching (newsletter), 236

Speced-l (listserver), 196

special-needs students, 62-65, 84, 181, 196, 223, 281
  Web sites for, 328-29

Spectrum Virtual University (Web site), 284

speech, parts of, 152

Stanford University Copyright and Fair Use Site (Web site), 134

Staroute Homework Helper (Web site), 276

starting pages, Web browser. *See* home pages, Web browser

States Homework Helper (Web site), 276

statistics, Canadian, 33

"Steps of the Solicitation" (online article), 265

Sticky Notes (communications program), 231

Stone Soup (Web site), 39

Storm Science (online resource), 151

St. Petersburg Times, 139

Stroud's Consummate Winsock Applications Page (Web site), 227

student portfolios, electronic, 58, 151

students, special-needs. *See* special-needs students

StudyWeb (Web site), 276

Stuffit (file decompression program), 220

subject trees, 92-95, 102, 126

SuffolkWeb Homework Helper (Web site), 276

Sunday Times, 138

"Surfing for ABC's" (lesson plan), 49

"Surfing Safely on the Internet" (lesson plan), 49

SurfWatch (filtering program), 68
  Web site, 69

Swarthmore College, 34

Switched-On Classroom, The (planning guide), 252

Symantec AntiVirus Research Center (Web site), 220

Sympatico, 240-41
  Web sites, 202, 277-78

Taconis, Kryn, 148

Tag-L (listserver), 196

TalkCity Education Center (Web site), 202

Tammy's Tech Tips (Web site), 58, 66

TCP/IP (Transmission Control Protocol/Internet Protocol), 244-45

Teacher2Teacher
  listserver, 196
  Web site, 196, 202

Teacher's Choice (Web site), 270

Teacher's Edition Online (Web site), 110

Teachers Helping Teachers (Web site), 114

Teacher Talk (Web site), 202

Teacher Topics (Web site), 110

Teaching and Learning on the WWW (Web site), 113

Teaching Students to Think Critically about Internet Resources (Web site), 129
teaching, Web sites, 331-34
technology, and education, 6-14, 26-27, 110, 112, 193, 262
Technology-Based Learning Network (Web site), 110
Technology Connection, 175
Technology in Education (Web site), 129
Teel Family's Homeschool Page, The (Web site), 282
telnet, 16-17, 85, 216-17, 227-28, 230, 238, 244-45
Template for Developing a WebQuest (Web site), 160
terminal emulation, 227
TESLK-12 (listserver), 196
text-based resources, 20
text files, 165, 219-20
Texture Land (Web site), 169
Texture Station (Web site), 169
Thinking Critically about World Wide Web Resources (Web site), 129
ThinkQuest Project, 24-25, 180
Tiger Mapping Service (Web site), 142
Tile.Net (Web site), 197
Time, 137
Times Newspapers Ltd. (Web site), 138
Time-Warner's Pathfinder (Web site), 137-38, 231
"Tips for Writing Grant Proposals" (Association of Supervision & Curriculum Development), 267
title bars, 87
toolbars
  Netscape Mail, 189-90
  Web browser, 81, 88
TopClass (course development tool), 285
top-level domains, 185
Tornado Web Page, 151
Tour Canada without Leaving Your Desk (Web site), 38
travel, 102, 140-43
treasure hunts. See scavenger hunts
Trumpet Winsock (communications program), 245
truncation, 122
TUCOWS (Web site), 91, 169, 171, 187, 220, 227, 232

tutorials, online, 25, 50, 126, 230
21st Century Problem Solving (Web site), 149

UCI Science Education Programs Office (Web site), 110
Ultimates, The (Web site), 102
Uniform Resource Locators (URLs), 84-86, 114, 116-17, 172, 218, 220, 228, 238
United States, 142
United States Geological Survey, 34
University at Albany Libraries (Web site), 259
University of British Columbia, 285
University of California at Berkeley, 20
University of Houston, 286
University of Illinois College of Education, 109
University of Minnesota, 228
University of New Brunswick, 283
University of North Dakota, 34
University of Pennsylvania African Studies Web Page, 146
University of Texas, 100
University of Twente, 283
University of Wisconsin Distance Education Clearinghouse (Web site), 287
Untangling the Web (Web site), 115, 127, 129
Urban Agricultural Notes (Web site), 46
Urban Education Web (Web site), 94
Urban Forest Centre (Web site), 46
URLs. See Uniform Resource Locators
USA Today (Web site), 138
Usenet. See newsgroups
Usenet Info Center Launch Pad (Web site), 201
US West Connected Schools Program (Web site), 270
Utahlink (Web site), 255

Vatican Exhibit, The (Web site), 132
video, 16, 216-17, 232-35, 238, 283, 285
Videoconferencing Site, The (Web site), 234
viewers, file, 217-18, 235-37
virtual events, 23, 40

The Teacher's Complete & Easy Guide to the Internet

Virtual High School Cooperative
Project, The (Web site), 284
Virtual Library Museums Page (Web
site), 129
Virtual Reality Markup Language
(VRML), 237
Virtual School for the Gifted, 280
Virtual Software Library (Web site),
224
Viruscan (antivirus program), 219
viruses, computer, 66, 219-20
volcanoes, 34
VRML (Virtual Reality Markup
Language), 237

Wacky Web Tales (online resource),
152
Walker, Doug, 60-61
Walkowiak, Karen, 40
Warner Brothers (Web site), 30
Washington Post (Web site), 138, 142
Washington University, 34
weather, 34, 151
Weather Channel, The, 34
Weather Mania (Web site), 151
WeatherNet (Web site), 151
Web66 WWW Schools Registry (Web
site), 173, 178, 262
Web-Based Course Development Tools
(Web site), 285
Web-Based Instruction Bookmarks
(Web site), 287
Web browsers, 15, 112, 116-17, 163,
216, 242-43
choosing, 82-84, 244-45
e-mail programs in, 82, 186-92, 197,
245
features of, 81-93, 95, 101, 171,
186-92, 197, 199-200, 217-18,
227-28, 231, 244-45
file viewers for, 217-18, 237
home pages in, 71, 84, 87-89, 99,
116
installing, 84
navigating with, 84-91, 113
newsreader programs in, 82, 199-
200, 197, 245
obtaining, 81-82, 187, 245, 247
plug-ins for, 81, 86, 216, 234-37
types of, 81-84, 91
using FTP with, 217-18
using telnet with, 227

See also bookmarks, Web browser;
HyperText Markup Language
WebCT (course development tool),
285
Web Developer's Virtual Library (Web
site), 173
Web directories. *See* subject trees
Web Doggie (Web site), 70
Weber-Malakov expedition, 26
Web Masters Reference Library, The
(Web site), 173
Web pages, 235
for bookmarks, 71
creating, 82, 161-81, 194, 196, 256,
258
downloading, 82, 84, 86-88, 238
saving, 82, 87
school, 13, 23, 39, 104, 133, 153,
163, 171, 173-79
student, 24, 50, 79, 114, 162, 175,
178-81. *See also* publishing, student
three-dimensional, 237
See also home pages, Web browser;
HyperText Markup Language
WebPhone (communications program),
231
Web-phone technology, 231-32
Web Places Clip Art Review (Web
site), 170
WebQuest: Does the Tiger Eat Her
Cubs? (Web site), 160
WebQuest Page, The (Web site), 160
WebQuest: Planet Earth Expedition
(Web site), 160
WebQuests, 115, 154-61
WebQuest: Searching for China (Web
site), 160
WebQuests in Our Future: The
Teacher's Role in Cyberspace
(Schrock), 160
Web Sense (Web site), 70
Web site editors. *See* HTML editors
WebSites and Resources for Teachers
(Web site), 110, 114
WebTabs (bookmark utility), 91
Webtalk (listserver), 196
Web Whacker (offline browser), 82,
238
Well-Connected Educator, The (online
publication), 117, 153, 270
whales, 56, 126
What Did You Do in the War,

Grandma (Web site), 148
Where the Wild Things Are (Web site), 100
White, George Abbott, 50
White Pine Software (Web site), 234
whole-class activities, 55
Willard, Nancy, 133
Windows 95, 63, 238, 241, 245
Windows to the Universe (Web site), 148
WinSite (Web site), 223
WinTelnet (telnet program), 227
WinZip (file decompression program), 220
Wired Magazine (Web site), 85
women's history, 150
Word Problems for Kids (Web site), 44
World Flags (Web site), 142
World Lecture Hall (Web site), 287
WorldView (VRML viewer), 237
World War II, 148-49
World War II Time Line (Web site), 148
World Wide Web
  accessing multimedia on, 243
  citing sources on, 134
  classroom use of, 112-61, 175, 181, 196, 216-17, 238, 251
  in distance education, 285
  and electronic postcards, 30
  evaluating sources on, 127-29
  and FTP, 217
  and Gopher, 228
  and the Internet, 15, 48
  as a learning tool, 78-79, 181, 262
  overview of, 79
  real-time communication through, 231
  as a research tool, 112-13, 277

searching of, 91-104, 124-26
and special-needs students, 62
in Internet training for teachers, 261
URLs, 85, 218
uses of, 15, 263
Web sites for learning about, 256-59, 261
See also publishing, student; Web browsers; Web pages, school; Web pages, student
World Wide Web Virtual Library— Geography (Web site), 143
Writers In Electronic Residence program, 19, 39
writing, 19, 39-40, 141, 149, 183, 193, 229, 281
WWWedu (listserver), 178, 196
WWW Viewer Test Page (Web site), 235

Yahoo (subject tree), 99, 102-03, 124, 126, 140, 143, 246, 259, 278
  chat, 231
  overview of, 92-94
  search engine links at, 93-94, 97
Yahooligans (subject tree), 94, 102, 126, 132, 141, 278
York University (Toronto), 39
You Can (Web site), 110
Youth in Action Network, 147-48
  Web site, 148
Yuckiest Site on the Internet (Web site), 154

ZDNet (Web site), 85
.zip (file format), 220
zipped files, 220
Z-Term (communications program), 249

About the Free CD-ROM

This comprehensive resource includes and extends the sites listed in Appendix B, by providing capsule summaries of hundreds of important education links for teachers and covering primary through secondary grade levels and more than fifteen curriculum areas. The CD-ROM will help you quickly link to special needs resources, technology planning resources, professional references for teachers, and activities for students.

Note that the Opera browser, included on the CD-ROM, is an evaluation copy. If you intend to use it on an ongoing basis, you will need to pay a modest registration fee. Information about Opera costs and alternative versions of the browser are available at **http://traviata.nta.no/opera.htm.**

1. To use this disc, your workstation must have a browser (e.g., Opera, Netscape, Internet Explorer, etc.) active and, ideally, you should be on the Internet.
2. You may install the Opera browser on your workstation directly from this CD.
3. This disc operates with Windows 3.1x, Windows 95, Windows 98, or Windows NT.
4. To begin using this CD, click on FORU.htm or open this file through your browser.

On this CD-ROM, you will find:

- Opera Browser in 16 and 32 bit format
- Over 1,000 carefully chosen live educational links on the Internet
- A section with beginner help files
- Lesson plan links and example lessons
- Assessment, Evaluation and Benchmark sites to help in your curriculum planning
- Tips 'n Techniques section to help you with accessing and downloading information from the World Wide Web

---

SUGGESTED MINIMUM REQUIREMENTS

- Windows operating system (ideally, Windows 95/98)
- 486 MHZ CPU or better
- 8 MB of memory or better (16 MB is ideal)
- 5 MB of available hard drive space (you will need more if you are storing picture and sound files from the Internet)
- 4x CD-ROM drive or better
- 640 x 480 or higher resolution monitor
- 256 (16 bit or better) color video card capability
- Mouse or similar pointing device